SOURCES FOR THE HISTORY OF BHUTAN

MICHAEL ARIS

SOURCES FOR THE HISTORY OF BHUTAN

Introduction to this Edition by

DR. JOHN A. ARDUSSI

MOTILAL BANARSIDASS PUBLISHERS
PRIVATE LIMITED • DELHI

First Indian Editon : Delhi, 2009
By arrangements with "Arbeitskreis für Tibetische und
Buddhistiche Studien, Universität Wien"

ISBN: 978-81-208-3409-5

MOTILAL BANARSIDASS
41 U.A. Bungalow Road, Jawahar Nagar, Delhi 110 007
8 Mahalaxmi Chamber, 22 Bhulabhai Desai Road, Mumbai 400 026
203 Royapettah High Road, Mylapore, Chennai 600 004
236, 9th Main III Block, Jayanagar, Bangalore 560 011
Sanas Plaza, 1302 Baji Rao Road, Pune 411 002
8 Camac Street, Kolkata 700 017
Ashok Rajpath, Patna 800 004
Chowk, Varanasi 221 001

Printed in India
By Jainendra Prakash Jain at Shri Jainendra Press,
A-45 Naraina, Phase-I, New Delhi 110 028
and Published by Narendra Prakash Jain for
Motilal Banarsidass Publishers Private Limited,
Bungalow Road, Delhi 110 007

Introduction

DR. JOHN A. ARDUSSI
(Senior Research Fellow,
University of Virginia Tibet Center)

It is a distinct pleasure to write an introduction to this new edition of Michael Aris's *Sources for the History of Bhutan* (hereafter abbreviated as *Sources*). The book was originally published as a microfiche supplement to Aris's PhD study published in 1979 as *Bhutan – The Early History of a Himalayan Kingdom* (hereafter abbreviated as *Bhutan*). The version of *Sources* updated here first came out in separate book form in 1986 in the Vienna University series Wiener Studien zur Tibetologie und Buddhismuskunde. Both *Bhutan* and *Sources* were groundbreaking studies of early Bhutanese history based on original documents, and represent the state of information available in 1979.

Sources consists of editions and translations of three important 17th - 18th century Tibetan language[1] documents relating to the history of Bhutan, plus a translation of a 17th century report on Bhutan written in Portuguese by a Jesuit monk who, with a colleague, passed through the country in 1627 on his way to Tibet. Quite by chance, the two priests were eye witnesses to the very first year of the Zhabdrung Rinpoche's newly founded Buddhist state (1725/6) that was to become the country now known as Bhutan.

Thirty years after *Bhutan* and *Sources* were first published, research on Bhutanese history is still an emerging field with few specialists, compared to the hundreds working on neighbouring Himalayan countries Tibet, Nepal, and Ladakh. However, a number of articles relevant to *Sources* have been written by other scholars, and important new source documents have become available for comparative study. In this introduction I plan to review several topics on which these new materials shed light, taking them up in the order in which Aris's essays were published. At the end, I have included a brief bibliography of these recent publications for the benefit of readers who may wish to refer to them.

Over the past forty years, conscious of the importance of preserving Bhutan's heritage and fragile cultural properties for future generations, the Royal Government of Bhutan and individual members of the royal family have devoted a great deal of attention to the development of institutions focused on preservation

[1] Notes on language: For the reader's benefit, in this introduction I have used simplified spellings for common names, but proper transliterations from Dzongkha and Tibetan of less familiar words and titles. Bhutanese use the term Choekey (*Chos skad*) to refer to literary Tibetan, the traditional written medium of Bhutanese monasteries brought from Tibet in earlier centuries.

and research. These include the Centre for Bhutan Studies founded in 1998, The Bhutan National Library & Archives (1967) and the National Museum (1968). The Centre for Bhutan Studies publishes a regular research journal called *Journal of Bhutan Studies*, and all of these institutes maintain on-line, Internet information and search portals that will greatly assist the work of future scholars.

I. The *Rgyal-rigs*, Written by Monk Ngag-dbang: A History of the Clans and Founding Families of Bumthang and Eastern Bhutan.

"If a man does not know his own family lineage
He is like a monkey playing in a boundless jungle."
(Bhutanese proverb)[2]

As readers of *Bhutan* will know, the *Rgyal-rigs* is the shortened title of an unusual genealogical study written by a monk descended from local nobility in Trashigang named "Monk Ngawang of the Byar", in the years after central and eastern Bhutan were forcibly incorporated into the Drukpa state between about 1648 and 1655. The chiefs of these districts, from Bumthang eastwards and south to the town now called Pemagatshal near the Indian frontier, had ruled over a population representing several ethno-linguistic strata different from the predominant Ngalong of western Bhutan.[3] The Sharchop (*Shar-phyogs-pa*) or 'Easterners' are distant kin to citizens of Tibetan Mon Yul and West Kameng in Arunachal Pradesh, whereas the early inhabitants of Bumthang included the so-called *Gdung* (pron. Dung), whose complex origin myths are tied to Tibet. The *Rgyal-rigs* and the subsequent history called the *Lo-rgyus* are their story.

The *Rgyal-rigs* was studied by Aris in *Bhutan* (1979) on the basis of a single manuscript which he edited and translated in *Sources*. Unfortunately, he was never able to travel to the eastern districts in question. In fact, few Westerners had ever been there. The translation, therefore, contained a large number of unidentified place names, and no map existed to provide the reader with geographical context. This may explain why, more than thirty years after its publication, Tibetologists, Indian historians, and other Himalayan history specialists have yet, in my view, to fully appreciate the fresh perspective that a close study

---

[2] *Mi rang kyi skye brgyud ma shes na // nags mtha' med 'byams pa'i 'spre'u 'dra //.* Choeten Norbu (2003): 1.

[3] Pommaret (1997).

of the *Rgyal-rigs* and the *Lo-rgyus* offer to the standard picture of the greater eastern Himalayan world based on Indian, Tibetan and Chinese sources.

In the years since 1979, Bhutan has become open to tourism and development, and good maps are available for the entire country. It is possible to identify many of the old place names mentioned in the *Rgyal-rigs* and to better visualize the events described. We now know that the complicated topography and river systems of eastern Bhutan go far to explain the rather fragmented distribution of communities mentioned in the *Rgyal-rigs*, many of which are located along upper mountain ridges. Over the centuries the locally prominent families dispersed and intermarried, extending branches southwards to the Duars along the Indian plains, upwards along the Gamri River (called Tawang River in Tibet) and eastwards to Dirang, well into what is now Arunachal Pradesh. Chapters 2 - 5 present what the author Ngawang could learn about their separate genealogical streams from oral accounts of elderly people and from the few relevant texts that he could locate.

The easterners' political organization was very different from that of western Bhutan under the Zhabdrung Rinpoche. There, after his founding in 1625/26 of the nucleus of what would become the Bhutan state, political and religious authority were effectively merged as a single institution under the well-known Buddhist principle called *chos srid zung 'brel.*[4] In eastern Bhutan society was based on old traditions of royal descent, including several strands of nobility (as described in the *Rgyal-rigs*) purportedly deriving from refugee princes of the 9th century Tibetan Yarlung monarchy, with the added feature, as Aris argues (less successfully in my view), of a kind of clan organization. Among the Tibetan princes whose Bhutanese connections are described in the *Rgyal-rigs*, Lha-sras Gtsang-ma (b. 800 CE), son of emperor Sad-na-legs, was most prominent.

Religious affiliation was another difference between east and west. Whereas the Drukpa school of Buddhism had been firmly established in western Bhutan since the 13th century, as late as the first half of the 17th century there were almost no Drukpa monasteries in eastern Bhutan. There, the main religious pioneers from Tibet had come from Nyingmapa and, in the far east, Gelugpa traditions.

From the time that the Zhabdrung Rinpoche took refuge in western Bhutan in 1616 until well into the 18th century, Tibet and Bhutan were either in a state of war or uneasy truce with each other. It was the continuation of a bitter sectarian political struggle that had impelled the Zhabdrung to leave Tibet in the first place.

---

[4] On this concept see Cüppers (2004) and earlier sources cited therein.

In the beginning, Bhutan's Tibetan antagonists were the kings of the province of Gtsang who ruled from Gyantse, and after 1642 fighting continued with the Gelugpa government of the Dalai Lamas in Lhasa.[5] The 5th Dalai Lama launched an army against Drukpa followers among the rulers of western Tibet. Bhutanese Drukpa emissaries were driven out of Nepal at the demand of Gelugpa adversaries. Even the famous *Blue Beryl* medical treatise written by the Tibetan Regent Desi Sangye Gyatsho contained a proscription against its use to heal Drukpa patients.[6]

The two countries competed throughout the Himalayas for sectarian advantage and territory. Numerous Tibetan armies invaded Bhutan, only to be repulsed. In defense, the Zhabdrung's deputies chose to annex eastern Bhutan into the Drukpa state. The conquest of eastern Bhutan in the 1650's by forces from the west was primarily focused on defeating or driving out followers of the Tibetan Gelugpa sect, but other local chiefs were also caught up in it. Responding to this, another military attack was launched by Tibet. It, too, was unsuccessful in that the Tibetans failed to recover control of their monasteries in eastern Bhutan. When the dust finally settled after a declared truce in 1679, a de-facto border between Bhutan and Tibet was created in the northeast. Tibet built a new fortress monastery at Tawang to head off further Bhutanese encroachment, and to serve as a new administrative centre for Tibetan Mon Yul. Other consequences were also significant, if unintended. The extended families of eastern Bhutan now straddled the new frontier between their lands along the Gamri River and in Mon Yul. In the late 20th century, Tawang became a focal point of contention in the border dispute in Arunachal Pradesh between India and China, but it seems to have been forgotten that the context of its creation was a border conflict between Tibet and Bhutan, not between Tibet and India.

The conquest of the local rulers in the east meant the end of their traditional authority. Although the chiefs who cooperated were more or less left in place, their powers were greatly diminished. Perhaps most important to monk Ngawang, as time passed and Drukpa institutions of authority strengthened, the oral traditions about the former eastern chiefs' once proud ancestry began to quickly die out. Even as he wrote, he bemoaned the wanton mixing of the eastern clans and the bored disinterest of young people in the old traditions.[7] It was to save that

---

[5] On this matter see Ardussi (1997).

[6] I thank Michael Aris's brother Anthony for bringing this to my attention.

[7] "*Mi srun gzu lum spyod pa'i shugs 'gros kyis // ya rabs che btsun rje 'bangs mtho dman med // rigs rus 'chol bar song ba'i dus nyid la // brgyud khungs bshad kyang don med ngal ba'i rgyu.*" *Sources:* 12-13.

record for posterity, and to express his aspiration to see the rise to power of a future king, that Ngawang claimed to have composed the *Rgyal-rigs*. More than a few Bhutanese today, I believe, would view the establishment of the monarchy in 1907 as a fulfillment of Ngawang's dream that "...at some future time, one of high family and lineage, noble and judicious, a descendant of the lord-kings [of eastern Bhutan] would come forth appointed by the heavens to rule the land, like a star shining in the daylight." (*Rgyal-rigs:* folio 2.b)

The two books *Rgyal-rigs* and *Lo-rgyus* are thus unique in many respects among Tibetological writings, a story written by the vanquished.[8] They are as close to what modern South Asian historians would call a 'subaltern' history as one is likely to find among Tibetological sources. The *Rgyal-rigs* was, as Ngawang wrote in his introductory poem, "a secret little song, a story I tell carefully only to men of nobility, on whose faces it might raise a smile, not one that I dare to repeat for the ears of all."[9]

The Date of the *Rgyal-rigs*

Given the sensitive issues of ethnicity, territory, power, and religion on which it touches, the *Rgyal-rigs* has not ceased to be a work of political interest. Even more so the *Lo-rgyus*, which is the second text in *Sources* attributed to the same author. A key question of relevance to the issue of historical accuracy is their date of composition. Were they written based on information from eye witnesses to the events of 1655-1685, or much later based on handed down traditions? I have studied this in an earlier publication (Ardussi 2007: 6-9) and concluded that the Earth-Male-Monkey year given near the beginning of the *Rgyal-rigs* and in the colophon refers to the year 1668, a mere decade after the final conquest period of eastern Bhutan, and not 1728 as consistently stated by Aris.[10] However, two other authors have put forward different dates, a Chinese Tibetan author arguing for 1608 and most recently a Bhutanese author for 1848. Of course, still other dates based on the recurring 60-year cycle are also possible. But which is best supported by the evidence?

Aris never addressed the issue of the date of composition anywhere in his writings, before his untimely death in 1999. It is unclear why he settled on 1728. The only evidence for this that I have seen is a handwritten note by an unknown Tibetan writer, on f. 50.a of the Tibet House manuscript that I have called MS **TibH**, which adds in cursive script above the date Earth Male Monkey, the

[8] Aris (1979: 94f) called it a work of protest.

[9] *Sources:* 12-14; Ardussi (2007: 10).

[10] Aris (1979: 94), etc

comment: *rab byung 12 / phyi lo 1728* i.e. "12th cycle, western year 1728." The original MS from which **TibH** is a photocopy came from Bomdila in Arunachal Pradesh, but we do not know by whom and when this note added, or using what information.

The argument for 1668 is based on a most important passage near the beginning of the *Rgyal-rigs* itself, one that was accidently omitted from Aris's edition and so was unknown to him. Just as *Sources* was going to print, the less defective edition of Dorje (1995) came into his hands. There Aris discovered the omission, but rather than address the question of the date he merely included a page of *Addenda and Corrigenda* slipped loosely into the book, in which he himself admitted that "The full implications of this new edition for my own work must await detailed study." Regrettably he never returned to this topic.

The missing passage found in all editions except *Sources* clearly gives the date when the *Rgyal-rigs* was written in the context of well known events of Bhutanese and Tibetan history.

> "According to the [work on chronology entitled] *Bstan rtsis gdan dus thun mong* of the scholar *Mkhas-grub* Lha-dbang Blo-gros, 'In the Fire-Male-Dragon year *Khri* Ral [pa can] died, and Glang Dar-ma became king.'[11] Also, *Lha-sras* Gtsang-ma came to Lho Mon [i.e. Bhutan] at that time. This is certain. Five years later, king Glang Dar-ma was killed by Lha-lung Dpal-gyi-rdo-rje. Ten years later, his sons 'Od-srungs and Yum-brtan fought amongst themselves. Then, from the above-mentioned Fire-Male-Dragon year until today's Earth-Male-Monkey year, a time of warfare with Dbus and Gtsang, 833 years have passed."[12]

---

[11] The passage is found on f. 5.b of this work, written in Bhutan by a Ladakhi scholar and confidant of the Zhabdrung Rinpoche: *me 'brug khri ral gshegs pa dang / dar mas rgyal po byas pa tshun //.* This text was reprinted in 1985 by the Bhutan National Library.

[12] Aris (1986) *Addenda and Corrigenda* to p. 24; *Dorje (1984)* 18; *TibH* 10.b-11.a: *lo'i nges pa ni mkhas grub lha dbang blo gros kyi bstan rtsis gdan dus thun mong las / me pho 'brug la khri ral gshegs pa dang / glang dar mas rgyal po mdzad pas tshun gsung pa dang / lha sras gtsang ma yang de'i dus la lho mon la phebs pa nges pa yin pas / de nas lo lnga la rgyal po glang dar ma lha lung dpal gyi rdo rjes bkrongs pa yin / de nas lo bcu la sras 'od srungs dang yum brtan gnyis 'khrugs pa yin / / gong gi me pho 'brug lo nas da lta'i dbus gtsang 'khrugs pa'i sa pho spre'u lo yan chad la lo grangs brgya phrag brgyad dang sum cu so gsum song /* Part of this passage is corrupted in *Lhasa (1988)*: 95.

As I pointed out in a previous study (Ardussi 2007: 8), of the two traditional dates for Tibetan Emperor Ral-pa-can's death one was the Fire Dragon year 836. Adding 833 years to this date (after the Tibetan manner of taking the starting date as the first year) yields the Earth Monkey year 1668 when the *Rgyal-rigs* was written. This I accept as the correct date. It is also consistent with the sentiments expressed by the author Ngawang about the position of the eastern Bhutanese in the near aftermath of their defeat.

In 1988, after *Bhutan*, *Sources*, and Dorje (1984) were all published, the well known Chinese Tibetan author Chab-spel Tshe-brtan Phun-tshogs produced an article on the topic of Mon Yul and its place in Tibetan history.[13] One of the main sources for his article was an edition of the *Rgyal-rigs* published with brief introduction in the same book, under the title *Mon Chos 'byung,* although the text of that work is almost identical to other editions of the *Rgyal-rigs*. His thesis was to prove from Tibetan sources that Mon Yul had always been an integral part of China. By this I presume he refers only to the modern Tibetan district of that name located northeast of Bhutan. But the location of "Mon" or "Mon Yul" is extremely vague in old Tibetan sources,[14] sometimes referring to places all along the Himalayan chain in what are now Ladakh, Nepal, Bhutan, and Arunachal Pradesh. Several places cited by Chab-spel as within "Mon Yul," such as Kyichu Lhakhang, Khaling and Mongar, have been part of Bhutan since the 17th century or long before. The author does not address these political complexities.
Both of these Tibetan-Chinese writings show evidence of careless editing and unfamiliarity with Bhutanese history. First, the title *Mon Chos 'byung* occurs nowhere in the text itself and appears to be made up for this publication. Secondly, the colophon is abruptly truncated at the point where the author, Monk Ngawang of the Byar's identity is about to be given, and so it is wrongly presented to have been written by two of the local rulers of eastern Bhutan who were in fact only sponsors of the work.[15] Lastly, Chab-spel Tshe-brtan Phun-tshogs has misinterpreted the date. Since the colophon was truncated, he had only to work with the date passage that was missing from the Aris edition. But there, for some reason he ignored the clear statement about adding 833 years, and instead made up his own number and erroneous interpretation: "... from the 9th century, when Lha-sras Gtsang-ma came to Mon Yul at about age 40, until the Earth-Monkey year of the 10th Tibetan era, 1608, when this history was written,

[13] Chab-spel Tshe-brtan Phun-tshogs (1988).

[14] Pommaret (1994, 1999).

[15] For the details see Ardussi (2007).

more than 700 years have passed during which some twenty-three generations of Lha-sras Gtsang-ma's descendants have ruled over the districts of Mon." (my translation)

Perhaps Chab-spel had not seen the *Bstan rtsis gdan dus thun mong* by Lha-dbang Blo-gros (1550-1633/4), whose own colophon written in Bhutan states that it was finished in 1616.[16] This fact alone would make 1608 an impossible date for the *Rgyal-rigs*. Or, perhaps he chose to interpret the phrase "warfare with Dbus and Gtsang" to mean "warfare between Dbus and Gtsang", i.e. the two provinces of central Tibet, which would have been true in 1608, but not in 1668. Or, was he influenced by a desire to not accept that when the *Mon Chos 'byung* (i.e. the *Rgyal-rigs*) was written, Bhutan and Tibet were at war with one another, which might dampen the impact of his nationalistic thesis on the historical relationship between Mon Yul and Tibet. In any case, 1608 cannot be accepted.

Yet another date has been put forward by a Bhutanese author, Choeten Norbu.[17] The author was a former educator at Sherubtse College in Kanglung, near the traditional eastern capital of Trashigang. Following a discussion of chronological issues, the author concludes that the *Rgyal-rigs* was written at the surprisingly late date of 1848. However, with due respect to Choeten Norbu's researches and knowledge of eastern Bhutanese oral history, I think that he has made a simple error. For some reason he has incorrectly read the starting point of the 833 year interval from the above passage of the *Rgyal-rigs* as a Fire-Dragon year when Prince Glang Dar-ma died, instead of his brother Ral-pa-can.[18] But the text does not say that, and so all the chronological difficulties that he addressed in consequence of that misreading go away.

Much work remains to be done on the history of central and eastern Bhutan. Oral traditions are still being recorded, and new historical sources occasionally come to light. The examination of material remains and early ruins will eventually contribute much to a better understanding of this part of Bhutan.

---

[16] See Ardussi (2007) for the details. This text was reprinted in 1985 by the Bhutan National Library.

[17] Choeten Norbu (2003):

[18] Norbu also accepts that Glang Ḍar-ma's death occurred in AD 906, whereas most sources place the event in 842 (e.g. Dung-dkar Rin-po-che (2002). *Dung dkar tshig mdzod chen mo:* 578).

II The *Lo-rgyus*: A History of Bhutan's Eastward Expansion during the Mid 17th Century

The colophon of this unusual and rare text identifies the author as "the old monk Wagindra" (i.e. Ngawang), whom Michael Aris accepts to be the same person as the author as the *Rgyal-rigs.* Based on the sequence of events, I would tentatively date the work to the period 1680-1690. As discussed above, it is a kind of continuation of the *Rgyal-rigs*. Whereas the latter describes the ancestry and spread of the eastern chieftains and their descendants, the *Lo-rgyus* tells the story of their defeat at the hands of the Bhutanese army launched during the 1650's from Punakha in the west, at the command of the civil ruler of Bhutan, the famous 3rd Druk Desi (*Sde-srid*) Mingyur Tenpa (*Mi-´gyur Brtan-pa*) (r.1667-1680). In the aftermath of this struggle, the imposing fortress Dzong of Trashigang was constructed high above the banks of the Gamri River on the site of an earlier castle named Beng-mkhar. From there, eastern Bhutan would be administered for the next 250 years.

The *Lo-rgyus* focuses on the course of the battles between the Bhutanese army from the west and the local forces, which included Monpa people fighting on behalf of the Gelugpa Lama of Merag. But the Merag Lama fled to Tibet, and upon their defeat the local chiefs took a public oath to convert their allegiance from the Yellow Hat faith to that of the Drukpa. The story concludes with a description of the peace and tranquility which followed in the districts of eastern Bhutan, and how the former general of the Bhutanese forces and his assistant, *Dbu-mdzad* Dam-chos Rab-rgyas and *Sku-drung* Pad-dkar Chos-´phel, established and justly administered the law of the land on behalf of their ultimate rulers, the Zhabdrung Rinpoche Ngawang Namgyal and his successors.[19] As his title would indicate and in keeping with Bhutanese tradition, *Dbu-mdzad* (Monastic Precentor) Dam-chos Rab-rgyas would appear to have been a monk before taking on the role of commander and administrator. He is a man about whom we wish we knew more.

III. The Bhutan Legal Code of 1729, by the 10th Druk Desi Tenzin Chogyal.

The importance of the Bhutan legal code of 1729 for the understanding of 17th - 18th century Bhutanese society cannot be overestimated. It contains

[19] Ironically, the Zhabdrung had died in 1651, but his death was being kept secret during this period of war with Tibet.

detailed information and policy statements relating to state administration, taxation policies and prescribed official behaviour.

The text translated by Aris was composed by the 10th Druk Desi Mipham Wangpo (1709-1738), who was the immediate reincarnation of the renowned 4th Druk Desi Tenzin Rabgye (1638-1696) and the the ruler of Bhutan during that era. It forms a supplement to the first formally written history of Bhutan called *Lho'i chos 'byung—History of the Southlands*, written during the years 1731-'59 by the 10th Je Khenpo or Chief Abbot of the state monastic system of Bhutan, Tendzin Chogyal (1700-1767), at the behest of Mipham Wangpo who did not live to see it completed.

The political context for this history was a period during the 1730's of intensely difficult relations between Bhutan and Tibet, during which Tibetan forces invaded Bhutan to settle a civil war then raging between two contending factions centered in Paro and Punakha valleys.[20] In the aftermath of this war, the rulers of Tibet and Bhutan attempted to establish normalized relations, for the first time since the Zhabdrung had come to Bhutan in 1616.

The *Lho'i chos-'byung* with the appended legal code had a quasi-political inspiration. It was written in part to explain the governing dilemma that had resulted from the Zhabdrung's untimely demise in 1651, leading to the factional conflict. Mipham Wangpo was instrumental in the effort to improve relations with Tibet, and was the first Bhutanese ruler to travel there since the state was founded. With the Manchu Ambans in Lhasa overseeing the peace efforts, the timely issuance of a Bhutanese legal code would no doubt have helped to demonstrate that Bhutan was not the lawless, troublesome state that her Tibetan enemies had hitherto portrayed.

The legal code of Mipham Wangpo continues a long tradition of Tibetan rulers issuing pronouncements on law or "legal edicts" *(bka'-khrims)*, which were codifications based on Buddhist canonical and moral principles and prescriptions of proper behaviour for the ministerial class. It is well established that such law codes drew upon those of earlier rulers, a primary motive being to show continuity and legitimacy to rule based on Buddhist theories of governance. The earliest versions are found in Tibetan documents from Dunhuang where they attach primarily to Tibet's great 7th century emperor and law-giver Songtsen Gampo. Cüppers has recently argued that a significant part of Mipham Wangpo's *bka'-'khrims* was copied from a similar law code from Tibet, the so-called 21-section

---

[20] The information in this paragraph is dealt with in Ardussi (1997) and in a forthcoming book.

"Guidelines for Government Officials" (Tib: *Glang dor gsal bar ston pa'i drang thig dwangs shel me long nyer gcig pa*) written in 1681 by the 5th Dalai Lama's regent Desi Sangye Gyatsho.[21] Mipham Wangpo himself claims that his work was based on legal codes of the early Tibetan monarchs and on an earlier Bhutanese law code issued by the First Druk Desi Tenzin Druggye (1591-1656). Not surprisingly, he does not mention any borrowing from the legal edict of the Tibetan Desi Sangye Gyatsho whom the Bhutanese viewed as a bitter and partisan enemy. The extent to which both law codes may have borrowed from older documents deserves to be studied in some depth.

The existence of even earlier Bhutanese legal codes is known from Choekey / Tibetan literature. The Zhabdrung Rinpoche himself issued a code entitled called *Clear Mirror of the Twofold System of Laws [religious and secular]* according to a Bhutanese biography published in 1720, nine years before Mipham Wangpo's law code was written.[22] No document with this title has so far turned up in Bhutanese private or monastery libraries. The law code attributed by Mipham Wangpo to the First Desi Tenzin Druggye is similarly missing.

An inscribed stone Bhutanese legal code outside the traditional winter capital at Punakha Dzong has long been known, however, although until recently no copy has been available for examination. In *Sources* (p. 8) Aris referred to this monument which he had not seen, but which had been reported to him as containing excerpts from Mipham Wangpo's legal code of 1729.

Recently, I was presented with a transcription of the Punakha slate inscription panels prepared by the Research and Development Division of the High Court of Bhutan. Based on my preliminary study, it would appear that the Punakha inscriptions contain not excerpts from the *bka'-khrims* of Mipham Wangpo, but rather an original legal code issued by the Zhabdrung Rinpoche Ngawang Namgyal himself! It bears the title *Khams gsum chos kyi rgyal po dpal ldan 'brug pa rin po che ngag gi dbang po phyogs thams cad las rnam par rgyal ba'i bka' khrims gser gyi gnya' shing*: "'The Golden Yoke of Legal Edicts' [as dictated] by the Dharmarâja of the Three Realms, the Glorious Drukpa Rinpoche Ngawang Namgyal." Further on in the preamble the author clearly states that "I, the Glorious Drukpa Rinpoche, the Dharmarâja, He who is Possessed of Magical Power, Vajra-Destroyer of Enemy Forces, have erected this of my own intent as lord and protector of the unruly and untamed beings in this Southern Land of Four

---

[21] Cüppers (2007).

[22] *Namthar of Gyalse Tenzin Rabgye:* folio 278.a, where the title is given: *Lugs gnyis kyi bka' khrims gtsang ma'i me long.*

Doors."[23] The colophon of this *bka'-khrims* also concludes in the voice of the Zhabdrung: "Because I, the Chos-rje ´Brug-pa must ensure that the Two-fold System [of religious and secular laws] is protected, [it is hereby ordained] that everyone, high and low, must unerringly obey the injunctions and prohibitions."

A study of this exciting new 17th century document must await a detailed examination of the inscriptions themselves. Superficially, it differs from the much longer 1729 legal code of Mipham Wangpo in that it is more clearly based on old Tibetan sources, citing as ancient precedents *The Six-fold Bka'-khrims* of Songtsen Gampo and *The Laws of Khri rtse ´bum bzher,* for example.[24]

IV. The Report on Bhutan of the Jesuit Priest Estevao Cacella (1627) "While Travelling to the Kingdom of Potente."

The fourth work in *Sources* rested unknown for nearly 300 years in the archives of the Vatican, until first studied briefly by C.H. Wessels in his 1924 book *Early Jesuit Travelers in Central Asia.* Wessels knew little about Bhutan and did not have the background or resources to understand the full importance of the document. Aris's useful translation and commentary in *Bhutan* (pp. 207 ff) first presented the text in its important historical context. A more complete translation has been published recently in the inaugural issue of *Journal of Bhutan Studies*.[25]

Readers may be interested to know that this Jesuit *Report* also sheds light on the origin of the name Bhutan, which quite capriciously came to be attached to the country of Bhutan. As shown in the *Report*'s title, the Jesuits were travelling to "The Kingdom of Potente." Aris did not recognize that this meant Tibet, not Bhutan. The spurious theory, accepted by Aris and many Indian historians that "Potente" was a corruption of Sanskrit Bhotânta (interpreted to mean "The end of Tibet', i.e. Bhutan) has been lately exposed in an interesting article by Romola Gandolfo, who shows in great detail how "Potente" originated as a peculiar name for Tibet on early European maps.[26] Even the name Bhutan once meant Tibet, as

---

[23] *Sgos su kha bzhi lho'i yul khams kyi sems can mu rgod mi bsrun pa rnams kyi skyabs dang mgon du / nged dpal ldan ´brug pa rin po che mthu chen chos kyi rgyal po bdud dpung ´joms pa'i rdo rjer bsam bzhin du bzhengs pa yin pas /*. The names Mthu-chen and Bdud-´joms rdo-rje were epithets of power that the Zhabdrung used of himself in his various writings and letters. *Kha bzhi lho'i rgyal khams* or Southern Realm of Four Doors was a traditional name for Bhutan.

[24] For more information on these texts, see Dotson (2006).

[25] Baille (1999).

evidenced by the French philosopher Voltaire's 18th century moral tale about the Dalai Lama whom he called Le Roi du Boutan.[27] In fact the Portuguese Jesuits reported that the indigenous name of the country was Cambirasi. Michael Aris could offer no useful explanation of this term (*Sources:* p.184 and fn. 14). I am fairly sure that it represents a garbled pronunciation of the old traditional name of Bhutan *Kha bzhi* or *Lho kha bzhi*, meaning "Southern Land of Four Doors."

Supplemental Bibliography of Recent Studies

Articles

Ardussi, John (1997). "The Rapprochement between Bhutan and Tibet under the Enlightened Rule of Sde-srid XIII Shes-rab-dbang-phyug (r. 1744-63)." *In* Helmut Krasser, et al, eds. *Tibetan Studies. PIATS 7 Graz 1995:* 17-27. Wien: Verlag der Österreichischen Akademie der Wissenschaften. (Reprinted in *Journal of Bhutan Studies* vol. 1, no. 1, 1999: 64-83).

_____ (2004). "The gDung Lineages of Central and Eastern Bhutan - A Reappraisal of their Origin, Based on Literary Sources." *In* Karma Ura & Sonam Kinga, eds. *The Spider and the Piglet. Proceedings of the First International Seminar on Bhutan Studies.* Thimphu, Centre for Bhutan Studies: 60-72. Develops a possible alternate interpretation of the origin of the gDung lineages, based on the *Rgyal-rigs*.

_____ (2007). "Notes on the rGyal rigs of Ngawang and the Clan History of Eastern Bhutan and Shar Mon." *In* Ramon N. Prats, ed. *The Pandita and the Siddha. Tibetan Studies in Honour of E. Gene Smith.* (Dharamshala (H.P.) India: Amnye Machen Institute): 1-11. A reappraisal of the authorship of the *Rgyal-rigs* based on newly available manuscripts, and a critical study of its date of composition.

_____ (2007a). "Preliminary Investigation of Bhutanese Castle Ruins and Caves Associated with Lha sras Gtsang ma" *In* John A. Ardussi & Françoise, eds. *Bhutan. Traditions and Changes.* Leiden: Brill.

Baille, Luiza Maria (1999). "Father Estevao Cacella's Report on Bhutan in 1627." *Journal of Bhutan Studies.* Vol. 1, no. 1: 1-35 (Thimphu: Centre for Bhutan Studies). Contains another, more complete translation than Michael Aris's, of the Portuguese original MS of Cacella's *Relação,* preserved in the Vatican Library

[26] Gandolfo (2004)

[27] Ibid: 114.

Chab-spel Tshe-brtan Phun-tshogs (1988). "*Mon yul ni sngar nas krung go'i mnga' khongs yin pa'i lo rgyus dpang rtags*." *In* Padma bsKal-bzang & Blo-bzang Tshe-brtan, eds. (1988) *Bod kyi lo rgyus rig gnas dpyad gzhi'i rgyu cha bdams bsgrigs* ('Selected Source Materials on Tibetan History and Culture') vol. 10, no. 1. Beijing, Mi-rigs dpe-skrun khang: 1-9. (Also included in the author's Collected Works or *gSung-rtsom Phyogs-bsgrigs:* Beijing, 1993, pp. 140-150). This article surveys Tibetan language sources, including the so-called *Mon Chos 'byung* (i.e. the *Rgyal-rigs*) to try to demonstrate that Mon Yul (including parts now within Bhutan) was since early times an integral part of China.

Cüppers, Christoph (2004) ed. *The Relationship Between Religion and State (chos srid zung 'brel) in Traditional Tibet.* Lumbini: International Research Institute.

_____ (2007). "Bstan 'dzin Chos rgyal's Bhutan Legal Code of 1729 in Comparison with Sde srid Sangs rgyas rgya mtsho's Guidelines for Government Officials." *In* John Ardussi & Françoise Pommaret (eds.). *Bhutan. Traditions and Changes.* Leiden, Brill: 45-52.

Dotson, Brandon (2006). *Administration and Law in the Tibetan Empire.* Unpublished D. Phil thesis, Oriental Institute, Oxford University.

Gandolfo, Romola (2004). "Bhutan and Tibet in European Cartography (1597-1800)." *In* Ura, Karma & Sonam Kinga, eds. *The Spider and the Piglet (Proceedings of the First International Conference on Bhutan Studies).* Thimphu: Centre for Bhutan Studies.

Pelgen, U. & T. Dorji (1997). "Lhasey Tsangma: Prince in Exile." In *Sherub Doenme—Academic Journal of Sherubtse College*, vol. 3 (pt. 1 & 2): 83-90. Kanglung, Bhutan.

_____ & Tenzin Rigden (1999). *Kengrig Namsum: A Historical Profile of Zhemgang Dzongkhag.* Zhemgang: Integrated Sustainable Development Programme / SNV. Contains oral traditional material relevant to the genealogical themes of the *Rgyal-rigs.*

Pommaret, Françoise (1994). "Entrance-Keepers of a Hidden Country: Preliminary Notes on the Monpa of South-Central Bhutan." *Tibet Journal,* vol. 19/3: 46-62. One of three recent articles by Pommaret on the ancient Mon people of Bhutan, their society and myths.

______ (1997). "Le pilier/mégalithe de Nabji au Bhoutan central: essai de compréhension d'un 'lieu surdéterminé'." *In* Samten Karmay & Philippe Sagant, (eds.) *Les habitants du Toit du monde.* Nanterre: Société d'ethnologie: 391-417.

_____ (1998). "Ethnic Mosaic: Peoples of Bhutan." *In* Schicklgruber, Christian & Françoise Pommaret, eds. *Bhutan Mountain Fortress of the Gods.* Boston, Shambhala.

______ (1999). "The Mon-pa Revisited: In Search of Mon." *In* Toni Huber (1999). *Sacred Spaces and Powerful Places in Tibetan Culture*. Dharamsala, LTWA: 52-73.

Tibetan / Chos-skad Sources

Choeten Norbu (2003). *The Garden of Mind Stretching Historical Account of Khardung Gyalpo.* (Choekey Title: *Slob dpon chos rten nor bu gyis mdzad pa'i 'khar gdung rgyal po'i lo rgyus rgyal rabs yid dbang 'phel ba'i skyed tshal*)." Thimphu: Centre for Bhutan Studies. (Monograph 5). A recent study by a former instructor at Sherubtse College and at the Institute of Language and Cultural Studies, Semtokha, of written and oral traditions about the ancestral origins of the Tshangla speaking peoples of eastern and southern Bhutan.

Zhabs-drung Ngag-dbang Rnam-rgyal (ca. 1651). *Khams gsum chos kyi rgyal po dpal ldan 'brug pa rin po che ngag gi dbang po phyogs thams cad las rnam par rgyal ba'i bka' khrims gser gyi gnya' shing zhe bya ba'i gtam*: (" 'The Golden Yoke of Legal Edicts', [as dictated] by the Dharmarâja of the Three Realms, the Glorious Drukpa Rinpoche Ngawang Namgyal.") This is the apparently original law code of Zhabs-drung Rin-po-che Ngag-dbang Rnam-rgyal (1694-1651), carved on slate tablets erected in front of the outer courtyard of Punakha Dzong.

Other Editions and Manuscripts of the Rgyal-rigs

Butters, Christopher & Khenpo Phuntshok Tashi (1992). Unpublished translation of the *Rgyal-rigs*, in the collection of The National Library of Bhutan.

Dorje (1984). *Dasho Tenzin Dorje* (Bstan-'dzin rDo-rje). *Bod rje mnga' bdag khri ral pa can gyi sku mched lha sras gtsang ma'i gdung brgyud 'phel rabs dang 'bangs kyi mi rabs mched khungs lo rgyus gsal ba'i sgron me.* np. An edition of the *Rgyal rigs* by Dasho Tenzin Dorje, as referred to in the "Addenda & Corrigenda" to *Sources.* This was also issued in 1985 under the auspices of the U.S. Library of Congress, with an English cover page, by Lama Rigzin Norbu. As I have shown elsewhere (Ardussi 2007), there are several significant deviations between this text and the version published by Aris in *Sources*, even though the latter was based on a copy made for Aris by Dasho Tenzin Dorje. I therefore treat this text as a distinct edition.

Lhasa (1988) = *Mon Chos 'byung.* *<<Rje 'bangs rnams kyi rigs rus kyi 'byung khungs gsal ba'i sgron me >> (Mon chos 'byung) zhes bya ba bzhugs so /.* Contained in Padma sKal-bzang & Blo-bzang Tshe-brtan, eds., (1988) *Bod kyi lo rgyus rig gnas dpyad gzhi'i rgyu cha bdams bsgrigs* (No. 1, General Series no. 10). Beijing, Mi-rigs dpe-skrun khang, pp. 87-130 . Reputed authors: *Lha-btsun* Ngag-dbang Phun-tshogs and Phyi-tshang Mong-khar-gyi rgyal-po. Date: none stated. The separate colophons of the individual sections preserve the more familiar title *Rgyal rigs 'byung khungs gsal ba'i sgron me.* The anonymous editor's preface tells us only that the source MS came from the state archives of the TAR *(Bod rang skyong ljongs yig tshags khang)*.

TibH *Gangs can bod du rje rgyal gnya' khri btsan / srong btsan sgam po khri srong lde'u btsan dang / lho phyogs mon du lha sras gtsang ma zhes / rnam par sprul pa'i skye[s] mchog de rnams kyi / gong ma rje'i gdung rabs 'byung khungs dang / 'og ma 'bangs kyi mi rabs chad tshul sogs / ng[e]s par gsal ba'i sgron me bzhugs so //.* Photocopy located in Tibet House, New Delhi, of an *dbu-can* MS in 50 folios. (However, the same illegible or missing folios from *LTWA* can be faintly read in this photocopy; they are in a different handwriting). Author (f. 49.b): *Byar gyi bandhe* Wa gindra (= Ngag-dbang). Date (f. 50.a): *sa pho spre'i lo hor zla brgyad pa'i yar tshes bzang po .*

LTWA[28] Second generation photocopy prepared from **TibH**, located in The Library of Tibetan Works and Archives, Dharamsala, as MS no. Ka 10-5845 (ff. 38, 45-47 said to be missing or illegible). I have not examined this photocopy directly and information was provided by to me by Lobsang Shastri. See also the listing in Dan Martin, *Tibetan Histories* (Serindia, 1997): Entry no. 265B.

CBS-1. An old, somewhat damaged MS copy of the *Rgyal-rigs*, in the possession of the Centre for Bhutan Studies, Thimphu, Bhutan. A photocopy of this MS was provided to me in 2007 by researchers at CBS.

Gelong Ngawang (2003). *The Lamp Which Illuminates the Origins of Royal Families.* (Choekey title: *Dge slong Ngag dbang mdzad pa'i rgyal rigs 'byung khungs gsal ba'i sgron me*). Thimphu: Centre for Bhutan Studies, 2003. A typeset version of the *Rgyal-rigs,* in Tibetan / Chokey, perhaps based on **CBS-1.**

[28] Information on this document was supplied in an email dated 12/25/00 from Lobsang Shastri of LTWA.

It is said to come from Bomdila, Arunachal Pradesh. A comparison of hand writing on the last page, and other peculiarities, confirm that it is the same manuscript as *TibH.*

Michael Aris: *Sources for the History of Bhutan*

ADDENDA AND CORRIGENDA

PAGE 2, line 8 from bottom: *For* "Text I: f.33a" *read* "Text I: f.6a"

PAGE 2, line 6 from bottom: *For "thos-pa" read "thod-pa"*

PAGE 4, line 2: *For* "Text IV" *read* "Text III"

PAGE 24, line 15 from bottom (*rGyal-rigs*, f.11b):
For "me kyis rtag par dpyad pa'i spyod yul du rag las pas so ||"
Read "me pho 'brug la khri ral gshegs pa dang | glang dar mas rgyal po mdzad pas tshun gsung pa dang | lha sras gtsang ma yang de'i dus la lho mon la phebs pa nges pa yin pas | de nas lo lnga la rgyal po glang dar ma lha lung dpal gyi rdo rjes bkrongs pa yin || de nas lo bcu la sras 'od srungs dang yum brtan gnyis 'khrugs pa yin || gong gi me pho 'brug lo nas da lta'i dbus gtsang 'khrugs pa'i sa pho spre'u lo yan chad la lo grangs brgya phrag brgyad dang sum cu so gsum song | rgya bod mkhas pa'i yang rtse rnams gling paṇ chen gyis bstan rtsi'i 'debs gter las kyang glang dar ma'i sras ni 'od srungs te || gdung rabs nyi shu thamṃ pa 'das gsungs pa dang || da lta'i sa pho spre'u lo yan chad la | lha sras gtsang ma'i gdung rabs kyang nyi shu rtsa gcig 'das nas da lta rtsa gsum gyi steng la yod | de nas blo gros shes ldan mkhas pa nyams myong rig rtsal la che ba rnams kyi brtag shing dpyad pa'i spyod yul du rag las pas so ||"

This reading has been obtained from an edition of the *rGyal-rigs* collated from three different manuscripts by *Drag-shos* bsTan-'dzin rDo-rje in 1984 and published under the title of *Bod-rje mnga'-bdag khri ral-pa-can-gyi sku-mched lha-sras gtsang-ma'i gdung-brgyud 'phel-rabs dang 'bangs-kyi mi-rabs mched-khungs lo-rgyus gsal-ba'i sgron-me* (n.p., n.d.). See pp. 18-19. The full implications of this new edition for my own work must await detailed study.

PAGE 152, line 12 (*bKa'-khrims*, f.111a): *After* "rdzong du 'thon mi chog |" *Insert* "yongs kyang rgyags mthun mjal gsos sogs sgrigs kyi byin mi chog | de phyin lam bsrung bka' rgya yod na ma gtogs | gzhan tshwa sman 'phrod rten gyi 'gro 'dug mi bkag cing so sor dgongs khrol byas gtong chog |"

I am indebted to Mr. Yoshiro Imaeda for pointing out this omission.

PAGE 168, bottom: The following notes to the *bka'-khrims* were omitted:

[74] The levy of *dbang-yon* as an additional form of taxation continued in Bhutan till quite recently. One of my informants described the institution of *dbang-yon* in this context as "an evil activity fixed in perpetuity" (*spros-ngan rgyun-'jag*).

[75] Shakabpa (1976 : 198) takes this tradition as applied to Mu-ne bTsan-po for an early example of Tibetan 'land reform' (*sa-zhing bcos-sgyur*). The claim, however, rests on nothing more than conjecture.

[76] DS (175): 'koot' (?)

[77] DS (176): "lug-rgyab = a sheep's load - possibly a kind of illegal tax imposed by minor local officials from the raiyots."

[78] This is an odd construction which I prefer to leave untranslated. LN suggests: *yar 'gro-chog-pa yang-na 'gro-ba'i zhor-la zer-ba-yin* |. DS (176): "in cases where (one) has to accompany the higher authorities (possibly the Deb or Dharma rajas)."

[79] DS (177): "in lieu of cash revenue".

[80] A silk fabric dyed yellow and printed with floral motifs.

81 The assessment of harvest-tax (*bsdu-khral*, see Glossary) is today based either on the area of the land in question or on its productive capacity, although it is not clear to me which circumstances have to obtain to determine the choice of system. In the former, the land is measured according to *glang-dor* ('a pair of oxen'), that is to say the area of land that can be ploughed in one day, starting at dawn and ending at midday (*nyin - gung*, actually about 2.0 pm). In the latter system, productive capacity was reckoned by the quantity of seed planted. This is known as *son-grangs* ("seed-number"). Five measures of seed (*son-bre*) are said to equal approximately one *glang-dor*. According to the quality of their land, taxpayers (*khral-pa*) are placed in one of three categories: maximum, intermediate or minimum (*khral-rab 'bring mtha'-ma*). New assessments (*zhib-rtsis*) could take place from time to time on the order of the ruler or district governor. Today the whole question of land-tax falls under the charge of the *Sa-khram Yig-tshang* at bKra-shis Chos-rdzong in Thim-phu.

The meat-tax and butter-tax referred to here were presumably levied from the pastoral communities in the north of the country in lieu of harvest-tax. I do not know how they were assessed. A useful account of Tibetan land-tax and the history of the various 'settlements' after 1740 is contained in Surkhang 1966.

82 The *she-ma* ('dairyman') is reckoned to be of a higher status than the *rdzi-bo* ('herdsman'). The former's work includes shearing yaks and curing hides, besides making cheese and butter. The latter is the one who actually goes around with the herd.

83 The colloquial words for slave in western Bhutan are 'zap' (masculine) and 'jham' (feminine). All slaves received their manumission in the 1950's.

84 I.e. in cash.

85 I.e. on his mother's or father's side of the family.

86 I.e. the bloodless food.

87 I am not sure of the meaning of *stong-rtsi zhabs-tog*. The phrase might allude to a fine for manslaughter (*stong*) incurred by the deceased and still outstanding.

88 The verb *brdung* (future of *rdung*, 'to pound') suggests the *pise* construction of most Bhutanese buildings.

89 One of the severest grievances was caused by the community being required to provide taxes and corvée for tax estates that stood empty, their liabilities still entered on the demand roll. Such 'empty estates' are called *rkang-stong* or *rtsa-stong-sa*.

90 'The Tenth Day (of the Month)', a popular ritual devoted to Padmasambhava. In extended form it takes place as an annual festival of sacred dance in the provincial capitals.

91 The *ma-ṇi-ba* (*ma-ṇi-pa* in Tibetan, 'manip' in Bhutanese vernacular) are wandering bards who carry around with them portable *stūpas* known as *bkra-shis sgo-mang*, the doors of which open up to show scenes illustrating the stories from their repertoire. In Tibet the *ma-ṇi-pa* used painted scrolls instead for this purpose. The 'licensed' bards referred to here were formally attached to government temples and monasteries, to which they would return in between their rounds of the villages. They no longer enjoy their former dispensation from taxes today and the whole custom is in some danger of disappearing. Apart from the common stock of stories deriving from Indian legends ('Gro-ba bZang-mo, Dri-med Kun-ldan, gZugs-kyi Nyi-ma etc.) they sing several items peculier to Bhutan, such as the life stories of the Ist *Zhabs-drung* and of 'Brug-pa Kun-legs. They also sing a great number of invocations based on the famous six-syllable *mantra* from which they derive their name.

92 DS (183):"...thrown into the water and then cremated."

93 I have avoided *dnar* for *las-sgo* here as the term probably includes the marts near the Tibetan border.

94 I am not sure of the exact sense of *gtan-tshigs* here, though it is clearly related to *gtsigs* in the 8th and 9th century inscriptions meaning 'decree'.

95 Literally, 'as his red ornaments'.

96 The famous minister of King Srong-btsan sGam-po.

97 Gods, humans and demi-gods (*lha, mi, lha-ma-yin*).

98 See Note 16 above

99 The Age of Truth (or Perfection).

100 Petech (1972:211 Note 75) points out that the term *rab-byung* (1747) is in contradiction to Earth Bird (1729) and that both years are incompatible with what he holds to be Mi-pham dBang-po's period of rule: 1730-1745. The dates given in LP's list, however, are 1729-1736 and in the preamble it is clearly stated that the decree was composed at the very beginning of Mi-pham dBang-po's reign. Earth Bird is therefore correct, while *rab-byung* may be taken as a simple error.

CONTENTS

PREFACE

The four works presented here have till now, and particularly in recent years, enjoyed a rather chequered career. They originally formed the second volume of the doctoral thesis I submitted in 1978 to the University of London. They were subsequently made available in the form of a microfilm supplement to my *Bhutan: The Early History of a Himalayan Kingdom* (Warminster and New Delhi, 1979). A few copies of the supplement were printed from the originals, paginated and bound for the benefit of those colleagues who were reviewing the main volume. It soon became clear, however, that the choice of microfiche as the medium of publication (a choice which had been determined only by the need for economy) was a major obstacle to the dissemination of these sources: most colleagues and students had strong inhibitions about using even as simple a piece of technology as a fiche reader! Many asked me to look again for a more conventional means of publication. This has now been made possible due to the help and kindness of Professor Ernst Steinkellner through the hospitality of his flourishing series, the Wiener Studien zur Tibetologie und Buddhismuskunde.

The book as now published is reproduced directly from the originals typeset by Aris & Phillips Ltd. The only changes are a few minor corrections and insertions, a reorganized structure (and consequent repagination) and the addition of a bibliography. These amendments were kindly made for me by Mr Philip Mudd, to whom I am indebted.

Among the critical notices which the first edition received, by far the most detailed comments were those provided by Professor J.W. de Jong in the *Indo-Iranian Journal.** The corrections and alternative readings he proposed have not been incorporated. Instead I should like to summarize them here for the benefit of readers, and I take this opportunity of thanking Professor de Jong most warmly for his valued attention:

Text I: f. 14b: on comparison with the form given on f. 29a, there is a case for correcting *lha'i khams-pa* to *lha'u khams-pa*.
Text I: f. 33a: for *Udayana* read *Śantānīka*.
Text I: f. 33a: for *tshe'i 'dus byas-nas* read *tshe'i dus byas-nas*.
Text I: f. 41a: *thong-pa* should not have been corrected to *thos-pa*, and the translation should read: "One does not break somebody's plough for the sake of the people".
Text I: ff. 41a, 43a &
Text II: ff. 18b, 19a: the phrase *tshug ma-thub-par* should be rendered throughout as "unable to bear, withstand".

Text III: f. 109a: a quotation from the *Sa-skya legs-bshad* which I had failed to identify is the one starting *blo-chung*: this is Bosson No. 12. Similarly:

Text III: f. 109b: *rgyal-po-nyid* is Bosson No. 202.

Michael Aris

Wolfson College, Oxford
September, 1985

* It may be useful to list here all the reviews which appeared: Alastair Lamb in *British Book News*, Nov. 1980; Charles Ramble in *Jl. of the Anthropological Society of Oxford*, xi (1980); Romila Thapar in *The Hindusthan Times*, 22 May 1981; K.R. Norman in *Modern Asian Studies*, 1981; Lama Chime Radha in *Jl. of the Royal Asiatic Society*, (1981), no. 2; R.C. Grey in *Asian Affairs*, xiii (1982); Luciano Petech in *Bull. of the School of Oriental and African Studies*, xlv (1982); J.W. de Jong in *Indo-Iranian Jl.*, xxiv (1982); Penny Walker in *The Middle Way*, (1982); D.B. Vohra in *The Times of India*, 7 Feb. 1982; Ernest Gellner in *Jl. of Asian Studies*, xli (1982); Sunanda K. Datta-Ray in *The Statesman* [Calcutta], 14 Nov. 1982; A.W. Macdonald in *Journal Asiatique*, (1983); Per Kvaerne in *Acta Orientalia*, xlv (1984); Anne Chayet in *Arts Asiatique*, xlv (1984).

ABBREVIATIONS

DS	Dousamdup (Zla-ba bSam-grub): English translation of Text IV (the Legal Code from *LCB* I) in the British Library
Dukūla	The autobiography of the 5th Dalai Lama (1617-82), vol. ka.
rGyal-rigs	*rGyal-rigs 'byung-khungs gsal-ba'i sgron-me* by Ngag-dbang, 1728 (Text I)
LCB I	*lHo'i chos-'byung* by bsTan-'dzin Chos-rgyal, 1759
LCB II	*lHo-phyogs nags-mo'i ljongs-kyi chos-'byung* by dGe-'dun Rin-chen, 1972
LN	*Slob-dpon* Nag-mdog (informant)
Lo-rgyus	*Lo-rgyus gsal-ba'i me-long* by Ngag-dbang, n.d. (Text II)
LP	*Slob-dpon* Padma-lags (informant)
PBP	The life of *Zhabs-drung* Ngag-dbang rNam-rgyal (1594-?1651) by *gTsang mKhan-chen*, vol. *nga* (*lHo'i skor*)
Relaçao	Cacella's account of his stay in Bhutan, 1627 (Text IV)
TD	bsTan-'dzin rDo-rje (informant)
Tohoku	*A Complete Catalogue of the Tibetan Buddhist Canons*
TR	sTobs-dga' Rin-po-che (informant)
*	Rejected spellings and omissions in the original texts are marked by asterisks and placed in the margin. Corrected spellings and reconstructions are given in the body of the texts themselves.
[ ]	Enclose matter not in the original, but are inserted in the English to make the sense clear.
[. . .]	Denote a lacuna.

BACKGROUND TO THE TEXTS

The works selected for inclusion have been chosen because of their value as crucial source material on the formative era of Bhutanese history, as they cover the entire period leading to the full emergence of the Bhutanese theocracy. Their relative brevity as compared with the other major works relevant to this period further suggested the convenience of presenting them here as a group of inter-related 'minor' texts. While the first two works in this collection have never before been available to modern scholarship, and are indeed hardly known even in Bhutan, the next two (which include a text translated from Portuguese) have been partially known from the work of White (1909) and Wessels (1924). Although these earlier writers fully realised their importance, neither of them were able to fit these works into the historical context with any degree of success, and the translations they provided were incomplete. To form something of a chronological sequence the works have to be read in the order: I, IV, II, III. The present order was determined by the close relationship of I and II and by the nature of IV as 'odd man out'.

I. *Sa-skyong rgyal-po'i gdung-rabs 'byung-khungs dang 'bangs-kyi mi-rabs chad-tshul nges-par gsal-ba'i sgron-me* (short title: *rGyal-rigs 'byung-khungs gsal-ba'i sgron-me*), *dbu-can* ms. in 54 folios measuring approx. 35 x 8½ cms. Author: the monk Ngag-dbang (Wa-gindra) of the Byar clan. Date: 1728.

I first heard of this work and No. II below in 1971 from *Drag-shos* bsTan-'dzin rDo-rje, former magistrate of bKra-shis-sgang rDzong, who was at that time employed at the Audit Office in the capital. He very kindly offered to secure copies for me from eastern Bhutan and after some months he succeeded in obtaining the manuscripts from which these copies were made. The copyist made no attempt to correct the many orthographic errors which had crept into the two works since the time of their composition and some effort has now gone into emending the more obvious mistakes. A few lacunae remain unfilled but not so as to cause serious disruption. bsTan-'dzin rDo-rje himself wrote down a few comments on the copy of this first work and these are given here in the notes under the abbreviation TD. *Slob-dpon* Padma-lags (LP) very kindly answered some specific queries in a letter dated 10/5/77. The work is uniquely important for its treatment of the ancient ruling clans and families of central and eastern Bhutan, particularly those clans which claimed descent from Prince gTsang-ma of Tibet (and which now no longer exist) and those families known as the gDung which still survive in the Bum-thang region today. I have already attempted to assess the quality of the work's historical testimony (Aris 1979: 83-139), and several unexpected references were found in Tibetan literature that shed light on its evidence. However, it should perhaps be pointed out again that the form of the work, particularly its division into apparently unrelated sections, seems to come from the fragmented nature of Bhutanese society itself. Although there are themes linking them together unconsciously, each of the sections 2 to 5 really stands on its own for its handling of a particular unit of rule, or rather of a collection of related units sharing a common myth. The Addendum provides a glimpse into how some of that 'sharing' seems to derive from the author's own search for unity in the face of multiformity. Apart from its supremely local character, the style and conception of the work owes much to the Tibetan *rgyal-rabs*.

II. *dPal 'brug-par lung lha'i gdung-brgyud-kyis bstan-pa'i ring-lugs / lho-mon-kha-bzhi-las nyi-ma shar-phyogs-su byung-zhing rgyas-pa'i lo-rgyus gsal-ba'i me-long; dbu-can* ms. in 24 folios, same measurements as I above. Author: Ngag-dbang. No date.

This is the second of the two works found for me by bsTan-'dzin rDo-rje, and its condition exactly matched that of I above. While the *rGyal-rigs* is a glorification of the ancient order in eastern Bhutan, this work is an enthusiastic narrative account of its destruction by a military campaign organised for the new 'Brug-pa government in the 1650's by *Krong-sar dPon-slob* Mi-'gyur brTan-pa. How the two works could have issued from the same pen remains something of an enigma. No doubt one reason can be found in the universal tendency to recognise and accept the powers that be once they are firmly established. Another is that the author was both a member of an ancient clan (the Byar) and a 'Brug-pa monk of the state monastery in bKra-shis-sgang rDzong. Furthermore, the *rGyal-rigs* seems to be a 'secret' work directed towards the sympathisers of the *ancien régime,* while the *Lo-rgyus* is clearly of a formal nature intended to win favour in the eyes of 'Brug-pa officialdom. They were probably written at different periods in the life of the author. The way in which several figures mentioned at the bottom of the pedigrees in Section 2 of the *rGyal-rigs* turn up here as protagonists in the struggle with the 'Brug-pa is particularly satisfying (see Aris 1979: Table V and the notes to both works). Unfortunately the geographical setting remains somewhat obscure and only the larger districts can presently be identified on the map. Nevertheless, the work is of great value, based as it is on a number of eye-witness reports and written in a most refreshing style, simple and direct. I know of no other work in Tibetan or Bhutanese literature which quite compares with it. The lack of a similar account of the 'Brug-pa expansion towards the west is much felt. The name of Mi-'gyur brTan-pa also figures prominently in that movement.

III. *dPal 'brug-pa rin-po-che mthu-chen ngag-gi-dbang-po'i bka'-khrims phyogs thams-cad-las rnam-par rgyal-ba'i gtam;* blockprint in 16 folios, occupying ff. 100b-115a in *LCB* I. Author: bsTan-'dzin Chos-rgyal, 1701-67 (*regn,* as 10th Head Abbot 1755-62). Date: 1729.

This is the Bhutan Legal Code of 1729 composed by bsTan-'dzin Chos-rgyal for and on behalf of the 10th *'Brug sDe-srid,* Mi-pham dBang-po, at the start of the latter's eight-year reign. Although this seems to be the first such code in Bhutan, it was by no means the only one. *Slob-dpon* Padma-lags informs me that he has personal knowledge of at least two others, both of which similarly took the form of decrees proclaimed by new incumbents to the position of *'Brug sDe-srid.* One may indeed wonder if these codes continued to hold force for very long after the reigns of their promulgators. Both Petech (1972:211 Note 75) and White (see below) appear to have thought that this particular code was the only example of its kind and that it enjoyed a constant validity through later Bhutanese history, the former referring to it as "the Bhutanese code of law (actually conduct rules for the ruling class)." The term *bka'-khrims* ('legal code', 'decree' or 'edict') as found in the above title has had an unbroken continuity from the time of the Tun-huang literature where it appears as *bka'grims* (cf. also *bka'grims-gyi yi-ge, bka'i khrims-yig,* Uray 1972:32). The only published text, however, which affords a parallel to this one seems to be 'The Edict of the C'os rGyal of Gyantse' (Tucci 1949: 745-6). In fact work on Tibetan law began only recently with Uray's most detailed study (1972) of the tradition of Srong-btsan as lawgiver. His researches will form the starting-point of any future approach to the question of the real codes of the 14th century and later. That sufficient material does survive to warrant an exhaustive study is quite clear from the notices given of certain legal texts by Kitamura (1965: No. 408), Yamaguchi (1970: Nos. 443-4) and especially by Meisezahl (1973: 222-65). Meanwhile, even if the code presented here cannot yet be properly set either in the context of the Bhutanese legal tradition or in the wider Tibetan tradition from which it stems, it does stand as a mine of information on the theory and practice of theocratic government in Bhutan. Two of the British colonial officers who had dealings with Bhutan realised its importance and commissioned their Tibetan assistants to translate it into English. A partial translation (or rather summary) can be found in Appendix I, 'The Laws of Bhutan', to White's book of 1909 (301-10). Sir Charles Bell employed the teacher 'Dousamdup Kazi' (Zla-ba bSam-grub) to translate the whole of the *lHo'i chos-'byung* wherein the code is preserved, and his type-script survives in the British Library (A2 19999.b.17). Both versions are marred by inaccuracies and omissions but were on occasion found useful for resolving certain problems of interpretation. The draft by 'Dousamdup' is generally better, though less fluent, and I give a few of his readings in the accompanying notes under the abbreviation DS, followed by the page number of his typescript. Of far greater value have been the glosses provided for me by *Slob-dpon* Nag-mdog, which he most graciously sent in a letter dated 11/12/75. Some of these I have reproduced in their original form in the footnotes and Glossary under the abbreviation LN. No attempt has been made to trace the undocumented quotations which sprinkle the text, besides those that turned up in the *Subhasitaratnanidhi* of Sa-skya Paṇḍita (the *Sa-skya legs-bshad,* Bosson's edition of 1969). The annotation of the translation has presumed a fair amount of 'Tibetological' knowledge on the part of the reader, and so my notes are generally confined to matters concerning Bhutanese institutions. Much of the text is written in a clipped 'civil service' idiom to the point of ambiguity or obscurity, and some license has therefore been used to bring out the meaning in certain passages. I have not checked the text against those excerpts of it which are said to be reproduced on slabs of slate set into a *stūpa* outside the *rdzong* of sPu-na-kha. (The *stupa* is known as the *rdo-ring* ('pillar'), presumably by analogy with the *Zhol rdo-ring* of lHa-sa.) A 'definitive' translation will only be possible when the later codes become available to supply sufficient parallels and contrasts.

IV. *Relação que mandou o p.^e Estevão Cacella Da comp.^a de Jesu ao p.^e Alberto Laercio Provincial da Provincia do Malavar da India Oriental, da sua Viagem pera o Catayo, até chegar ao Reino do Potente.* 15 folios, ms. in Portuguese (29 x 20 cms.). Preserved in the Archivum Romanum Societatis Iesu where it has the catalogue no. $627\frac{4}{x}$. An account by Cacella of his stay in Bhutan, written at the court of *Zhabs-drung* Ngag-dbang rNam-rgyal at the temple of lCags-ri on 4th October 1627. It is not in the author's handwriting and must be a copy sent to Rome from India.

The translation of Cacella's *Relação* (or rather the bulk of it which recounts his stay in Bhutan) has been made from a photocopy kindly provided by the Society of Jesus in Rome. It would have been impossible to include this interesting document here but for the help of Dr. Thomas Earle, University Lecturer in Portuguese, Oxford, who also supplied the following comment: "The Jesuits sometimes wrote highly literary reports of their activities, especially their 'cartas anuas', but this is clearly not one of them. It is only a report of work in progress, as Cacella explains in para. 1. The report is not especially well put together, as after a rather sententious summing-up on ff. 13-14 (omitted in our translation) he remembers that he has failed to tell the Provincial about the geography of Cambirasi [= Bhutan, see Note 14]. I think the omitted para. is intended as a summing-up, because it begins 'This is the state of things in which we are at present' and he goes on to ask for the blessing of the Provincial, which he does again at the very end of the report. Where Cacella does attempt higher flights, as in the para. we have omitted, he is rather unclear and difficult to follow. The vocabulary seems straight-forward, apart from the few oriental words he uses. On the whole I would guess that this report was somewhat hastily written." (letter dated 29/3/77.)

The value of this document lies chiefly in the fact that by a stroke of pure good fortune it contains a detailed account of Cacella's meeting with *Zhabs-drung* Ngag-dbang rNam-rgyal (1594-?1651), the founder of Bhutan. Cacella and his fellow Jesuit, Cabral, spent several months in the *Zhabs-drung's* company in 1627 and the account corroborates several passages in the biographies of the *Zhabs-drung* (*PBP* and *LCB* I, ff. 12a-54a) which I point out in the notes. The only person who has given serious notice of the *Relação* to date is Wessels (1924: Ch. 5 and Appendix II). Although he made a brave attempt to relate the evidence to Bhutanese institutions, unfortunately Wessels only had the secondary material deriving from British authors to hand, and so the significance of the work from the point of view of the Bhutanese material was of course lost on him. However, his book is still basic reading for those who wish to see Cacella's account in the wider context of Jesuit missions to Tibet and Central Asia. It also has to be read for its narrative of our Jesuits' approach journey to Bhutan and for their doings in Tibet, both of which lie outside the present interest. One question which still remains unresolved is whether Cacella and Cabral can be identified with the men from 'Purdhu-kha' (Portugal) who brought a gift of firearms to the *Zhabs-drung*. See *PBP*, ff. 96b-97a, *LCB* I, ff. 34b-35a and the discussion in Aris 1979: 289-90 n. 14.

TEXT I

(Ia) ***sa skyong rgyal po'i gdung rabs 'byung khungs dang 'bangs kyi mi rabs chad tshul nges par gsal ba'i sgron me bzhugso //***

(Ib) na mo Ārya lo ki sho ra dharma rā dza bho dhe sa twa ya //

rgyal kun thugs rje gcig 'dus lhag pa'i lha //
mtha' khob bod kyi ma rig mun gling 'dir //
gang 'dul thabs kyis* cir yang skur ston pa'i // *kyi
spyan ras gzigs dbang mgon la phyag 'tshal lo //

gang de'i snang brnyan* sgyu ma'i zlos gar las // *bsnyen
sna tshogs sprul pas 'dzam gling skye 'gro 'phel //
sangs rgyas bstan pa (2a) phyogs mthar rgyas pa'i phyir
rgya gar mi rigs lha las* sprul pas chad // *la
bod kyi mi rnams spre'ur gyur pas spel //
de dag dge ba'i thabs mchog stsol ba* ni // *ba'i
rgya gar yul du mang pos bskur ba'i rgyal //
gangs can bod du rje rgyal gnya' khri btsan //
srong btsan sgam po khri srong* lde** btsan dang // *sring **sde
lho phyogs mon du lha sras gtsang ma zhes //
rnam par (2b) sprul pa'i skye mchog de rnams kyi //
gong ma rje'i gdung rabs 'byung khungs dang //
'og ma 'bangs kyi mi rabs chad tshul sogs //
nges* par gsal ba'i sgron me 'di ni spor // *nge
'phags yul gangs can bod kyi chad khungs rnams //
lo rgyus* bstan bcos kun la mthong thos dang // *rgyud
'jig rten rgan rabs mkhas pa'i ngag rgyun* bzhin // *brgyun
kun gyi go bde nyer mkho cung zad tsam //
brjod par spro yang snyigs dus skye bo rnams //
mi srun gzu lum spyod pa'i shugs 'gros kyis //
ya rabs che btsun rje 'bangs mtho dman* med // *man
rigs rus 'chol* bar song ba'i dus nyid la // *'cho
brgyud khung bshad kyang don med ngal ba'i rgyu //

(1a) The Lamp which Illuminates with Certainty the Origins of Generations of 'Earth-Protecting' Kings and the Manner in which Generations of Subjects Came into Being is contained [herein].

(1b) *nama Āryalokeśvara-dharmarājabodhisattvaya*

I bow down to the powerful protector
Avalokiteśvara,
The 'superior deity' in whom the compassion
of all Jinas is united
And who by his method of converting in all
situations shows himself in
forms everywhere
In this ignorant and dark land of Tibet,[1] a
barbarous border region.
Having manifested his various visible forms
Out of the dance of illusion, beings in the
world increased.

(2a) So that the Buddha's teachings might spread
in all directions,
The human race in India was emanated from the
gods and thus generated and
The humans of Tibet were transformed from
monkeys and spread.
As for those who bestowed on them the finest
method of attaining virtue,

In the country of India King Mahāsaṃmata,
In Tibet, the Land of Snow, the Lord-King
gNya'-khri bTsan[-po],
Srong-btsan sGam-po and *Khri* Srong-lde-btsan;
and
In Mon to the South, the Divine Prince
gTsang-ma, so it is said.
The origins of generations of lords above
And the manner in which generations of subjects
beneath [them] came into being,

(2b) [All of whom were under the authority] of these
excellent emanated beings,
Is recited in this *Lamp which Illuminates with
Certainty.*
A needful account in brief, that all can
understand well, of
The geneses in India and in Tibet, the Land of Snow,
According with all the stories and *shastra* read
and heard
And the oral traditions of wise old men of the
world,
Will be enlarged upon by discourse. As a result,
however, of the
Malicious and rash conduct of beings in the Age
of Degeneration
There is no distinction between noble lords
and their subjects.
At [this] very time when families and lineages
have become disordered
Even though ancestral origins are explained, it is
the cause of useless sloth.

'on kyang ma 'ongs (3a) dus kyi skabs 'ga' re //
rigs rus mngon mtho dpa'* mdzangs blo gros ldan // *dpa'i
gnam bskos stobs kyis sa la dbang sgyur ba'i //
rje rgyal brgyud pa nyin skar byung srid na //
dgyes pa'i 'dzum zhal snyan gyi dga' ston dang //
(4b5)[1] ya rabs pho mnyam khrol mor gleng ba'i gtam //
kun gyi rna ba'i thos rgyar mi spobs kyang //
mgrin dbyangs gsang ba'i glu chung 'di ltar len //

1. A considerable muddle in the original pagination is evident at this point and continues till 6bI.

(3a) However, if at certain times in the future
One of high family and lineage, noble and judicious,
A descendant of the Lord-Kings who governed the earth
From the power of their being appointed by heaven, can come forth like a star that appears in daytime,

(3a2) Then for the sake of joyful smiles and a feast for the ears

(4b5) I sing the tune of a secret little song in this manner,
Even though I do not dare to address to the audience of all ears
This discourse which is given so as to be intelligible to nobles of equal standing.

SECTION I

(5a) de yang mdo sde padma dkar po las lung bstan pa bzhin / sngon
sangs rgyas bcom ldan 'das zhal bzhugs pa'i dus su / bod gangs can
gyi gling phyogs 'dir ri lung * sa gzhi thams cad la mtsho chen po *klung
'khyil* zhing chags nas yod pa la / sangs rgyas bcom ldan 'das kyis / *khyil
spyan ras gzigs la lung bstan pa bka' stsal pa / spyan ras gzigs kyis
kyang zhal gyis bzhes shing / thugs bskyed smon lam gyi stobs dran
pa tsam la / kong chu lag* kha phye nas mtsho thams cad der thim *rlag
nas sa gzhi lag mthil ltar chags shing sā* la'i nags chen po byung bar *sa
gyur pas / de nas 'phags pa spyan ras gzigs dbang phyug dang / jo
mo sgrol ma'i thugs rjes brgyud bskul nas / spre'u byang chub sems
dpa' dang / brag srin mo gnyis bza' (5b) mir 'doms pa dang / spre'u
phrug drug skyes pa las rims pa 'phel nas / spre'u phrug lnga brgyar
song ba dang / 'phags pa spyan ras gzigs kyis / skye bo gzhon nu
lang tsho dar la babs pa shin tu mdzes pa cig tu sprul nas / sprel tsha
rnams kyis khyed kyis gzugs byad mdzes pa de ci las byung zer bas /
mi des mi dge ba bcu spangs pa'i chos bshad pas spre'u tsha rnams
kyis kyang de bzhin nyams su blangs pas / de rnams kyang rims par* *pas
mi la gyur to // de nas 'phags pa spyan ras gzigs kyis / spre'u rgan
byang chub sems dpa' la 'bru sna lnga gnang nas / spre'u gyur pa'i
mi rnams kyis so nams kyi las la 'jug ste lo thog smin pa dang / sus
thob dang hab* thob byas pas 'thab cing rtsod** pa dang / steng na *has **btsod
rje dpon med / 'og na 'bangs kyi rim pa med pas (6a) [. . . . .] [1] //
lan zer nas / khong rang thams chad kha mthun* gyis rje dpon 'tshol *thun
ba'i 'dun ma 'grigs pa dang / 'phags pa spyan ras gzigs kyi thugs rje
'od zer gyis / rgya gar gyi rgyal po dmag rgya* pa'i bu tha chung *brgyab
ru pa skye bskul* ba dang / bod kyi mi rje dpon 'tshol du phyin pa *bskug
rnams dang lha ri rol pa'i rtser phrad pas / bod kyi mi rnams kyis /
rgyal po la khyed gang nas yin zer dris pas / de dus rgya bod skad
ma go bas / rgyal po mdzub* mo gnam la ker ba dang / khong rnams *mdzum
kyis 'di ni gnam las yong ba'i lha yin pa 'dug zer nas / gnya' ba la
khri bzos nas 'khur yong bas / rgyal po'i ming yang rje gnya' khri
btsan por btags so // bod kyi rgyal po la snga ba de yin no // rgyal
po de'i rigs rus kyi 'byung khungs ji ltar yin zhe na / sngon rgya
gar 'phags pa'i yul gyi rgyal po la snga ba rje mang po bkur ba'i
rgyal po yin pa dang / de nas gdung brgyud rims par* ded** pa'i *omitted **'dod
rgyal rabs la / rgyal po bha (6b) ra dhwa dza dang / go'u ta ma
gnyis byung ste / go'u ta ma nyes* pa med pa la / nyes par bsgrags *mnyes
nas / gsal shing gi rtse la bskyon pa las khrag (3a2)[2] gi thig lɛ 'dzag
pa la smon lam btabs pas sgo nga gsum du gyur pa / bu ram shing

1. A passage appears to have been omitted here.
2. Pagination error continues.

SECTION I

(5a) Now then,[2] according to the prophecy given in the *Puṇḍarīka-sūtra,*[3] at the
time when the Buddha Bhagavan was living, there was a great lake which
had come forth swirling on top of all the mountains, valleys and ground in
this region of Tibet, the Land of Snow. Whereupon the Buddha Bhagavan
commanded Avalokiteśvara and he, agreeing, opened up the effluent of the
Kong-chu river simply by recollecting the power of a 'visualizing prayer'.
The entire lake sunk away there and so the ground appeared forth [as clear]
as the palm of one's hand. A great forest of *Sāla* trees arose and then Ārya
(5b) Avalokiteśvara and the Lady Tara [transformed themselves into] a monkey
bodhisattva and a rock demoness. Coming together as husband and wife,
they begat six monkey children who gradually increased. When there were
five hundred monkey children, Ārya Avalokiteśvara transformed himself
into an extremely handsome and mature youth. The monkey grandchildren
asked him: "Where does your beautiful appearance come from?" So the
man explained to them the doctrine of abstaining from the ten evil deeds.
Accordingly, after the monkey grandchildren had themselves practised it,
they too gradually turned into humans.

Then Ārya Avalokiteśvara gave five kinds of grain to the old monkey
bodhisattva and so the monkeys who had become humans started upon
agricultural work. When the harvest ripened, they each scrambled to obtain
what they could, fighting and quarrelling. Since there was no lord-chief
(6a) above and no graded order of subjects below, [someone] replied: [" . . . "]
So with universal accord they held consultations during which it was
decided to search for a lord-chief. Thereupon, induced by the rays of
compassion of Ārya Avalokiteśvara, Ru-pa-skye [Rūpati] who was the
youngest son of King dMag-rgya-pa [Udayana] met those Tibetans who
had gone in search of a lord-chief on the peak of lHa-ri Rol-pa. The
Tibetans asked the king: "Where do you come from?" Since at that time
Indians did not understand the language of Tibet, the king raised his
finger to the sky and so they said: "This person seems to be a god who
has come from the sky." So making a throne of their necks, they bore him
off. The king's name was therefore fixed as *rJe* gNya'-khri ('Neck-throne')
bTsan-po. He was the first king of Tibet. If it be asked: "What was the
origin of this king's family and lineage?" [the answer is as follows:] In
former times the first king of the sacred land of India was the Lord
Mahasaṃmata Raja. In the dynasty of the line of his descendants who
(6b) followed each other successively there appeared Kings Bharadvāja and
Gautama, these two. Gautama, while innocent, was declared guilty and

lo ma'i* seb tu bzhag pas / rgyal bu khye'u chung gsum du gyur pa *lo'i *for* lo ma'i
la / gdungs brgyud rims par 'phel ba'i bu ram shing pa'i rgyal rabs
ḅrgyud pa dus kyi dbang gis* grong khyer chen po ser skyar** gnas *gi **skya
shing ming sring lhan du sdebs pa las byung ba'i brgyud pa la / shā
kya chen mo / shā kya li tsa byi / shā kya ri brag* pa zhes rgyal rigs *grag
gsum du dgyes pa las / rje gnya' khri btsan po de ni / shā kya li tsa
byi'i brgyud pa yin no // gnya' khri btsan po'i gdung rabs nyi shu
rtsa (3b) lnga la / rgyal po lha tho tho ri gnyan btsan* byon pa yin / *lha tho tho'i snyan shal
de nas gdung rabs lnga la / rgyal po srong btsan sgam po byon pa
yin / de nas gdung rabs lnga la / rgyal po khri srong lde* btsan byon *sde
pa yin / rgyal po khri srong lde* btsan la sras mu ne btsan po / mu *sde
khri btsan po / sad na legs gsum 'byung ba'i / sad na legs kyi sras /
khri ral pa can / lha sras gtsang ma / glang dar ma gsum byung ba'i /
khri ral pa can ni / snying rje padma dkar po'i mdo las lung bstan
pa'i phyag na rdo rje'i sprul pa yin / de nyid rgyal sar bskos nas
'dzam bu gling cha gnyis la dbang sgyur nas / stobs dang mnga'
thang* lha'i longs spyod mnyam zhing / 'u zhang rdo'i** gtsug lag *'thang **'u shang mdo'i
khang chen mo rgya 'phibs* dgu thog dang bcas pa bzhengs / sangs *'bigs
rgyas kyi bstan pa dar zhing rgyas pa'i phyir du / dge 'dun gyi sde
chen po / (4a) 'dul grwa bcu gnyis / bshad* grwa bcu gnyis / sgom *bshed
grwa bcu gnyis la sogs pa / bod dbus gtsang khams yan chod du /
chos sde chen po sum bcu so drug btsugs* / rgya gar nas paṇḍi ta** *gtsug **panti ta
da' na sh'i la la* sogs pa'i paṇḍi ta** mang po spyan drangs nas / *omitted **panti ta
bod kyi lo tsā ba rnams dang chos thams cad skad* gsar** bcad *skar **gsang
kyis* sgyur du bcug cing dam pa'i chos dar zhing rgyas pa dang / *kyi
khyad par du'ang dge 'dun pa re la 'bangs mi khyim bdun bdun
bsnyen bskur la sbyar zhing / rgyal po nyid kyi dbu'i ral pa la ras
yug btags / de'i steng* la dge 'dun rnams bzhugs bcug cing / sangs *stengs
rgyas kyi bstan pa la bkur sti khams che ba bla na ma mchis par
mdzad pa las / mnga' 'bangs rnams la dka' las che tsam byung ba
dang sdig blon rnams blos ma rangs par / dbas* rgyal to re dang / *dbabs
(4b) cog ro legs sgra gnyis kyis / rgyal po bkrongs nas chos khrims
bshig pa'i 'dun ma byas pas / cog ro legs sgra na re / rgyal po
bkrongs kyang / lha sras gtsang ma dang / blon chen dpal gyi yon
tan yod pas / chos khrims bshig mi thub zer ba la / dbas* rgyal to *dbab
res nga la thabs yod zer nas / bod dbus gtsang gi mo ma brtsis pa
thams cad la nor rdzas kyi rngan pa byin nas / thams cad kha
mthun par smras du bcug pa la / lha sras gtsang ma da lo bod khams
'dir bzhugs na / rgyal po* dang lha sras gnyis kyi sku tshe la bar chad *rgul
yong nyen che* ba dang / khyad par du bod** khams 'dir nad *tsha **khod
yams* dang / mu ge dus 'khrugs (6b1)[1] la sogs pa yong ba 'dug zer *yam
nas / thams cad kha mthun par smras du bcug nas smras pa dang /

1. **Pagination error continues.**

(3a2) impaled on the top of a pointed stake. As drops of blood dripped forth he said prayers over them, causing them to turn into three eggs. These were placed in between the leaves of a sugar-cane tree and turned into three little infant princes. When the line of their descendants had proliferated successively, [it became known as] the lineage of the Bu-ram-shing-pa (Iksavāku) dynasty. From force of circumstances [its members] came to reside in the great city of Ser-skya (Kapilavastu) and in the lineage which arose as a result of brothers and sisters cohabiting there issued forth the three royal families of the so-called 'Mahā-Śākya', the 'Śākya-Licchavī' and the 'Śākya Ri-brag-pa'. As for *rJe* gNya'-khri bTsan-po, he was of the Śākya-Licchavī lineage.

(3b) In the twenty-fifth generation after gNya'-khri bTsan-po there came forth King lHa-tho-tho-ri gNyan-btsan. Then, after five generations, King Srong-btsan sGam-po came forth. Then, after five generations, King *Khri* Srong-lde-btsan came forth. King *Khri* Srong-lde-btsan had three sons: Mu-ne bTsan-po, Mu-khri bTsan-po and Sad-na-legs. Of these, Sad-na-legs had three sons: *Khri* Ral-pa-can, *lHa-sras* gTsang-ma and Glang Dar-ma. Of these, as for *Khri* Ral-pa-can, he was the emanation of Vajrapāṇi as prophecied in the *Karuṇapuṇḍarīka-sūtra.*[4] After he had been raised to the royal throne and had gained power over the [remaining] two-thirds of the world, his strength and dominion equalled that enjoyed by the gods. He built the great temple of 'U-zhang-rdo with a Chinese roof and nine stories.
(4a) In order to cause the doctrine of the Buddha to flourish and increase, he established thirty-six great religious communities throughout dBus-gtsang in Tibet and as far as Khams; these included twelve colleges of the *Vinaya*, twelve colleges of scriptural study and twelve colleges of meditation, [all of them] great monastic communities. He invited many pandits from India, including the pandit Danasila; together with the Tibetan translators, he caused them to render all the scriptures [into Tibetan] by means of the 'new language' [devised for the translation of Buddhist tests]. So the holy *dharma* flourished and increased. In particular, seven households of his subjects were appointed [to provide for] the honour of each member of the *sangha* and the king himself caused the monks to sit upon a length of cotton [the end of] which he attached to the tresses of his own head.

As a consequence of his paying enormous and unsurpassed honour to the doctrine of the Buddha, his subjects were faced with quite considerable difficulties. Thereupon the sinful ministers became obstinate to the extent
(4b) that dBas-rgyal To-re and Cog-ro Legs-sgra – [these] two – held consultations about how they would destroy the religious law after killing the king. Cog-ro Legs-sgra said: "Even if the king should be killed, there still remain the Divine Prince gTsang-ma and the Chief Minister dPal-gyi Yon-tan. It would therefore be impossible to destroy the religious law." To that dBas-rgyal To-re replied: "I have a solution." He gave rewards in the form of wealth and goods to all the (female?) diviners and astrologers throughout dBus-gtsang in Tibet and forced them to say with universal accord: "If the Divine Prince gTsang-ma resides this year in this realm of Tibet, there

dbas* rgyal to re kyis** / rgyal po'i snyan du gsol pas / rgyal po'i *dbabs **kyi
zhal nas / gcung gtsang ma rang da lo nged rang rnams kyi sku chags
bsangs pa dang / lho mon gyi mnga'* 'bangs mi sde rnams kyi yul *mngal
khams ji ltar yod dang bde sdug ci 'dra yod gzigs pa la phebs pas
chog zer ba bzhin lho spa gro* phyogs la 'phebs pa dang / yang *spa dro
dbas* rgyal to re dang / cog ro legs sgra gnyis kha mthun nas / rgyal *dbabs
to re dang / cog ro legs sgra gnyis kha mthun nas / rgyal po'i btsun
mo ngang tshul ma dang / blon chen dpal gyi yon tan gnyis / rgyal
po ma mkhyen par gsang thabs kyis* 'dod pa (7a) spyad nas / nal *kyi
bshams 'dug zer nas phra ma bcug pas / btsun mo ngang tshul ma
ha las* te lcebs te shi bas / rgyal po phra ma la gsan nas / blon chen *les
dpal gyi yon tan me dpung chen po'i nang la cug nas bkum pa dang /
sdig blon gnyis kyis* glags rnyed** nas / rgyal po 'bras chang gsol *kyi **snyed
nas gzims pa la / dbu lhag par skor nas bkrongs so // de nas glang
dar ma rgyal sar bskos nas / gtsug lag khang dang / sku gsung thugs
kyi rten rnams bshig cing / dge 'dun gyi sde rnams* stor ste khyi ra *rnam
byed du ma nyan pa* rnams gsad / chos sgyur 'phro rnams bcad nas *omitted
paṇḍi ta* rnams rang yul du log / sangs rgyas kyi bstan pa ming *panti ta
tsam yang med par byas pas / lha sa'i gnas bdag ma cig dpal lhas
thugs rgyud bskul nas / lha lung (7b) dpal gyi rdo rjes* rgyal po *rje
glang dar ma bkrongs so // // de la sras 'od srungs dang / yum
brtan* gnyis 'byung ba sku nar son nas / rgyal srid la ma cham par *yum bstan
dbu ru dang / g.yo ru so sor phye nas lo bcu gnyis bar du 'khrugs
pas / rgyal krims dang chos khrims gnyis ka med par mun pa'i gling
lta bur gyur nas / lo bdun cu tsam song ba dang / sangs rgyas dang
'phags pa spyan ras gzigs kyi thugs rje brtse* bas gzigs nas / gangs *rtse
can mun pa'i gling du sangs rgyas kyi bstan pa me ro smad nas langs
te / stod nas gso zhing bar du dbus gtsang la dar zhing rgyas pa'i
ngang tshul byung ba las / bstan pa'i me ro smad nas langs pa ni /
bstan pa bsnubs pa'i dus gtsang rab gsal / g.yo dge 'byung / dmar
shākya mu ni dang gsum / dpal chen chu bo rir* sgom zhing yod *ri
tsa na / btsun (8a) pas khyi ra byed pa mthong nas lo rgyus* dris *rgyud
pas / rgyal pos bstan pa med par byas pa'i gtam thos pas / khong* *kho
gsum dngangs skrags nas 'dul ba'i chos rnams dri'u la bkal nas mdo
smad khams la bros nas gnam rdzong brag la sgom zhing bzhugso //
de'i dus su yul tsong* khar skyes pa'i bon gzhon nu rmu gsal gshen *btsong
'bar* zer ba'i byis** pa de phyugs 'tshor phyin pas / snang gsal lha *mu zu gsal 'bar **byi
khang zer ba'i lha khang zhig ral song ba'i nang gi sdebs bris logs la /
dge slong rab tu byung ba'i gzugs brnyan* yod pa mthong bas / byis *bsnyan
pa de snang ba shin tu spro dga' bskyed nas / nye logs na rgan mo
rgas shing khok pa 'khar ba la bsten pa cig yod pa de la / de ci'i
gzugs brnyan* ci yin zer nas dris pas rgan mo na re / nga na chung *bsnyan
gzhon nu'i dus na / dge slong (8b) rab tu byung ba zer ba cha lugs

is a danger that impediments will arise in the lives of both the king and the
(6b1) Divine Prince gTsang-ma. In particular also, pestilence, famine, troubled times and so forth will come to this realm of Tibet." He said this [to the diviners and to the astrologers] and having forced them to speak these words with universal accord, they were spoken. Thereupon dBas-rgyal To-re reported them to the king who declared: "This year my younger brother gTsang-ma may depart in order to remove our obstacles and in order to see what the subjects and communities in lHo Mon are like and to enquire into their welfare." When, in accordance with these words, he [gTsang-ma] had departed[5] in the direction of lHo sPa-gro, once again both dBas-rgyal To-re and Cog-ro Legs-sgra agreed and spread a slander, saying: "The King's queen, Ngang-tshul-ma, and *Blon-chen* dPal-gyi Yon-tan – [these] two –
(7a) have secretly indulged their lust and fornicated without the king's knowing it." On account of this, the queen Ngang-tshul-ma became terrified and, committing suicide, she died. The king, paying heed to the slander, had *Blon-chen* dPal-gyi Yon-tan placed on a great pyre and killed. Having accomplished their purpose, the two sinful ministers twisted the king's head round and killed him while he was sleeping after he had drunk rice beer.

Then, after Glang Dar-ma had been raised to the royal throne, he destroyed the temples and the body, speech and mind-supports. He scattered the monastic communities and killed those [monks] who refused to hunt. He stopped the remaining work of translating the scriptures and so the pandits returned to their own countries. The doctrine of the Buddha was abolished,
(7b) not even its name remaining, so that lHa-lung dPal-gyi rDo-rje killed Glang Dar-ma, his spirit having been roused by *Ma-gcig* dPal-lha, the guardian deity of lHa-sa.

He [Glang Dar-ma] had two sons, 'Od-srungs and Yum-brtan. When they grew up they fell out over the government and, having split into a 'central wing' and a 'left wing' they contended over a period of twelve years, so that [the country] became like a land of darkness, devoid of both state and religious law. When about seventy years had elapsed, the Buddha and Ārya Avalokiteśvara looked down with loving compassion and so the circumstances arose whereby in the land of darkness the ashes of the Buddha's doctrine were revived from sMad, nourished from sTod and caused to flourish and prosper in dBus-gtsang. As to how the ashes of the Buddha's doctrine were revived from sMad: At the time when the doctrine was being caused to decline, gTsang Rab-gsal, g.Yo dGe-'byung and dMar Śākyamuni – [these]
(8a) three – who were at dPal-chen Chu-bo-ri meditating, saw a monk who was hunting and asked him his story. Hearing an account of how the king was abolishing the doctrine, the three of them became terrified and, having loaded up a mule with the volumes of the *Vinaya,* they fled to mDo-smad-khams and stayed at gNam-rdzong-brag meditating.

At that time a child called rMu-gsal gShen-'bar, who was a young Bon [-po] born in the district of Tsong-kha, set off to pasture his cattle and [came to] a temple which had gone to ruin called sNang-gsal lHa-khang.

de bzhin gyi sde mang po yod pa yin te / glang dar mas* chos kyi *ma'i
bstan pa bsnubs* pa'i** tshun chad med pa yin zer ba / byis pa na *brnubs **pa'i nas
re / de dus kyi dge slong rnams sa cha gzhan la 'thor song ba med
dam zer bas / rgan mo na re / gzhan la yod med mi ma shes / dpal
chen chu bo ri nas bros song ba'i dge slong gsum da lta mdo khams
gnam rdzong brag la bzhugs yod zer gyi 'dug zer bas / byis pa de
de'i mod nyid la gnam rdzong brag la song nas / gtsang rab gsal /
g.yo* dge 'byung / dmar shākya mu ni gsum dang mjal nas gus *yo
pa'i btud cing /* chos 'dul ba la lhag par dad pas rab tu byung te / *lhag par
ming dge slong rab gsal du btags / phyis thugs rab gsal* zhing chos *che zhing
kyi sde snod thams cad thugs su chud pa'i (9a) bla chen dgongs* *dgong
pa rab gsal du mtshan yongs su grags pas / dbus bsam yas nas yum
brtan gyi sras brgyud tshana ye shes rgyal mtshan dam pa'i chos la
dad pa bskyed nas / klu mes shes rab tshul khrims* la sogs pa mi *klu med tshul khrims shes rab
bcu rab tu 'byung bar brdzangs pas / bla chen dgongs pa rab gsal
las rab tu byung nas chos rgyun dbus gtsang spel ba las / bstan pa'i
me ro smad nas langs pa de la zer ba yin 'dug / stod nas gso ba ni /
glang dar ma'i sras 'od srung dang / yum brtan* gnyis byung ba las / *bstan
'od srung gi sras / mnga' bdag dpal 'khor btsan / de'i sras bkra shis
rtsegs pa dpal dang / skyid lde nyi ma mgon gnyis byung ba'i /
skyid lde nyi ma* mgon gyi sras / dpal gyi mgon / lde btsug mgon / *nyi ma omitted
bkra shis mgon gsum byung (9b) bas / bkra shis mgon gyi sras /
'od kyi rgyal mtshan / srong nge dang khor* re gnyis byung bas / *kho
srong* nges gu ger mtho lding lha khang bzhengs / kho rang mkhan *song
slob* med par rab tu byung nas bsnyen par rdzogs / mtshan lha bla *blob
ma ye shes 'od du btags / sras gnyis kyang rab tu byung du bcug /
rgyal srid gcung* lha lde la gtad / de la sras gsum byung ba'i bar pa
byang chub 'od yin / lha bla ma ye shes 'od dang / lha btsun byang
chub 'od mes dbon* gnyis kyis / rin chen bzang po la sogs pa'i bod *dbos
phrug* nyi shu rtsa gcig rgya gar yul du btang nas lo tsa' slab cing *'phrug
dam pa'i chos bod du sgyur bcug / khyad par du rin chen gser la ma
brtsis* shing / rang nyid kyi lus srog la'ang phangs pa med par sdod *'phrug
su bcug nas / rgya gar nas paṇḍi* ta lnga brgya'i (10a) gtsug rgyan *panti ta
jo bo rje dpal ldan A ti sha zhes mtshan nyi zla ltar yongs su grags
pa de nyid mnga' ris* gung thang du spyan drangs nas chos kyi 'khor *ri
lo bskor ba dang / de nas rim pas dbus gtsang du phebs nas / sangs
rgyas kyi bstan pa rin po che dar zhing rgyas pa nam mkha'i mtha'
dang mnyam par gyur ba'i rgyun dus ding sang gi bar du yod pa de
yin no // zhes rgyal rigs 'byung khungs gsal ba'i sgron me las / gangs
can bod du mi brgyud spel zhing rje rgyal spyan drangs nas sangs
rgyas kyi bstan pa dar zhing rgyas pa'i le'u ste dang po'o //

When he saw the picture of a monk on the wall-paintings inside, the child experienced a feeling of extreme happiness. There was an old lady close by, supporting herself on a stick, and he asked her: "What is this picture and who does it depict?" The old lady replied: "When I was young there were
(8b) many communities of so-called 'monks' [who used to wear] that kind of costume. There have been none since Glang Dar-ma caused the doctrine to decline." The child said: "Weren't the monks of that time scattered to some other area?" The old lady replied: "Nobody knows whether or not they are somewhere else. It is said [however] that there are three monks now resident at mDo-khams gNam-rdzong-brag who fled from dPal-chen Chu-bo-ri." At that very instant the child went off to gNam-rdzong-brag and on meeting gTsang Rab-gsal, g.Yo dGe-'byung and dMar Śākyamuni – [these] three – he bowed down to them with devotion. Having surpassing faith in the *dharma* and in the *Vinaya,* he was ordained monk and given the name of *dGe-slong* Rab-gsal. Later his mind became exceedingly clear (*rab-gsal*) and, having absorbed all the *piṭaka* of the *dharma* into his mind,
(9a) he became widely renowned under the name of *Bla-chen* dGongs-pa Rab-gsal. In dBus bSam-yas, Tshana Ye-shes rGyal-mtshan, who was the descendant of Yum-brtan, having gained faith in the holy *dharma,* he sent ten persons including Klu-mes Shes-rab Tshul-khrims to be ordained monks. They were ordained by *Bla-chen* dGongs-pa Rab-gsal and so the continuity of the *dharma* was spread to dBus-gtsang. It is this [sequence of events] which is called "the revival from sMad of the doctrine's ashes"

As for "the nourishing [of the doctrine] from sTod": Of the two sons which Glang Dar-ma had, 'Od-srung and Yum-brtan, 'Od-srung's son was *mNga'-bdag* dPal-'khor-btsan. Of the two sons which he had, bKra-shis rTsegs-pa-dpal and sKyid-lde Nyi-ma-mgon, the latter had three
(9b) sons: dPal-gyi-mgon, lDe-btsug-mgon and bKra-shis-mgon. Of the sons which bKra-shis-mgon had, 'Od-kyi rGyal-mtshan and both Srong-nge and Khor-re, it was Srong-nge who built the mTho-lding temple in Gu-ge. Without abbot or teacher, he became a monk and took his final ordination. He was given the name of *lHa-bla-ma* Ye-shes-'od. He made his two sons become monks too. He handed the government over to the younger brother lHa-lde. The latter had three sons of whom the middle one was Byang-chub-'od. *lHa-bla-ma* Ye-shes-'od and *lHa-btsun* Byang-chub-'od, both grandfather and grandson, sent twenty-one Tibetan boys including Rin-chen bZang-po to India. Having studied to be translators, he made them translate the holy *dharma* into Tibetan. In particular he compelled [himself] to live without regard for precious gold and without sparing his
(10a) own life [in order to] invite from India to mNga'-ris Gung-thang the crown-ornament of five hundred pandits, *Jo-bo-rje dPal-ldan* Atiśa, whose name is as widely renowned as the sun and the moon. He 'turned the wheel of the *dharma*' [there] and then proceeded by stages to dBus-gtsang and so the precious doctrine of the Buddha came to flourish and prosper. That its continuity which reached the very limits of the sky should continue to exist up to present times is [due to] this [sequence of events].

This is the first section from *The Lamp Which Illuminates the Origins of Royal Families* concerning how, after the human race had come to be spread in Tibet, the Land of Snow, a lord-king was invited and the doctrine of the Buddha flourished and prospered.

SECTION II

(10a4) // de nas yang rgya gar 'phags pa'i yul dang / gangs can bod du byung ba'i stobs kyis 'khor los bsgyur ba'i rgyal po* rim par byon pa'i gdung rabs kyi 'byung khungs rgyas pa ni / rgyal rabs* gsal ba'i me long dang / dpag bsam ljon pa / rgyal (10b) rabs khug pa rnams la gsal bas* 'dir ma bkod / de yang rgyal rabs gsal ba'i me long las kyang / lho phyogs mon gyi rgyal po rnams / lha sras gtsang ma'i gdung brgyud yin gsung 'dug pa dang / da lta na'ang rgyal rigs dang mi sde thams cad kyi gtam rgyun la'ang / rgyal rigs thams cad rgyal mkhar mi zim pa las so sor 'gyes pa'i gleng gtam kho na kun mthun kyang / 'ga' re nas so sos 'dod gtam nga rgyal gyi nga yin khyod min zer ba dang / la las ni ma go ba'i hol spyod gzu lum gyi gtam lha sras gtsang ma nas sras brgyud gdung rabs bcu tsam re bgrang nas de'i bu nga yin zer nas nges rtags* kho na smras pa dang / la las ni sras brgyud rim pa'i* ming 'di yin 'di min zer nas / brtsod cing rang rang so so'i 'di rang yin zer ba ni / ma rig blun rmongs* shes rig med pa (IIa) kho na yin te / dper na mi gcig la'ang ming mang po yod pa* kun gyis shes pa de bzhin / pha mas chung dus bkra shis mnga' gsol nas btags* pa'i ming dang gces par bskyang nas 'phangs pa'i ming dang / bya ba'i gnas skabs dang gzugs byad* la dpag pa'i ming dang / che sar bkur ba'i zhe* sa che brjod kyi ming dang bcas ji snyed yong bas gcig 'dzin pa ni dpyad dka'o // la las lha sras gtsang ma lho mon du phebs nas lo grangs tsam 'das dang / gdung rabs tsam song gi khungs ma chod par sras brgyud rim pa 'di yin 'di man gyi 'byung khungs nges rtags ltar brjod pa ni / nga rgyal khengs shing dregs pa'i bab col* gyi gtam gzu lum kho na yin pas** rjes su mi 'brang 'tshal lo // // dper na lo'i nges pa ni mkhas grub lha dbang blo gros kyi bstan brtsis gdan dus (IIb) mthun mongs las / me kyis rtag par dpyad pa'i spyod yul du rag las pas so // // de nas yang gong du bshad pa'i 'phros las / lha sras gtsang ma dpon g.yog lnga tsam lho brag phyogs la byon rtsis yin kyang / sngon gyi smon lam dbang gis* gtsang phag ri phyogs nas spa gro** gnam mtho-ng* dkar po la phebs / der zhag kha shas bzhugs pa'i bar la bud med shin tu mdzas shing lang tsho dang ldan pa zhig rtse grogs brten nas / lha sras nyid tshur phebs pa'i rjes la / phyis bu med de las ma nges pa'i bu yan pa gcig btsas pa dang / 'ga' res nas lha sras gtsang ma'i sras yan po yin pa 'dra zer ba'i bu brgyud / da lta spa gro'i* rgyal gdung zer ba dang / thim phu'i gdung 'brog rus che ba rnams yin zer ba'i 'phros gtam re yang zer gyi 'dug / de nas rim pas thim phu (12a) gzhung / thed lung chu pho chu mo dbang 'dus pho brang bar grong zam pa rgal nas shar lung sgor mo la sleb / de nas* kho dwangs kha / sngan* lung mang sde lung / kheng / rta li / sbu li / stung la sbi / zhong dkar mol ba lung pa rnams rim pas bgrod cing /

*stobs kyi 'khor lo sgyur ba'i rgyal po
*rab
*ba'i
*rtag
*pas
*mongs
*ba
*btag
*byas
*zhes
*bcol **pa'i
*gi **dro
*thong
*dro'i
*de nas pas
*ngan

SECTION II

Now, since the extended account of the origins of successive generations
of *bāla-cakravarti-rājas* who appeared in India and in Tibet, the Land of
(10b) Snow, has been made clear in the *rGyal-rabs gsal-ba'i me-long,* the *dPag-bsam*
jon-pa and in the *rGyal-rabs khug-pa,*[6] it is not included here. Now even in
the *rGyal-rabs gsal-ba'i me-long* it is said that the kings of Mon to the south
are of the lineage of the Divine Prince gTsang-ma[7] and even at present times
the oral traditions of the royal families and of the public are also all in perfect agreement in their versions of how all the royal families came to be
separately diffused from [the direction of] the Mi-zim-pa[8] royal castle. Some,
however, give arrogant versions based on their individual desires, saying: "It
is I, not you". Others give misunderstood accounts which are unexamined
and ill-considered; having counted about ten generations of the Divine Prince
gTsang-ma's issue they say: "I am that person's son", telling this as sure
evidence. Others say: "These are the names of the successive descendants.
Those are not." This quarrelling and saying of "It is exactly this" by each
(11a) one differently is just ignorant, foolish and uneducated. For example, just
one person can have many names and can be known to everyone in this
manner: by the name given to him in his childhood by his parents at the
ceremony of wishing him auspicious success and by the name they used
when looking after him lovingly and succouring him; by the names given
according to the circumstances of his work and his physical appearance;
and by his honorific name given to him in eulogy as a mark of respect for
his high position, and so on – as there are so many it would be difficult to
examine them all in order to hold to one of them. Other people speak
unfoundedly of a certain number of years having elapsed since the Divine
Prince gTsang-ma came to lHo Mon and of a certain number of generations
having gone by. Such declarations as: "The successive descendants [of our
ancestors] are these, not those", given as with certain proof of their origins,
are just arrogant and proud talk that is rash and ill-considered and so I ask
(11b) you not to concur with them. For example, with regard to chronological
accuracy, it is said in the *bsTan-brtsis gdan-dus mthun-mongs* of *mKhas-*
grub lHa-dbang Blo-gros: "To examine by means of 'fire' [the number 3]
depends on the object of enquiry (?)."[9]

Now – in continuation of that which has been explained above –
although the Divine Prince gTsang-ma in a party of about five persons
including the Lord and his attendants had intended to proceed in the
direction of lHo-brag, due to the power of his aspirations made in previous
lives, from the direction of Phag-ri in gTsang he went to gNam-mthong
dKar-po[10] in sPa-gro. While residing there for some days he cohabited with
an extremely beautiful young girl as his play-mate and when the Divine
Prince himself had proceeded on his way, that girl later gave birth to an
unclaimed son of uncertain paternity and some people said that he was
probably the illegitimate son of the Divine Prince gTsang-ma. Nowadays
some legends are still told of how the important clans of the so-called
rGyal-gdung of sPa-gro and of the gDung-'brog of Thim-phu[11] are the
descendants of that son. Then in stages he [gTsang-ma] proceeded by way
(12a) of the central region of Thim-phu, the Chu-pho and Chu-mo rivers[12] of
the Thed valley, and dBang-'dus Pho-brang. Having crossed the bridge of
Bar-grong[13] he arrived at sGor-mo in the Shar district. Then he travelled
in stages through Kho-dwangs-kha, sNgan-lung, Mang-sde-lung, Kheng, rTa-
li, sBu-li, sTung-la-sbi and Zhong-dkar Mol-ba-lung-pa.[14] When he arrived

sku ri chu la sleb pa dang / chu bo'i stod smad gang la ltas kyang
zam pa med par ha las te ci drag thugs nas bsam blo zhig btang* *'thong
bas / lha sras kyi thugs la ngas lung phyogs 'di la gnas shing dbang
sgyur ba'i skal* ba yod na zam pa** tshug par gyur cig zer ro // *bskal **par
gnam lha la dmod bor nas / shing sdong gcig bcad cing sgyel bas /
chu phan tshun sbrel ba'i zam pa lta bur byung bas / chu bo rgal
nas lcang bum du sleb cing skor ri'i lab* rtsa rgal nas / snga tshang *lam
gi sa cha dang she ri chu rgal nas ba geng bre mi he long / (12b)
rtseng mi'i* sa cha rnams rim par bgrod nas byams mkhar la sleb / *ma'i
tshang zam gyi zam pa las 'thon te mug ltang mkhar thum bur zer
ba'i spang logs la sleb cing log nas bltas pas / gong ri grang ma'i chu
rgyud de lung pa'i har yangs shing dwangs sangs pa* 'dugs pas / lha *ba
sras thugs nyams* spro ba'i rnam pa zhig byung nas dngul gyi mda' *nyam
zhig yod pa de 'phangs pa'i chu byung ba da lta'i gser sgom zer ba
de yin no // de nas wang ser kung par sleb nas phyogs mthar gzigs
pas lung pa dwangs spro ba yod kyang / mi dang grong zhing re
gnyis las med pas der bzhugs ma spro // de dus lho mon gyi lung
phyogs sa cha gang la'ang / rgyal (13a) po khyi kha ra thod dang
mnyam po yong ba'i mi 'thor bu res bzung ba'i khyim zhing* 'thor *khyin zhin
bu re las med pa las / lha sras kyang phebs cing bzhugs ma spro bar
rim pas 'di phyogs la phebs pa yin 'dug / de nas lha sras nyid kyis* *kyi
mi rnams la mi dang yul grong gang la mang dang / sa gzhi* gang la *zhi
bzang zer nas dris pas / mi rnams kyis la 'og yul gsum dpal mkhar
bzang zer bas / rim pas dpal mkhar du phebs nas bzhugs pas / bod
khams la sdig rgyal dang sdig blon rnams kha mthun nas sangs rgyas
kyi bstan pa bshig pa'i skabs yin zer ba'i skad cha thos byung ba
dang / bod yul dang thag nye ba'i gshis* kyis der bzhugs ma spro *shis
bar 'brong mdo gsum btsan mkhar la phebs nas / rgyal mkhar
bzung ba'i 'os* gang la 'dug gzigs (13b) pas / mi zim pa'i sa cha de *'od
chu brag gis skor zhing lung* pa'i 'dus che la sa btsan pa 'dug *lus
dgongs nas der phebs pas / de na A mi don grub rgyal zer ba'i mi
zhig gis bdag byas pa'i mi khyim zhig 'dug pa la / lha sras kyis don
grub rgyal la gsungs pa / khyed rnams 'dir yong nas mi rabs tsam
song / rigs rus lung phyogs gang nas yin zer bas / don grub rgyal
kyis smras pa / yul phyogs bod nas nga'i pha ma'i dus la yong
ba yin / rigs rus ni slob dpon padma'i dngos slob A mi* byang *ma
chub 'dre bkol rlangs* lha gzigs kyi** brgyud pa / byar po'i yul *rmyang **kyis
du yod pa pha spun nang 'khrugs nas mnga' 'bangs dbang rgyu
ma byung ba las 'dir yong ba yin / zer ba'i lo rgyus* zhib par zhus *brgyud
pas / lha sras kyang yid ches* nas der gnas bcas nas bzhugs *che
(14a) pa A mi don grub rgyal dang rigs brgyud gcig pa ni /
deng* sang sde phag mo gru** pa 'am / sne gdong*** gong ma *der **grub ***sdong
chen mo zer ba dang rus gcig pa yin 'dug / A mi* don grub rgyal *ni

at the sKu-ri Chu river, wherever he looked upstream or downstream there
was no bridge. He was surprised and, pondering in his mind what would be
best done, the Prince said to himself: "If I have the fortune to reside in this
region and gain control of it, may I [first] erect a bridge." Sending up a
prayer to the God of Heaven,[15] he felled and toppled a tree trunk so that
it became like a bridge joining both sides of the river. Crossing the river he
arrived at lCang-bum[16] and then passed over the top of the sKor-ri[17] Pass.
After travelling in stages through the lands of sNga-tshang, crossing the
(12b) She-ri Chu river and then [having proceeded] through Ba-geng Bre-mi-he-
long and the lands of rTseng-mi, he arrived at Byams-mkhar.[18] Leaving
the bridge of Tshang-zam he came to the open surface of the pasture called
Thum-bur at Mug-ltang-mkhar[19] and looked back. The course of the
Grang-ma'i Chu river of Gong-ri formed a broad and clean valley and so the
Divine Prince had a feeling of happiness and discharged a silver arrow he
had, causing a stream to appear [where the arrow came down]; it is the
place called gSer-sgom nowadays. Then he arrived at Wang-ser-kung-pa[20]
and looking around in all directions he saw that although the valley was
clean and pleasant, there were very few inhabitants, settlements and fields
and so he did not feel inclined to reside there. Since at that time throughout the regions of lHo Mon there were no more than a few houses and
fields which had been appropriated by the small number of people who had
(13a) come in company with King Khyi-kha Ra-thod,[21] when the Divine Prince
also came he had no desire to stay there and so proceeded by stages in
this direction. Then the Divine Prince himself asked the people, saying:
"Where are there many people and settlements and where is there good
land?" The people replied: "dPal-mkhar in La-'og Yul-gsum[22] is good."
So he went in stages to dPal-mkhar and resided there. When he came to
hear talk of how it was a time in Tibet when the sinful king[23] and sinful
ministers had agreed among themselves to destroy the teachings of the
Buddha, he did not feel inclined to reside in that place due to its close
proximity to Tibet and so he went to bTsan-mkhar in 'Brong-mdo-gsum.
(13b) Looking around for a suitable place to take for a royal castle, he thought:
"That land of Mi-zim-pa is surrounded by water and rocks, the valley is
rich and the site is strong," and so he went there. At that place there was a
habitation owned by a man called *A-mi* Don-grub-rgyal[24] and the Divine
Prince said to Don-grub-rgyal: "How many generations have passed since
you people came here? Which family, clan and region are you from?"
Don-grub-rgyal said: "We came in my parents' time from the land of Tibet
As for our family clan it is of the lineage of *A-mi* Byang-chub 'Dre-bkol of
the Rlangs lHa-gzigs [clan] who was the direct disciple of the *ācārya*
Padma[sambhava].[25] Due to a quarrel with my paternal siblings who were
in the country of Byar-po,[26] the control that I should have gained over
our subjects was not forthcoming and because of that we came here." As
he told this story in detail the Divine Prince believed him and so, having
(14a) settled there, he took up residence. As to the family lineages which are the
same as that of *A-mi* Don-grub-rgyal, nowadays[27] [that of] the so-called
sDe[-srid] Phag-mo-gru-pa [otherwise called] the *sNe-gdong Gong-ma
Chen-mo* is of the same clan. bSod-nams dPal-skyid,[28] the daughter of
A-mi Don-grub-rgyal, was taken as wife by the Divine Prince gTsang-ma and

gyi bu mo bsod nams dpal skyid / lha sras gtsang ma'i btsun mor
blangs pas / sras khri mi* lha'i** dbang phyug dang / gces bu *mi'i **omitted
mthong legs btsun gnyis 'khrungs nas sku nar son pa dang / mi
khyim yul grong 'thor bu re yod pa rnams la dbang sgyur nas rgyal
mkhar brtsigs pas / bod chos rgyal gyi gdung zhes grags pa cher song
ba dang / khri mi lha'i dbang phyug / la 'og yul gsum nas blon 'bangs
rnams kyis rje dpon spyan* drangs nas phebs pa / phyis sras rgyud *omitted
rnams lha'i khams pa la bzhugs pas khams pa jo bo zer ba'i ming de
las grags pa yin / (14b) gces bu* mthong legs btsun rgyal mkhar mi *pu
zim pa bzung ba'i sras khri brtan dpal dang / gong dkar rgyal dpal
bskyed* dar gnyis mnyam por 'khrungs pa'i sras mtshe** ma gnyis *skyed **'tshem
yin / sras gsum sku nar son pa dang / yab kyis gsungs pa / khyed
gsum gyi gnyen byed pa la lung phyogs 'di la gnyen zla che cher
med pa las / sngon rgya gar gyi yul du rigs rus gcig la / shākya* *shā kā
chen mo / shākya ri brag pa / shākya li tsa byi la sogs pa ming so
sor btags nas gnyen du sdebs pa ltar / khyod rang gsum yang de ltar
gyis* shig** gsungs*** nas / de yang gnas skabs dang bstun nas rus *gyi **shis ***gsung
kyi ming btags ba la khri brtan dpal / sras kyi thog mar 'khrungs
pa'i rje rgyal po ltar bkur* bas** na rus kyi ming la rje zer cig / *bskur **bar
gong dkar rgyal dang dpal bskyed* (15a) dar gnyis sras mtshe** ma *skyis **'tshem
gnyis mnyam por sbyar nas 'khrungs pas* na rus kyi ming la sbyar** *pa'i **byar
zer cig gsungs nas / gong dkar rgyal kho long stod kyi rje dpon du
spyan drangs nas byon / khri brtan dpal gyi rgyal sa bzung bas sras
gnam bskos lde / de nyid kyis yab mes gong ma rnams kyi yig
tshang la gzigs shing phyag srol* ji lta ba** bzhin dpe blangs nas *sros **omitted
mdzad pas / lung phyogs phal* cher mnga' 'bangs la 'dus shing *pher
dbang sgyur / sras yang gung ri rgyal / lha bzang dar / gnam sa
'bangs*/ dpal ** mthong legs bzhi 'khrungs nas sku nar son zhing *bang **dpel
stobs mnga' thang che ba'i skad sgra lung pa* mtha' dag la thos *omitted
pa dang / de'i sngon thog tsam la bod yul du rgyal po glang dar
ma'i sras 'od srung dang yum brtan gnyis rgyal srid la ma cham par
(15b) dbu ru dang g.yo* ru so sor phye** nas lo bcu gnyis kyi bar *g.yu **'phye
du 'khrugs pas / 'od srung pham nas mnga' ris stod du bros pa'i
blon 'bangs rnams lho mon* gyi phyogs su 'thor nas yong pas mi *smon
rnams kyis yul grong phal cher de dus btab pa yin pa 'dug / de'i
sngon la mi dang yul grong cher med pa dang / rje 'bangs kyi rim
pa med par 'thab cing rtsod* pa las / sngon gyi smon lam shugs *brtsod
byung lta bu thams cad kha cham nas / rgyal mkhar mi zim par rje
dpon gdan 'dren zhu bar phyin pas / rgyal po gnam bskos sde'i zhal
nas khyod rnams 'dir ci la yong gsungs // nged rnams bod chos kyi
rgyal po'i gdung yod zer ba nas rje dpon zhu bar yong ba yin zer
bas / rgyal po'i zhal nas de ni rten 'brel* shin tu legs so // gsungs *'bres
nas / gung ri rgyal 'dir rgyal (16a) mkhar bzung ba la 'dir sdod cig /

so both Khri-mi lHa'i-dbang-phyug and gCes-bu mThong-legs-btsun were
born. When they grew up they gained control over the few habitations and
settlements which existed and built a royal castle. When the fame of the
so-called 'Clan of the Tibetan *Dharmarājas'* had become great, Khri-mi lHa'i-
dbang-phyug was invited by the officers and subjects from La-'og Yul-
gsum as their chief and he went there. [29] Later the name of the so-called
Khams-pa Jo-bo' [clan] [30] achieved renown from the fact that his
descendants resided in the domain of the gods (*lha'i khams-pa*?). The son of
(14b) gCes-bu mThong-legs-btsun who took control of the Mi-zim-pa royal castle
was Khri-brtan-dpal. There were also the sons Gong-dkar-rgyal and dPal-
bskyed-dar who were two twins born together. When these three sons grew
up, their father said: "Since for the marriages of you three there are none
really fit for matrimonial alliance in this region, so just as in India in
previous times there were applied various names to one family - i.e. the
Mahā-Śākya, the Śākya Ri-brag-pa, the Śākya-Licchavī and so on who then
intermarried – so also should you three do likewise." Then, giving clan
names in accordance with their individual circumstances, he said: "Call
Khri-brtan-dpal by the clan name of rJe [31] ('Lord') in order to honour him
(15a) like a lord-king, being the first-born of my sons. Call both Gong-dkar-rgyal
and dPal-bskyed-dar by the clan-name of sByar ('Attached') since they were
born as two twins attached to each other." Gong-dkar-rgyal was invited as
the lord-chief of Kho-long-stod and went there. The son of Khri-brtan-dpal
who took control of the royal site [of his father] was gNam-bskos-sde. He
looked to the records of his ancestral forebears and, taking their custom as
an example just as they used to be, [32] he acted accordingly and so
subjugated most regions and gained power. His sons, Gung-ri-rgyal, lHa-
bzang-dar, gNam-sa-'bangs and dPal-mthong-legs, [these] four, were born.
They grew up and accounts of their great strength and power were heard in
all the valleys.

At a time just prior to these events, 'Od-srung and Yum-brtan, the two
(15b) sons of King Glang Dar-ma, had not been in accord over the government and,
separating into a central wing and a left wing, they had contended over a
period of twelve years. After 'Od-srung had been defeated he fled to
mNga'-ris sTod [33] and his officers and subjects were dispersed in the
direction of lHo Mon and it seems that it was at that time that most of the
settlements were established by these people who had come. Previous to
that there had not been many people or settlements and in the absence of
a graded order among ruler and subjects they disputed and quarrelled. Then,
as if by the power of their former aspirations [made in previous lives], they
all came to agreement and set off for the Mi-zim-pa royal castle in order to
extend an invitation to a lord-chief. King gNam-bskos-sde said: "Why have
you come here?" "We have come to ask for a lord-chief since it is said that
there is a clan of the Tibetan Dharmarājas [here]", they said. "Then that is
a very good auspice", said the king. "Let Gung-ri-rgyal stay here so as to
(16a) take control of the royal castle in this place. May the other sons depart to

sras gzhan rnams blon 'bangs so so'i blo dang sbyar nas gdan 'dren
gang du zhu ba'i sar song la / blon 'bangs rnams byams dang snying
rje thabs mkhas kyi sgo nas skyongs* shig gsungs nas / bkra shis *sgyongs
smon lam* gyi rgyas btab cing dngos po yo byad** sna tshogs kyi *omitted **yod byed
rdzong ba mdzad pas / lha bzang dar nyi ma che* rigs la gdan *tsha
drangs / gnam sa 'bangs nyi ma chung rigs la gdan drangs / dpal
mthong legs smad gdung bsam la gdan drangs nas byon pas / de
rnams so so'i sras brgyud rim* par bgyis pa ni / de dus rgyal po *chu
rnams yul grong gcig tu nges pa mi 'dzin par / blon 'bangs rnams
kyi yul grong skor nas bzhugs pa yin 'dug / lha bzang dar che rigs
la byon pa'i sras / stong gsum rgyal po / de'i bu (16b) som rgyal /
som dar / som bzang / som bzang gi bu / bla ma dang / 'od 'bar /
bla ma'i bu rgyal gdung 'jig stang la / de nyid kyi was chur thum
nang mkhar la rgyal mkhar brtsigs* shing / gnas mo chen chung
blangs pas chen mo'i bu rgya nag dang ma ku gnyis byung / chung
ma'i bu rin bzang / dpal bzang / grags pa bzang / bsod nams 'bum* *'bu ma
bzhi byung bas / skya sa mkhar gyi sa cha gsal la dwangs* shing *dangs
phu mda' 'brel pa nyam dga' ba yod pa las / khong pha bu rnams
kha cham nas der rgyal mkhar brtsigs shing rgyal sa bzung nas / de
las so sor 'gyes pa las rgyal po snga tshang phyi tshang zer ba de las
byung ba yin / rgya nag gi bu / ham po dang / grags pa gnyis yin /
ham po'i bu lha dar / de'i bu rdor chos dbang / des mkhar nang du
'thon rgyal mkhar (17a) brtsigs shing der sdod / de'i bu gsang bdag
dang / dpal bkra shis gnyis yin / dpal bkra shis kyi* bu / dar 'jam *omitted
dang / chos 'jam gnyis yin / chos 'jam gyi bu / rdor tshe dbang /
de'i bu lha dbang / mi dbang gnyis / lha dbang gi bu / dar 'jam / de'i
bu nor bu dbang rgyal dang / ngag dbang nor bu gnyis / yang rdor
tshe dbang / rtseng mi'i blon 'bangs rnams kyi rje dpon du gdan
drangs yong nas / tshan lnga shing mkhar la rgyal mkhar bzung nas /
chung ma* blang pa'i** bu / kun thub / de'i bu rgyud stong ldan *mo **ma'i
dang dbang bstan 'dzin grags pa'i bu brgyud mkhar nang dang / mu
sde nor bu sgang la yod pa'i* rgyal rigs** rnams yin / gong du bshad *omitted **rtsigs
pa'i chung ma'i bu / rin bzang gi bu brgyud rim par 'gyes pa be tsha
nang mkhar gyi rgyal rigs (17b) rnams yin / bsod nams 'bum* skya *bum
sa mkhar du rgyal mkhar bzung nas sdod pa'i bu / dngos 'bum dang /
chos 'bum gnyis yin / dngos 'bum gyi brgyud pa spun mang tshan
gyi rgyal rigs rnams yin / chos 'bum gyi bu / sgrub pa dang / sgo la
gnyis yin / sgrub pa'i bu / rang po dang rdor* bzang / rdor bzang** *rdos **omitted
gi bu / bang nge dang khri mi gnyis yin / de gnyis kyi* bu brgyud *bkyis
rim par 'gyes pa / da lta skya sa mkhar / khas mkhar / mug ltang
mkhar / skyed mkhar / the nang sbi la yod pa rgyal* rigs rnams yin / *rgyag
khri mi'i* bu / nyi ma bzang / de'i bu sangs rdo rje yin / des 'dre *mi
spong la song nas rgyal mkhar brtsigs nas btsan sa bzung ba'i bu
rgyud rim par bgyes nas* 'dre spong gi rgyal rigs rnams yin / sangs *omitted

whatever places they are invited according to the intentions of the subjects and officers and may they protect the subjects and officers by clever means with love and compassion," he said. Sealing the matter with prayers of good auspice, he sent them off with a variety of goods and chattels. lHa-bzang-dar was invited to Nyi-ma Che-rigs. gNam-sa-'bangs was invited to Nyi-ma Chung-rigs. dPal-mthong-legs was invited to lower gDung-bsam; and so they went off. As to the successive issue of their various descendants: At that time the kings did not take control of single settlements decisively but instead they circulated around the settlements of the subjects and officers,
(16b) residing there [each by turn]. The son of lHa-bzang-dar who went to Che-rigs was sTong-gsum rGyal-po. His sons were Som-rgyal, Som-dar and Som-bzang. Som-bzang's sons were Bla-ma and 'Od-'bar. Bla-ma's son was rGyal-gdung 'Jig-stang-la who built a royal castle at Was-chur Thum-nang-mkhar.[34] Acquiring a senior and junior wife, two sons of the senior, rGya-nag and Ma-ku, came forth and four sons of the junior, Rin-bzang, dPal-bzang, Grags-pa-bzang and bSod-nams-'bum came forth. Since the land of sKya-sa-mkhar was clear and pure and its connected upper and lower parts were pleasant, they, father and sons, came to an agreement and building a royal castle in that place they took control of a royal site. The so-called 'Kings of sNga-tshang [and] Phyi-tshang'[35] arose from among their various issue. The sons of rGya-nag were Ham-po and Grags-pa, [these] two. The son of
(17a) Ham-po was lHa-dar and his son was rDor Chos-dbang who proceeded to mKhar-nang and, building a royal castle, resided there. His sons were gSang-bdag and dPal-bkra-shis, [these] two. The sons of dPal-bkra-shis were Dar-'jam and Chos-'jam, [these] two. The son of Chos-'jam was rDor-tshe-dbang. His sons were lHa-dbang and Mi-dbang. The son of lHa-dbang was Dar-'jam.[36] His sons are (?) Nor-bu dBang-rgyal and Ngag-dbang Nor-bu, [these] two. As for rDor-tshe-dbang, he was invited [to act] as the chief of the officers and subjects of rTseng-mi and came there. Having taken control of a royal castle at Tshan-lnga Shing-mkhar, Kun-thub, the son of the junior wife he married [there, was born]. The descendants of his progeny, sTong-ldan[37] and dBang bsTan-'dzin Grags-pa, are the royal families who are at mKhar-nang and Mu-sde Nor-bu sGang.

The successive issue of the descendants of Rin-bzang, the son of the
(17b) junior wife mentioned above, are the royal families of Be-tsha Nang-mkhar. bSod-nams-'bum took control of a royal castle at sKya-sa-mkhar and resided there. His sons were dNgos-'bum and Chos-'bum, [these] two. The descendants of dNgos-'bum are the royal families of sPun-mang-tshan. The sons of Chos-'bum were sGrub-pa and sGo-la, [these] two. The sons of sGrub-pa were Rang-po and rDor-bzang. The sons of rDor-bzang were Bang-nge and Khri-mi, [these] two. The successive issue of the descendants of these two are now the royal families who are at sKya-sa-mkhar, Khas-mkhar, Mug-ltang-mkhar, sKyed-mkhar and The-nang-sbi. The son of Khri-mi was Nyi-ma-bzang. His son was Sangs-rdo-rje. Having gone to 'Dre-spong he built a royal castle and took control of the stronghold. Having proliferated successively, his descendants are the royal families of 'Dre-

rdo rje'i bu / zla'u la / des mong sgar (18a) du yong nas rgyal mkhar
brtsigs shing sa gzhis bzung ba'i bu / rgyal po nor bu dbang phyug
dang / dbang drag gnyis yin / bang nge'i* bu sngo seng / de'i bu tshe *spang de'i
dbang / de'i bu tshe ring dbang chen / de'i bu* rgyal po yin // // *omitted
gnam sa 'bangs* nyi ma chung** rigs la byon pa'i bu brgyud la / *bang **chu
me gdung stong gsum zer ba'i rgyal po spun gnyis byung ba'i / me
gdung gi bu / sman khyi dang / thos pa / sman khyi'i* bu / bya ku *khyi
dang* / nya ku / de las so sor 'gyes pa wang ser kum pa'i rgyal rigs *omitted
rnams yin / thos pa'i bu / gser gdung dang ldan pa / gser gdung beng
mkhar bkra shis sgang la byon nas / rgyal mkhar brtsigs shing rgyal
sa bzung ba'i* bu khu na / de'i bu kha khas / dngos / rgya mtsho *omitted
bang gsum byung ba'i dngos kyi bu brgyud (18b) grong stod kyi
rgyal rigs rnams yin / rgya mtsho bang gi bu brgyud grong smad kyi
rgyal rigs rnams yin / kha khas kyi bu brgyud rang ci mkhar las
yong ba'i rgyal rigs rnams yin / ldan pas* gcen mkhar du song nas *pa'i
rgyal mkhar brtsigs nas* blon 'bangs la** dbang sgyur nas / rje *omitted **omitted
dpon mdzad pa'i bu thub sbi / de'i bu brgyud la cho ka rdo rje /
mgon po rdo rje / senge rdo rje gsum yin / cho ka rdo rjes* rgyal *rje
mkhar bzung nas* rgya gar rdo rong rwa dza dang 'phrul thabs *omitted
bsdur bas cho ka rdo rje rgyal nas de* tshun chad nas** rgya'i las *de las **omitted
sgo la dbang sgyur ba yin / cho ka rdo rje'i bu / khyi rog / rdos /
rgyas mtsho* gsum yin / khyi rog gi bu / bla ma / de'i bu lha mo *rgyal tsho
A chi / de'i bu rdo rje phan pas / de'i bu zu gi / de'i bu brgyud gcen
mkhar la yod / rdos kyi bu dngos grub dang / bla ma grags pa /
dngos (19a) grub kyi bu rgyal mtshan / de'i bu nor bu rgyal po dang
gsang grags / nor bu rgyal po'i bu* rgyas mtsho / de'i bu khyi rog *omitted
dpal yin brgyud chad / gsang grags kyi bu tshe dbang / de'i bu* *omitted
rin chen rgyal po dang / karma rgyal po gnyis yin / bla ma grags
pa'i bu brgyud phra sgom gyi rgyal rigs rnams yin / spun chung ba
rgyas mtsho / kha gling gi blon 'bangs rnams kyis* gdan drangs nas / *kyi
kha gling mkhar la byon nas rgyal mkhar brtsigs shing / blon 'bangs
dang* rgya gar gyi** las sgo la*** dbang sgyur nas / stobs mnga' *omitted **gi ***omitted
thang che bar byung ba dang / phyogs mtha'i mi sde thams cad der
'dus* pas** da lta'i kha gling gi Ar tshan zer ba'i yul tshan rnams *dus **pa'i
de yin pa 'dug / rgyas mtsho'i bu / rgyal bu / de'i bu brgyud bsod
nams dpal 'byor / de'i sras che ba chos kas / chung ba rgyas bsam
grub / chos* kas kyi sras tshe (19b) g.yang / tshe g.yang gi sras che *cho
ba / rgyal bu / chung ba bla ma don grub / rgyal bu'i sras / padma
rgyal po / padma rgyal po'i sras / gces bu / bsod nams dbang / khri
mi gsum yin / gces bu'i* bu bkra shis dar rgyas dang / sing po gnyis *pu'i
yin brgyud pa chad / khri mi'i* bu bde ba'i brgyud chad / bsod *mi
nams dbang la brgyud pa med / bla ma don grub kyi sras / sangs
rgyas po / nor bu rgyal po / karma tshe ring / 'brug rgyal po bzhi

(18a) spong. The son of Sangs-rdo-rje was Zla'u-la. [38] Having gone to Mong-sgar, he built a royal castle and took control of an estate. His sons are the *rGyal-po*(s) Nor-bu dBang-phyug and dBang-drag, [39] [these] two. The son of Bang-nge was sNgo-seng. His son was Tshe-dbang. His son was Tshe-ring dBang-chen. His son is rGyal-po. [40]

Among the descendants of gNam-sa-'bangs, who had gone to Nyi-ma Chung-rigs, there came forth two brothers, the kings called Me-gdung and sTong-gsum. The sons of Me-gdung were sMan-khyi and Thos-pa. The sons of sMan-khyi were Bya-khu and Nya-khu. The successive issue from them are the royal families of Wang-ser-kum-pa. [41] The sons of Thos-pa were gSer-gdung and lDan-pa. [42] gSer-gdung went to Beng-mkhar bKra-shis-sgang, [43] built a royal castle and took control of a royal site. His son was Khu-na. His sons, Kha-khas, dNgos and rGya-mtsho-bang, [these] three, came forth. The descendants of dNgos are the royal families of Grong-
(18b) stod. [44] The descendants of rGya-mtsho-bang are the royal families of Grong-smad. The descendants of Kha-khas are the royal families who come from Rang-ci-mkhar. lDan-pa, having gone to gCen-mkhar, built a royal castle, gained power over the officers and subjects and acted as lord-chief. [45] His son was Thub-sbi. Among his descendants there were Cho-ka rDo-rje, mGon-po rDo-rje, and Senge rDo-rje, [these] three. [46] After Cho-ka rDo-rje had taken control of a royal castle he vied in magical skill with the Indian rDo-rong Rwa-dza; [47] Cho-ka rDo-rje won and thereafter the Indian *duars* were in a state of subjugation. [48] The sons of Cho-ka rDo-rje were Khyi-rog, rDos and rGyas-mtsho, [these] three. The son of Khyi-rog was Bla-ma. His son was lHa-mo A-chi. His son was rDo-rje Phan-pas. His son was Zu-gi. His descendants are at gCen-mkhar. [49] The sons of rDos were dNgos-grub and *Bla-ma* Grags-pa. The son of dNgos-grub was
(19a) rGyal-mtshan. His sons were Nor-bu rGyal-po and gSang-grags. The son of Nor-bu rGyal-po was rGya-mtsho. His son was Khyi-rog-dpal and then the lineage expired. The son of gSang-grags was Tshe-dbang. His sons were Rin-chen rGyal-po and Karma rGyal-po, [these] two. The descendants of *Bla-ma* Grags-pa are the royal families of Phra-sgom. The youngest brother, rGyas-mtsho, having been invited by the officers and subjects of Kha-gling, he went to Kha-gling-mkhar and built a royal castle. He brought under his power the officers and subjects and [also] the Indian *duars*, and when his strength and dominion became great all the communities from every direction assembled there and so the present so-called Ar-tshan districts of Kha-gling seem to be those [places where they settled]. [50] The son of rGyas-mtsho was rGyal-bu. His descendant was bSod-nams dPal-'byor. His
(19b) elder son was Chos-kas and his younger son rGyas-bsam-grub. The son of Chos-kas was Tshe-g.yang. The elder son of Tshe-g.yang was rGyal-bu and his younger son was *Bla-ma* Don-grub. The son of rGyal-bu was Padma rGyal-po. The sons of Padma rGyal-po were gCes-bu, bSod-nams-dbang and Khri-mi, [these] three. The sons of gCes-bu were bKra-shis Dar-rgyas and Sing-po, [these] two, and then the lineage expires. The son of Khri-mi was bDe-ba [51] and then the lineage expired. bSod-nams-dbang had no lineage. The sons of *Bla-ma* Don-grub, Sangs-rgyas-po, Nor-bu rGyal-po, Karma Tshe-ring and 'Brug rGyal-po, [these] four, came forth. The sons of

byung ba'i / karma tshe ring gi bu / bstan 'dzin rgyal po dang* / *omitted
bstan 'dzin dbang 'dus / bstan 'dzin dbang 'dus kyi bu /
ngag dbang bsam 'phel/ngag dbang bsam 'phel gyi bu /
ngag dbang phun tshogs dang / bsod nams 'brug rgyal gnyis yin /
bsod nams 'brug rgyal gyi bu / 'brug bde legs / 'brug rgyal po'i* *po
bu / bang ga / rgyal po bsam (20a) grub / ba man gsum yin / bang
ga'i bu / sngon la / de'i bu bla ma rgyal po / ngag dbang bsam grub /
karma bstan 'dzin yin pas brgyud chad / seng ge rdo rje'i bu brgyud
rim par 'das pa'i brgyud pa la / U rgyan dang / rgyas dar gnyis
byung / rgyas dar gyi bu / rgyal po dang las kyi / rgyal po'i bu /
rgyal bkra shis / de'i bu tshe ring dang nor bu dbang gnyis yin / de'i
bu brgyud sdom mkhar la yod pa'i rgyal rigs rnams yin / las kyi'i* *kyi
bu ngag dbang / de'i bu pho brang dang nag seng gnyis yin / de'i bu
brgyud btsan mkhar gyi rgyal rigs rnams yin / rje dpal mthong legs
gdung bsam la byon nas blon 'bangs dang rgya gar la dbang sgyur
nas / stobs mnga' thang che bar byung zhing / btsun mo blangs pas
sras 'od bar byung / de'i bu tsha bo chang po / de'i (20b) bu brgyud
rim par 'das pa'i bu brgyud la* / bstan na dang / bang tsho zer ba'i *rim
rgyal bu spun gnyis rgyal srid la ma cham par 'khrugs pas / bang
tsho pham nas yul 'thon song ba'i bu brgyud gung gdung rgyal po
dang / gzhong dkar stong phu la yod pa'i rgyal rigs rnams yin /
gdung bsam mon yul stong gsum la* yod zer ba'ang / de'i dus la *omitted
'thor ba yin 'dug / gong du brjod pa'i me gdung gi gcung po stong
gsum / de'i sras stong rab / de gnyis kyis gcen mkhar dang sgam ri
lung pa ra ti / phong mi khang pa mkhar la sogs par rim par phebs
kyang / rgyal sa bzung ma thub par mthong rong wa ma spang
gdung la yul bzung nas re zhig der sdad / de nas slar log nas mkhar
gdung la yul bzung sdod pa'i bu brgyud mkhar gdung gi rgyal (21a)
rigs rnams yin / yang gong du bshad pa'i 'phros las / gong dkar
rgyal kho long stod smad kyi blon 'bangs rnams kyi rje dpon du
gdan drangs nas kho long stod la 'phebs / rgyal mkhar brtsigs shing
mnga' 'bangs mi sde thams cad la stobs shugs* che ba'i sgo nas *shug
dbang sgyur nas / btsun mo che ba dpal 'dren skyid / rdor 'dzom
pa / A thung skyid /g.yang dpal mo bzhi yang khab tu blangs /
btsun mo che ba dpal 'dren skyid las / sras mthong legs dpal dang /
btsun gong rgyal gnyis 'khrungs pa dang mo nga rgyal langs nas /
rgyal po la'ang* zlo / btsun mo gzhan gsum phyir bton nas rang *langs
rang so so'i yul du log btang ba'i rtsis byas pa la / rgyal pos ma
nyan par bzhag pa dang / btsun mo gsum (21b) gyis kyang sems
chung gi dngos nas btsun mo che ba'i g.yog mo'i tshul ltar bzung
nas sdod pa'i / zla dus 'khor ba dang btsun mo gsum la'ang rgyal
po'i sras lus la chags pa dang / gtso* rgan stong 'dus dar** gyis*** *gtsor **dur ***gyi
shes nas / btsun mo gsum la gsang gtam phan tshig smras pa /
khyed gsum la rgyal po'i sras lus la yod pa btsun mo che bas* shes *ba'i

Karma Tshe-ring were bsTan-'dzin rGyal-po and bsTan-'dzin dBang-'dus.
The son of bsTan-'dzin dBang-'dus was Ngag-dbang bSam-'phel. The sons
of Ngag-dbang bSam-'phel are Ngag-dbang Phun-tshogs [52] and bSod-nams
'Brug-rgyal, [these] two. The son of bSod-nams 'Brug-rgyal is 'Brug bDe-legs.
(20a) The sons of 'Brug rGyal-po were Bang-ga, rGyal-po bSam-grub, and Ba-man,[53]
[these] three. The son of Bang-ga was sNgon-la. His sons were Bla-ma
rGyal-po, Ngag-dbang bSam-grub and Karma bsTan-'dzin and then the
lineage expired.

In the lineage that passed down successively among the descendants of Seng-ge rDo-rje there came forth U-rgyan and rGyas-dar, these two. The sons of rGyas-dar were rGyal-po and Las-kyi. The son of rGyal-po was rGyal-bkra-shis. His sons were Tshe-ring [54] and Nor-bu-dbang. Their descendants are the royal families who are at sDom-mkhar. The son of Las-kyi was Ngag-dbang. His sons were Pho-brang [55] and Nag-seng, [56] [these] two. Their descendants are the royal families of bTsan-mkhar.

Having gone to gDung-bsam, *Lord* (*rJe*) [57] dPal mThong-legs gained
power over the officers and subjects and [also] the Indians and his strength
and dominion became great. After marrying a consort, a son, 'Od-bar, came
(20b) forth. His son was Tsha-bo Chang-po. In the lineage that passed down
successively among his descendants the two princely brothers called
bsTan-na and Bang-tsho were not in accord over the government and they
contended. Bang-tsho was defeated and departed from the home. His
descendants are the kings of Gung-gdung [58] and the royal families who are
at gZhong-dkar sTong-phu. [59] They are also said to be at gDung-bsam Mon-yul sTong-gsum [60] and it was at that time that they were scattered there.

sTong-gsum was the younger brother of Me-gdung who is mentioned
above. His son was sTong-rab. [61] Although they both went in stages to
gCen-mkhar, sGam-ri-lung-pa Ra-ti, Phong-mi Khang-pa-mkhar and other
places they were unable to take control of a royal site and so they seized
a home at mThong-rong Wa-ma sPang-gdung and for a time resided there.
Then, having returned, they seized a home at mKhar-gdung [62] and their
(21a) descendants who reside there are the royal families of mKhar-gdung.

Now, in continuation of what was explained above, Gong-dkar-rgyal went
to Upper Kho-long having been invited as the chief of the officers and
subjects of Upper and Lower Kho-long. Having built a royal castle and
brought under his power all the subjects and communities by means of
great force, he brought to his court the senior consort dPal-'dren-skyid, and
rDor-'dzom-pa, A-thung-skyid and g.Yang-dpal-mo, [these] four. When the
sons mThong-legs-dpal and bTsun-gong-rgyal, [these] two, were born to
dPal-'dren-skyid, the senior consort, she became proud and vied [63] even
with the king. As for her plan to expel the other three consorts and send
them back each to their various homes, the king would not listen and
(21b) retained them. The three consorts, however, because of their genuinely
humble disposition, kept on behaving in the manner of servants to the
senior consort. When the months had elapsed and when the king's sons had
also been generated in the bodies of the three consorts, the headman sTong-'dus-dar, knowing [64] about it, spoke useful words in secret to the three
consorts. "If the senior consort knows that you three have the king's sons
in your bodies there is great danger that she will try to harm you on account

nas ngan sems phrag dog gi gnod pa skyal nyen che bas bag gzon legs
par gyis shig zer bas / btsun mo gsum gyis* kyang de bzhin byas / *gyi
zla grangs tshang rim* gyi sras po re re btsas pa dang / btsun mo *rin
che bas* tshor gyi dog nas / rdor 'dzom pas** btsas pa'i sras po de / *ba'i **pa'i
zo ba* gyas kyi nang du gsang nas gsos / A thung skyid kyi sras po *zo ba de
de gzeb ma stung gi nang du sbas nas gsos /g.yang dpal mo'i sras
(22a) po de / sa dong wang gi nang du 'gab nas gsos pas / gsum ka
gzugs byad* bzang shing bskyed yang che bar byung nas 'gro 'grul *byas
shes shing gtam 'thol re smra shes pa dang / btsun mo chung ba
gsum gyis* kyang btsun mo che bas gnod pa skyel** gyis dogs*** *gyi **skyal ***dog
nas / blon 'bangs rnams kyis* bran nas bu chung gsum khrid cing *kyi
gong dkar drung du phyin nas smras pa / btsun mo che ba'i phra
dog la 'jigs nas sbas gsang thabs mkhas kyis* gsos** pa'i sras*** *kyi **bsos ***pa'i
gsum po 'di yin zer bas / rgyal po thugs dgongs shin tu dgyes shing sras omitted
bud med shes rab kyi rang bzhin yin zer ba bden par 'dug gsungs* *gsung
nas / sras gsum po rim pas phang du blangs shing mgo la btsugs* *'rdzus
btsugs* re mdzad nas / dus ma 'ong pa na gtam rgyun ngo mtshar *'jus
che zhing ya mtshan pa'i phyir du sras gsum po'i (22b) mtshan ma'i
ming dang rus kyi ming so sor btags dgos gsungs nas / rdor 'dzom
pa'i bu snod yas kyi nang du gsang nes gsos* ba yin pas na / ming *bsos
gsang sde btsan du btags* / rus kyi ming la yas sde zer / A thung
skyid kyi bu snod stung gi nang du sbas nas gsos* pa yin pas na /
ming sbas sde btsan du btags* / rus kyi ming la stung sde zer / g.yang *btag
dpal mo'i bu sa dong wang gi nang du 'gab* nas gsos** pa yin pas *gab **bsos
na / ming 'gab* sde btsan du btags** / rus kyi ming la wang ma *gab **btag
zer cig / da dung bu gsum nar ma son gyi bar du legs par bskyangs
shig gsungs nas / yum gsum la bza' btung mkho ba'i yo byad* dpag *byed
tu med pa gnang ngo / de nas sras lnga nar son zhing dpa' brtul lang
tsho dar la babs nas / stobs mnga' thang che bar song ba dang / yab
gong (23a) dkar rgyal yang thugs dgyes pa'i nga rgyal langs nas /
blon 'bangs rnams la khral 'u lag gi rgyun che bar btsugs shing / lung
pa'i phu las sha khral / mda' las nya khral / tshong pa lam 'grul las
lam khral tshugs* len pa dang / blon 'bangs rnams dka' las che bar *tshug
len pa dang / blon 'bangs rnams dka' las che bar byung ba dang /
thams cad kha mthun gyis ngo log nas / gong dkar rgyal yab sras
rnams rgyal mkhar las bton* btang ba dang / log yong nas re** zhig *gton **ri
rgyal mkhar mi zim par bzhugs pa'i skabs der / sngar nas rje dpon
gdan 'dren ma zhus pa'i mi rnams kyis / lha sras gtsang ma'i gdung /
gong dkar rgyal gyi sras rnams yod par shes nas / rgyal mkhar mi
zim par yong nas / gong dkar rgyal gyi drung du zhus pas / nged kyi
yul du rje dpon med par 'thab (23b) cing brtsod pa'i sdug bsngal
yod pas* de sel ba'i phyir du / sras rnams nged** so so'i yul phyogs *pa'i **ded
kyi rje dpon la zhus dgos zer bas / gong dkar rgyal gyi zhal nas /
mthong legs dpal nga rang gar sdod kyi sa gzhi zung ba la bzhag

of malicious envy. So take careful heed," he said. The three consorts therefore did so. When the number of months had come to an end and they each
gave birth to a son, fearing that the senior consort would perceive it, the
son whom rDor-'dzom-pa had given birth to was reared secreted inside a
(22a) *g.yas* trough. The son of A-thung-skyid was reared hidden inside a *stung*
pannier. The son of g.Yang-dpal-mo was reared concealed in a *wang* pit.[65]
The three of them were born of fine appearance and when they grew bigger
and knew how to walk about and suddenly began to speak words, the three
junior consorts were fearful that the senior consort might do them an injury
and so the officers and subjects, knowing about it, went before Gong-dkar
[-rgyal] and said: "These are the three sons who in fear of the jealousy of the
senior consort have been reared by clever means in secret hiding." The king
was overjoyed and declared: "It is [commonly] said that women are of the
true nature of wisdom and it would seem to be true." He took up the three
sons in succession on his lap and patted each on the head. "In order that in
times to come the legend may be wondrous and strange, it is necessary to
(22b) give personal names and clan names to the three sons individually," he
said. "Since the son of rDor-'dzom-pa was reared secreted (*gsang*) in a *yas*-
vessel give his name as gSang-sde-btsan[66] and call his clan name Yas-sde.
Since the son of A-thung-skyid was reared hidden (*sbas*) inside a *stung*-
vessel give his name as sBas-sde-btsan and call his clan name sTung-sde. Since
the son of g.Yang-dpal-mo was reared concealed (*'gab*) in a *wang*-pit give his
name as 'Gab-sde-btsan and call his clan name Wang-ma. Now guard the
three sons well until they grow up," he said. To the three mothers he gave a
limitless supply of food, drink and requisites. Then when the five sons grew
up, became brave and attained youthful manhood, their strength and
(23a) dominion increased and their father, Gong-dkar-rgyal, in his joy bursted
with pride. So he established in large measure a regular custom of taxation
and corvée among the officers and subjects; he introduced and collected a
meat-tax from the upper part of the district, a fish-tax from the lower part
and a road-tax from the traders who travelled the roads. When great
difficulties arose for the officers and subjects they unanimously revolted
and Gong-dkar-rgyal, father and sons, were expelled from the royal castle.
At the time when, having returned [to their original home] they were
residing at the Mi-zim-pa royal castle, those people who had previously not
invited a chief, knowing that the sons of Gong-dkar-rgyal were of Prince
gTsang-ma's clan, they came to the Mi-zim-pa royal castle. In front of
Gong-dkar-rgyal they declared: "There being no lord-chief in our country
(23b) there is suffering on account of quarrels and contentions and so in order to
remove it (i.e. the suffering) we must request your sons [to act] as the
lord-chiefs of our various districts." Gong-dkar-rgyal said: "I must keep
mThong-legs-dpal in order to control the estates wherever I stay. Take away

dgos / bu gzhan rnams khyed rang blon 'bangs so so 'i blo dang sbyar
nas khrid cig gsungs pas / yas* sde gsang sde btsan / sa gling rgyan *yang
mtshams la gdan drangs nas byon / stung sde sbas sde btsan / zang
lung pa la gdan drangs nas byon / wang ma 'gab* sde btsan / gang *gab
zur stod la gdan drangs nas byon / sras rnams so sor 'gyes pa'i rjes
su / yab gong dkar rgyal yang thugs mkhyen stobs kyi mdzad
khyon* rlabs che ba'i bshams ra sgrigs pa dang / sngar nas mi zim *khyod
pa'i rgyal mkhar 'dzin mkhan gnam bskos (24a) lde'i* thugs ji ltar *sde
yong mi shes bsam nas / gong dkar rgyal yab sras gsum ri gzhung
thang ngos* la phebs nas gnas gzhi bcas bas / de'i nye 'khor na yod *sngos
pa'i mi sde thams cad kyang sngon gyi smon lam shugs byung lta
bur* rang dbang med par mnga' 'bangs la 'dus** pa dang / gzhan *bu'i **'dud
yang yul grong mang po zhi rgyas dbang drag gi sgo nas mnga' 'bangs
la bcug cing / stobs mnga' thang che bar byung nas / sgo khyi yang
stag la byas pa'i rdo phong bug* pa phug nas gtags pa'i bshul da *phug
lta'ang 'dug / gong dkar rgyal gyi sras / mthong legs dpal / de'i sras
rgyal gdung dar / de'i sras ngam bzang la / de'i sras sprang po dar /
btsan 'dus la / Ong ma gsum byung ba'i / sprang po dar gyi pha nor
che dgu thams cad khyer nas / shar dom (24b) kha la song nas stobs
shugs che ba grub thob spyod pa lta bus / mi sde thams cad mnga'
'bangs la bchug cing rgya'i las sgo la dbang sgyur nas stobs mnga'-
thang che bar byung ba'i bu brgyud* shar dom kha dang / mur *brgyud
shing la yod pa'i ba spu rnams yin / bar ma btsan 'dus la* tsha se *btsan 'dul
la song nas rgyal mkhar bzung nas blon 'bangs la dbang sgyur ba'i
bu / btsan gong la dang / lag sdum pa de gnyis kyi bu brgyud so sor
'gyes pa / tsha se dang / yu rung / khang pa / phyi mung / zla gor la
yod pa'i byar pa'i rigs thams cad de'i brgyud pa yin no // chung ba
Ong ma U dza rong la song nas / rgyal mkhar bzung nas blon 'bangs
la dbang sgyur nas rje dpon mdzad pa'i bu / dpal 'bum dang / bzang
dar / lu btsan gsum byung ba las so sor 'gyes (25a) pa / U dza rong
dang / gtor ma gzhong / yong ka la / lcags mkhar bzung / ku ri smad /
rgya ras zur / byog kang / ngang la / khom shar / ne to la / kheng* *khyed
rigs rnam* gsum la yod pa'i byar pa'i rigs thams cad byar Ong ma'i *rnams
bu brgyud yin no // yang zur du bshad* na / dpal 'bum gyi bu *phye
brgyud la / gser 'bum* / dngos 'bum*/dar 'bum* gsum byung ba'i *bum
gser 'bum* gyi bu / thur skye / de'i bu rdo rje grags pa / de'i bu *bum
las kyi bang dang / padma dbang / las kyi bang gi bu / bstan 'dzin
bsod nams dang / bstan 'dzin grags pa yin / 'di gnyis kyi bu brgyud
dang / dngos 'bum* dang dar 'bum* gyi bu brgyud U dza rong yod *bum
pa rnams yin / gong du brjod pa'i 'phros las / yas* sde gsang sde *yang
btsan / sa gling rgyan mtshams (25b) du blon 'bangs rnams kyis* *kyi
gdan drangs nas byon te / rgyal mkhar brtsigs shing rgyal sa bzung
ba'i bu brgyud la yas sde su na zer ba'i dpa' mdzangs blo gros thabs
la mkhas pa zhig yong ste / des* sgam ri'i chu rgyud phan tshun gyi *de'i

with you the other sons in accordance with the various desires of your
officers and men." Yas-sde gSang-sde-btsan was invited to Sa-gling rGyan-
mtshams and departed. sTung-sde sBas-sde-btsan was invited to Zang-lung-
pa and departed. Wang-ma 'Gab-sde-btsan was invited to Upper Gang-zur
and departed. After the sons had dispersed in different directions, their
father, Gong-dkar-rgyal, through the strength of his perceptions also
prepared a plan of extensive action and thinking that he could not know
(24a) what would arise in the mind of gNam-bskos-lde [his nephew] who had
acted from previous times as the castellan of Mi-zim-pa, Gong-dkar-rgyal
father and sons - three [in all] - went to a pasture at Ri-gzhung and
founded a settlement there. All the communities that were in the vicinity
of that place were gathered together as subjects with no freedom [of
choice], as if the force of aspirations made in previous lives had been
accomplished, and furthermore many districts and villages were subjugated
by peaceful, enriching, strong and fierce means and so his strength and
dominion became great. Using a tiger as a guard dog, he tied it to a
boulder in which he had pierced a hole, the gap of which exists even at
present. The son of Gong-dkar-rgyal was mThong-legs-dpal. His son was
rGyal-gdung-dar. His son was Ngam-bzang-la. His sons, sPrang-po-dar,
bsTan-'dus-la and Ong-ma - [these] three - came forth. Of them, sPrang-
(24b) po-dar, taking with him all his patrimony and his most precious
possessions and having gone to Shar Domkha, subjugated all the
communities with great energy as in the manner of a *mahāsiddha* and
gained power over the Indian *duars*. His descendants, whose strength and
dominion became great, are the *ba-spu* ('*Babu*') who are at Shar Domkha and at Mur-shing. [67]

The middle son, bTsan-'dus-la, after going to Tsha-se, took control of a royal castle and gained power over the subjects and officers. The descendants of his two sons, bTsan-gong-la and Lag-sdum-pa, dispersed in different directions and their lineages are [preserved by] all the Byar-pa families who are at Tsha-se, Yu-rung, Khang-pa, Phyi-mung and Zla-gor.

The youngest son, Ong-ma, after going to U-dza-rong, took control of a
royal castle and, gaining power over the subjects and officers, acted as their
chief. After his sons, dPal-'bum, bZang-dar and Lu-btsan - [these] three -
had come forth they spread in different directions. The descendants of
(25a) Byar Ong-ma are all the Byar-pa families who are at U-dza-rong, gTor-ma-
gzhong, Yong-ka-la, lCags-mkhar-bzung, Ku-ri-smad, rGya-ras-zur, Byog-
kang, Ngang-la, Khom-shar, Ne-to-la and Kheng-rigs rNam-gsum.

Now if it should be explained additionally, among the descendants of dPal-'bum there came forth gSer-'bum, dNgos-'bum and Dar-'bum, [these] three [brothers?] and of them, the son of gSer-'bum was Thur-skye. His son was rDo-rje Grags-pa. His sons were Las-kyi-bang and Padma-dbang. The sons of Las-kyi-bang were bsTan-'dzin bSod-nams and bsTan-'dzin Grags-pa. The descendants of these two and the descendants of dNgos-bum and Dar-'bum are those who are at U-dza-rong.

In continuation of what was said above, Yas-sde gSang-sde-btsan was
(25b) invited by the officers and subjects to Sa-gling rGyan-tshams and went
there. Building a royal castle he took control of a royal site. Among his
descendants there came forth a certain courageous and wise person who
was intelligent and clever in skilful means called Yas-sde Su-na. He
gained power over all the communities, the officers and subjects on both
sides of the course of the sGam-ri Chu river and then since he also built a

mi sde blon 'bangs thams cad la dbang sgyur nas bu na la'ang rgyal
mkhar brtsigs shing lam khral bsdu bas stobs mnga' thang che bar
byung nas / sngon gyi dus su sa brtsi ri brtsi la ma cham par / yas
sde su na la gtug nas bgo shag byas pa yin zer ba'i gtam rgyun / dus
ding sang* gi bar la'ang 'dug / de'i bu brgyud rim par 'gyes pas sa *gsang
gling rgyan mtshams dang / dga' gling mkhar mi / 'phong mi / ra ma
geng ra / khre phu / stag tshang la yod pa'i yas sde rgyal rigs thams
cad (26a) yas sde su na'i bu brgyud yin no // // yang de'i bu brgyud
la yas sde yang phan zer ba / 'phong mi blon 'bangs rnams kyi rje
dpon du gdan drangs nas yong bas / de nyid rje dpon gyi bya ba
mdzad pa la / rig* rtsal shin tu che shing 'phrul thabs la mkhas pas *rigs
pha rol gyi dgra bo thams cad zil* gyis gnon zhing / rku 'phrog *gzil
khrims 'gal gyi gnod pa thams cad las* bsrungs bas na / blon 'bangs *omitted
rnams kyis* ming yang yas sde bsrungs ma dar zer nas mtshan yongs *kyi
su grags pa stobs mnga' thang che ba byung / de'i bu bsod nams
rgyal po / sa na / 'tsheng rgyal po / rgyal bu don grub bzhi byung
bas / bsod nams rgyal po rgyal mkhar bzung ba'i brgyud / glang
khyim gyi yas sde rgyal rigs rnams (26b) yin* / sa na dang** *omitted **omitted
rgyal bu don grub gnyis kyis zer khyim bzung ba'i bu brgyud
breng khyim gyi yas sde rgyal rigs rnams yin [1] / 'tsheng* rgyal pos *'tshengs
khang pa mkhar bzung ba'i bu brgyud khang pa mkhar gyi yas sde
rgyal rigs rnams yin / de las yang zur du bshad* na / 'tsheng** *phye **'tshengs
rgyal po'i bu / som bzang / de'i bu som rgyal / karma rgyas / rdor
tshe ring gsum / rdor tshe ring gi bu / sgo nu / de'i bu dag pa / de'i
bu lug dkar / de'i bu* dkon dbang yin / gong du bshad pa'i 'phros *omitted
las / stung* sde sbas sde btsan / zangs lung pa / 'dus stung mkhar *stong
la 'phebs nas rgyal mkhar bzung nas blon 'bangs la dbang sgyur bas
sras / thom pa dang som dar gnyis byung bas / thom pa'i bu brgyud
(27a) la stung* sde As mang zer ba brtul phod shin tu che ba grub *stong
thob kyi spyod pa lta bus / ngam grog g.yang sa chen po brags zer
tog la sogs pa las sngar med pa'i lam bton zhing / dag pa be mi sa ri
yul grong thams cad la dbang sgyur nas stobs mnga' thang che ba* *ba'i
byung ba'i khral gyi rgyun da lta'ang yod zer gyi 'dug / de'i bu
brgyud so sor 'gyes pa khyi nyil / kham nang / bu ri gyang phu /
zangs lung pa / kha 'thor dag pa be mi la yod pa'i stung* sde'i rigs *stong
thams cad stung* sde As mang gi bu brgyud yin no // // yang *stong
gong du brjod pa'i 'phros las / wang ma 'gab* sde btsan gyis / *gab
sgang zur stod la yong nas rgyal mkhar wang ma mkhar brtsigs nas
rgyal sa bzung zhing / blon 'bangs 'thor bu re yod pa la kha lo sgyur /
de'i bu gnyis byung ba'i / che ba gung la rgyal / chung ba dpal la
(27b) dar yin / rgyal mkhar wang ma mkhar de / sa cha zur chod du
song ba dang / blon 'bangs yang cher mi 'dus shing / longs spyod

1. This sentence is repeated.

royal castle at Bu-na and collected road-tax his strength and dominion became great. There is a legend still existing at present which says that in previous times they [his subjects] fell out with each other over the question of the delineation of their agricultural land and pastoral land and so the matter was brought before Yas-sde Su-na who made [suitable] divisions. His descendants spread successively and so all the Yas-sde royal families who are at Sa-gling rGyan-mtshams, dGa'-gling-mkhar-mi, 'Phong-mi, Ra-ma-geng-ra, Khre-phu and sTag-tshang are the descendants of Yas-
(26a) sde Su-na.

Now among his descendants there was one called Yas-sde Yang-phan who was invited to act as the chief of the officers and subjects of 'Phong-mi and so went there. As for the performance of his work as chief, his skill in learning was very great and as he was clever in magical [or mechanical?] devices he conquered all external enemies. Because he guarded (*bsrungs*) against all injuries that transgressed the law [such as] robbery, the officers and subjects called him by the name of Yas-sde bSrungs-ma-dar, a name everywhere renowned, and his strength and dominion became great. His sons, bSod-nams rGyal-po, Sa-na, 'Tsheng rGyal-po and rGyal-bu Don-grub, [these] four, came forth. The descendants of bSod-nams rGyal-po who
(26b) took control of a royal castle are the Yas-sde royal families of Glang-khyim. The descendants of Sa-na and rGyal-bu Don-grub who took control of Zer-khyim are the Yas-sde royal families of Breng-khyim. The descendants of 'Tsheng rGyal-po who took control of Khang-pa-mkhar are the Yas-sde royal families of Khang-pa-mkhar.

If it should be explained in even greater detail, the son of 'Tsheng rGyal-po was Som-bzang. His sons were Som-rgyal, Karma-rgyas and rDor-tshe-ring, [these] three. The son of rDor-tshe-ring was sGo-nu. His son was Dag-pa. His son is Lug-dkar. [68] His son is dKon-dbang.

In continuation of what was said above, sTung-sde sBas-sde-btsan went to 'Dus-stung-mkhar [69] in Zangs-lung-pa having taken control of a royal fort he gained power over the officers and subjects. His sons, Thom-pa and Som-dar, [these] two, came forth. Among the descendants of Thom-pa there was
(27a) one called sTung-sde As-mang whose bravery was very great and whose behaviour was like that of a *mahāsiddha*; he laid out roads which had previously not existed from Ngam-grog, g.Yang-sa Chen-po, Brags-zer-tog and so forth and having gained power over all the Dag-pa districts and villages of Be-mi and Sa-ri his strength and dominion became great. It is said that the tradition of his [right to] taxes exists even at present. His descendants dispersed in different directions and all the sTung-sde families who are at Khyi-nyil, Kham-rang, Bu-ri Gyang-phu, Zangs-lung-pa, Kha-'thor and Dag-pa Be-mi are the descendants of sTung-sde As-mang.

Again, in continuation of what was said above, Wang-ma 'Gab-sde-btsan, having come to sGang-zur-stod and built the royal castle of Wang-ma-mkhar, he took control of the royal site and ruled the few officers and subjects who
(27b) were there. Of his two sons that came forth, the elder was Gung-la-rgyal and the younger was dPal-la-dar. As for the royal castle of Wang-ma-mkhar, when its land had become split up and when the officers and subjects no

yang dkon tsam byung ba dang / bu chung ba dpal la dar / lha sa
bsam yas nas yong ba'i sgom chen gsum dang chas nas / Ar po gnyis
khrid nas / lha sa bsam yas mjal ba la song nas / bod kyi sgom chen
gnyis dang bcas lo rog phyogs nas slog te / shar them spang la sleb
pa dang / sgom chen gnyis kyis wang ma dpal la dar la zhe sa che
brjod byas nas / lha btsun zer nas bos pas / them spang gi gtso rgan
A rgyal zer bas* / lha btsun zer ba'i ming gi rgyu mtshan ci yin zer *ba'i
ba las / sgom chen rgan pa na re / lha btsun chos rje* zer ba de / *mrjod
sngon gyi bsam yas kyi rgyal po khri srong lde* btsan gyi sras *sde
brgyud yin pas na / lha btsun zer ba yin zer bas / (28a) gtso rgan
A rgyal yid ches nas / 'o na de ltar yin na nged rang gi rje dpon gyi
glo* kha dkar kha nag kha gnon la bzhugs dgos zer nas / blon *do
'bangs rnams kyis bkur zhing / rgya'i las sgo la* dbang sgyur bas / *omitted
ba spu zer ba de rgya skad kyi ming btags pa yin / dga' re nas them
spang ba spu'i chad khungs bsam yas nas yin zer ba yang / wang ma
dpal la dar bsam yas phyogs nas yong ba la* brten** nas zer ba yin / *las **rten
them spang la chad pa'i ba spu wang ma dpal la dar gyi brgyud pa
yin no // wang ma 'gab sde btsan / pha spad gnyis kyang / rgyal
mkhar wang ma mkhar bzhags nas / kha gling lung pa'i mjug / man
chod lung pa la song nas / gdung rus che ba'i lo rgyus* bshad pa *brgyud
dang / der mi 'thor bu re yod pa rnams kyis* kyang bkur sti cher *kyi
byas pas / rgya gar (28b) gyi mi rnams kyis* bkur zhing las sgo la *kyi
dbang sgyur bas longs spyod che bar byung 'dug pa dang / da lta'i
man chod dang / gzhan la yod pa'i wang ma'i rigs thams cad /
wang ma gung la rgyal gyi brgyud pa yin no // 'dir yang 'phros las /
la 'og yul gsum rgyal rigs jo bo rnams kyi brgyud khungs kyang
cung zad brjod par bya'o // de las* yang rgyas pa** ni jo bo na rim *omitted **par
gyis blon 'bangs la dbang sgyur zhing rgyal sa bzung nas mdzad
khyon* rlabs chen gyis stobs mnga' thang che bar byung ba'i *khyod
gleng gtam rgyas* pa ni / jo bo sras brgyud mkhyen dpyod che *rgyal
ba rnams kyi phyag gi deb* ther yig cha la gsal bas** 'dir ma bkod / *debs **ba'i
nye bar brgyud pa'i rim pa ni / lha sras gtsang ma rgyal mkhar mi
zim par phebs nas / sras gnyis byung ba'i sras che ba khri mi lha'i
dbang phyug / la 'og yul gsum du blon 'bangs (29a) rnams kyis rje
dpon du gdan drangs nas phebs pa'i sras lha mgon / de'i sras bkra
shis bsod nams / de'i sras tshe dbang rnam rgyal / de'i sras dpal
'byor bzang po / de'i sras nam mkha' bsod nams / de la sras bdun
byung ba'i che ba gong dkar rje yin / de yis lha'u kham par byon
nas rgyal sa bzung ba'i kham pa jo bo zer ba'i ming yongs su grags
pa de las byung ba yin 'dug / sras bdun las gcig shar sde rang gi rje
dpon du gdan drangs nas phebs pa'i sras brgyud shar sde rang gi jo
bo rnams yin 'dug / zhib par ni yig cha dang gtam rgyun mthong
thos med pa las 'dir ma bkod / gong dkar rje'i sras dzo ki dang

longer assembled there in great number and when even its riches had
become rather scarce, the younger son dPal-la-dar set off with three
meditators who had come from lHa-sa and bSam-yas. Taking a couple of
menials with him he went [on pilgrimage] to see lHa-sa and bSam-yas and
then together with two Tibetan meditators came back by way of Lo-rog.
When they reached Shar Them-spang the two meditators addressed Wang-
ma dPal-la-dar in most respectful terms. As they addressed him saying
lHa-btsun' the headman of Them-spang called A-rgyal said: "What are the
grounds for this name *'lHa-btsun'*?" The elder meditator replied: "As for
the form of address *'lHa-btsun Chos-rje'*, since he is a descendant of the
(28a) ancient king of bSam-yas, *Khri* Srong-lde-btsan, he is called *'lHa-btsun'*."
The headman A-rgyal believed him and said: "Well, if that is so, he must
reside [here] as a lord-chief to suppress the Glo Kha-dkar and Kha-nag." [70]
The officers and subjects honoured him and since he gained power over
the Indian duars he was given the Indian name of Ba-spu (*Babu*). Although
some say that the Ba-spu of Them-spang [71] had their origin in bSam-yas, it
is said so however due to the fact that Wang-ma dPal-la-dar had come there
from the direction of bSam-yas. The Ba-spu born in Them-spang are the
lineal descendants of Wang-ma dPal-la-dar.

Wang-ma 'Gab-sde-btsan, both father and son, also abandoned the royal
castle of Wang-ma-mkhar and went to the district of Man-chod at the lower
end of the Kha-gling district. When they delivered an account of their great
clan, the few people who were there paid them great respect and so the
(28b) Indian people honoured them and they gained power over the *duars* and
their wealth became great. All the Wang-ma families who are at present in
Man-chod and elsewhere are the lineal descendants of Wang-ma Gung-la-
rgyal. [72]

I will also speak briefly here in continuation [of the passage above] [73]
about the ancestral origins of the Jo-bo [clansmen] who are the royal
families of La-'og Yul-gsum. Since a more extended version containing a
full account of how the successive Jo-bo, having gained power over the
officers and subjects and taken control of a royal site, came to enjoy great
strength and dominion due to their far-ranging endeavours has been
clarified in the personal documentary records of the Jo-bo descendants
who possessed great discernment, [the details of these records] are not
included here. As to the succession of their close lineal descendants:
After Prince gTsang-ma went to the Mi-zim-pa royal castle, two sons
(29a) appeared of whom the elder, Khri-mi lHa'i-dbang-phyug, was invited as
chief to La-'og Yul-gsum by the officers and subjects and so he went there.
His son was lHa-dgon. His son was bKra-shis bSod-nams. His son was Tshe-
dbang rNam-rgyal. His son was dPal-'byor bZang-po. His son was Nam-mkha'
bSod-nams. Of his seven sons that came forth the eldest son was Gong-dkar-
rje. Having gone to lHa'u Kham-pa [74] he took control of a royal site and it
was from there that the widely renowned name of Kham-pa Jo-bo arose. Of
the seven sons one was invited as chief to Shar sDe-rang and went there. His
descendants are the Jo-bo of Shar sDe-rang. As to the details, since I have
not seen or heard the written records and oral traditions, they are not
included here. [75] The sons of Gong-dkar-rje were Dzo-ki and bTsun-cung

btsun cung / btsun cung gi sras rgyal mtshan grags pa byung / des
bu ri gyang phu nas stung* sde min bla ma skyid btsun mor blangs *stong
pas / (29b) sras che bar rgyal po dar / lhun grub / ku nu / gsum
byung ba'i / rgyal po dar gyis* rus po mkhar bzung nas bse ru'i *gyi
rje dpon mdzad / lhun grub kyis ber mkhar bzung nas shar tsho'i
rje dpon mdzad / kun nus kham pa rang du bzhugs nas / yab kyi
rgyal sa bzung ste lha'u'i rje dpon mdzad / lhun grub kyi sras jo bo
sangs rgyas cung / de'i sras sangs rdo rje / la kra / dge shes / kra'u
bzhi byung ba'i / kra'u sgam ri lung pa'i blon 'bangs rnams kyis rje
dpon du* gdan drangs nas ra ti la phebs / sangs rdo rje'i sras jo bo *omitted
dar rgyas kyis / ram geng ra nas U sen rgyal mo blangs nas bzhugs
pa'i skabs der / grub thob thang stong rgyal po bsod snyoms la
byon pa nang du gdan drangs nas bsnyen bkur phun sum* tshogs *gsum
par mdzad cing / 'bras chang tshim par drangs pa gsol ba'i rjes la
'bras (30a) chang gis ka' pa li bkang nas grub thob kyis nam mkha'
la 'phangs pas / chang ma 'bor bar grub thob kyi phyag la babs pa
jo bo dar rgyas la gnang ste / chang 'thung gang thub gyis dang rten
'brel gyi rtags khyad par can yong gsungs pas / jo bo dar rgyas kyis
chang ka' pa li drug rdzogs par 'thung / gcig las phye kha lus pa
dang grub thob kyi zhal nas / khyod la bu bdun yong ba 'dug ste /
gcig gis* phan mi thog / bu drug pa las gcig sa bcu'i byang chub *gi
sems dpa' bshad grub kyi bstan pa 'dzin zhing sems can gyi 'gro don
dpag tu med pa zhig 'ong ba 'dug gsungs nas / ka' pa li chang gi
bkang nas / 'o jo bo chen po ka' pa li 'di ni mkha 'gro ma 'gro ba
bzang mo'i dbu thod yin pas / shin tu 'gangs* che khyod la dad *gangs
pa'i rten du bzhag (30b) go gsungs nas gnang / de nas gzhan yang
grub rtags bton pa'i rten khyad* par can rnams kyang gnang ngo // *khyed
grub thob kyi lung bstan pa bzhin sras bdun byung ba'i / che ba
bkra shis dar rgyas / de 'og bsod bzang / gsum pa / rgyal po dar /
sangs rdo rje / dgos cung rnams yin / jo bo bkra shis dar rgyas
kyis* rgyal sa mdzad / jo bo gsum pas thams cad mkhyen pa dge *kyi
'dun rgya mtsho* dpal bzang po las / rab tu byung zhing mdo *mtsho'i
sngags la sbyangs pa mdzad cing phul du phyin pas / mtshan yang
blo bzang bstan pa'i sgron me* gsol nas bshad sgrub** kyi bstan pa *med **omitted
'dzin zhing / grub thob kyi spyod pa lta bus / shar stag lung / me
rag sag stengs / Ar rgya gdung la sogs par dgon gnas mang po btab
cing 'gro don rgyas par byung ba dang / jo bo gzhan bzhi pos kyang
spa'u gdung byam (31a) mkhar / shar nub / sgreng mkhar bcas
bzung ba'i brgyud pa da lta yod pa'i jo bo rnams yin no / sras tha
chung ni lung bstan bzhin chung dus* nas 'das / jo bo bkra shis dar *du
rgyal* gyi sras / bkra shis bzang po / de'i sras sa 'dzin / de'i sras *rgyal
sangs rgyas grags pa / chos mdzad / dar rgyas gsum byung ba'i /
sangs rgyas grags pa'i sras jo bo karma / de'i sras phun tshogs dang* / *omitted

The son of bTsun-cung, rGyal-mtshan Grags-pa, came forth. He took as his
(29b) wife sTung-sde Min-bla-ma-skyid[76] from Bu-ri-gyang-phu and so rGyal-po-
dar, the eldest son, lHun-grub and Ku-nu, [these] three, came forth. Of
these, rGyal-po-dar took control of Rus-po-mkhar and so acted as the lord-
chief of bSe-ru, lHun-grub took control of Ber-mkhar[77] and acted as lord-
chief of Shar-tsho and Ku-nu, staying in Kham-pa itself, took control of the
royal site of his father and acted as the lord-chief of lHa'u. The son of lHun-
grub was Jo-bo Sangs-rgyas-cung. His sons, Sangs-rdo-rje, La-kra, dGe-shes
and Kra'u, [these] four, came forth. Kra'u, having been invited as chief by
the officers and subjects of sGam-ri Lung-pa, went to Ra-ti. At the time
when Jo-bo Dar-rgyas, the son of Sangs-rdo-rje, had taken U-sen from Ram-
geng-ra as his queen and was residing [there?], he invited to his home the
mahāsiddha Thang-stong rGyal-po[78] who was going around begging alms
and performed him excellent works of veneration. After he had consumed
(30a) some rice-ale which had been served him to his full satisfaction he filled a
skull-cup with some rice-ale and the *mahāsiddha* threw it into the sky. He
gave to Jo-bo Dar-rgyas the ale which fell into his hands without spilling
and said: "Drink as much ale as you can and a special sign of the omens
will come forth." Jo-bo Dar-rgyas completely drank up six skull-cups of
ale. When half remained from a [further] cupful the *mahāsiddha* declared:
"It seems that you will have seven sons but one will be of no use. Of the
six [remaining] sons one will be a *bodhisattva* of the tenth stage who will
uphold the teachings pertaining to explanations of the doctrines and their
realisation, and who will be of infinite benefit to sentient beings." Filling
the skull-cup with ale, he said: "Oh, Great Jo-bo! Since this skull-cup is the
cranium of the *ḍākinī* 'Gro-ba bZang-mo it is extremely valuable. I leave it
(30b) with you as the support of your faith" and he gave it to him. Furthermore
he then also gave him special relics which had brought forth signs of realisation. In accordance with the prophecy of the *mahāsiddha,* seven sons came
forth of whom the eldest was bKra-shis Dar-rgyas and below him bSod-
bzang, gSum-pa, rGyal-po-dar, Sangs-rdo-rje and dGos-cung. Jo-bo bKra-
shis Dar-rgyas controlled the royal site. Jo-bo gSum-pa received his ordination from the Omniscient dGe-'dun rGya-mtsho dPal-bzang[79] and as he
pursued the study of the *sūtras* and *tantras* and attained perfection therein
he received the name of Blo-bzang bsTan-pa'i sGron-me. Upholding the
teachings of explanation and realisation, and in behaviour like a *mahāsiddha,*
he founded many monasteries at Shar sTag-lung,[80] Me-rag Sag-stengs,[81]
Ar-rgya-gdung[82] and so on, accomplishing extensive benefit to beings.[83]
(31a) The other four Jo-bo took control of sPa'u-gdung,[84] Byam-mkhar,[85] Shar-
nub,[86] sGreng-mkhar and so forth and their lineal descendants are the Jo-
bo who are there at present. The youngest son died at an early age in
accordance with the prophecy.[87] The son of Jo-bo bKra-shis Dar-rgyas
was bKra-shis bZang-po. His son was Sa-'dzin. His sons, Sangs-rgyas Grags-
pa, Chos-mdzad and Dar-rgyas – [these] three – came forth. The son of
Sangs-rgyas Grags-pa was Jo-bo Karma. His sons were Phun-tshogs and

'dzom pa dbang / phun tshogs kyi sras brgyud ber mkhar 'og ma'i jo bo rnams yin / 'dzom pa* dbang gis A'u gdung du sa bzung nas rje dpon mdzad pa'i sras sangs rgyas rdo rje dang jo bo sri thar gnyis yin / jo bo dar rgyas kyi sras / karma rdo rje dang jo bo sde pa gnyis yin / karma rdo rje'i* sras brgyud ber mkhar gong ma la yod pa'i jo bo rnams yin / sngon dus sgam ṛi lung pa ra ti la / rje dpon (31b) rim pas yul mkhar bzung ma thub par 'thon song ba dang / blon 'bangs rnams gros sdur byas nas / la 'og yul gsum nas kham pa jo bo gdan 'dren* du phyin pas / de'i dus su** la 'og yul gsum la / jo bo ku nu / lhun grub / rgyal po dar gsum gyis* rje dpon mdzad nas yod pa las / ber mkhar nas jo bo lhun grub kyi sras* sangs cung / de'i bu skya'u la rgya mtsho gdan drangs yong nas / ra ti la rgyal mkhar bzung zhing rje dpon mdzad pa'i bu bla ma / de'i bu brgyud rim par 'gyes pa'i rgyal mkhar bzung mkhan mi rabs brgyad la jo bo kham pa zer ba byung nas brgyud chad / pha spun so sor 'gyes pa'i bu brgyud da lta ra ti sgam rir* yod pa'i kham pa jo bo'i rigs yin zer ba thams cad skya'u la rgya mtsho'i bu brgyud yin no // rgyal rigs 'byung khungs (32a) gsal ba'i sgron me las lha sras gtsang ma'i gdung brgyud la rigs rus kyi ming so sor btags nas / lho phyogs mon gyi lung phyogs so sor 'gyes shing rje dpon mdzad pa'i le'u ste gnyis pa'o //

*omitted

*rje

*dren **su tsho la

*gyi

*omitted

*ri

SECTION III

(32a2) // da ni bum thang* sde bzhi'i gdung rnams kyi chad khungs 'byung tshul kyang brjod par bya'o // de nas sngon rgyal po khyi kha ra thod dang mnyam po yong ba'i mi ser 'thor bu re yod pa rnams rje dpon med par 'khrugs cing brtsod pa las / khong rang rnams kha mthun gyi rje dpon 'tshol ba'i rus chen rgyal rigs med pas rje dpon ma rnyed par / gnam* lha 'o de gung rgyal mchod cing gsol ba btab pas / 'o de gung rgyal gyis bka' bsgos nas / lha'i bu gu se lang ling lha'i rmu thag la 'jus nas / U ra la bab po 'od du zhun* nas / bud med ye shes (32b) kyi mkha' 'gro'i mtshan dang ldan pa bsod nams dpal 'dren gyi lhums* su bzhugs nas rdzus skye lta bur 'khrungs pa'i phyir / bar snang gi sgra las /'o bu 'di ni lha'i bu yin pa'i gdung rabs mang po'i bar du rje dpon byed par 'gyur ro zer ba'i sgra / yul de'i mi dpon gyi skye dman 'dzom pa sgron gyis* thos pa dang / de ltar yong na mi sde la dbang sgyur nas mo la mthong* bkur mi yong bsam pa'i gdug rtsub kyi nga rgyal langs nas smon lam log par btab kyang / lha'i bden pa'i* mthus / lha'i sprul pa'i gdung 'khrungs / mtshan lha mgon dpal chen gsol nas / mi sde'i yul khams la dbang sgyur nas rje dpon mdzad pa'i sras lha bzang

*stang

*gnas

*zhu

*lhum

*gyi

*'thong

*par

'Dzom-pa-dbang. The descendants of Phun-tshogs are the Jo-bo of Ber-mkhar 'Og-ma. 'Dzom-pa-dbang took control of land at A'u-gdung and acted as chief. His sons were Sangs-rgyas rDo-rje and Jo-bo Sri-thar – [these] two. The descendants of Karma rDo-rje are the Jo-bo who are at Ber-mkhar Gong-ma.

(31b) In previous times when the successive lord-chiefs at Ra-ti in sGam-ri-lung-pa had been unable to take control of the district castle and had departed, the officers and subjects discussed the matter and then went to invite a [member of the clan of] Kham-pa Jo-bo. At that time in La-'og Yul-gsum there were Jo-bo(s) Ku-nu, lHun-grub and rGyal-po-dar acting as lord-chiefs. At their invitation sKya'u-la rGya-mtsho, the son of Sangs-cung who was the son of Jo-bo lHun-grub, came and, taking control of the royal castle at Ra-ti, acted as lord-chief. His son was Bla-ma. After eight generations of royal castellans called Jo-bo Kham-pa had come forth among his successive descendants, the lineage died out. The descendants of the paternal siblings who spread in different directions [or who issued collaterally?], that is those said to be of the Kham-pa Jo-bo families that are now in Ra-ti sGam-ri, are all the descendants of sKya'u-la rGya-mtsho.

(32a) This is the second section from *The Lamp which Illuminates the Origins of Royal Families* concerning how, after individual names were given to the families and clans descended from the Divine Prince gTsang-ma, these came to be spread in the different parts of Southern Mon and became lord-chiefs.

SECTION III

(32a2) Now I shall speak about the history of the origins of the *gDung* [families] of the four districts of Bum-thang.[88]

Now then, in previous times after the few subjects who came in company with King Khyi-kha Ra-thod had, in the absence of a lord-chief, contended and quarrelled, they searched for a unanimously chosen chief. Since there was no royal family [among them belonging to] a great clan they did not find a chief and so they worshipped and supplicated the God of Heaven 'O-de Gung-rgyal. 'O-de Gung-rgyal enjoined saying: "The divine son Gu-se Lang-ling, having grasped the divine *rmu*-cord, will descend to U-ra" and he melted into the light. After he [Gu-se Lang-ling] had resided in the womb

(32b) of bSod-nams dPal-'dren, a woman who possessed the marks of a *ḍākinī* of gnosis, in order that he might be born as if by a miracle a voice from space declared: "Oh! This boy is a divine son and for many generations [his descendants] will come to act as lord-chiefs." When 'Dzom-pa-sgron, the wife of the headman of that place, heard it she thought that if it should come to pass in such a manner no honour would be paid to her after [Gu-se Lang-ling] gained power over the community and so malicious arrogance arose in her and she uttered maledictions. Due, however, to the power of divine truth the divinely emanated *gDung* was born. After receiving the name of lHa-mgon dPal-chen he gained power over the community's

rgyal[1] / (33a) de'i sras gdung grags pa dbang phyug byung nas / de
la sras med par snyung gzhi drag pos thebs nas grongs khar thug pa
dang / blon 'bangs rnams kyi smras pa / gdung rin po che nyid mya
ngan 'das nas / nged rnams kyi re ltos su la re zer nas smre sngags* *smres ngag
'don pas / gdung grags pa dbang phyug gi zhal nas / nga nad 'di las
ma thar par tshe'i 'dus byas nas khyed rang rnams nga dran pa'i
dus byung na / bod yul dbus kyi gzhung yar lung grong mo che la
song nas / mon gyi shing 'bras stong kha dog legs pa khyer nas byis
pa mang po'i khrod du stor cig / stong mang po gang gis zin pa de
lha'i rnam 'phrul yin pas* de gdan 'dren zhus las / khyod rang *pa'i
rnams kyi rje dpon bcol zhig zer nas 'das so // de nas (33b) blon
'bangs rnams kyis kyang lo lnga tsam song ba dang / sngon nas
rje dpon gdung gi kha chems bzhin / U ra pa mi lnga stong gi 'bras
bu khyer nas yar lung du de* ltar phyin pas / yar lung gi sa cha de *omitted
lag mthil ltar mnyam shing yul sde che ba lta bas mi ngom pa 'dug /
kha chems bzhin lha'i 'phrul pa* gar yod ni ma shes pa dang / yul *omitted
grong mang po bshal nas phyin pas / grong mtshams kyi thang zhig
la byis pa mang po tshogs nas rtsed mo rtses kyi 'dug pa dang /
khong 'tshol mkhan mi lngas / gnam gyi lha mchod cing dmod* bor *smod
nas / byis pa mang po 'dzom pa'i khrod du stong kha shas skyur
btang bas / byis pa gzhan rnams sngar nas mthong ma myong ba'i
shing 'bras mthong* ba dang / thams cad ha las te 'thu ma shes par *'thong
ha re lus pa dang / de'i nang nas (34a) byis pa mtshar zhing mdzas
pa lta na sdug pa / yan lag khyug bde ba hrig ge ba zhig gis skad* *bskad
cig la shing 'bras thams cad hub kyis* blangs nas bsdus pas / 'tshol *kyi
mkhan lnga po yang sngar nas lung bstan pa'i byis pa de yin par
'dug bsam nas yid ches so // de dus bod mon gnyis ka'i skad ma go
ba dang / mi lnga pos lag brda* byas nas shing 'bras de byis pa *rda
gzhan la byin / da rung yod khyod la ster ro zer ba'i brda byas nas
stong bstan* pas / byis pa des stong byis pa gzhan rnams la sbyin *bsten
nas / kho rang la da rung dgos zer nas lag pa gdeng nas yong ba
dang / mi lnga pos stong bstan* zhing tshur tshur khrid yong nas *bsten
lkog tu sleb pa dang / gsang thabs kyis* rtsid phad nang du bcug *kyi
cing 'khur yong nas / U ra zhang ma'i la la slebs* pa (34b) dang / *sleb
rtsid phad kha 'phye nas bltas pas / byis pa lha'i bu 'dra ba de zhal
'dzum mu le ba byas langs nas 'thon byung ba dang / bcug pa'i snod
stong rtsid phad sprugs* pas bod kyi rtsa chun po zhig yang tshud *sprug
'dug pa der 'thon song ba* las skyes nas / dus da lta'i bar du yang *omitted
bod kyi* rtswa** sa cha gzhan la med pa zhang ma'i la la rtswa *kyis **rtsa
sgor ba cig yod do / byis pa des U ra la gdan drangs nas rje dpon du
bkur nas ming yang lha dbang grags pa btags nas / sku nar son zhing
blon 'bangs la dbang sgyur ba dang / lha dbang grags pa rang nyid

1. This sentence is repeated.

(33a) territory and acted as lord-chief. His son was lHa-bzang-rgyal. His son,
gDung Grags-pa dBang-phyug came forth and, having no son, when he was
afflicted with an illness and was on the point of dying the officers and
subjects said: "After you, Precious *gDung,* have died, in whom should we
place our hope?" Saying this they lamented. *gDung* Grags-pa dBang-phyug
said: "As I am not going to survive this illness, after the composite substance
of life [has dissolved], when the time comes that you remember me go to
Yar-lung Grong-mo-che [89] at the centre of dBus in the country of Tibet
and taking with you some nicely coloured *stong* [90] fruit of Mon, drop these
among a large crowd of children. Since the one who seizes many *stong* is
(33b) [my] divine emanation invite and appoint him your lord-chief." Saying
this he died.

Then when about five years had elapsed for the officers and subjects, in
accordance with the will which the lord-chief *gDung* had previously given,
five men of U-ra went in that manner to Yar-lung taking with them some
stong fruit. The territory of Yar-lung was as flat as the palm of one's hand
and the great district was so beautiful that they could not gaze at it long
enough. They did not know where the divine emanation was and so in
accordance with the will they went roving through many villages. In the
pasture on the outskirts of a certain village there were many children
assembled and playing, whereupon the five searchers worshipped the God
of Heaven and cast prayers up to him. They then scattered some of the
stong into the large crowd of children assembled there. When the children
other [than the one who was to be chosen] saw fruit which they had
never seen before they were so amazed that they were unable to pick
(34a) them up, being left wonder-struck. Among them a child who was fine
handsome and lovely to behold, agile in limb and sharp-sighted, in an
instant seized and gathered up all the fruit in handfulls. The five searchers
therefore thought: "The child about whom the prophecy was previously
given seems to be this one" and so they believed in him. At that time the
languages of Tibet and Mon were not mutually understood and so the five
men made gestures as if to say: "Give those fruit to the other children.
There are more and we shall give them to you." Indicating this, they
showed the *stong.* The child gave his *stong* to the other children and,
saying that he wanted more, came forward with his hands open. Showing
him the *stong,* the five men led him further and further away and when
they arrived at a place of concealment they stealthily put him inside a yak
hair bag and carried him off. On arriving at the pass of Zhang-ma'i La in
(34b) U-ra they opened the yak hair bag and looked inside. The child who was
like a divine son stood up smiling and came out. When the empty
receptacle, the yak hair bag into which he had been put, was shaken a
bundle of Tibetan grass which had also been put into it came out and
grew [in that place]. Even up to present times there is at Zhang-ma'i La a
patch of this Tibetan grass which does not exist in any other place but
this. [91]

The child was invited to U-ra, installed as lord-chief and given the name of lHa-dbang Grags-pa. When he grew up he gained power over the officers and subjects. At the time when lHa-dbang Grags-pa was himself a child,

byis pa'i dus / pha ma gnyis ka'i ming phan* tshun 'bor re rna bas *phun
thos pa tsam ma gtogs* rigs rus che chung ji ltar yin sogs dran pas *togs
mi zin pa nas / [. . . .][1] pha ma'i* ming bton ste** de'i byis pa*** *ming **omitted
stor ram ma stor zer nas yar lung du rtsad gcod par (35a) btang ***pa'i
bas / de'i rigs rus khungs chod do / de* ji ltar yin zhe na / glang dar *de'i
ma'i sras mnga' bdag 'od srungs / de'i sras mnga' bdag dpal 'khor
btsan myang stod du snyags kyis bkrongs nas rgyal srid 'thor ba'i
skabs / sras bkra shis brtsegs pa dpal dang / skyid lde* nyi ma mgon *sde
gnyis kyang / stod mnga' ris dang dbus gtsang du 'thor song bas /
bkra shis brtsegs pa dpal gyi sras / dpal lde* / 'od lde* / skyid lde* *sde
gsum byung ba las / rim par gyes* nas** dpal lde sras brgyud yar *'gyes **omitted
lung du chags pa'i jo bo kun dga' grags pa dang / yum dpal mo
'dzom gnyis la* sras bzhi yod pa'i tha chung hur rgol la gar song *omitted
cha med du stor ba de yin par nges shing / chos rgyal gyi* gdung *gyis
kho na nyid yin pas na / blon 'bangs rnams kyang (35b) dga' zhing
mgu la rjes su yid rangs* nas / chos 'khor nas A lce sgron 'dzom *rang
btsun mor blangs nas phul bas / sras grags pa dbang phyug / lha
dbang bkra shis / phun tshogs don grub gsum byung ba nas / rim
par 'gyes pa'i sras brgyud / chu smad gdung dang / rgya tsha / sdom
mkhar / dur dang / ngang / bum thang* la yod pa'i gdung thams *stang
cad de'i brgyud pa yin no // kheng rigs rnam* gsum dang / gzhong *rnams
sgar mol ba lung pa la'ang / U ra gdung gis* dbang sgyur nas gdung *gi
grags pa* dbang phyug lo re bzhin khral bsdu ba la yong ba dang / *pa dang
zur du dpon mo bkra shis dbang mor bsten pa'i sras nyi ma dbang
rgyal byung ba nas sras brgyud rim par 'gyes pa / stung la sbi / go
zhing / phang mkhar / ka lam ti / nya mkhar dang / kheng rigs
rnam* gsum la yod pa'i gdung (36a) thams cad dang / gzhong sgar *
mol ba lung pa la yod pa'i yong lam rje zer ba thams cad kyang
de'i brgyud pa yin no // // yang bum thang* sde gzhi gdung dang / *stang
yong* lam rje'i chad khungs lugs cig la ni / bon thang la 'od dkar *yang
gyi yig gter dang / gzhong sgar mol ba lung phyogs dang / gdung
bsam mon yul stong gsum gyi gleng gtam ngag rgyun la ni / me rag
sag stengs 'brog pa'i mes po* rnams sde pa ya bu bzang po gsang *mepho
nas / mtsho sna bse ba mkhar las yul 'thon nas yong skabs gnam
gyi lha la mchod cing gsol ba* btab nas yong bas / sum cu rtsa *omitted
gsum gyi pho brang nas lha dbang po brgya* byin gyis / lha'i bu *rgya
gu se lang ling lho gdung mtsho skar ma thang gi lha la stongs
grogs gyis bka' bsgo* brdzangs pas / rmu'i yul du phebs nas re zhig *sgos
der bzhugs shing rmu'i rje (36b) dpon mdzad pas / ming* yang *mi
rmu btsan lha gnyan chen por btags / de nas shar gangs ri dkar po'i
rtse la phebs nas gzigs pas / ri mtho la mdzas pa wang seng gi ri bo
de mthong nas der phebs shing / gnas yangs shing rgya che la

1. A passage appears to be missing here.

apart from just hearing the names of both his parents being called out here
and there, he had no recollection as to whether his family and clan were
great or small. [Some people] were therefore sent off to Yar-lung in order
to make an investigation by mentioning the names of his parents and
(35a) asking whether or not their child had been lost. So the origin of his clan
was substantiated. If it be asked "What was it like?" [the answer is as
follows:] The son of Glang Dar-ma was *mNga'-bdag* 'Od-srungs. At the
time when royal government declined after his son, *mNga'-bdag* dPal-'khor-
btsan, had been killed in Myang-stod by sNyags, his sons, bKra-shis
brTsegs-pa-dpal and sKyid-lde Nyi-ma-mgon - [these] two - were also
dispersed to dBus-gtsang. After the sons of bKra-shis brTsegs-pa-dpal,
[namely] dPal-lde, 'Od-lde and sKyid-lde - [these] three - had come forth
they gradually spread and the descendants of dPal-lde appeared at Yar-
lung.[92] Among them *Jo-bo* Kun-dga' Grags-pa[93] and the mother dPal-
mo-'dzom - [these] two - had four sons of whom it seemed certain that he
[lHa-dbang Grags-pa] was the youngest who had been lost in a sudden raid
without news of where he had gone. Because he was of the very same clan
as the *Dharmarājas* the officers and subjects were happy and glad and they
(35b) rejoiced. From Chos-'khor they fetched *A-lce* ('The Lady') sGron-'dzom
as his consort and offered her to him and so the sons Grags-pa dBang-
phyug, lHa-dbang bKra-shis and Phun-tshogs Don-grub - [these] three -
came forth. Their descendants who gradually spread, [i.e.] all the *gDung*
[families] who are in Bum-thang [including] the Chu-smad *gDung* and
[those of] rGya-tsha, sDom-mkhar, Dur and Ngang, are of their lineage.
The *U-ra gDung* having also gained power over Kheng-rigs rNam-gsum[94]
and gZhong-sgar Mol-ba-lung, *gDung* Grags-pa dBang-phyug came annually
to collect taxes and in private he lived with *dPon-mo* ('Chieftainess') bKra-
shis dBang-mo of whom the son Nyi-ma rNam-rgyal came forth. His
descendants gradually spread and all the *gDung* [families] who are in Kheng-
rigs rNam-gsum, [i.e. those of] sTung-la-sbi, Go-zhing, Phang-mkhar,
(36a) Ka-lam-ti and Nya-mkhar and also all the so-called *rJe* [families of] Yong-
lam who are in gZhong-sgar Mol-ba-lung-pa are of his lineage.

Now, according to one version of the origins of the *gDung* [families] of
Bum-thang sDe-bzhi and of the *rJe* [families] of Yong-lam, [i.e.] according
to the treasure-writing of Bon Thang-la 'Od-dkar and the oral tradition of
stories told in the vicinity of gZhong-sgar Mol-ba-lung and of Mon-yul
sTong-gsum in gDung-bsam, the ancestors of the pastoral people of Me-rag
[and] Sag-stengs left their home at mTsho-sna bSe-ba-mkhar, concealing
[their departure] from *sDe-pa* Ya-bu bZang-po. As they went they worshipped and supplicated the God of Heaven so that from the palace of the
Trāyastriṃśat Heaven Indra the ruler of the gods despatched the divine
son Gu-se Lang-ling, commanding him to assist the god of [the lake at] lHo
gDung-mtsho sKar-ma-thang.[95] So he [Gu-se Lang-ling] went to the land
(36b) of rMu,[96] stayed there for a time and acted as the lord-chief of rMu, being
given the name of rMu-btsan lHa-gnyan Chen-po. Then having gone to the
summit of Gangs-ri dKar-po to the east he looked and saw a tall and
beautiful mountain, the mountain of Wang-seng and so he went there.

nyams* dga' ba mu ku lung mtsho mo la pho brang gzhal yas khang *mnyam
bkod nas / snang srid lha srin sde brgyad kyi sde dpon mgo nag mi'i
skyabs mgon mdzad cing bzhugs pa la / shar phyogs nas bud med lang
tsho rgyas shing shin tu mdzes pa'i A ya cig gdung bsam mkhar rgyal
po'i bag ma la yong ba mtsho 'gram la zhag nyal ba'i nub mo / mtsho
de'i nang nas sbrul dkar po zhig 'thon bag ma de la* gom** nas song *omitted **'gom
ba dang gnyid* gsad / de nas gdung bsam la sleb pa dang bu gcig *gnyis
skyes* ba las pha med par bar las byung ba dang / ming yang bar *skye
skyes btags (37a) nas / gzugs byad nar son pa dang / rgya'i las sgo
la phyin pas / ngas gtsang long pa'i mtsho gram la slebs pa dang /
bar skyes de lha btsan gyi bu yin pa'i gshis* kyis / ngas gtsang long *shis
pa'i klu bdud kyi cho 'phrul bstan nas rgya la ma thar ba dang /
khyim du log nas A ma la nga su'i bu yin dris pas / A mas slab ma
nyan / g.yo thabs kyis sgo nas dris pas A mas smras pa / khyod ni
mu ku lung lha btsan mi ma yin gyi bu yin pas na / klu bdud kyis* *kyi
cho 'phrul bstan nas lam bkag pa yin zer bas / byis pa bar skyes de
nyid kyis / de ma thag tu mu ku lung mtsho 'gram gyi rtsar song
nas / A pa la 'o* dod 'bod pas / mtsho'i nang nas skyes pa gzhon *'od pa yin 'dod
nu lang tsho* dar la** babs pa dar dkar gyi gos gyon zhing / dar *tshod **ba
dkar thod bcing pa'i rtse la (37b) yid bzhin gyi nor bus brgyan pa
zhig 'thon yong nas / khyod kyi pha ni nga yin pas don ci dgos
nas yong ba yin zer bas / ngas gtsang long pa nas lam ma thar ba'i
lo rgyus zhib par smras pas / pha na re 'o de ltar yin na ngas khyod
la dmag dpung zhig ster* ro zer nas / smyug ma'i dong pa kha bcad
pa cig byin byung nas / ngas gtsang long pa'i mtsho'i gram la ma
sleb bar du kha ma 'phye cig zer nas btang bas / bar skyes kyi bsam
pa la 'di ci yin nam ma shes bsam nas / lam bar khre phu la sleb pa
dang / yid ma ches bar smyug dong kha 'phye nas bltas pas dug
sbrul* kha shas der song ba dang / yang la 'ur kha bcad nas / smyug *sprul
dong de khyer nas ngas gtsang long pa'i mtsho 'gram la sleb pa dang
kha 'phye bas / de'i nang nas sbrul rigs* mi gcig** pa sa gzhi*** *rig **ci ***zhig
gang bar (38a) 'thon nas / skad cig de nyid la mtsho brtol nas bye
ma'i thang skam shar re ba byung ba dang / de'i dkyil na zangs chen
cig kha sbub nas yod pa mthong ba dang / gzhon nu bar skyes des* / *de
der song shing kha slog* nas bltas pas / de'i nang nas klu bdud *slob
kyi* g.yog mo nang sgur ma cig yod pa des / zangs skyogs kyis *kyis
gzhon nu bar* skyes kyi dpral bar rgyab nas der gsad pas klad pa *bang
de nya gcig gis zos pas / bar skyes mi ma yin gyi bu yin pa dang /
kho'i rnam par shes pa* de nya la 'dzul nas nya la gyur to / de nas *omitted
nya de grang ma'i chu dang ku ri chu gzhong sgar* mol ba'i chu *dkar
rnams la rims pas bzhugs cing / de nas phyang khos kyi* chu la *kyis
mdzegs pas / phyang khos kyi nya rwa* la tshud nas / pho rengs *omitted
gcig gis* khyer nas yong / mi'i skad gtam smras (38b) pa dang / *gi

Having built a palace at [the lakeside of] Mu-ku-lung mTsho-mo, a broad,
extensive and pleasant place, he resided as the chief (*sde-dpon*) of the
'Eight Classes of *lHa-srin* [Belonging to] the Visible World' and as the
protector of the 'black-headed ones', the humans. At that time a girl in the
fullness of youth, a most lovely beauty, who was coming from the east as
the bride of the king of gDung-bsam-mkhar, slept the night at the side of
the lake. During the night a white snake came out from within the lake and
when it went away after crawling on her she awoke. When she arrived at
gDung-bsam she gave birth to a son who was given the name of Bar-skyes
('Born Interjacently') since he had come forth interjacently without a
(37a) father. When he grew up he set off for the Indian *duars*. On arriving at the
lakeside of Ngas-gtsang-long-pa, on account of the fact that Bar-skyes was
the son of a *lha-btsan,* the *nāga*-devil of Ngas-gtsang-long-pa displayed
magical apparitions and so he did not reach India. Having returned to his
house he asked his mother: "Whose son am I?" His mother would not hear
of telling him but when he asked her cunningly, the mother said: 'since you
are the son of the hon-human *lha-btsan* of Mu-ku-lung, the *nāga*-devil displayed
magical apparitions and so the road was blocked." The child Bar-skyes therefore
immediately went himself to the lakeside of Mu-ku-lung and called out loudly [97]
for his father's help. From within the lake a mature youth wearing clothes of
(37b) white silk and adorned with a wish-fulfilling gem at the top of his bound turban
of white silk came forth and said: "Since I am your father I have come to fulfil
whatever it is that you want." After [Bar-skyes] had recounted in detail the
story of how he could not proceed on his way beyond Ngas-gtsang-long-pa the
father said: "If that is the case I shall give you an army". Giving him a bamboo
tube with a closed opening he said: "Do not open it until you have arrived at
the lakeside of Ngas-gtsang-long-pa" and he sent him off. Bar-skyes thought to
himself: "I don't know what this is" and so when he reached Khre-phu halfway
on his path he opened up the bamboo tube and looked inside disbelievingly.
Some poisonous snakes came out and so he quickly closed it up again. Carrying
the bamboo tube off with him he arrived at the lakeside of Ngas-gtsang-long-pa
and opened it up. Different kinds of snakes came out from inside, filling the
(38a) ground and at the very instant they reached the lake in a flash it became a dry
sandy plain. On seeing in its centre a great copper vessel which was there
turned upside down, the young Bar-skyes went there, turned it over and looked.
Coiled inside was a maid servant of the *nāga*-devil who hit the young Bar-skyes'
forehead with the copper vessel, killing him there. His brain was eaten by a
fish and since Bar-skyes was the son of a non-human his consciousness entered
the fish and so he became a fish. Then the fish stayed by turns in the Grang-
ma'i Chu river, the Ku-ri Chu river and the gZhong-sgar Mol-ba'i Chu river
and then, having climbed up the river of Phyang-khos it entered a fish-net of
(38b) the Phyang-khos people and was carried off by a bachelor. Since it spoke to

za ma nus par chu bkang sa'i wa nang la bzhag pas / nyin* cig pho *nyon
rengs de zhing las la song nas log yong ba dang / khyim nang la mi
med pa la chu* len nas bzhag 'dug / yang nyin cig thab** kha la me *me **thabs
phu nas bzhag 'dug pa las / pho rengs* de ci yin nam bsam nas *reng
nyams* mi dga' bar zhing las la song ba ltar byas te log yong nas *nyam
khyim gyi zur cig las gsang nas ltas pas / wa nang gi nya'i khog pa'i
nang las byis pa dpa' zhing khyug bde ba zhig 'thon nas / me phu
chu len gyi* bya ba byas pas / pho rengs** de'i bsam pa la byis pa *gyis **reng
de kho'i bu tshab byas dgos bsam nas / nya'i pags pa'i sob de thab
nang gi me la skyur btang bas me tshig pas / byis pa 'dzul sa ma
snyed par de gar lus song bas mi la gyur to // kho mi ma (39a) yin
gyi bu yin pa'i gshis* kyis / mthu stobs dang dpa'** rtsal shin tu *shis **dpal
che ba sus kyang 'gran* par mi nus pa byung bas na / ming** yang *'gram **mi
ral pa stobs can du grags shing / de nyid kyis I tung la zer ba'i sa
btsan po* zhig la mkhar rtsigs nas / U ra dang mol ba lung pa la *pa
sogs pa'i yul khams mi sde thams cad la dbang sgyur nas / stobs
mnga' thang che bar byung ba dang / grags tshad mi zin par / zhang
po'i yul phya li mthong ba'i phyir du stong phu'i ri'i sa bcad nas
brdal dgos zer nas ri bcad pas / bud med shes rab kyi rang bzhin
can gcig* gis** smras pa*** / ri mthon po bcad pa las mi mthon *tsam **gyi ***pas
po bcad na sla zer bas / tshig de'i don blon 'bangs rnams kyis rig
nas / ral pa stobs can de g.yo thabs kyis* bslus nas / kar** sbi'i *kyi **ka ra
(39b) thang la gser gyi mda' rtses byed kyi 'dug / ltas mo la 'gro
dgos zer khrid yong nas / snying khar mda' rgyab nas der bsad* *gsad
pa'i kha chems la / khyed rang rnams nga dran pa'i dus yong na
nga'i skye ba bod yul gyi gzhung yar lung grong mo che la yong
rgyu yin pas* khyed rang rnams 'gron** bu khyer la shog cig *pa'i **gron
'gron bu de byis pa mang po 'dzom pa'i khrod du stor cig 'gron bu
'ub gyis 'dus nas khyer ba de nga'i skye ba yin no zer nas 'das so /
de nas lo gcig gnyis song ba dang rje 'bangs kyi rim pa med pa las /
steng nas 'phrog* 'og nas brkus pa las / 'khrugs cing brtsod pas** *'phrog cig **pa'i
yul khams thams cad mi bde bar gyur pa las / sngon gyi rje'i kha
chems dran nas / mi lnga 'gron bu khyer nas / bod gzhung yar lung
grong mo cher phyin nas byis pa mang po tshogs pa'i sar 'gron* *gron
bu stor nas khrid yong ba dang / gong du bshad pa'i U ra pa mi
lnga pos stong gi* 'bras bu stor nas brkus yong ba ni / don cig ming *gyis
gi (40a) rnam* grang yin 'dug / de ji ltar zhe na / U ra pa dang mol *rnams
ba lung pa* rnams kyis yar lung du rje dpon gyi skye ba 'tshol du *pa'i
phyin pa dang / gdan drangs nas U ra la byon lugs yab mes* gong *med
ma rnams kyi rigs brgyud kyi 'byung khungs / phyi gdung lha
dbang grags par mtshan gsol ba sogs ngo bo gcig pa kho na yin
'dug kyang / mdzad pa so sor rnam pa mi cig pa lta bu'i gtam rgyun
smras pa de ni / khong lha klu mi ma yin gyi* bu yin pas na / so *gyi pa'i
so'i mthong snang tsam ma gtogs ngo bo cig pa kho na nyid yin no //
zhes rgyal rigs 'byung khungs gsal ba'i sgron me las / bum thang
sde bzhi'i gdung rnams kyi chad khungs 'byung tshul bshad pa'i* *omitted
le'u ste gsum pa'o //

him in human speech he could not eat it and so he kept it inside a trough in
the ground filled with water. One day the bachelor went to work in the fields
and when he came back [he saw that] water had been fetched and left in the
house although it was empty of people. Again one day a fire was left burning
in the hearth. Wondering how this had happened and feeling disturbed, the
bachelor pretended to set off for his work in the fields and then returned and
watched in concealment from a corner of the house. From inside the belly of
the fish that was in the trough there emerged a strong and agile child who
performed the work of fetching water and lighting a fire. The bachelor thought
how he would like to make the child his adopted son and so he threw the
empty fish skin into the hearth fire and it burnt. Since the child, being unable
to find anything to enter, was left in that condition, he became human. Due to
(39a) the fact that he was the son of a non-human his strength and skill in combat
was exceedingly great and nobody could challenge him. On account of this
he was renowned by the name of Ral-pa sTobs-chen ('Strong Locks'). Having
himself built a castle at a fastness called I-tung La, he gained power over all
the lands and dominions of U-ra, Mol-ba-lung and so forth. His strength and
dominion became great and his renown immeasurable. In order to see his
uncle's home at Phya-li [98] he said that the ground of the mountain of sTong-
-phu should be cut down and spread out and so it was cut down. A lady
possessing the nature of wisdom [99] declared: "It is easier to cut down a
tall man than it is to cut down a tall mountain." Having grasped the meaning of these words the officers and subjects beguiled Ral-pa sTobs-chen by
(39b) cunning means and said to him: "They are playing with a golden arrow on
the pasture of sKar-sbi. You must go and see the show." After they had led
him there he was shot with an arrow in the heart and killed. As his last will
he said: "When the time comes that you remember me my incarnation will
have come to Yar-lung Grong-mo-che at the centre of the country of Tibet.
So you bring some cowrie shells and come there. Scatter the cowries into a
large crowd of children assembled there. The one who gathers the cowries
in handfulls and carries them off is my incarnation." Then he expired. When
one or two years elapsed, on account of there being no hierarchy of lord
and subjects, acts of seizure were committed from above and acts of theft
from below. The resulting quarrels and contentions caused all the districts
to fall into a state of unhappiness. Then, remembering the last will of their
former lord, five men took some cowries and went to Yar-lung Grong-mo-
che, the centre of Tibet, and scattered the cowries in a place where there
were many children assembled. Their escorting [of the chosen boy] and the
theft of [lHa-dbang Grags-pa] by the five men of U-ra after scattering the
stong fruit as described above are of the same sense but there is a varying
(40a) enumeration of names. If it be asked how this could be, [that is to say how
can one reconcile the different] ways in which the people of U-ra and those
of Mol-ba-lung went to Yar-lung in search of the incarnation of their lord-
chief and, having brought him forth, how he came to U-ra, [he] the source
of the family lineages of the ancestral forebears, and how he later received
the name of *gDung* lHa-dbang Grags-pa and so on, [the answer would be
that these differing versions] are of the very same substance but the oral
traditions regarding his various actions appear diverse. This is simply due to
the fact that since he was the son of a non-human *lha-klu* [he assumed
different appearances in] the sight of different persons. Apart from this
[the stories] are of exactly the same essence.

This is the third section from *The Lamp Which Illuminates the Origins of Royal Families* in which is explained the ancestral origins of the *gDung* [families] of the four districts of Bum-thang.

SECTION IV

(40a5) da* ni lho phyogs mon lung shar phyogs kyi dpon chen / *de
(40b) zhal* ngo kheng po zer ba'i brgyud khungs kyang cung *zhel
zad brjod par bya'o // de yang gong du bshad pa'i 'phros las / rgyal
po glang dar mas sangs rgyas kyi bstan pa bshig* cing snubs pa'i dus / *shig
lha sa'i gnas bdag ma gcig dpal gyi lha mos / lha lung dpal gyi rdo rje
la lung bstan zhing rgyud bskul ba dang / nyin cig rgyal po glang dar
ma lha sa'i phyi skor du skyo bsangs la phebs nas / rdo ring gi yi ge
la gzigs cing bzhugs pa'i skabs lha lung dpal gyi rdo rje sngags chas
phod ka phu dung gi nang du mda' gzhu bcug nas gar stabs 'cham
zhing yod pas thams cad de la bltas nas g.yeng ba dang / phu dung
gnyis kyi nang las mda' gzhu kha sprad* nas rgyal po'i** dpral bar *sbrad **po
rgyab ste der bkrongs te bros* song ba dang su yin ma shes / rjes *brol
snyags nas bdas pas ma zin / de (41a) nas lha lung dpal gyi rdo rje
yer pa'i brag la song nas sgom sgrub byed pa'i tshul du bzhugs shing /
rkang rjes* rnams bya zin zhing dkrogs na, bya thal gyis rkang *rje
rjes bsub nas sdod pa dang bded mi* rnams der yong nas / mi 'di *'das mo
ni man pas rkang pas rgyu 'grul med pa yun ring po song 'dug zer
nas log song ba dang / mi blo* gros can nyams che ba gcig gis logs *lo
yong nas / lha lung dpal gyi rdo rje'i snying kha'i thad kyi brang la
spar mo* bkab nas bltas** pas / snying*** 'phar**** 'phar spar ba *sprar **ltas ***snying la ****phar
shes nas dmangs* kyi don la sgos kyis thod** pa mi bcag zer nas *mangs **thong
gzhan la ma bshad* par log song ba dang / lha lung dpal gyi rdo rje *shad
der g.yang grog za nas tshug ma thub* par khams la bros song ba *thob
las / khong gi sku mched* rdo rje spun drug yang so sor kha 'thor *chen
nas bros song ba (41b) las / stobs ldan la ba rdo rje / mgar ba khye'u
rdo rje / g.yang rtsal spre'u* rdo rje gsum / gtsang pha ri** phyogs *sprul 'u **phag rig
las spa gro* rgyud nas rim pas bum thang** la slebs pas / sngar de *dro **stang
na rgyal po khyi* kha ra thod dang mnyam po yong ba'i mi brgyud *omitted
dang grong zhing 'thor bu re yod pa rnams kyi yul bshal nas song /
khong spun gsum gyi bsam pa la / bod kyi dpon rigs rus yin pas na* / *nas
rigs rus kyi mthong* bkur re byed mi yong ba bsam pa la byed mi *'thong
ma byung nas / stobs shugs che tsam gyi ngos kha lo sgyur dgos
bsam pa la / sngar nas rje 'bangs kyi rim pa mtho man med pa las
bstod bkur byed ma nyan pa dang / spun gsum ci drag la thug nas
gros bsdur byas shing / zhi ba thabs gyi sgo nas gang la gang 'dul
mi sde'i blo dang sbyar* nas byas pas (42a) kha la nyan tsam byung *byar
ba dang / stobs ldan la ba rdo rje / stang lung pa la song nas yul

SECTION IV

(40a5) Now I shall speak briefly about the ancestral origins of the so-called *Zhal-*
(40b) *ngo Kheng-po,* chiefs of the eastern districts of the Southern Mon Country.
Now then, in continuation of what was explained above, at the time when
King Glang Dar-ma was destroying the teachings of the Buddha and causing
them to decline, the guardian deity of lHa-sa, *Ma-gcig* dPal-gyi lHa-mo, made
a prophecy to lHa-lung dPal-gyi rDo-rje and roused his spirit. One day when
King Glang Dar-ma had gone for his diversion to the outer circulating road
of lHa-sa and was standing looking at the writing on the pillar, lHa-lung dPal-
gyi rDo-rje, having placed a bow and arrow in the broad sleeves of a tantric
costume, performed the steps of a dance [before him]. When everyone
watching him was diverted he fixed the arrow in the bow [having taken
them out] from within his two sleeves and, firing off at the king's forehead,
killed him there. He fled and nobody knew who he was. Those who hastened
(41a) after him in pursuit did not catch him. lHa-lung dPal-gyi rDo-rje then went
to the rock of Yer-pa and stayed there as if performing meditation. His
foot-prints were taken over by birds who churned them up and covered
them with droppings. As he stayed there the pursuers came up. "It is not
this man; a long time has elapsed without his moving around on foot", they
said. As they were returning, however, one [from among them] who was
intelligent and noble-minded came back and placed his hand on lHa-lung
dPal-gyi rDo-rje's chest at a point over his heart and looked. Knowing that
the pulse of his heart was beating [rapidly with fear on account of his
guilt] he said: "For my own part I shall not break his skull for the sake of
the common weal".[100] He went back without telling the others. Feeling
great fear[101] in that place, lHa-lung dPal-gyi rDo-rje was compelled to flee
to Khams.

After this his brothers, the Six Vajra Brothers, also scattered in different
(41b) directions and fled. sTobs-ldan La-ba rDo-rje, mGar-ba Khye'u rDo-rje and
g.Yang-rtsal sPre'u rDo-rje,[102] [these] three, arrived in Bum-thang in stages
by way of sPa-gro from the direction of gTsang Pha-ri. They proceeded,
roving through the villages of the few people who were there with their
habitations and fields who descended from those that had come there in
previous times with King Khyi-kha Ra-thod. In their minds the three
brothers thought that since they were from the families and clans of
Tibetan chiefs, a few people would come forward to do honour to their
families and clans but no such people arose. As for their thinking that they
should rule by means of some considerable force, due to the fact that from
previous times [in Bum-thang] there had been no high and low grades
between a lord and his subjects, [the people] would not hear of showing
them respect. Thereupon the three brothers fell to wondering what would
be best done and so they held a discussion and [decided that] by peaceful
means each should convert in the manner best suited to him in accordance
(42a) with the will of the communities. So when some compliance at least was
shown, sTobs-ldan La-ba rDo-rje went to the district of sTang, established

mkhar* btab cing sa gzhi bzung ba'i** bu brgyud rim par je 'thor *repeated **bas
song zhing dpon por gyur ba'i bu brgyud yin no / / g.yang rtsal
spre'u rdo rje bum thang* du yul mkhar btab cing sa gzhi bzung / *stang
bu brgyud rim pas pha las bu drag* pa byung nas bum thang** chos *grags **stang
'khor dpon po zer / stobs mnga' thang che ba ming yongs su grags
pa de byung ba yin 'dug / chos 'khor dpon po spa gro* nas yin zer *dro
ba'ang gtsang pha*ri phyogs las spa gro** rgyud nas yong ba las *phag **dro
zer ba yin 'dug / mgar ba khye'u rdo rje sa gtsang la ri mtho zhing
bod yul thag nye ba bod mon gnyis kyi mtshams / sha mar thud
gsum dang 'bru sna 'dzom pa'i las sgo la long spyod pa'i phyir bod
mon mtshams kyi* (42b) 'brog bzung ba'i bu brgyud** da*** lta'i *gyi **omitted ***omitted
mtshams pa'i 'brog rigs mtho ba rnams yin 'dug / yang spun gsum
lho brag phyogs las yong ba / kha rtsing las kyi rdo rje / pho mtshar
grags pa rdo rje / smras mkhas* spyang rig** rdo rje gsum ku ri *khas **spyod rigs
lung du sleb nas / gros bsdur byas pas / kha rtsing las kyi* rdo rje *omitted
na re nged* rang gsum mnyam po sdod** nas / pha ma'i lugs *red **stod
kyis* sa gzhi** bzung nas mi sde la dbang sgyur ba zhig byed dgos *kyi **gzhis
zer bas / pho mtshar grags pa rdo rje na re / de bzhin byas na lung
phyogs 'di la mi dang grong zhing 'thor bu re las med pas / nged* *red
rang spun gsum bya spyod kyi rlabs 'dir byed* rin mi chog / lung *byas
phyogs so sor song* nas pho res stobs shugs kyi sgo nas mnga' *bsong
'bangs btsol* nas yul mkhar bzung dgos zer bas / spun gsum de la *btsal
kha cham nas / kha rtsing las kyi rdo rje (43a) 'du rang gi smad
tshi rab stong phu zhang tshan yong nas mi sde* la dbang sgyur *lde
bas / mi zim pa'i rgyal mkhar bzung mkhan rgyal po yong la phan
gyi sems la phog nas / khong nas 'khrugs pas yong la phan gyis* *gyi
tshugs* ma thub par yul las 'thon song ba las / de'i mi sde thams *tshug
cad kyang kha rtsing las kyi* rdo rje'i 'og tu bcug go / de'i bu *omitted
brgyud so sor gyes* pa tshi rab stong phu zhang tshan** dang / *'gye **mtshan
mu hung shes ro gsar rnying* la yod pa'i dpon chen zer ba'i rigs *snying
thams cad kha rtsing las kyi rdo rje'i* bu brgyud yin no // pho *rdo rje'i repeated
mtshar grags pa rdo rje ku ri lung stod smad thams cad la dbang
sgyur ba* brgyud pa da lta'i ku** ri lung gi dpon chen zhal ngo *bas **sku
thams cad pho mtshar grags pa rdo rje'i bu brgyud so sor 'gyes pa'i
brgyud pa yin no // smras mkhas spyang rig* rdo rjes gzhong sgar *cad rigs
mol ba (43b) lung pa song nas thabs mkhas g.yo 'phrul sna tshogs
kyis kha lo sgyur nas mi sde thams cad mnga' 'bangs la bcug cing
pho ngar khengs* pa byung bas na / rus kyi ming la 'ang kheng* *mkheng
po zer nas btags cing / stobs shugs che ba byung ba'i* bu *bas
brgyud / gzhong sgar* dang tog ka ri / the mung / phya li / *dkar
nya rtsis sogs la yod pa'i kheng* po'i rigs thams cad smras mkhas *kheng
spyang rig* rdo rje'i bu brgyud so sor gyes** pa'i brgyud pa yin *cad rigs **'gyes
no // rgyal rigs 'byung khungs gsal ba'i sgron me las / lha lung
dpal gyi rdo rje'i sku mched rdo rje spun drug lung phyogs so sor
song nas / dpon po gyur ba'i le'u ste* bzhi pa'o // *te

a district castle and took control of an estate. His descendants gradually increased and are the descendants who became chiefs (*dpon-po*). g.Yang-rtsal sPre'u rDo-rje established a district castle in Bum-thang and took control of an estate. His descendants gradually came forth, the sons exceeding the fathers, and the so-called *Bum-thang Chos-'khor dPon-po,* [103] this universally renowned name [of those possessing] great strength and dominion, arose. Although the *Chos-'khor dPon-po* are said to be from sPa-gro, it is said so because [g.Yang-rtsal sPre'u rDo-rje] came by way of sPa-gro from the direction of gTsang Pha-ri. mGar-ba Khye'u rDo-rje, in order to enjoy the mart where meat, butter and cheese, [these] three, and various kinds of grains abounded close to the country of Tibet on the border of Tibet and Mon, [surrounded by] pure land and lofty mountains,
(42b) seized the pasture-land on the Tibet-Mon border. His descendants are at present the important pastoral families of mTshams-pa.

Furthermore, the three brothers who came from the direction of lHo-brag, (i.e.) Kha-rtsing Las-kyi rDo-rje, Pho-mtshar Grags-pa rDo-rje and sMras-mkhas sPyang-rig rDo-rje, [these] three, having arrived in Ku-ri-lung, held a discussion. Kha-rtsing Las-kyi rDo-rje said: "We three residing together must gain power over the communities after taking control of an estate in the manner of our parents." Pho-mtshar Grags-pa rDo-rje said: "If we should act in that manner, since there are not more than a few people with their habitations and fields in this district, it is insufficient for the timely performance here of extensive activity by us three brothers. We must take control of district castles after going to different areas and individually searching for subjects with vigour and strength." The three
(43a) brothers agreed to this and so Kha-rtsing Las-kyi rDo-rje came to Tshi-rab sTong-phu Zhang-tshan in the lower part of 'Du-rang and gained power over the communities. This aroused King Yong-la-phan, the castellan of the royal castle of Mi-zim-pa; contending with him, Yong-la-phan was unable to inflict any damage and so departed from his home. After this all the communities of that place were brought under the subjugation of Kha-rtsing Las-kyi rDo-rje. His descendants who spread in different directions, [i.e.] all the families of the so-called *dPon-chen* ('Great Chiefs') who are in Tshi-rab sTong-phu Zhang-tshan and in Mu-hung Shes-ro gSar-rnying are the descendants of Kha-rtsing Las-kyi rDo-rje.

Pho-mtshar Grags-pa rDo-rje gained power over all the upper and lower parts of Ku-ri-lung. His descendants, at present all the *dPon-chen Zhal-ngo* ('Chief Nobles') of Ku-ri- lung [104] are of the lineage of the descendants of Pho-mtshar Grags-pa rDo-rje who spread in different directions.

(43b) sMras-mkhas sPyang-rig rDo-rje went to gZhong-sgar Mol-ba-lung-pa and after imposing his rule through various clever means and cunning designs all the communities were made subject. Since he came forth strong and proud (khengs-pa), he was given the clan name of Kheng-po [105] and his descendants who came forth with great vigour, [i.e.] all the Kheng-po families who are in gZhong-sgar, Tog-ka-ri, The-mung, Phya-li, Nya-rtsis and so forth, are of the lineage of the descendants of sMras-mkhas sPyang-rig rDo-rje who spread in different directions.

This is the fourth section from *The Lamp Which Illuminates the Origins of Royal Families* [which explains how] the brothers of lHa-lung dPal-gyi rDo-rje, the Six *Vajra* Brothers, went to different districts and became chiefs.

SECTION V

(43b4) // da ni 'og ma 'bangs kyi mi rabs chad khungs 'byung tshul
dang rigs kyi ming yang brjod par bya'o // de yang sngon gangs can
bod du mi* brgyud spel ba'i pha rgan byang chub sems dpa' de / *omitted
bu brgyud rim* par phel** (44a) zhing / rus rigs bzhi ru 'phye ba *rims **'phel
la / se dang rmu / ldong dang stong ste bzhi'o // de las so sor 'phye
ba la / se las byu* legs kyi** bu bzhi srid / rmu las ko le phra*** *byus **omitted ***khra
brgyad* srid / ldong las rus chen bco brgyad srid / stong las rje *brgyal
bzhi khol* brgyad srid ces pa / se las 'gyes pa'i rus rigs bzhi ni / *kho las
rgyal nang rje / 'gro gang nyer ba / 'og gog btsan / bde stong se dang
bzhi'o // stong las rje bzhi khol brgyad so sor 'gyes pa'i rus kyi ming
ni / cog la ram pa rje / rtsang rje thod dkar rje / te tsom* snyal po *tsog
rje / snyags rje thog sgrom* rje dang bzhi'o // 'bangs ni dmar dang *sgom
dmar ma dang / snyal* dang snyal dben rngog dan khrog / rtog dang *snyel
sbas te brgyad yin no // rmu las ko le* khra brgyad so sor 'gyes pa'i *las
rigs rus kyi ming ni ngam* dang snubs dang gzhung dang smon / 'gar *dbab
dang dkar dang (44b) snyos dang ngan lam ste brgyad yin no //
ldong las rus chen bco brgyad so sor 'gyes pa'i rus kyi ming ni / cog
dang cog rtse cog ro dang / 'brom dang khyung po zla ba dang /
'bring dang lha lung lha rtse dang / brang* dgos pa khu na dang / *brang na
nya dang tshe spong lu nag dang / snying* dang pho gong thag *snyid
bzang la rus chen bco brgyad zer ba yin / sngon gyi dus su gangs
can bod kyi rigs rus ming gi rtsa ba de rnams las med kyang phyis
nas mi brgyud yul khams lung phyogs so sor 'gyes pa las / bya ba'i
gnas skabs dang sbyar ba'i rus kyi ming dang yul skad so so'i smras
gtam gyi skad zur chag pa dangs rigs rus kyi so sor lta bur snang ba
yin 'dug / khyad par du 'ang lho mon kha bzhi'i lung phyogs 'di
nyid kyi mi rnams bod yul nas lho mon la yong nas yun ring po* *yul rin po
ma song bas / gong du brjod pa'i rigs rus kyi brgyud pa kho na
(45a) nyid yin 'dug kyang / lho mon gyi lung phyogs 'dir / rgya
bod kyi lugs ltar rigs rus la mtho dman gyi dbye ba med cing
mthong* bkur che bar mi 'dzin pa las yig cha la ma bkod** pa dang *'thong **bkos
khungs ma chod pa yin 'dug / lho mon nyi ma shar phyogs 'di
nyid la pha tshan so sor 'phye ba'i rus kyi ming / dang ri* / skye *perhaps ngang ri
stong / yu sbi / ri bsangs / ba gi / glang la / chur nang / shar ro /
ra ma / nya mi / gnam sa / skom mo / rlon mo / rog mo / mkhar
mo / khu mo / brag mo / skyid mo / seng po / rong bu / mthong
re / geng ra / snying len / zur / gter ci / nga rig la sogs pa'i rus kyi
ming ji snyed yod pa dang / de bzhin lho mon shar phyogs kyi lung
phyogs gang la 'ang so so'i yul skad dang bstun* pa'i rus kyi ming *bstan
ji snyed yod pa sha stag yin kyang / 'dir khungs ma chod* pa las *mchod
(45b) 'di tsam las yi ger ma bkod do //

// 'ga'* re nas so sos gtam rgyun smras pa la las 'byung khungs lha'i *'gag
rmu skas* dang gser dngul gyi phya** thag la 'jus nas mi'i yul du *skad **dpyad
babs pa yin zer ba'i gleng gtam phal cher gyis yongs su grags pa de
ni bon lugs kyi yig gter gyi gtam rgyun yin nam / sangs rgyas byang
sems rnams kyis 'gro ba'i don du sprul pa'i snang brnyan* rigs rus *snyan

SECTION V

(43b4) Now I shall speak about the history of the ancestral origins of generations of subjects beneath [the rulers] and also about their family names.

Now then, the descendants of the old father Bodhisattva who propagated
(44a) the human race in former times in Tibet, the Land of Snow, gradually increased and were divided into four clan-stocks: [106] Se and rMu, lDong and sTong – [these] four. As for their separate classification: It is said that from the Se there were the 'Four Sons of Byu-legs'; from the rMu there were the 'Eight Ko-le-phra'; from the lDong there were the 'Eighteen Great Lineages'; and from the sTong there were the 'Eight rJe-bzhi-khol'. The four clan-stocks which issued from the Se were [Se-gong] rGyal-nang-rje, 'Gro-gang Nyer-ba[-se], 'Og-gog bTsan[-se] and ['Og-ma] bDe-stong-se – [these] four. The clan names of the 'Eight rJe-bzhi-khol' who issued variously from the sTong were Cog-la Ram-pa-rje, rTsang-rje Thod-dkar-rje, Te-tsom sNyal-po-rje and sNyags-rje Thog-sgrom-rje – [these] four. Their subjects were the dMar and the dMar-ma, the sNyal and the sNyal-dben, the rNgog and the Khrog, the rTog and the sBas – [these] eight. The family and clan names of the 'Eight Ko-le-phra' who issued variously from the rMu were Ngam,
(44b) sNubs, gZhung and sMon; 'Gar, dKar, sNyos and Ngan-lam – [these] eight. The clan names of the 'Eighteen Great Lineages' who issued variously from the lDong were Cog, Cog-rtse and Cog-ro; 'Brom, Khyung-po and Zla-ba; 'Bring, lHa-lung and lHa-rtse; Brang, dGos-pa and Khu-na; Nya, Tshe-spong and Lu-nag; sNying, Pho-gong and Thag-bzang – these are the so-called 'Eighteen Great Lineages'

Although no more than these roots of the family and clan names of Tibet, the Land of Snow, existed in previous times, later on after the human race had spread to different districts in the country, there appeared clan names conforming to the circumstances of their deeds, [deriving from] the corrupted speech of various local dialects and [in accordance with] the different natures of the families and clans. In particular, as it is not long since the people of this area of lHo Mon Kha bZhi came from the country of Tibet to lHo Mon, they are of the very same lineage as those [Tibetan]
(45a) families and clans mentioned above. However, in this area of lHo Mon there are no high and low divisions among the families and clans as in the manner of India and Tibet and since they were not upheld with great honour they are not mentioned in the records and are unsubstantiated. The clan names which differentiate the families [of subjects] in this Eastern Province of lHo Mon are: Dang-ri [or Ngang-ri?], sKye-stong, Yu-sbi, Ri-bsangs, Ba-gi, Glang-la, Chur-nang, Shar-ro, Ra-ma, Nya-mi, gNam-sa, sKom-mo, Rlon-mo, Rog-mo, mKhar-mo, Khu-mo, Brag-mo, sKyid-mo, Seng-po, Rong-bu, mThong-re, Geng-ra, sNying-len, Zur, gTer-ci, Nga-rig and so on – there are numerous clan names. [107] Thus although they represent all the numerous clan names which accord with the various local dialects prevailing throughout the area of the Eastern Province of lHo Mon, since they cannot be
(45b) substantiated here, no more than just this has been put in writing.

As for the version which most stories make universally renowned according to which some people, in recounting the various oral traditions say that the origins [of their ancestors lay in a] descent to the land of humans after grasping the divine *rmu*-ladders and the gold and silver *phya*-cords [108] – is this a legend based on the treasure-texts of the *Bon* tradition? Or is it said of the Buddhas and Bodhisattvas whose manifested forms, emanated for the sake of beings, were born among the scions of these families and clans?

de rnams kyi bu brgyud la 'khrungs nas / rtags* bcu yon tan brgyad* la sogs pa'i sgo nas 'gro ba'i don mdzad cing / dbon sras rim par dbu 'phang gong na 'phags shing chos kyi 'khor lo rgyun chad med par skor ba la zer ba yin nam /* yang na 'jig rten gyi lha chen po tshangs pa dang / dbang phyug la sogs par pha mes gong ma na rim nas lung phyogs thams cad kyi mgrin gcig* tu lo re bzhin mchod cing (46a) gsol ba las / mgon skyabs dang stongs grogs mdzad pa'i phyir du lha'i bu'i rnam par sprul pas / gong du brjod pa'i rigs rus de rnams la 'khrungs shing / stobs kyi 'khor lo sgyur nas yangs pa'i rgyal khams thams cad bde skyid kyi dpal la bkod cing / sras gdung brgyud rim pas sa chen kun la dbang sgyur zhing stobs mnga' thang gong du* 'phags pas lha'i longs spyod kyi dpal la ji srid yun ring du spyod cing / lha'i rnam par sprul pa'i snang brnyan dngos su bstan pa las ya mtshan pa'i gtam rgyun yongs su grags pa* yin nam / de dag ni skye bo phal pa rnams kyis* rtogs par dka' zhing bsam pa'i yul las 'das pas / skye bo dam pa mkhyen dpyod phul du phyin zhing mngon par shes pa mnga' ba rnams kyi spyod yul du* snang ngo // zhes rgyal rigs 'byung (46b) khungs gsal ba'i sgron me las / 'og ma 'bangs kyi mi rabs kyi 'byung khungs* dang rigs rus so sor 'phye ba'i le'u ste lnga pa'o //

*tag
*brgyas
*omitted
*omitted
*omitted
*omitted
*kyi
*omitted
*omitted

[According to this interpretation] having acted for the welfare of beings by means of the Ten Signs,[109] the Eight Qualities[110] and so forth their descendants were gradually exalted on high and turned the wheel of the *Dharma* unceasingly. Or else is it [based on] the famous legends which marvel at the true appearance of the manifested forms of divine emanations? [According to these legends] the great gods of the world, Brahmā, Īśvara and so forth, whom successive forbears annually worshipped and supplicated
(46a) as with the single voice of all districts, therefore emanated divine sons who were born in the clans mentioned above for the sake of protecting and assisting [these forbears]. Turning the 'wheel of strength', they established all the wide kingdoms in the glory of happiness and so successive members of their sons' lineages gained power over the whole earth and acted for periods as long as possible in the glorious state of divine plenty on account of their strength and dominion being exalted on high. It is difficult for the majority of people to understand [the truth of] these [various interpretations] and as it exceeds the scope of their minds, it is perceived [only] within the sphere of activity of those sacred beings whose discernment is perfect and who possess super-sensible cognition.

(46b) This is the fifth section from ***The Lamp which Illuminates the Origins of Royal Families*** [in which is explained] the origin of generations of subjects beneath [the rulers] and which classifies their various families and clans.

CONCLUDING VERSES AND COLOPHON

(46b1) smras pa //

gangs can lho phyogs mon khams shar gling 'dir //
sngon nas rim par byung ba'i skye ba yis //
rje 'bangs rigs kyi* chad khungs gleng ba'i gtam // *omitted
brtag par ma dpyad yi ger ma bkod pas //
gtam rgyun khungs bcad yi ge 'thor bu 'dus //
legs par sgrigs pa'i mun gsal sgron me 'di //
mkhas pa'i gral bsnyegs rlom pa'i nga rgyal dang //
snyan grags gtam gyi 'dod pa ma yin par //
ma 'ongs rjes 'jug dus kyi phyi ma la //
ya rabs mkhas btsun bzang po rim byon tshe //
sngon med 'byung khungs deb* ther 'di gzigs pas // *debs
zhal bgad rtse mo'i zhal 'dzum 'phye ba dang //
gzu lum (47a) nga rgyal 'joms pa'i dpa'* bo de** // *dpa'i **ste
ma rig* mun pa sel ba'i sgron me yin // *rigs
pho mnyam gzhon pa phan tshun smra* ba'i gtam // *omitted
lhag bsam rnam par dkar bas* 'di sgrigs pas // *omitted
kun 'dus tshig la lhag chad 'gal 'khrul rnams //
mkhas mchog blo gros spyan yangs bzod par bzhes //
rnam g.yeng nor dang 'dzol ba'i cha mchis pa //
mkhyen dbang dag gis gzigs nas bcos par gsol //
zhes dang //

CONCLUDING VERSES AND COLOPHON

(46bI) It is declared:

In this eastern region of the Mon country
south of the Land of Snow
The beings who appeared successively in
previous times
Did not examine or put in writing
The stories that recount the origin of
the families of lords and subjects;
So oral traditions have been substantiated
and a few documents collected.
This properly compiled *Lamp Which Illuminates
Darkness*
Did not arise from boastful pride in aspiring
to the rank of scholars
Or from desire for reputation and celebrity,
But rather that in the future, after the
time of our successors,
When noblemen who are learned, honourable
and good succeed each other by turn,
On seeing this unprecedented record of origins
Their smiles may open at the peak of laughter

(47a) And that this hero which defeats stupidity and
pride
May be a lamp which removes the darkness of
ignorance.
A discourse which young men of equal standing
tell each other,
Since this work was compiled out of purest
devotion
May excellent scholars who have understanding
and broad outlooks show forgiveness for
The omissions, exaggerations and delusions in the
words of this all-inclusive work.
On seeing those sections which contain slips,
faults and errors
Erudite persons are requested to correct them.

kha gling gi rgyal rigs bslab gsum sde snod 'dzin pa mkhyen pa la mi rmongs pa'i lha btsun ngag dbang phun tshogs dang / phyi tshang mong sgar* gyi rgyal rigs dpa'** mdzangs*** brtul phod che zhing khungs btsun pa'i rgyal po dbang grags dang / phyi tshang skya sa mkhar gyi rgyal rigs shes bya blo gros rgyas shing smra ba stong sde'i* ru dar la mkhas pa'i rgyal po dang / phong mi'i yas sde'i rgyal (47b) rigs 'phrul thabs sgyur rtsal la mkhas pa'i chos mdzad lug* dkar dang / shar phyogs sde rang gi rgyal po mi chos yon tan drug dang / thabs bzhi'i mnga' brnyes* 'phrul thabs kyi 'khor lo sgyur ba'i jo bo A bzang dang / de dag rnams kyis so sos nas lhag bsam rnam par dkar bas gsung gis bskul ba las / shes rig sbyangs brtson gyi yon tan dang mthong thos nyams* myong rig rtsal gyi spobs pa gang yang med kyang / gsung rigs gyen zlog ma nus par byar gyi bende wa gindras ming gis sngon byung gi rgyal rabs dang / phyis byung gi yig cha 'thor bu rnams so so nas 'dus shing / rgan rabs kyi gtam rgyun gyi khungs legs par dpyad cing gcig tu bsdus pa* 'di ni phur bu zhes pa** sa pho spre lo'i hor zla brgyad pa'i yar tshes bzang po la / gza' dang skar ma'i sbyor ba phun gsum tshogs (48a) shing lang tsho dpal gyi nyi mas gang ba'i nyin / rgya bod kyi 'dun sa bkra shis sgang gi pho brang gzhal yas khang gi zur khang du zin bris su bkod pa las / thog mar yi ge'i lam du spel ba po śnga tshang bkra shis sding mkhar gyi rje rigs chos mdzad nor bu dar rgyas kyis* bris pa dge legs phyogs dus gnas skabs thams cad du dar zhing rgyas la yun ring du gnas par gyur cig /
Om swa sti dha rmā ra dza ni rmā kā ya na ma /

*omitted **dpal ***bdzangs
*de
*klu
*banyes
*mnyam
*pa'i **pas
*kyi

gangs can ljongs 'dir dpal ldan rgyal ba'i bstan //
chos srid rnam pa zung gis gong nas gong //
spel mdzad sngon byon chos rgyal mes* dbon ni //
yab sras brgyud par bcas la phyag bgyi'o //
gang de'i gdung rabs mtha' bzhir 'gyes pa yis //
rgya bod lho mon rgyal khams 'dzin pa dang //
dgos 'dod kun 'byung las sgo'i sgo* phye nas //
rnam mang skye 'gro'i re ba (48b) skong ba'i gtam //
ya rabs gong ma'i gsung ngag dri med dang //
dngos bzhugs rgan mgo'i rgyud tshig drang* po'i don //
phyogs lhung 'dod dbang spong ba'i lhag bsam gyis //
mchog gsum dbang du bzhugs pa'i tho chems bris //

*me
*go
*drag

lHa-btsun Ngag-dbang phun-tshogs [111] of the royal family of Kha-gling, upholder of the *Pitaka* and the Three Precepts, unimpaired as to knowledge; *rGyal-po* dBang-grags [112] of the royal family of Phyi-tshang Mong-sgar, of great honour and bravery and of noble ancestry; rGyal-po [113] of the royal family of Phyi-tshang sKya-sa-mkhar, of extensive knowledge and understanding, skilled in rhetoric; [114] *Chos-mdzad* Lug-dkar [115] of the royal family
(47b) of the Yas-sde [clan] of Phong-mi, skilled in the dexterous use of magical means; Jo-bo A-bzang, King of sDe-rang in the east, [116] who has gained the power of the Six Virtues of Worldly Religion [117] and of the Four Methods,[118] and who turns the Wheel of Magical Means; [119] – having been individually exhorted in speech by these persons out of purest devotion, although possessing no confidence at all in learning acquired by the diligent study of knowledge or in any proficiency born of the personal experience of things seen and heard, but being unable to resist what was said to me, I Wagindra [=Ngag-dbang] by name, a monk of the Byar [clan], collected together from different places the few royal histories of former times and records of later times and also carefully examined the grounds for the oral traditions of elders; and so this work which combines all these accounts was put into draft form during the auspicious second half of the eighth Hor month of the Earth Male Monkey Year called 'The Dagger' [=1728], a time of
(48a) excellent planetary and astral conjunction when the days were filled with the youthful sun, in a side building of the palace of bKra-shis-sgang, the meeting-place of India and Tibet. [120] The one who first distributed it in written form was *Chos-mdzad* Nor-bu Dar-rgyas of the noble family of sNga-tshang bKra-shis-sding-mkhar, who wrote it out. May its virtuous qualities flourish and increase in all circumstances of place and time and may it enjoy a long duration.

Om swasti dharmarājanirma[na] kayanama
[I] bow to the former Dharmarājas,
grandfathers and grandsons,
Together with their father-son lineage,
who spread
From height to height the teachings of the
glorious *Jina*
In this Land of Snow by combining religious
and secular spheres.
[This] story [has recounted] how their
succeeding generations which had spread
to the four limits
Came to take control of realms in India,
Tibet and lHo Mon and how,
Having opened the doors to the trade-marts
from where all wishes and wants came forth,
(48b) They fulfilled the hopes of many kinds of beings.
[This] testamentary record which is sustained by
the power of the Three Jewels was written
From devotion which rejects partiality and
the force of personal desires
On the basis of the unblemished discourses
of ancestral nobles and on
The just and traditional words of elders in person.

ADDENDUM

[I]

(48b2) / de yang rgyal brgyud zur tsam bshad pa ni / rgyal po srong* btsan sgam po / khri lde gtsug brtan**/ de'i brgyud khri srong lde* btsan / de'i bu mu khri btsan po / ma rung btsan po / bzhi khri btsan po / khri ral pa rnams yin / bzhi khri btsan po'i brgyud pa mon* yul la 'og yul gsum la byon pa yin / de nas rgyal mkhar mi zim pa la babs pa yin / mi zim pa la mi rabs lnga drug sdod pa yin / de nas shar sde* rang rgyal po dang / sgam ri radhi rgyal po dang / snga tshang phyi tshang rgyal po dang / sngon la srin mi rgyun mi'i rgyal po dang / beng mkhar / kha gling / gdung* bsam / de tsho'i rgyal po mi (49a) zim pa las 'gyes pa yin / mi zim pa'i rgyal po khun dang zer ba dang / thum bi zer ba gnyis yod pa'i khun dang gi bu gser gdung / thum bi'i bu ldan bu yin / gser gdung dang ldan bu gnyis kyi thog la mi zim pa nas babs ste / gser gdung gis* beng mkhar bzung / mkhar la btsan sa** brag chen yod / phyi'i lcags ri'i grang ma chu dang mi thi gnyis kyis bskor ba yod / las sgo ni sgam ri nya'u chung gser mi yod / phu ni tsheng phu'i 'og la sdod pa yin / de nas mkhar gcen mkhar 'di / sngar dang po ni rgyal po stong rab kyis bzung ba yod / stong rab kyi mag* pa sbyar pa da las bu yin / stong rab kyi brgyud pa chad nas mag* pas bzung ba yin / de nas rgyal po ldan bu* ni mi zim pa nas gcen mkhar la babs pa yin / ldan bus* zer ba la /

*spong **khri sde btsug bstan
*sde
*yon
*sdi
*bdung
*gi **pa
*smag
*smag
*bu'i
*bu'i

chos rgyal gdung brgyud nga rang yin //
bu ri stag gi mgo* stog yin // *go
gcen mkhar stag gi sked pa yin //
smad gdung bsam 'di rkang bsten gyi mdzub (49b) mo* yin // *mtsho mo
[1] gdung bsam stag gi 'jug ma yin //
ri sa pha sgam 'byung mo 'di rgyab rten* gyi ri bo yin // *bstan
sgom la 'brog gsum gser gyi gzhong pa 'dra //
sgam ri mdo bzhi yid* bzhin nor bu 'dra // *yin
beng mkhar 'di srin yul gyi sgo bsrung 'dra //
gcen mkhar 'di ka ta rgyug pa'i shong lam yin //
kha khra* rgyug pa'i chu lam yin // *khrag
mi lam rgyug pa'i gsang lam yin //
rgya bod 'gro ba'i lam 'gags yin //
'di las ma gtogs gzhan las 'gro sa med //
phu yon phu gser gyi yol ba* brkyang** ba 'dra ba 'dug // *la **rkyang
mda' ldom gzi ni glang chen 'dra ba 'dug //

zhes gsungs so //

1. The following two lines are taken from † below where they do not appear to belong.

ADDENDUM : Brief Records of the Yo-gdung Wang-ma Clan [121]

[I. The Ruling Families of Beng-mkhar and gCen-mkhar and their Lineages]

(48b2) Now, as for a brief additional explanation of the royal lineages: King Srong-btsan sGam-po; *Khri* lDe-gtsug-brtan; his descendant *Khri* Srong-lde-btsan; his sons were Mu-khri bTsan-po, Ma-rung [=Mu-rum] bTsan-po, bZhi-khri bTsan-po and *Khri* Ral-pa[-can]. The descendants of bZhi-khri bTsan-po [122] went to La-'og Yul-gsum in Mon-yul. Then they came down to the royal castle of Mi-zim-pa. They stayed for five or six generations at Mi-zim-pa. Then the Kings of Shar sDi-rang, the Kings of sGam-ri Radhi, the Kings of sNga-tshang [and] Phyi-tshang, the ancient Kings of Srin-mi [and] rGyun-mi [123] and the Kings of Beng-mkhar, Kha-gling and gDung-
(49a) bsam – all these spread forth from Mi-zim-pa. There were two kings of Mi-zim-pa called Khun-dang and Thum-bi of whom Khun-dang's son was gSer-gdung and Thum-bi's son was lDan-bu. [124] During the lifetimes of both gSer-gdung and lDan-bu they came down from Mi-zim-pa and gSer-gdung took control of Beng-mkhar. For [the site of] a castle there was a great rock stronghold. The outer wall [formed by] the Grang-ma Chu river encircled it to [the distance of] two *mi-thi*. [125] As for [his] *duars*, [he] had [those of] sGam-ri Nya'u-chung gSer-mi (?). As to the top part [of the Beng-mkhar district?], he resided below Tsheng-phu.

Now, as regards the castle of gCen-mkhar, in previous times it was first controlled by King sTong-rab. sTong-rab's son-in-law was sByar-pa [126] Da-las-bu. When sTong-rab's lineage [127] died out, the son-in-law took control [of gCen-mkhar]. Then, as for King lDan-bu, he came down from Mi-zim-pa to gCen-mkhar. lDan-bu declared:

"I am the descendant of the Dharmarājas.
Bu-ri is the tiger's head.
gCen-mkhar is the tiger's waist.
(49b) Lower gDung-bsam is the toe attached to the [tiger's] foot.
gDung-bsam is the tiger's tail.
The mountain-land of Pha-sgam-'byung-mo is the 'support-mountain' [of the tiger?].
sGom-la 'Brog-gsum is like a golden trough.
sGam-ri mDo-bzhi is like a wish-fulfilling gem.
Beng-mkhar is like the door-guard of a demon-land.
gCen-mkhar is the ridge-way where the *ka-ta* [128] run.

It is the waterway where the Kha-khra run.
It is the secret way where the path of humans run.
It is the check-post on the way to India [or] Tibet:
There is no other way than this.
The top of the district, Yon-phu, is like a golden curtain spread out.
The lower end of the district, lDom-gzi, is like an elephant."

Thus he spoke.

'di'i dus su 'bum pa yer la tshong 'dus btsugs ste / rgya'i A tsa ra dang bod pa khams pa / mon yul gyi mi thams cad 'dzom pa yin no† // rgyal po* ldan bu la bu gsum yod pa'i che** shos*** mchog ka rdo rje / de'i 'og ma mgon po rdo rje / chung (50a) shos seng ge rdo rje // mchog ka rdo rje yab sras kyi the skor sor gdub bskur ba tsam gyis kyang gnyer kha thub* pa yin no //

*bu **bche ***shog

*thum

[II]

de nas yo* gdung wang ma rnams kyi rgyal rabs bshad pa ni / rgyal mkhar mi zim pa nas pha ma'i lung bstan dang bstun te / las sgo yo gdung la babs pa yin* / de nas 'brug pa kun mkhyen padma dkar po'i slob ma bla ma bkra shis dbang zer ba lung bstan mdzad nas gnang ba yin* / de nas bla ma bkra shis dbang dang yo gdung wang ma yon mchod gnyis kyis* rgya gar rtswa mchog grong gi gnas sgo phye nas / rgya bod / hor khams pa / stod mnga' ris* man chad kyis gnas mjal la 'dzom sa yin / de nas las sgo sa* gzhi thams cad kyi** bdag po yo* gdung wang mas byed pa la / spun so sor ma 'chams ste / yo gdung wang ma / dog shing wang ma ya (50b) ran wang ma / rgyal gdung sman mkhar gyi wang ma de tsho las sgo'i rtsa ba las ma 'chams par / yo gdung wang mas gcen mkhar rgyal po mchog ka rdo rje las* srid tshol nas / dmag bkug ste rgyal gdung sman mkhar la dmag rgyab ste / thams cad gtor brlag gtang nas / las sgo rtsis len te / gcen mkhar ba la las sgo sbyin pa'i rtsa ba 'di yin / mchog ka rdo rje yan chad ni khong gis las sgo mi thob / de nas bu mo btang ste gnyen yang byas* pa yin /

*yong

*. . . pha ma'i lung bsten te / las sgo dang bstun nas yo gdung . . .

*. . . lung bstan / mdzad nas nang ba yin /

*kyi

*rigs

*omitted **kyis

*g.yo

*la

*byes

In his time a market was established at 'Bum-pa-yer and the A-tsa-ra(s) [129] of India, the Tibetans, the Khams-pa(s) and all the people of Mon-yul gathered there.

King lDan-bu had three sons of whom the eldest was mChog-kha rDo-rje,
(50a) below him mGon-po rDo-rje and the youngest Seng-ge rDo-rje. [130] Simply by sending out their thumb-rings mChog-ka rDo-rje, father and sons, could ensure [that] heed [would be paid to their commands].

[II. The Yo-gdung Wang-ma Clan - Introduction]

Now, as for the royal lineage of the Yo-gdung Wang-ma [clan] : In accordance with the prophecy of [their] parents, [members of this clan] came down to the *duar* of Yo-gdung. Then the disciple of the *Omniscient 'Brug-pa* Padma dKar-po [131] called *Bla-ma* bKra-shis-dbang made a prophecy. Then *Bla-ma* bKra-shis-dbang and the [chief of the] Yo-gdung Wang-ma, both priest and patron, opened up the way to the holy shrine of the Indian Kuśinagara [132] so that it is [at present] the meeting place of pilgrims from India and Tibet, Hor and Khams(-pa) and [from all those areas] below sTod mNga'-ris. Then when the Yo-gdung Wang-ma was acting as the owner of all the *duar* lands, the cousin-brothers [within the clan] fell into contention
(50b) with each other and so the Yo-gdung Wang-ma, the Dog-shing Wang-ma, the Ya-ran Wang-ma and the Wang-ma of rGyal-gdung sMan-mkhar – all these [sub-clans] – quarrelled over the question of the *duars.* As a result the Yo-gdung Wang-ma tried to win power from mChog-ka rDo-rje, King of gCen-mkhar and, drawing up his forces, battle was fought at rGyal-gdung sMan-mkhar. When all had been brought to destruction [on the side of the Yo-gdung Wang-ma], [mChog-ka rDo-rje] took over charge of the *duars.* This was the cause of [their] having to give the *duars* to the people of gCen-mkhar. In the times after mChog-ka rDo-rje they did not [re-] gain the *duars.* Then a girl [of the Yo-gdung Wang-ma] was sent [to marry into the ruling family of gCen-mkhar] and so they became kinsmen. [133]

[III]

de nas yo gdung wang ma'i brgyud pa* rim par las sgo thob tshul *. . . wang mas
dang / sa bcad kyi tshams gzhan yang gnas rtswa* mchog grong gi** *rtsa **gis
gnas sgo bye* tshul zur tsam bkod pa ni / sngon thog mar dkar *dbye
rgyud bla ma kun mkhyen ngag dbang nor bu de nyid kyis* mdzad *kyi
pa'i dus su wang ma ge gser rgyal po dang gtso rgan dung bu yin /
(51a) de'i rjes su bla ma bkra shis dbang rgyal kyis mdzad dus wang
ma lnga rigs rgyal po dang gtso rgan gsang gus yin / de'i rjes su bla
ma Om bu kun bzang gis* mdzad dus su wang ma phrong rgyal po *gi
dang gtso rgan la pas yin / rje de'i rjes su bla ma dge slong dmags
'dus kyis* mdzad dus wang ma rin chen rgyal po dang gtso rgan ru *kyi
pa yin / de'i rjes su bla ma 'brug pa kun legs kyis* mdzad dus wang *kyi
ma kun rgyal po dang gtso rgan spen da yin / de'i rjes su bla ma
sku'i skyes dang thugs dam pad dkar* gyis mdzad dus wang ma *thugs gdams dpe dkar
bstan nyi rgyal po dang gtso rgan rdo las yin / de'i rjes su bla ma
sku'i skyes dang dpon slob ngag dbang bkra shis gnyis kyis* mdzad *kyi
dus wang ma chos rgyas dang gtso rgan zo gi yin / de'i rjes su [bla
ma sku'i skyes dang dpon slob ngag dbang bkra shis] skye pa rnam
rgyal 'phrin las gnyis kyis mdzad dus / wang ma nor bu dar rgyas kyi
bu gsum las che ba ko li rgyal po / bar ma smin drug dbang rgyal /
chung ba ka rma dbang rgyal gsum / gtso rgan bkra shis yin / kar rdzi
shes rab 'brug rgyas 'di rnams yin no // de'i rjes su (51b) bla ma
bstan 'dzin rgyal pos* mdzad dus / wang ma ko li gyi bu gsum las *po'i
che ba nor bu rgya mtsho dang / bar ma bkra shis srid thal / chung
ba cu pas gsum / gtso rgan ngag dbang tshe ring de'i bu sprul rgyal
yin / de'i rjes su bla ma sku drung shar phyogs 'dra'os* mdzad dus / *'dra'o'i
wang ma nor bu rgya mtsho'i bu gsum las che ba tshe dbang rgyal
po / bar ma 'brug dbang rgyal / chung ba ngag dbang 'phrin las yin /
gtso rgan bstan 'dzin 'brug rgyal yin / de'i rjes su bla ma bsam grub
dang bla ma . . .[1] / wang ma tshe dbang rgyal po'i* bu gnyis las che *spod
ba 'brug rnam* rgyal dang chung ba rdo rje** bar ma 'brug dbang *snam **sdor rjes
rgyal gyi* bu gnyis las che ba srid thal nor bu dang chung ba bkra *gyis
shis srid thal / gtso rgan bsam* bstan 'dzin yin / de'i rjes su bla ma *sams
. . .[2] /

[III. The Lineage of the Yo-gdung Wangma]

Now, as for a brief account of the lineage of the Yo-gdung Wang-ma [III], the manner in which they gradually acquired *duars* [V], the boundaries of their land-holdings [IV] and also the manner in which the way to the holy shrine of Kuśinagara was opened up [IX]: In previous times, at the beginning, during the period of the dKar-rgyud Bla-ma, the Omniscient Ngag-dbang Nor-bu [134] himself, the Wang-ma was Ge-gser rGyal-po and the *gtso-rgan* [135] was Dung-bu. [The list of the successive incumbents to the positions of (1) *Bla-ma,* (2) *Wang-ma* and (3) *gTso-rgan* may be set out in tabular form as follows:]

		Bla-ma	Wang-ma	Gtso-rgan
	(1)	Ngag-dbang Nor-bu	Ge-gser rGyal-po	Dung-bu
(51a)	(2)	bKra-shis dBang-rgyal	lNga-rigs rGyal-po	gSang-gus [+*Kar-rdzi* [136] Padma-rus-gnam-sa ?]
	(3)	Om-bu Kun-bzang	Phrong rGyal-po	La-pas
	(4)	*dGe-slong* dMags-'dus	Rin-chen rGyal-po	Ru-pa
	(5)	'Brug-pa Kun-legs [137]	Kun rGyal-po	sPen-da
	(6)	*Bla-ma* sKu'i-skyes [138] & Thugs-dam Pad-dkar [139]	bsTan-nyi rGyal-po	rDo-las
	(7)	*Bla-ma* sKu'i-skyes & *dPon-slob* Ngag-dbang bKra-shis	Chos rgyas	Zo-gi
	(8)	? Skyes-pa & rNam-rgyal 'Phrin-las	Nor-bu Dar-rgyas & his sons: 1) Ko-li rGyal-po, 2) sMin-drug dBang-rgyal 3) Ka-rma dBang-rgyal	bKra-shis +*Kar-rdzi* [140] Shes-rab 'Brug-rgyas
(51b)	(9)	bsTan-'dzin rGyal-po	Ko-li & his sons: 1) Nor-bu rGya-mtsho 2) bKra-shis Srid-thal, 3) Cu-pas	Ngag-dbang Tshe-ring & his son: sPrul-rgyal
	(10)	*sKu-drung* Shar-phyogs 'Dra-o	Nor-bu rGya-mtsho & his sons: 1) Tshe-dbang rGyal-po, 2) 'Brug dBang-rgyal 3) Ngag-dbang 'Phrin-las	bsTan-'dzin 'Brug-rgyal
	(11)	bSam-grub & ?	Tshe-dbang rGyal-po & his sons: 1) 'Brug rNam-rgyal, 2) rDo-rje 3) (?) 'Brug dBang-rgyal and his sons: 1) Srid-thal Nor-bu & 2) bKra-shis Srid-thal.	bSam bsTan-'dzin
	(12)	?	?	?

[IV]

de nas rgyal po wang ma bdag gis* yo gdung rgyal mkhar nas (52a) rgyal sa thob tshul 'di'i sa mtshams ni / stod skyi shing rung nas man chad / mu ris sgam phug nas man chad / jo bo sha wang nas man chad / rdo mchod rten* nas tshur / tur pa nas yan chad / nye ring ngang rgyu nas yan chad / ti ki ri rdo phug nas yan chad / dngul gum ba nas man chad / phrang phrang ba lab rtsa nas man chad / 'di rnams thams cad wang ma bdag gi sa yin no //

*gi

*mchor brten

[V]

de nas yang wang ma bdag gi las sgo'i sa mtshams 'di yin bya ba'i 'dzin tho* ła / thog mar sbo ka li sa phyogs kyi stod go ma ri / shar pas ki pa ra / khe sha zu li / nub phyogs ma / khyir zan / hal da sba ri / sbe ta na / za lugs sba ri / sdi ga las sdob li bar gzhung / gling zan / mo long dga' / bar gtsong / sgam ri ka ta / sdo bskor par / khang zu li / wag (52b) zam sba ri / no sgor / shing ging sba ri / shams nyi ya / kho kho ra sdob li stod / phan tsho / shab kha / spu la / yang shar phyogs nye'u li nas man chad / sbar da nas tshur / ga ga ri zan nas* tshur / bzo ya chu nas nub phyogs / brong dgon chu nas nub phyogs / da khu bha nas nub phyogs / dho kha shing nas nub phyogs / bhu la zu li nas shar phyogs / nye ri chu phran nas yar phyogs / shu ka la nas shar phyogs / gho na bar nas sdong gos shar phyogs / bhu li sdob li nas shar phyogs / shu ba pur / bhos sprog chu nas shar* phyogs** / 'di rnams wang ma bdag gi dbang ba'i sa yin / bdag gi rgya'i sa dang ming dang sa mtshams tshang* ngo //

*thog

*omitted

*shis **omitted

*'tshang

[VI]

de nas tha khur gyi rgyud las sngar dang po thog mar tha khur phur gtum pa / de'i bu Ur ka / de'i bu la'u zi / de'i bu mas na / de'i bu kong ga / de'i bu (53a) khong thabs / de'i bu the kha ra / de'i bu sham lung / de'i bu sham za / de'i bu lo khin bar / de'i bu sho na

1. A name seems to be missing here.
2. Names omitted.

[IV. The Boundaries of the Yo-gdung Wang-ma Principality]

(52a) Now, as for the boundaries of the royal lands which I King Wang-ma, from [my] royal castle of Yo-gdung, acquired in such manner: [All the land] 1) below sKyi-shing-rung at the top; 2) below Mu-ris-sgam-phug; (3) below Jo-bo Sha-wang; 4) hitherward from rDo-mchod-rten; 5) above Tur-pa; 6) above Nye-ring-ngang-rgyu; 7) above the stone-cave of Ti-ki-ri; 8) below dNgul-gum-ba; 9) below the top of the pass of Phrang-phrang-ba; – all these [districts] are the land belonging to me, Wang-ma.

[V. The boundaries of the Yo-gdung Wang-ma *duars*]

Now, furthermore, in the inventory (*'dzin-tho*) specifying the boundaries of the *duars* that belong to me, Wang-ma: First of all, Go-mari at the top of the sBo-ka-li district; to the east: Ki-pa-ra [and] Ke-shazu-li; the western [*duars*]: Khyir-zan, Hal-da-sba-ri, sBe-ta-na [and] Zalugs-sba-ri; in the central region between sDi-ga and sDob-li: Gling-zan, Mo-long-dga', [141] Bar-gtsong, sGam-ri-ka-ta, sDo-bskor-par, Khang-zu-li,
(52b) Wag-zam-sba-ri, No-sgor, Shing-ging-sba-ri [and] Shams-nyi-ya; above Khokho-ra-sdob-li: Phan-tsho, Shab-kha [and] sPu-la; furthermore, [all the land] below Nye'u-li [142] in the east; hitherward from sBar-da; hitherward from Ga-ga-ri-zan; westwards from the bZo-ya River; westwards from the Brong-dgon River; westwards from Da-khu-ba; westwards from Dho-kha-shing; eastwards from Bhu-la-zu-li; upwards from the Nye-ri Stream; eastwards from Shu-ka-la; eastwards from Gho-na-bar to (?) sDong-gos; eastwards from Bhu-li-sdob-li; eastwards from Shu-ba-pur and (?) the Bhos-sprog River. These [*duars*] are the land ruled over by me, Wang-ma. My Indian lands, their names and boundaries are complete [in number herein].

[VI. The Lineage of the Tha-khur]

Now, from among the lineage of the Tha-khur: [143] At first in previous times to begin with [there was]: 1) Tha-khur Phur-gtum-pa; 2) his son Ur-ka; 3) his son La'u-zi; 4) his son Mas-na; 5) his son Kong-ga; 6) his son
(53a) Khong-thabs; 7) his son The-ka-ra; 8) his son Sham-lung; 9) his son Sham-za; 10) his son Lo-khin-bar; 11) his sons Sho-na-ram, Por-ya- pha'o-la

ram / por ya pha'o la / tha khur A nas / spun gsum yin* / 'di rnams bdag gi tha khur gyi brgyud yin tshang ngo* //

*spun sum yin wrongly placed after sho na ram.
*'tshang go

[VII]

de nas dang po nye ba li gyi las sgo shor ba'i* rgyu mtshan ni / gdung bsam pa'i* tsha'o shag ci yang rgyas dang / khres phug pa'i tsha bo la na spun gsum gnyis ma cham nas / rgyal sa gcig la rgyal po gnyis mi 'thad* pa 'dug zer nas / sho rgyan rgyab pas la na spun gsum pham nas gsod* dgos pa byung / gsod* pa dang srog nor dngul phor byin nas btang bas / yang dngul phor 'di lam du sbas bzhag nas (53b) log te yo gdung wang ma'i rtsar yong nas las sgo gcig dgos pa 'dug zer nas bslangs* byung / de nas nye ba li de las shor ba yin no //

*bas
*pas
*thad
*bsod
*blongs

[VIII]

sngon dang po chos rje* 'brug pa sku gsar byon pa'i skabs su / rgya gar las sgo med pa'i dus / rgyal po wang ma bdag gi* las sgo las / mo long dga' zer ba'i* las sgo 'di / 'brug pa sku gsar byon pa'i skabs dus su / phud du 'bul ba'i las sgo yin no //

*rjes
*gis
*bas

[IX]

bla ma bkra shis dbang rgyal*gtso byas nas / wang ma lnga** rigs* rgyal** po dang gtso rgan gsang*** gus dang / kar rdzi padma rus gnam sa yin / 'di rnams kyis* gnas rtswa** mchog grong* gi gnas tshol phyin nas brnyed** de / rtswa mchog grong gi gnas kha 'di dag* rnams kyis** thob nas de las tshur mjal ba byung ngo //

*rgyas **nga
*rig **rgyal rgyal ***bsang
*kyi **rtsa
*omitted **brnyen
*bdag **kyi

(54a) gong gsal mdzad bzang rnam dkar rta bdun 'od //
tshul min kunda'i nags ljongs kun bcom zhing //
dge legs padmo'i ze'u brtas pa ni //
gangs can bod* rigs bkra ba khyod kyis** dran //

*omitted **kyi

[and] Tha-khur A-nas who are (?) three brothers. These are all of the lineage of my Tha-khur [subjects, and the list] is complete.

[VII. The Loss of the Nye-ba-li *duar*]

Now, as for the reason for the loss in previous times of the *duar* of Nye-ba-li: The gDung-bsam-pa cousin Shag-ci Yang-rgyas and the Khre-phug cousins, [i.e.] the three La-na brothers – these two [parties] – were not in accord and as it was said to be unfit for two kings [to exist] where there was place for only one king, lots were cast with dice. The three La-na brothers lost and it became necessary to kill them. When they had been killed, [Shag-ci Yang-rgyas?] was given a silver cup, the "life-wealth" [of the La-na brothers?] and sent on his way. As for this silver cup, he left it
(53b) hidden by the road and then returned and came to where the Yo-gdung Wang-ma was. He begged [him] saying: "I want a *duar*." Then Nye-ba-li was lost as a result of it. [144]

[VIII. The Grant of the Mo-long-dga' *duar* to Zhabs-drung I (?)]

In previous times when the new embodiment [145] of the 'Brug-pa Hierarchs came forth, at a time when he did not have any Indian *duars*, it was the *duar* called Mo-long-dga' which I, King Wang-ma, offered as a special donation from among my own *duars* at the time when the new embodiment of the 'Brug-pa Hierarchs came forth.

[IX. The Discovery of Kuśinagara]

With *Bla-ma* bKra-shis dBang-rgyal at the head, the Wang-ma was lNga-rigs rGyal-po, the *gtso-rgan* was gSang-gus and the *kar-rdzi* was Padma-rus-gnam-sa (?) These persons went in search of the holy shrine of Kusinagara and found it. When they had found the holy shrine of Kusinagara, from that time onwards it has been [possible to] see it.

(54a) Remember, you fortunate beings of Tibet,
the Land of Snow,
How the white light of the sun in the good
deeds related above
Conquered the whole of this chaotic forest-
land of jessamines
And so caused the anthers of the lotus of
virtue to swell. [146]

Notes to Text I

1. It is interesting to note that the author here seems quite content to regard the area of Bhutan as part of Tibet (see also f. 5a below). Elsewhere he makes a clear distinction between Bod (Tibet) and Mon (Bhutan).
2. This section is a summary of Tibetan history from its legendary origins in the pre-dynastic period down to the restoration of Buddhism in the middle years of the 11th century. It is a standard account derived apparently from a reading of the *rGyal-rabs gsal-ba'i me-long* by bSod-nams rGyal-mtshan (c. 1373). As it covers well known ground that lies outside the scope of this study, no comments are offered.
3. Tōhoku No. 111.
4. Tōhoku No. 112 (?)
5. dGe-'dun Rin-chen claims this occurred in *'das-lo* 1779: *lcags-bya*, i.e. A.D. 841 (*LCB* II, f. 68a). This is the same date as that given by Bu-ston (f. 130b) for the assassination of Ral-pa-can which is now thought to have happened in c. 836. On the whole tradition of gTsang-ma's sojourn in Bhutan see Aris 1979: 83-114.
6. The *rGyal-rabs gsal-ba'i me-long* is undoubedly the same work as that referred to in note 2 above. I cannot identify the *dPag-bsam ljon-pa*, nor the *rGyal-rabs khug-pa*. My informant *Slob-dpon* Padma-lags insists the latter means 'The Recurrent History' (as in *bskal-pa bar-gyi khug-pa bco-brgyad*, 'the eighteen recurring (lit. 'looped') *kalpas* of the middle'). However, another interpretation would suggest that the phrase refers to all the other written sources used by Ngag-dbang, taking *khug-pa* as 'found' or 'obtained' (see Jaschke's dictionary).
7. No such statement is found in the *rGyal-rabs gsal-ba'i me-long*. However, it is found in the *bShad-mdzod (lho-phyogs mon-gyi rgyal-po rnams / mnga'-bdag rtsang-ma'i gdung-rgyud yin* / f. 85b). The two works probably became confused in Ngag-dbang's memory.
8. This important place seems to be located just south of sKur-stod, but see Aris 1979: 101.
9. LP: */ me zhes-pa grangs gsum-gyi ming / gsum-gyi sgyur-bkod-kyis brtags-shing dpyad-par-bya'o // zhes-pa'i don yin-pa-'dra /* (" 'Fire' [the third of five elements] is the [symbolic] word for number three. The meaning seems to be: 'Examine and enquire by means of a triple calculation (?).' ") This does little to bring out the sense of the quotation or its relevance for the argument. The *bsTan-brtsis* referred to is well known to Bhutanese scholars as one of the principal texts of their astrological tradition. Its author, lHa-dbang Blo-gros of the 'Brug-pa school, was the chief master of *Zhabs-drung* Ngag-dbang rNam-rgyal. The Jesuits Cabral and Cacella met him at lCags-ri in 1627 (*Relação*, f. 9), the place where he composed the *gDan-dus mthun-mong* (*LCB* I, f. 29b).
10. A village situated in the upper reaches of the sPa-gro valley.
11. On these two clans, perhaps tribes (also the Wang-gdung and Mi'i-rgyal-mtshan who similarly claimed descent from gTsang-ma) see Aris 1979: 88, 123.
12. More commonly known as the Pho-chu and Mo-chu ('Male River', 'Female River') which meet at the *rDzong* of sPu-na-kha.
13. This iron-chain suspension bridge was built by Thang-stong rGyal-po (see f. 85 of his *rnam-thar* where the place is called Bag-grong). The bridge is no longer standing but a pile of the original chains is still to be found on the river-bank.
14. Kho-dwangs-kha and sNgan-lung are sub-districts of Shar. rTa-li, sBu-li and sTung-la-sbi are villages in the Kheng district. Zhong-dkar (or -sgar) lies due east of Kheng. Mol-ba-lung (-pa) must be a sub-district of gZhong-sgar. Up to this point in the story Ngag-dbang has been attempting to harmonise the tradition of gTsang-ma's arrival in Bhutan by way of sPa-gro with the other tradition that claimed he came by way of lHo-brag (Aris 1979: 87). Having now arrived in eastern Bhutan, the story picks up the oral traditions relating to gTsang-ma peculiar to this area of the country. From here onwards the names of most of the villages and districts mentioned in the text remain unidentified. I never had occasion to visit this part of the country and my informants from this area were generally very vague about locations. It is hoped that this serious gap will be filled at some future date.
15. The God of Heaven is surely 'O-de Gung-rgyal (see ff. 32a, 33b, 36a below and Aris 1979: 126-7). *LCB* II (f. 68b) provides a synopsis of the story; it has *dmod-btsugs* for *dmod-bor*.
16. lCang-bu (loc. cit.)
17. Ku-ri'i La (loc. cit.)
18. 'Jam-mkhar (loc. cit.) For the folk etymology of this name see bSod-nams bZang-po's oral account in Aris 1979: 92.
19. Mu-tang-mkhar (loc. cit.)
20. Wang-seng (loc. cit.)

21. See Aris 1979: 60-82.
22. The three villages (*yul gsum*) of La-'og, in the vicinity of rTa-wang rDzong, are: Shar-tsho, bSe-ru and lHa'u (*Vaiḍūrya Ser-po*, p. 396). On the Jo-bo clan of La-'og Yul-gsum, see ff. 28b-31b below.
23. Glang Dar-ma.
24. *A-mi* Don-grub (*LCB* II, loc. cit.)
25. In the Gangtok recension of the ***Rlangs po-ti bse-ru*** which recounts the ancestral legends of the Rlangs clan, Byang-chub 'Dre-bkol is the principal hero of the story and is presented as the incarnation, not the disciple, of Padmasambhava (Stein 1962: 79, 84). The tradition which claimed him as the forebear of Don-grub-rgyal may have arisen from the fact that they share the same, rather unusual title of *A-mi* (or *A-mes*) which appears to mean *yogin* (Stein 1959a: 404-5 note 33). Another member of the Rlangs clan who has legendary associations with Bhutan is dPal-gyi Seng-ge, considered one of the twenty-four disciples of Padmasambhava. dPal-gyi Seng-ge is said to have received the initiation of Vajrakīla from the Guru at the shrine of sTag-tshang in sPa-gro. His remains were entombed in a large stūpa inside a cave which can still be seen there today. The *gnas-yig* of sTag-tshang refers to the tomb as *sku-gdung ril-por bzhugs-pa'i mchod-rten* ("the stūpa where his entire body remains"). Kong-sprul, however, claims in his *gTer-rnam* (f. 22b) that it was a quite different person of the same name and clan who is associated with sTag-tshang, namely Rlangs dPal-gyi Seng-ge 'the Later' (*phyi-ma*). This person was the son of Byang-chub 'Dre-bkol. No doubt the story appears also in the ***Rlangs po-ti bse-ru*** applied to one or other of the dPal-gyi Seng-ge. I do not have access to this work at present but according to Stein (1962: 98) its account of dPal-gyi Seng-ge 'the Earlier' is closely modelled on that of Byang-chub 'Dre-bkol himself (or vice versa).
26. Byar-po is a Tibetan district some miles to the north-east of Bhutan; it appears as Byar in Ferrari (1958: 51, 127 note 261) and as Bya-yul in Wylie (1962:93, 174 note 552). The Bya clan associated with this district appear to have had a connection with the ancient seat of royal power in Yar-lung (*Blue Annals*, Vol. *BA* f. 11b), a fact which Haarh (1969: 210-11) has made much of. The leaders of the clan were generally appointed governors not only of Bya-yul but of all the surrounding districts from the time of Sa-skya rule down to at least the time of Phag-mo-gru-pa rule in Tibet (*Blue Annals*, Vol. *BA* ff. 11b-14a). Don-grub-rgyal in our text, if he is an historical figure at all, may perhaps have come from this clan, not the Rlangs. His title of *A-mi* is also applied to one of the members of the clan, *A-mi* Bya-nag Chen-po (Wylie op. cit., 94 and *Blue Annals*, Vol. *BA*, f. 12a). One is also tempted to look for a connection between the Byar clan of eastern Bhutan (see below) and the Bya clan of Bya-yul (or Byar, Byar-po). Unless, however, the link were derived merely from a borrowing of a name, it is difficult to imagine how a single clan structure could have cut across the distinct ethnic and linguistic identities of the two people.
27. The Phag-mo-gru-pa rulers had of course long disappeared by the time this work was written in 1728. The statement therefore derives from misapplied hindsight on the part of the author, or else it appears as a quotation from an earlier textual source written at the time of Phag-mo-gru-pa supremacy.
28. bSod-nams dPal-bskyed (*LCB* II, f. 68a).
29. It may be noted that Khri-mi ('the Enthroned') lHa'i-dbang-phyug, who appears to be the eldest son, goes off to seek his fortune while his younger brother, gCes-bu ('the Beloved Son') mThong-legs-btsun, remains with his father and succeeds him. In the next generation, however, it is the eldest of three sons who succeeds while the younger two fulfill their destinies elsewhere. As Allen (1976:267) has pointed out, the principle of primogeniture does not provide the norm for all periods and areas in the Bodic-speaking world.
30. See ff. 28b-31b below.
31. See f. 20a and Aris 1979: 100-1, 138.
32. This is quite a common theme in histories dealing with the dynastic period in Tibet.
33. This is the general name for western Tibet. It should be written sTod mNga'-ris. I can find no passage in any Tibetan history to corroborate the tradition that the followers of 'Od-srung were dispersed to Bhutan.
34. Or perhaps Was-chur-thum Nang-mkhar, 'The Inner Castle of Was-chur-thum' (cf. Be-tsha Nang-mkhar, f. 17a below).
35. The pairing of these names may be compared to those below of Nyi-ma Che-rigs / Chung-rigs, Glang-khyim / Breng-khyim (and Zer-khyim?), Be-mi / Sa-ri, Kha-gling Phyi-'khor / Nang-'khor, Las-pa / Los-pa and Srin-mi / rGyun-mi. (See also the Addendum [I] (f. 48b) for further mention of the kings of sNga-tshang and Phyi-tshang.)

36. I would identify this figure with King Dar-'jam of sNga-tshang, one of the first rulers of eastern Bhutan to submit to the 'Brug-pa authorities (*Lo-rgyus*, f. 10a). He was among the group of rulers that took the oath of allegiance at the conclusion of the campaign (op. cit., f. 21b). His sons may well have been alive at the time when the *rGyal-rigs* was composed.
37. This must be King sTong-ldan (or sTobs-ldan) of rTseng-mi, cousin to Dar-'jam, another supporter of the 'Brug-pa who took the oath of allegiance (*Lo-rgyus*, ff. 12a, 20a, 21b).
38. This is King Zla'u-la of Phyi-tshang of which Mong-sgar, his capital, must be a part (*Lo-rgyus*, ff. 10a, 21b and the next note). *Zla'u* is the common Bhutanese contraction of *Zla-ba*, 'moon'.
39. "King dBang-grags of the royal family of Phyi-tshang Mong-sgar, of great honour and bravery and of noble ancestry", according to the colophon (f.47a) where he is listed among those who requested the composition of the *rGyal-rigs*.
40. "rGyal-po of the royal family of Phyi-tshang sKya-sa-mkhar, of extensive knowledge and understanding, skilled in rhetoric" (f. 47a below), another of those who requested Ngag-dbang to write the *rGyal-rigs*.
41. Cf. *Lo-rgyus*, f. 17b and f. 36b below ("the mountain of Wang-seng").
42. According to the Addendum I (f. 49a), Khun-dang (sic) and Thum-bi (sic) were the fathers, not the sons, of gSer-gdung and lDan-bu (sic) respectively.
43. bKra-shis-sgang is actually the name of the fort built much later at Beng-mkhar by *sKu-drung* Pad-dkar Chos-'phel (*Lo-rgyus*, ff. 17a, 19b, 22a).
44. Grong-stod and Grong-smad appear to be hamlets at Beng-mkhar. A king of Grong-stod appears in the *Lo-rgyus*, his name spelt Slang-sga (f. 12b), Glang-nga (f.16a) and lHa-lnga (f. 22a).
45. The Addendum [I] (f. 49a) suggests that King lDan-bu (sic) gained power at gCen-mkhar by displacing the son-in-law (from the Byar clan) of King sTong-rab, the latter having apparently died without issue. sTong-rab is presented here as lDan-bu's cousin (see f. 20b below).
46. I translate *bu-brgyud* tentatively as 'descendants', but the meaning may be simply 'sons'. The Addendum [I] (ff. 49a-50a) claims that mChog-ka rDorje (sic), mGon-po rDo-rje and Seng-ge rDo-rje were the sons of lDan-bu.
47. The rDo-rong Rwa-dza here is without doubt the Rāja of Darrang, a tributary chief of the Ahom kings. It is not clear in Devi's study (1968: 197) whether the office existed prior to 1616 when a certain Bali Narayan was appointed, Darrang having just been reclaimed from Mogul expansion in this area. Basing her account on an earlier British study by Wade, she maintains that soon after 1616 an unsuccessful Bhutanese campaign was launched to try and regain control of lands lost to the Darrang Rāja. The Bhutanese rulers are oddly referred to as the "Deva-Dharma Rajas", surely an allusion to the *Zhabs-drung* and *sDe-srid*, institutions which had not yet been properly established. *Zhabs-drung* Ngag-dbang rNam-rgyal himself arrived as a refugee only in 1616. On later relations between the Darrang Raja and the Bhutanese see Bhuyan (1933:123, 181), Devi (1968:200-209) and Gait (1926:207).
48. On Cho-ka rDo-rje's annexation of certain *duars* belonging to the Yo-gdung Wang-ma clan, see the Addendum [II] (f.50b).
49. One of these descendants, King Sangs-rgyal (-rgyas)-po of gCen-mkhar, was killed during the 'Brug-pa campaign (*Lo-rgyus*, ff. 15a, 16a).
50. One of the two (or in some records, three) *duars* that are situated in the Darrang district is that of Khaling, spelt Kulling in Pemberton (1839:15) and Killing in Devi (1968:205). The *duar* must have taken its name from that of the village of Kha-gling whose ruler, rGyas-mtsho, is claimed here to have annexed it.
51. This is presumably King bDe-ba of Kha-gling. The account of his dispute with a certain 'Brug-rgyal forms the introduction to the story of the 'Brug-pa campaign (*Lo-rgyus*, ff. 2a-b, 11b, 16b).
52. "*lHa-btsun* Ngag-dbang Phun-tshogs of the royal family of Kha-gling, upholder of the *Piṭaka* and the Three Precepts, unimpaired as to knowledge", one of those that requested the composition of the *rGyal-rigs* (f. 47a below).
53. Ba-man (lit. 'non-cow') is the name for the mithun, here used as somebody's personal name.
54. King Tshe-ring of 'Dom-mkhar (sic) was the enemy of his cousin, King Pho-brang of bTsan-mkhar (*Lo-rgyus*, f.15b).
55. Pho-brang A-chi, King of bTsan-mkhar (*Lo-rgyus*, ff. 15a-16b) is also described as king of rKang-lung (f. 12a). King Chang-lo-dpal of Kha-gling and he were "father and son" (*pha-spad*, f. 16b), apparently only in a figurative sense.

56. This person is not to be confused with *Bla-ma* Nag-seng of Me-rag (*Lo-rgyus*, ff. 12a, 17b-18a). He and King Pho-brang were allies of the dGa'-ldan-pa (= dGe-lugs-pa).
57. It is not possible to say whether *rJe* here is a clan name or a title (see Aris 1979: 100).
58. On the recalcitrant king of Gung-gdung see the *Lo-rgyus*, ff. 22b, 24a.
59. On the king of sTong-phu, one of the first rulers to be defeated by the 'Brug-pa campaign, see the *Lo-rgyus*, ff. 9b, 24a.
60. See f. 36a below.
61. Cf. the Addendum [I] (f. 49a) and note 45 above.
62. TD: *mkhar-dung* (sic) *zer-bar rdzong-shul yod / de'i mi-rnams bros-zur rta-dbang phyogs-su sa bcags* [=bcas]*-pas ming-yang mkhar-dung zer-gyi-'dug* / ("There is a ruined fort at the place called mKhar-dung. The people of that place fled secretly (?) and, settling in the area of rTa-dbang, (their new home) is also called mKhar-dung.")
63. LP: / *zlo-ni 'gran-pa'i don yin-pas* / ("*zlo* has the sense of *'gran-pa*, 'to contend, vie'.")
64. See the Glossary under *bran(-pa)*.
65. The words (*g.*)*yas*, *stung* and *wang* are Tsangla for *zo-ba* ('trough, pail'), *gzeb(-ma)* (a box or pannier made of split cane) and *sa-dong* ('earth pit') in the western Bhutanese dialects (and Tibetan?). The syntax makes use of the common construction whereby a noun may be classified by a succeeding noun for the sake of clarity or rhetoric (e.g. *pho-brang gzhal-yas-khang*). See also *snod-yas* and *snod-stung* below (f. 22b). The device is used with effect here in order to establish the etymology of the clan names Yas-sde, sTung-sde and Wang-ma. The legend may be compared to that of 'Od-srungs in, for instance, the *rGyal-rabs gsal-ba'i me-long*, f. 95a.
66. The names of the three half-brothers carry obvious allusions to those of the Tibetan kings *Khri* Srong-lde-brtsan (b. 742) and *Khri* gTsug-lde-brtsan (b. 805).
67. For a quite different and more authentic picture of the origins of these rulers, see the passages quoted from the histories of 'Gos Lo-tsa-ba and dPa'-bo gTsug-lag in Aris 1979: 101-2.
68. "*Chos-mdzad* Lug-dkar of the royal family of the Yas-sde [clan] of Phong-mi, skilled in the dexterous use of magical means" (f. 47a-b below), one of those who requested the composition of the *rGyal-rigs*.
69. See Aris 1979: 106.
70. The Kha-nag ('Black-Mouths') are the Aka tribals of the Kameng district of Arunachal. Kennedy 1914 (quoted in Elwin 1959: 438 note 1) derives the word Aka, meaning 'painted', from their custom of decorating their faces with a mixture of pine-resin and charcoal. The Kha-dkar ('White-Mouths') are still unidentified. Both are termed Glo-pa (or Klo-pa), a vague term applied to all the tribals of this region. The Kha-khra ('Striped-Mouths') are mentioned on f. 49b below in the Addendum [I]. They also remain unidentified. Elsewhere the term Kha-khra is used to signify the early inhabitants of Bhutan itself (Aris 1976:628 note 66). All the terms carry a strong pejorative tone (LP: *sems-can bsad-pa dge-bar rtsi-mkhan klo kha-dkar kha-nag yin-'dug* / "The Klo Kha-dkar and [Klo] Kha-nag are people who consider it a virtue to kill sentient beings." Note also *kla-klo* = 'barbarian'.) The Klo-pa best known to the Tibetans are those living south of Kong-po where Thang-stong rGyal-po consecrated 'a *stūpa* to suppress the *Klo*' (*Klo kha-gnon-gyi . . . mchod-rten*, f. 120a of his biography. See also ff. 72a-76b on his activities among the Klo-pa). These are divided into the same three groups mentioned above. (Wylie 1962: 178 note 583).
71. 'Tembang' of the maps, five miles east of Dirang Dzong. The Them-spang people can probably be identified with the 'Themongs' with whom the Sherdukpens traditionally intermarried. The legend recounting how this custom came to an end is given in Paul 1958:24-25.
72. For the records of the Yo-gdung Wang-ma clan see the Addendum [I – IX] (ff. 48b-53b below).
73. See f. 14a above.
74. Cf. *lha'i khams-pa*, f. 14a above.
75. This must surely have been a disappointment to Jo-bo A-bzang, King of sDe-rang (Dirang), who was among those who encouraged the composition of this work (see f. 47b below). On Padma Gling-pa's meeting with a King of Dirang see Aris 1979: 106
76. This name does not look right. However, as a member of the sTung-sde clan of Bu-ri-gyang-phu (see f. 27a above), the lady's marriage to the hereditary chief of the Jo-bo clan is a clear example of how political affiliations could be determined, and indeed sought, through marriage alliances.
77. TD: *ber-mkhar zer-ba-de be-mkhar zer-gyin-yod / rgyal-ba tshangs-dbyangs rgya-mtsho'ang de-la 'khrungs* / ("The place called Ber-mkhar is now called Be-mkhar. *rGyal-ba* Tshangs-dbyangs rGya-mtsho [6th Dalai Lama, 1683-? 1706] was even born there,") See Aris 1979: 162-3.

78. Evidence for the activity in this area of the great bridge-building saint Thang-stong rGyal-po (1385-1464) is found in his standard biography by 'Gyur-med bDe-chen. Although it does not seem to contain an account of his visit, the area of Shar-mon is prophecied on f.41a to be one of the districts where he would be active. Again at the end of the work (f. 170a) we read that sKyabs-pa bZang-po, his great-nephew (?), carried on the saint's work in Shar-mon. The legend recounted here is still current and has been recorded by Sarkar (1975:32) who adds the information that the household of Jo-bo Dar-rgyas in Ber-mkhar is known as Bu-bdun ('Seven Sons').
79. This is the 2nd Dalai Lama (1475-1542).
80. TD: *shar stag-lung zer-ba-la deng-sang-gi bar-yang rdzong-dpon-re rta-dbang grwa-tshang-nas bskos-kyi-yod* / ("Even at present a *rdzong-dpon* is appointed by the monastic college of rTa-dbang [to control the monastery/fort] called Shar sTag-lung.") This is the 'Talung Dzong' of the maps, a few miles north-east of Kalaktang in the Kameng Frontier Division. "From there [sTag-lung] he went to Assam and met the king. The king received him cordially, promised him all help and donated him land in the plains in Odalguri and Amratola areas." (Sarkar 1975: 34)
81. bKra-shis rTse-gling dGon-pa in Sag-stengs and dGa'-ldan rTse-gling dGon-pa in Me-rag (loc. cit.). bsTan-pa'i sGron-me is said to have died in the latter place at the age of ninety-nine.
82. For the legend of this monastery's foundations, see Sarkar (op. cit., 33) where it is spelt 'Ariakdun' and is said to be located half a mile from lHa'u, eight miles east of rTa-dbang.
83. Sarkar (op. cit., 35-41) provides short sketches of the lives of nine incarnations of bsTan-pa'i sGron-me who have succeeded each other up to the present day. Most important of these, from the point of view of the present study, was the fourth in the line, 'Lote Gyatso', who can be identified with the *Me-rag Bla-ma* Nag-seng who played such an important role on the dGe-lugs-pa side during the war with the 'Brug-pa authorities of western Bhutan (*Lo-rgyus*, ff. 12a, 17b-18b).
84. TD: A'u-dung
85. TD: Byang-mkhar
86. TD: Sha-nu
87. Jo-bo Sangs-rgyas 'Od-zer of La-'og Yul-gsum, who is mentioned on f. 95b of Padma Gling-pa's autobiography, must have been a contemporary or near contemporary of these seven sons.
88. The content and significance of this section have been discussed at some length in Aris 1979: 115-39. Notes 89 to 99 below deal with a few points which remain untreated in that discussion.
89. Grong-mo-che may simply mean "the great settlement" (of Yar-lung). Cf. *yul-sde che-ba*, f. 33b below.
90. I cannot identify the fruit referred to here. Notice how the fruit become cowrie shells (*'gron-bu*) in the variant tradition of gZhong-sgar and gDung-bsam (f. 39b below) and dice (*sho*) in the modern version of bSod-nams bZang-po (Aris 1979:133).
91. The same patch of grass was pointed out to me by my porters when I crossed the Zhang-ma'i La pass between sTang and U-ra in 1970.
92. This does not accord with the *rGyal-rabs gsal-ba'i* me-long (ff. 98b-99a) where we read that the *Yar-lung Jo-bo* descended from 'O-lde (brother of dPal-lde) through his son Khri-chung who settled at Yar-lung.
93. Unidentified in the Tibetan records.
94. LP informs me that "the three divisions (?) of Kheng" (Kheng-rigs rNam-gsum) are those of Phyi-'khor, Nang-'khor and mTha'-ma-phyogs-'khor (sp ?).
95. This place, visited by Padma Gling-pa (f. 62a of his autobiography), is probably crucial to the *gDung* complex discussed in Aris 1979: 115-39. According to *Slob-dpon* Padma-lags, just as the Klo-pa tribals in the vicinity of the holy shrine of Tsa-ri are considered by Tibetans to be the 'retinue' (*'khor-ba*) of the goddess Zhing-skyong dBang-mo, so also are the Dag-pa people of eastern Bhutan regarded as the retinue of Jo-mo Re-ma-ti who has her shrine at this place called gDung-mtsho ('Origin Lake'). The mithun (*ba-man*) is said to be the animal specially associated with this goddess and the Dag-pa observe a sacred trust to look after it on her behalf. They have to invoke her through various rituals when they are engaged in working with mithuns. The sacred character of the mithun is celebrated by all the tribal peoples of Arunachal and Nagaland and no doubt the beliefs of the Dag-pa (and Mon-pa ?) in this respect derive from an early pre-Buddhist form of mithun-worship. 'Jigs-med Gling-pa provides a very interesting account of the mythological origins of the mithun and the hybrid *rgya-tsha* in Chapter 3 of his *gTam-tshogs* (f. 32b).

96. Unlike the last place, this is probably a mythical land (Stein 1959b:55). From rMu-yul the god returns again to the eastern marches of Bhutan. Gangs-ri dKar-po ('The White Snow Mountain') is not identifiable but the mountain of Wang-seng is surely related to Wang-ser-khum-pa/-khung-pa (f. 18a above and *Lo-rgyus*, f. 17b). One would like to see a connection too with 'Jumu Wang-sing' (= ? *Jo-mo* Wang-seng) who is the meat-eating, blood-drinking 'god of the forests' for the Sherdukpen people. Elwin (1958:243) records the myth which tells how this god had an argument with 'Konchosum' (the *Triratna* personified) over the sacrifices owed to him(her ?) by the Jiji, the ancient non-Buddhist priest of the Sherdukpen. A compromise was reached.

97. LP kindly provided the correct reading of this phrase from f. 5b line 2 of his copy of the MS.

98. This should perhaps be Phyang-khos, the 'uncle' being his adoptive father, the batchelor of Phyang-khos.

99. Cf. f. 22a above.

100. The *rGyal-rabs gsal-ba'i me-long,* which is the source for this story, has *spyi'i tha-ba-la / dgos-su shol mi-bcog* (f. 95a). The meaning of *shol* here is quite uncertain, and my emendation of *thong-pa* to *thod-pa* in the text is most tentative.

101. The phrase *g.yang-grog za-nas tshug ma-thub-par* is also problematic. LP suggests that *dogs-pa za-nas sdod ma-tshugs-par* ("being unable to stay, feeling fear") might be a better reading.

102. See Aris 1979: 139.

103. See *ibid.* 118-19. The *Chos-'khor dpon-po* is almost the only one of the hereditary offices mentioned in this section known from other sources and still remembered today in local traditions.

104. The *dPon-chen Zhal-ngo* of Ku-ri-lung may perhaps have included lHa-bu-dar, the *dPon-po* of Rag-sa, and Dar-ma, the *dPon-chen* of sKyi-gling (*Lo-rgyus,* f. 8b).

105. There is probably a connection between the name of this clan and that of the Kheng district which adjoins gZhong-sgar.

106. The following classificatory schema of the Tibetan clans (or tribes) appears to be a summary of Chapter 4(2) of the *bShad-mdzod* (ff. 90b-92a), entitled *'Og-ma 'bangs-kyi mi-rabs bshad-pa'i le'u* ("The Chapter which Explains the Generations of Subjects Beneath [the Rulers]"), a title which Ngag-dbang seems to have borrowed for this section of the *rGyal-rigs.* Allowing for variants, the names which follow have therefore been corrected in order to conform to those found in the *bShad-mdzod.* The structure and content of the schema in its basic form have been examined by Tucci (1949: 713-17), Stein (1959b: passim) and Haarh (1969:279-88). The schema of the *bShad-mdzod* itself has been studied by E. Gene Smith in his Appendix I to Lokesh Chandra's edition of that work ('The tribal structure of the world as outlined in the *Bsad mdzod yid bzhin nor bu*').

107. As in the case of the ruling clans in eastern Bhutan (the Jo-bo, rJe, Byar, Yas-sde, sTung-sde and Wang-ma), none of these names are remembered today.

108. See Aris 1979: 125-6.

109. LP informs me that the 'Ten Signs' are the product of yogic attainment in the *Mahāmudra* system of meditation. They divide into the following groups: (A) 'Five external signs manifested after gaining control of the *prāṇa* of the five elements' (*phyi-rol-du 'byung-ba lnga'i rlung zin-pas rtags lnga*) consisting of (1) 'smoke, by controlling the earth-*prāṇa*' (*sa-rlung zin-pas du-ba*); (2) 'mirage, by controlling the water-*prāṇa*' (*chu-rlung zin-pas smig-rgyu*); (3) 'burning, by controlling the fire-*prāṇa*' (*me-rlung zin-pas me-khyer*); (4) 'a lamp, by controlling the wind-*prāṇa*' (*rlung-gi rlung zin-pas mar-me*); and (5) 'a clear, cloudless sky, by controlling the sky-*prāṇa* (*nam-mkha'i rlung zin-pas sprin-med nam-mkha' dwangs-pa*). (B) 'Five special signs of fixedness' (*brtan-pa khyad-par-gyi rtags lnga*) consisting of: (1) 'sight of the earth's golden surface' (*gser-gyi sa-gzhi mthong-ba*); (2) 'silver-like clarity of body' (*lus dngul-bzhin dwangs*); (3) 'great strength and speed' (*stobs che-zhing 'gro-ba mgyogs*); (4) 'non-perception of physical happiness' (*lus bde-zhing yod-pa mi-tshor*); and 'sight of the *Tathāgatas'* heaven and the realms of the six classes of beings' (*de-bzhin-gshegs-pa'i zhing dang rigs-drug-gi gnas mthong-ba*).

110. This is another numerical category relating to certain yogic attainments. LP, however, was unable to supply a complete list in this case.

111. See f. 19b above.

112. See f. 18a above.

113. See f. 18a above.

114. The odd phrase *stong-sde'i ru-dar* (lit. 'wing-banners of the thousand-districts') is found in the *bShad-mdzod* (ff. 253b, 261b). Gene Smith translates it as 'rhetoric', though it is not clear how the term has acquired this figurative sense. LP takes the whole phrase in

which it appears quite literally and suggests either 'skilled in the means of spreading forth many military divisions' (*dmag-gi sde mang-po 'phel-ba'i thabs-la mkhas-pa'i*) or else 'skilled in the experience of causing many companies (?) of one's own side to flourish and prosper' (*rang-phyogs-gi sde-tshan mang-po dar-zhing rgyas-pa'i byus-la mkhas-pa'i*).

115. See f. 26b above.
116. See f. 29a above.
117. Unidentified, but perhaps related to the *mi-chos gtsang-ma bcu-drug* ('Sixteen Pure Rules of Human Conduct'). See *LCB* I, f. 103a , also Note 34 to Text III below.
118. 'Pacifying, enriching, overpowering and destroying' (*zhi rgyas dbang drag*).
119. The term *'phrul-thabs* seems to refer in this text to mechanical devices used in warfare, whose operation is linked to the activity of the guardian divinities.
120. The *bShad-mdzod* (f. 99b) describes the district of Gru-shul, situated just beyond the north-eastern corner of Bhutan, as "the meeting-place of India, Tibet and Mon, [these] three" (*rgya bod mon gsum-gyi mdun* [= 'dun]*-sa*). It seems practically certain that Ngag-dbang was familiar with the *bShad-mdzod*. (Cf. notes 7, 106 and 114 above.)
121. It is not known when the Addendum was composed, who its author really was or when it was appended to the manuscript of the *rGyal-rigs* from which the present copy was made. The author refers to himself as "I, Wang-ma" (f. 52a-b) or "I, King Wang-ma" (ff. 51b, 53b). It can be assumed that he was the hereditary ruler of the Wang-ma clan which was introduced above (ff. 22b, 23b, 27a-28b) in a manner that accords very little with the information provided here. Until the geographical picture becomes clearer the lines between the two texts will remain obscure and muddled. The problem is further exacerbated by the fact that the author of the Addendum seems to have been barely literate, the style is crude and several ambiguities remain unsolved. Moreover, since the work was aimed at a local audience that was perfectly familiar with local institutions and customs, no explanation of these is given and we are left to guess their nature as best we can.
122. bZhi-khri bTsan-po is a fictitious name and the list of Tibetan kings in which it appears is muddled in the extreme. However, because the name precedes that of *Khri* Ral-pa-can in the list, we may conjecture that the person referred to is actually *lHa-sras* gTsang-ma, brother of Ral-pa-can, whom Ngag-dbang and all his informants claimed to be the true ancestor of the Bhutanese clans.
123. All these 'kings' have been introduced above in the *rGyal-rigs* proper, with the exception of those of Srin-mi/rGyun-mi. This is the only reference to the place I can find. The name is comparable to all the other 'paired' names in this area (see note 35 above) and particularly to 'Senjithongji', the local name of the 'Sherdukpen' people of Kameng.
124. See f. 18a-b above.
125. *mi-thi* should perhaps be corrected to *mig-mthong* (lit. 'eye-sight'), a vague measurement of distance used in Bhutan. See for instance the autobiography of Padma Gling-pa, ff. 62b-63a.
126. I.e. "of the Byar clan".
127. See ff. 20b-21a above.
128. Perhaps *khwa-ta*, 'crow' or 'raven'.
129. Sanskrit *ācārya* ('teacher'), a term usually applied to the clown dressed as an Indian who performs during festivals of sacred dance, but here applied to Indians in general.
130. See f. 18b above.
131. On Padma dKar-po (1527-92), the greatest scholar of the 'Brug-pa school, see Aris 1979: 205-6.
132. This is the temple of Hajo near Gauhati in Assam. See *ibid.* 112-14.
133. As a result of this arrangement, the Yo-gdung Wang-ma seem to have regained control of their *duars*. See [V] below.
134. I.e. Padma dKar-po.
135. Village headmen are still called *gtso-rgan* in eastern Bhutan.
136. See [IX] below.
137. The only evidence that 'Brug-pa Kun-legs (1455-1529) was ever active in this part of the country is found in the passage from the *rnam-thar* of Kun-dga' rGyal-mtshan quoted in Note 9 to the *rGyal-rigs*.
138. The name means 'the re-incarnated lama'. He may have been sNyan-grags (or Rin-chen) dPal-bzang of sDing-po-che. See Note 10 to the *rGyal-rigs*.
139. This person is the same as the Thub-brtan Pad-dkar mentioned in the *Lo-rgyus* (f. 5a-b), a contemporary of *Zhabs-drung* Ngag-dbang rNam-rgyal who had control of certain 'Brug-pa monasteries in eastern Bhutan.

140. The *kar-rdzi* may have been the official who had charge of the ruler's herds of cattle (*rdzi-bo* = 'herdsman').
141. See [VIII] below.
142. See [VII] below.
143. *Thakur* ('Lord') is an honorific used in addressing certain people of the Brahmin caste in Bengal. It is not clear who the Thakur here referred to are. Their names should eventually help to identify them with one of the Indian border peoples of this area.
144. The sense of this whole passage is ambiguous and the translation remains tentative.
145. LP suggests this might be *Zhabs-drung* Ngag-dbang rNam-rgyal.
146. This elegant verse could not have been written by the same person who composed the Addendum.

TEXT II

(Ia) *dPal 'brug par lung lha'i gdung brgyud kyis* bstan pa'i ring lugs* / lho mon kha bzhi las nyi ma shar phyogs su byung zhing* rgyas pa'i lo rgyus** gsal ba'i me long bzhugs so //*[1] *kyi *lug *omitted **rgyud

(Ib) na mo wa gindra An na dhā dza ya //

'dzam gling yangs pa'i sa chen la chos srid stobs kyis* 'khor los** bsgyur* ba'i chos kyi rgyal po Ngag-dbang rNam-rgyal ba la / snying nas gus pa'i spyi bos* phyag bgyi'o // de'i bstan pa'i ring lugs gangs can lho phyogs kyi nyi ma shar phyogs su byung ba'i tshul cung zad* brjod par bya'o // de yang sngon shar phyogs kyi rgyal khams (2a) 'dir / sde srid chen po gtsang pas mnga' 'bangs btsugs nas dbang sgyur zhing yod pa'i skabs la / ri bo dga' ldan pa'i phyag* mdzod sde pa nang so** A bos g.yo 'phrul sgyu ma'i 'khrul 'khor du ma shams nas / byang mtsho kha sngon mo nas (sog po)[2] rgyal po rda las bha dur gyi dmag bkug* nas / sde srid chen po gtsang pa* phab rgyal** srid 'phrog te mnga' 'bangs thams cad la dbang sgyur nas yod pa'i skabs der / kha ling (2b) rgyal po bde ba dang / 'brug rgyal gnyis rgya'i las sgo'i sa cha dang mnga' 'bangs kyi rtsa ba las ma cham par / ri bo dga' ldan pa'i sde srid la zhu bar phyin pas / lha sa gzhung nas mi sna dpon chen gnyis gnang byung ba khrid nas kha ling du sleb pa dang / mi sna dpon chen gnyis kyi drung du kha ling rgyal po bde ba dang / 'brug rgyal gnyis kyi tshig bden rdzun sdur bas / de dus rgya bod dang lho mon rnams phan* tshun cher ma phrad cing brda ma mjal* ba'i gshis** kyis byung khungs kyi lo rgyus* ji ltar bshad kyang / mi sna dpon po gnyis kyis* mon pa'i** skad ma go bar / bod skad shes pa'i lo tsa*** ba* dgos zer ba bzhin / 'brug rgyal gyi ngos nas bod kyi 'brug pa'i bla ma thub bstan pad dkar gyi bu bla ma rnam* sras rdo rje / bde ba'i phyogs nas la 'og yul gsum gyi lta* wang bla ma** chos dbyings rgya mtsho gnyis kyis lo tsa byas nas / bden rdzun khru sbyangs (3a) zhib par sdur bas / tshig bden rdzun 'dra ba yin 'dug kyang / bod pa dang mon pa khyad par gyi skad kyi sgyur stabs snyan 'jebs dang bstun / 'brug rgyal gyi ngos nas gsal dwangs* ngos khungs chod pa'i tshig don bshad byung ba dang / mi sna dpon po gnyis kyang yid mgu ba lta bu sems la bsam pa'i rnam pa byung ba dang / rgyal po bde ba yid ma rangs pa'i phra dog gis kun blangs te / g.yo 'khrul gyi phra ma sems kyis* bshams nas / g.yo thabs kyi sgo nas mi sna dpon po gnyis la phra ma zhu ba la / khyed dga' ldan pho brang gnam dga' ldan sa dga' ldan gyi dpon po yin kyang / khyed la ni bsnyen bkur shabs tog dang tshogs chang drang mkhan mi gcig

Marginal notes: *kyi **lo; *sgyur; *bo'i; *bzad; *phyags **nag song; *bkun; *omitted **sral; *phun; *'jal **zhis; *rgyud; *kyi **po'i ***tsa'i; *omitted; *rnams; *lto **omitted; *dangs; *kyi

1. The title has been reconstructed from that found in the colophon (f. 24a-b). Only the final part, starting with *nyi ma shar phyogs,* is written on the title page. This does not make sufficient sense by itself.
2. *sog po* has been added below the line in a different hand.

(1a) ***The Clear Mirror [containing] the Story of How the Order Prophesied to the [School of the] Glorious 'Brug-pa by Its Divine Lineage Came and Spread in the Eastern Province of the Sun Within the 'Southern Mon Country of Four Approaches'*[1] is contained [herein].**

(1b) Obeisance to Ngag-dbang-rNam-gryal![2]
I bow my head with heartfelt devotion to the *Dharmarāja* Ngag-dbang
rNam(-par)-rgyal(-ba) who turns the wheel of power pertaining to religious
and secular authority on the broad surface of the world. I shall speak briefly
about the manner in which the order of his teachings came to the Eastern
Province of the Sun south of the Land of Snow.
(2a) Now, at the time when the Great *sDe-srid* gTsang-pa had in previous times
subjugated and gained power over this realm of the Eastern Province, the
treasurer of the Ri-bo dGa'-ldan-pa, *sDe-pa Nang-so* A-bo, having prepared
many deceitful and cunning plots, summoned the army of the [Qośot] Mongol
king Dalai Batūr from Kukunor and the Great *sDe-srid* gTsang-pa was over-
(2b) thrown, his rule seized and all his subjects overpowered.[3] At that time King
bDe-ba of Kha-ling[4] and 'Brug-rgyal, [these] two, were in total disaffection
over the question of the land and subjects of the Indian *duars* and so they
went to submit the case to the *sDe-srid* of the Ri-bo dGa'-ldan-pa. They were
granted two envoy officials from the lHa-sa government [to try their case]
and having brought them along with them, they arrived at Kha-ling where
the substantiality of the words of both King bDe-ba of Kha-ling and of
'Brug-rgyal were judged before the two envoy officials. At that time, due
to the fact that the peoples of India, Tibet and lHo Mon had not had much
intercourse and so did not understand each other's languages, despite whatever manner was used to explain the accounts of the origins [of the dispute],
the two envoy officials said they required interpreters who knew the
Tibetan language as they themselves did not understand the language of the
Mon-pa. Accordingly, on 'Brug-rgyal's side *Bla-ma* rNam-sras sDo-rje, the
son of the *bla-ma* of the Tibetan 'Brug-pa, Thub-bstan Pad-dkar,[5] and, on
(3a) bDe-ba's side, the *lTa-wang Bla-ma* Chos-dbyings rGa-mtsho of La-'og
Yul-gsum, both acted as interpreters. On investigating and judging in detail
the substantiality of their accounts, it appeared they were the same. However, in accordance with the euphony [that can be achieved] in translating
between the Tibetan and Mon-pa languages, when, on 'Brug-rgyal's side,
the purport of his argument in proof of his case was explained with clarity,
it appeared that the two envoy officials, for their part, seemed contented
in their minds. Whereupon King bDe-ba experienced resentful jealousy and
having mentally prepared a deceitful imputation, he cunningly declared it
to the two envoy officials, saying: "Although you are the officials of the
dGa'-ldan Pho-brang – the sky dGa'-ldan, the earth dGa'-ldan – there is not

kyang min 'dug / bla ma rnam sras la ni A ma bu mo mang po tshogs nas nyin re bzhin tshogs chang nyin mtshan khor* mo ster gyi 'dug / khyed la ni (3b) min 'dug pas nga'i khyim du gdan drang* so zer nas / rgyal po bde ba'i khyim la khrid nas / zas kyi sna rigs mi gcig pa mang pos bsnyen bkur dpag tu med pa dang / lhag par du 'bras chang gi* yang snying dang A** rag la sogs skoms kyi rigs / dpag tu med pa drangs* zhing** blud pas / dpon po gnyis kyang chang gyi gzi byin bskyed pa'i gtam sna tshogs smra ba dang / rgyal po bde ba'i bsam pa la da ni glags* brnyed par 'dug snyam nas / yang phra ma zhus pa da len nged kyi khyim du gdan 'dren zhus nas bza' gtung gi bsnyen bkur phran bu tsam zhu ba ma gtogs / bla ma rnam sras la* tshogs chang 'dren mi bu mo mtshar zhing mdzas pa lha'i bu mo 'dra ba tshogs chang 'dren mkhan ni mi 'dug zer bas / dpon po gnyis kyis* de lta bu'i bu mo mdzas pa rang yod dam zer bas / yul stod dar ma dar phi la nges par rang yod zer bas / dpon po gnyis (4a) kyis* nged kyang ji ltar yod lta bar 'gro dgos zer nas / dpon g.yog* 'khor bcas chang gis ra ro nas gom pa 'khyor zhing phyin pas / na chung bu mo mdzas ma mang po yod pa'i nang na / bla ma rnam sras kyi brtse* grogs bu mo lha mo 'dra ba gnyis khrid nas / ki ki ngar sgra sgrogs cing yongs bas bla ma rnam sras kyi bsam pa la / nyes med kyi bsam pa la / nyes med kyi bu mo la de ltar byed pa mi 'os bsam nas / ma bzod* par ki ki'i 'khus** lan btab* pa las / mi sna lding** dpon bstan srung zer bas nged la mi ma rtsi bar 'khus* lan de ltar btab las thag chod dam zer nas yongs bas / bla ma rnam sras kyis grwa pa rtogs* ldan gnyis khrid nas khyim nang las phyir thon yong bas / lding* dpon bstan srung dpon g.yog 'khor bcas kyis* grwa pa rtogs** ldan gnyis der bsad*** do/ bla ma rnam sras kyis* kyang lding** dpon bstan srung gi snying kha'i (4b) thad du gri shugs che ba btsug pas shi yod dam bsam nas sngangs skrags cing bros pas / lding dpon la mtshon bsrung zab mo yod pa'i gshis* kyis** ma shi ba'i skad cha thos kyang / ri bo*** dga' ldan pas* skos pa'i dpon po yin pa nas / phugs su rtsad gcod kyi nag gcod drag po yong* bsam nas / la 'og yul gsum du phyin / ku ri lung pa las rgyud nas song bas / krong sar rdzong du sleb dpon slob mi 'gyur brtan* pa mjal / skad cha gleng mo zhib par 'dri ba gnang ba bzhin / lan rim par zhu bas / dbu cog cog tsam yang yang mdzad nas / khyed bla* ma rin po che'i sku gzhogs** su mjal bar 'gro dgos pa 'dug gsungs nas / dpon slob rin po che'i phyag phyir byas nas phyin pas / spung thang du sleb sde pa dbu mdzad chen* mos sna khrid mdzad nas / bla ma rin po che (5a) ngag dbang rnam rgyal gyi zhabs drung du sleb nas phyag 'tshal zhing zhal mjal ba'i mod la / spyan ras gzigs dngos su yin no snyam pa'i snang ba byung zhing mi mched pa'i dad pa thob / zhabs drung rin po che zhal nas bla ma rnam sras la bka' stsal pa / khyod yul dang skye sa gang nas

*kho
*drangs
*gyi **omitted
*dwangs **zhings
*zhings
*sa
*kyi
*kyi
*g.yogs
*rtse
*zod **khus
*btabs **ding
*khus
*rtog
*ding
*kyi **rtog ***gsad
*kyi **dir
*shis **kyi ***omitted
*pa'i
*yongs
*bstan
*blad **gzhog
*chon

even a single person doing you honour and service or plying you with ale,
whereas there are many ladies and girls gathered who are serving ale to
(3b) *Bla-ma* rNam-sras every day, continuously night and day. Since there is
nobody doing this for you, I shall invite you to my house." After being
conducted to King bDe-ba's house they were accorded infinite honour with
many different kinds of food and, in particular, they were plied and served
with limitless kinds of drink including the finest rice ale, spirits and so forth,
so that when the two officials recited various drunken stories King bDe-ba
thought to himself: "Now I have got my chance." Once again he spoke
slanderously, saying: "Now then, having invited you to my house, apart
from doing you slight honour with food and drink I haven't any ale-servers
such as the fine and beautiful girls who are like the daughters of gods whom
Bla-ma rNam-sras has for his ale-servers." The two officials said: "Does he
really have such beautiful girls?" "He definitely has them at the top of the
district at Dar-ma-dar-phyi", said [the King]. The two officials said:
(4a) "We too must go and see what they are like," and so they set off, the lords
and their servants together with a retinue, reeling along in a drunken stupor.
From a home where there were many beautiful young girls they took off
with them, shrieking "Ki ki!" as they went, two of *Bla-ma* rNam-sras'
sweethearts who were like goddesses, so that *Bla-ma* rNam-sras thought to
himself: "It is unlawful to do such a thing to innocent girls." Unable to
bear it, he returned the insult of the shouts of "Ki ki!" Whereupon the
envoy called Captain bsTan-srung came forward saying: "Are you resolved
to return the insult in that way, having no regard for me as a person?"
Bla-ma rNam-sras came out from inside the house, taking with him two
yogin monks, and Captain bsTan-srung, the lord with his servants together
with the retinue, killed the two *yogin* monks there. For his part, *Bla-ma*
(4b) rNam-sras stuck a knife with great force into the region of Captain bsTan-
srung's heart and thinking: "Is he dead?", took fright and fled. Although
he heard news that since the Captain had a powerful protective amulet
against weapons he had not died, he thought that as he [the Captain] was
an officer who had been appointed by the Ri-bo dGa'-ldan-pa he himself
would eventually have to face severe punishment as the result of an enquiry
and so he went to La-'og Yul-gsum. Proceeding by way of Ku-ri-lung(-pa)
he came to Krong-sar rDzong and saw *dPon-slob* Mi-'gyur brTan-pa.[6] In
accordance with the detailed questions he was asked on the news, he gave
his answers turn by turn and [the *dPon-slob*] simply nodded his head again
and again and then declared: "You must go and have an audience with the
Precious Bla-ma." Acting as a servant of the *Precious dPon-slob* he departed
and so arrived at sPung-thang.[7] Guided by the *sDe-pa Great Precentor*[8] he
(5a) came into the presence of the *Precious Bla-ma* Ngag-dbang rNam-rgyal and
made his obeisance. At the instant he saw him, the notion came to him
that he must be Avalokiteśvara in person and he gained steadfast faith.
Zhabs-drung Rin-po-che said to *Bla-ma* rNam sras: "Where is your home
and birth-place? For what purpose have you come here?" *Bla-ma* rNam-

yin / 'di ru don ci la yong gsungs pas / bla ma rnam sras kyis* lan *kyi
zhu ba / bdag gi* pha'i yul ni dbu gzhung rnam rgyal rab brtan** *kyi **bstan
rtse nas yin / ming la thub bstan* pad dkar zer ba yin / nga rang gi *brtan
skye sa ni shar phyogs tsha se zer ba nas yin / nga'i A pa grwa sding* *ding
po* che nas 'brug pa sprul sku snyan grags** dpal*** bzang *dpon **grag ***dpa'
gis* shar phyogs mon yul du grags pa'i dgon lag yod pa thams cad *gi
kyi bdag 'dzin du bla ma skos* nas btang ba yin / bdag kyang phas *bkod
'dzin pa'i dgon lag rnams kyi (5b) bdag 'dzin byas nas sdod pa las /
dga' ldan pho brang gi sku tshab dang / kha ling rgyal po rnams kyi
mig la babs po rang ma 'byung ba nas / bla ma rin po che'i sku
gzhogs su 'di phyi'i skyabs gnas zhu ba la yong ba yin* zhus pas / *yomg yin
bla ma rin po che'i zhal nas / khyod kyi pha thub bstan* pad dkar *brtan
de / nged gdan sa ra lung la yod dus / yar* 'brog snang dkar rtse'i *yam
pho brang nas / sde pa khri dpon zhu ru byung ba dang bstun / yar* *yam
'brog sgang gsum gyi gdul* bya la** nged dpon slob sgar chen *'dul **omitted
btegs nas phyin dus kyi ma ṇi'i dge bskul ba chen po thub bstan* *brtan
pad* dkar gyi bu yin 'dug gsungs** nas thugs dgyes dgyes mdzad *dpad **gsung
de / dpon slob thugs yid gcig tu 'dres / gtsug phud kyi skra phud
phul bas / dpal ldan 'brug pa'i bstan pa spel zhing mi 'jigs pa'i ming
yang gnam sa'i rdo rje btag / de nas rim pas dbang lung man ngag
thams cad gnang nas rdo rje 'dzin pa'i go 'phangs la bkod bkra shis
mnga' (6a) gsol mdzad cing / sku gsung thugs kyi rten dang chos* *mchos
chas la sogs pa dpag tu med pa gnang nas / nyi ma* shar phyogs *omitted
su chos kyi bstan pa spel ba 'gro ba'i don kho na nyid yin kyang /
khyad par du shar phyogs kyi yul khams der / dpon po mang zhing
cig 'og tu cig mi 'dzul ba'i nga rgyal dregs pa dang ldan zhing / drag
po'i khrims kyi ma gcun* pa'i ma rung mu rgod mtha' khob kyi yul *bcun
khams der / bka' khrims drag pos ma gcun* par / zhi ba'i sgo nas *bcun
chos kyi bstan pa'i ring lugs spel ba la shog rgya cher mi yong ba
'dra lags zhus pas / zhabs drung rin po che'i zhal nas / phyis 'jug
nga'i bstan pa lugs gnyis kyis sgo nas / shar phyogs kyi rgyal khams
der dar zhing rgyas pa'i* lung** bstan yod pas / de dus khyed rang *khang **omitted
snying khams ma chung bar* de ltar bgyis shig** gsungs pas / bla *par **shis
(6b) ma rnam sras yang yid* ches** shing snying nas gus pa'i *yi **che
phyag 'tshal zhing zhabs spyi bor blang nas krong gsar du log go /
de nas lo gsum song ba dang / sngar bum thang chos 'khor dpon po
sbyin bdag gi rtsa ba yin pa la / rgyu rkyen gyis bskul nas dpon
slob mi 'gyur brtan* pa'i** bka' la mi rtsi bar ngo log pa dang / *bstan **pa
dpung chen lan gnyis gsum bar du bcug* kyang glag** ma 'khel*** *bcugs **glags *mkhas
par log pas / dpon slob kyi thugs dgongs la bla ma'i lung bstan
yod pa bzhin bcas la mi 'dul ba dpe mi srid snyam nas / zhi ba'i
sgo nas g.yo thabs kyi 'phrul* 'khor rnam** pa mang po thugs la *sphrul **rnams
bkram nas pho nya ba mngag* gzhug** nub chu stod nas chos *mnga' **zhu

sras replied:[9] "My father's home is in rNam-rgyal Rab-brtan-rtse in dBu-
gzhung. His name is Thub-bstan Pad-dkar. My birth-place is Tsha-se in the
Eastern Province. From Grwa sDing-po-che my father was appointed
bla-ma and sent by the 'Brug-pa incarnation sNyan-grags dPal-bzang [10] to
take charge of all the branch monasteries [11] that existed in the so-called
'Eastern Province of Mon-yul'. After I had also stayed in charge of the
(5b) branch monasteries which my father had controlled, I did not find favour
in the eyes of the representatives of the dGa'-ldan Pho-brang and the
King of Kha-ling and so on account of this I have come before the
Precious Bla-ma to seek refuge." The *Precious Bla-ma* said: "With regard
to your father Thub-bstan Pad-dkar – while I was at my seat of Ra-lung
the *sDe-pa Khri-dpon* ('Myriarch') made me a request after coming from
[his] palace of sNang-dkar-rtse in Yar-'brog; [12] when we, lord and
disciples, had in compliance [with this request] established a great camp
among the devotees of Yar-'brog sGang-gsum and were going around, he
Thub-stan Pad-dkar, was a great exhorter to the virtue of the *ma-ṇi*
recitation – and you are his son!" He rejoiced and the minds of the lord
and disciple intermingled. [*Bla-ma* rNam-sras] offered his tonsure and
was given the name of gNam-sa'i rDo-rje ('*Vajra* of the Sky and Earth')
[as a mark of] his being fearless in spreading the teachings of the Glorious
'Brug-pa. Then he was gradually given all the initiations, authorisations
(6a) and instructions and installed in the dignity of a '*Vajra*-holder'. An
auspicious installation ceremony was performed and he was given an
infinite number of body, speech and mind-supports, religious objects and
so on. [*Bla-ma* rNam-sras] said: "To propagate the *dharma*'s teachings to
the Eastern Province of the Sun would certainly be for the welfare of
beings. In particular, however, in that region of the Eastern Province there
are many chiefs and they are possessed of the pride and arrogance whereby
one will not subordinate himself to another. It does not seem that the
propagation of the order of the *dharma*'s teachings by peaceful measures will
meet with a great deal of success in that atrocious and barbarous border
region that has never been subdued by fierce laws unless it *is* [first]
subdued by means of [such] fierce laws." *Zhabs-drung Rin-po-che* said:
"Since there is a prophecy that in the future my teachings shall flourish
and increase in that realm of the Eastern Province by means of the dual
system, [13] at that time you must act according [to the prophecy] without
(6b) losing courage." *Bla-ma* rNam-sras believed him and having made obeisance
with heartfelt devotion and placed [Ngag-dbang rNam-rgyal's] feet on his
head, he returned to Krong-gsar.

Then when three years had elapsed, the *Chos-'khor dPon-po* [14] of Bum-
thang who had previously been the most important patron [of the 'Brug-pa
in eastern Bhutan] was compelled by [various] circumstances to rebel,
paying no heed to the order of *dPon-slob* Mi-'gyur brTan-pa. Although a
great host was despatched up to two or three times, being unable to destroy
him it returned. The *dPon-slob* thought to himself: "According to the
existing prophecy of the [*Zhabs-drung*] *bla-ma,* it is inconceivable that he
should not be subdued." Having prepared in his mind many kinds of cunning
plots that would employ peaceful measures, he despatched a messenger and
summoned *Chos-mdzad* rGyal-mo from Nub Chu-stod: [15] On commanding
her to employ various methods, *Chos-mdzad* rGyal-mo declared: "The

mdzad rgyal mo* bkug nas / thabs sna tshogs pa byed dgos pa'i bka' *ma
bsgo bas / chos mdzad* rgyal mos nga bas chos 'khor dpon po dang *omitted
thag nye ba chu smad gdung bsod nams dbang po yod pas / bka'
bsgo (7a) ba bzhin gyi g.yo thabs ngas kho* la** slab po zer nas *khol **omitted
bka' bsgo ba bzhin slab pas bsod nams dbang pos kyang nga bas
gnyen sha khrag* gis** 'brel bas*** / sdom mkhar mi dpon *khri **omitted ***sas
dbang thob yin pas bka' bsgo ba bzhin g.yo thabs kho la byed du
bcug go zer nas / sdom mkhar dbang thob la dpon slob mi 'gyur
brtan pas bka' bsgo ba bzhin slab* pas / 'grub pa'i nus nga las med *sleb
kyang / bka' phebs gang gsung ba bzhin gyi thabs sna tshogs pa
rnams / nga'i zhang po lcags mkhar gnas po mar rgan la sogs pa'i
pha tshan rnams chos 'khor dpon po'i bka' blon nang ma yin pas /
bslu* E tshug lta'o zer nas song ngo / de nas dbang thob kyis** *bslus **kyi
kyang dpon slob mi 'gyur brtan pas thabs sna tshogs pa bka' bsgo
ba bzhin zhang po nang blon rnams la smras pa / khong rnams yid
ches nas bka' ji ltar gnang ba bzhin nged rnams kyis* 'grub bo zer *kyi
nas khas blangs so / de nas dbang thob* kyis** kyang rim (7b) par *omitted **kyi
'ded nas sngar gyi gtam rgyus rnams / dpon slob mi 'gyur brtan pa'i
snyan du zhus pas / dpon slob kyi* zhal nas da ni dpung chen *mi kyi
bcug go gsungs nas / spung thang bde ba* can** nas dmag dpon *na **chen
chen mo gnyer pa 'brug rnam rgyal gyis* gtsos pa'i tsho** chen *'brug rnams pa'i **mtsho
gyi dpung chen dang / wa can mnga' og shar rus dge gling nyi shor
dga' seng bcas pa'i dmag bkug nas / mang sde lung pa'i dmag dang
bcas dpon slob mi 'gyur brtan pas* dmag dpon mdzad / bla ma *pa'i
rnam sras kyis* dmag rgyab sna po byas nas / bum thang chos *kyi
'khor yur ba zhing gi rdzong la dmag gis bskor nas / 'tshang kha
rgyab pa dang / sngar gi nang blon khas len pa rnams kyis* sna *kyi
len byas nas yur ba zhing gi rdzong bcom pas / chos 'khor dpon
po rnams sngangs skrag cing mi kyang rta kyang re byas nas bod du
bros so / de nas mnga' 'bangs mi sde yul 'khor dang / bum thang
sde bzhi thams cad mnga' 'og tu bcug / padma gling pa'i sku gdung
la sogs pa'i rten khyad par 'phags pa dang / nor rdzas kyi rigs bye
brag (8a) dpag tu med pa brtsis blang nas / bya dkar rdzong la
rdzong gi shom ra sgrigs* nas rdzong bdag la gnyer pa long ba *'grigs
bskos* pa gnang bas** / der tshogs pa'i mi thams cad kyis *bskod **ba'i
smras* pa / E ma mi 'di ni mig long ba rkang pa zha bas dpon po *smas
mi yong zer bas / dpon slob mi 'gyur pa'i* zhal nas / sngon gyi *pas
las 'phro lung bstan la yod pas / sngon bum thang lcags mkhar du
rgya gar gyi rgyal po sindhu ra dza zhes bya ba byung ba la / Orgyan
padma 'byung gnas kyis* dus ma 'ong pa na khyod mig long ba *kyi
rkang pa zha ba gcig tu skyes nas / bum thang 'dir dbang bsgyur
ba'i dpon du 'gyur ro // zhes lung bstan la yod gsungs bas thams cad
yid ches so / der dmag dpung thams cad* 'khrugs pa las rgyal zhing *thams cad la

Chu-smad gDung bSod-nams dBang-po [16] is closer to the *Chos-'khor dPon-*
(7a) *po* than I am and so I shall tell him to use cunning means in accordance with
your command." So she spoke to him in accordance with the command but
bSod-nams dBang-po also declared: "The *sDom-mkhar Mi-dpon* [17] dBang-
thob is closer related by flesh and blood [i.e. on his mother's side, to the
Chos-'khor dPon-po] than I am and so I shall make him use cunning means
in accordance with the command." [However] on speaking to *sDom-mkhar*
dBang-thob in accordance with the command given by *dPon-slob* Mi-'gyur
brTan-pa, he [dBang-thob] said: "Although there is nobody better able to
accomplish it than myself, as for the various measures that are to be
employed in accordance with whatever orders are given, since my maternal
uncle the Landlord of lCags-mkhar [18] together with his paternal relatives
including the elderly matrons are the household officials of the *Chos-'khor*
dPon-po, I shall try and see if I can entice them." Having said this he
departed. Then dBang-thob also spoke to his maternal uncles who were the
household officers about the various measures which *dPon-slob* Mi-'gyur
brTan-pa had commanded. Believing him they agreed, saying: "We shall
fulfill the order just as it has been given." Then dBang-thob, having
(7b) proceeded [to Krong-gsar] by stages, reported to *dPon-slob* Mi-'gyur brTan-
pa the recent news and so the *dPon-slob* declared: "Now a great force must
invade." Having summoned the great force of the Tsho-chen [19] from sPung-
thang headed by the commander-in-chief *gNyer-pa* 'Brug rNam-rgyal [20] and
the soldiers of the district under Wa-can, [21] [namely those of] Shar
Bus[-pa'i-sa] dGe-gling, Nyi-shor and dGa'-seng, *dPon-slob* Mi-'gyur brTan-
pa acted as commander of the troops of Mang-sde-lung and other places.
With *Bla-ma* rNam-sras acting as the battle guide, the soldiers surrounded
the fortress of Yur-ba-zhing [22] in Bum-thang Chos-'khor and when they
stormed it the household officials who had previously given their consent
took them in and the fortress of Yur-ba-zhing was defeated. The *Chos-'khor*
dPon-po's party took fright and with a horse apiece they fled to Tibet. Then
the subjects, the communities and villages – all of Bum-thang sDe-bzhi –
were brought to subjugation. Having taken charge of the relics of Padma
Gling-pa [23] and other highly esteemed sacred objects and also infinite kinds
(8a) of articles of wealth, arrangements for [building] a fortress at Bya-dkar
rDzong were prepared and the 'Blind Steward' was appointed *rdzong-bdag.* [24]
So all the people assembled there said: "Alas, this person is blind and lame
and so will not do as chief." *dPon-slob* Mi-'gyur said: "It is contained in a
prophecy that there is a karmic bond with former times. An Indian king
called the Sindhu Rāja came to Bum-thang lCags-mkhar in previous times
and Padmasambhava of O-rgyan declared to him: 'You will be reborn in the
future as a blind and lame man and become a chief gaining power here in
Bum-thang,' and this is contained in the prophecy." [25] On saying this,
everyone believed him.

blo bde bar ngal so zhing yod pa'i skabs la / sngar nas zhabs drung
rin po che lung bstan pa bzhin / dus (8b) la babs pa dang shar ku
ri lung du rag sa'i dpon po lha bu dar de nyes pa med par / skyi-
gling* gi dpon chen dar ma dang / gzhung phag gi gdung gyi rgyal *gli
po dga' ba gnyis kha mthun nas bsad* pa dang / de'i yug sa ma *gsad
rengs* mo dang / blon 'bangs rnams kyis len byed dgos bsam pa la *reng
ni stobs mnga' thang gis* ma thub par ci drags la thug nas yod *gi
pa'i skabs 'dir / 'brug pa'i dpung chen bum thang la sleb nas chos
'khor dpon po bcom pa'i skad cha thos pas / rag sa'i mo rengs* *reng
mo dang / 'bangs rnams shintu dga' nas dpung chen gdan 'dren
zhu ba la / pho nya brdzangs pas dkyil sgar du sleb byung bas
dang / dpung* (9a) chen gyi kha 'khyogs nas ku ri lung du phyin *dpun
pas / rgyal po dga' ba dang / dpon chen dar ma gnyis kyis dmag
dpung gi lam du bsu nas 'thab pas skad cig nyid la khong gnyis
dmag pham nas skrag cing bros pas / dpon po gang yod rnams lag
tu tshud nas btson* du bzung khong gnyis mnga' 'bangs mi sde *brtson
dang / ku ri lung stod smad thams cad mnga' 'og tu bcug nas /
gleng gleng du rdzong btab nas ming yang lhun grub rtse btags /
rdzong dpon bla ma 'brug phun tshogs bskos* pa gnang nas / *bskod
dpung chen shar kho long phyogs la kha 'khyogs pas / kho long pa
rnams 'jigs shing skrag nas 'babs zhus kyi mnga' 'og tu 'dus shing /
dong sti bkra shis yang rtse rdzong btab pas / 'jigs grags kyis
'brong mdo gsum zangs lung pa phan tshun chad kyi 'bab zhus
(9b) byas so / de nas dpung chen tshur log nas smin rgyal yul
gsum sleb pa dang / stong phu rgyal po stobs mnga' thang che
tsam byung bas / mol ba lung pa la shugs drag brtsong ba dang
gzhong sgar kheng po rnams blo ma rangs par / rgyab rten zhu ba
la gros bsdur byas nas chos mdzad dkar po gdung / dpung chen
gdan drangs pa la smin rgyal yul gsum la song nas / dmag dpon
gnyis la zhu ba la nged kyi yul du rdzong sa btsan* zhing lung pa brtsan
mang po'i / sa 'dus che ba yod pas der byon pa zhu zer bas / dmag
dpon gnyis kyis* kyang zhal gyis bzhes nas / dpung chen gyi kha *kyi
'khyogs pa tsam la / sngon las chos 'khor dpon dang ku ri lung gi
dpon stobs 'byor rgya che ba rnams skad cig nyid la bcom pa'i skad
cha thos pa'i 'jigs grags la sngangs shing skrag nas / lam bar (10a)
gyi rtsa bar mang po'i dpon khag mi sde thams cad 'jigs shing dpa'
khum nas mnga' 'bangs su bzhag* go / stong phu rgyal pos 'thab** *zhag **thab
ra'i mtshon* cha** bzos*** nas rgol ba'i sham ra grigs pa la / *btson **cha chab ***zos
dpung chen 'gro ba'i zhor gyi skad cig de nyid la ming med du
brlag par byas nas / gzhong sgar du sleb pas / snga tshang phyi
tshang gi rgyal blon 'khor dang bcas pa phyogs ris gnyis su phye
nas / 'thab cing brtsod nas 'khrugs pa'i skabs yod pa la / dpung
chen gyi stobs la gnyis ka ha las 'das nas / sngon nas skyabs mgon

At a time when all the troops were happily resting there after winning
(8b) victory in battle, the time came for the fulfilment of the prophecy which had
formerly been given by *Zhabs-drung Rin-po-che.* Without having committed
any crime, lHa-bu-dar the chief of Rag-sa in Ku-ri-lung to the east, was killed
by both Dar-ma the great chief [26] of sKyi-gling and King dGa'-ba of gZhung
Phag-gi-gdung [27] who had agreed on this among themselves. Thereupon his
widow and the officers and subjects thought they should retaliate but as
their strength and power were not sufficient for this they fell to wondering
what would be best done. At this point they heard the news that the great
force of the 'Brug-pa had arrived in Bum-thang and had defeated the *Chos-'khor dPon-po* and so the widow of Rag-sa and the subjects were overjoyed
(9a) and despatched messengers to invite the great force. When they arrived at
the central camp, the great force set off and went to Ku-ri-lung. Both King
dGa'-ba and the great chief Dar-ma engaged the army on its path and fought.
Both their armies were instantly defeated and taking fright they fled. Their
remaining officers fell into the hands [of the invaders] and were imprisoned.

The subjects and communities of both of them and all of Upper and
Lower Ku-ri-lung were subjugated. In time a fortress was built and given the
name of lHun-grub-rtse. [28] *Bla-ma* 'Brug Phun-tshogs was appointed *rdzong-dpon.*

When the great force set off in the direction of Kho-long in the east, the
people of Kho-long took fright and were brought together in subjection after
they had made acts of submission, and the fortress of bKra-shis Yang-rtse [29]
at Dong-sti was established. Frightening rumours caused the people of all
(9b) parts of 'Brong-mdo-gsum and Zang-lung to make acts of submission. Then
the great force turned back and came to sMin-rgyal Yul-gsum. At that time
the King of sTong-phu's [30] strength and dominion was quite considerable
and he had been violently oppressing the people of Mol-ba-lung. There-upon the Kheng-po [31] people of gZhong-sgar, being disaffected, held a
discussion in order to request support and so *Chos-mdzad* dKar-po-gdung
went to sMin-rgyal Yul-gsum in order to invite the great force. In his
submission to the two commanders he said: "Since in our country there is
strong ground for a fortress and the land of its many districts is rich,please
come there." For their part the two commanders agreed and so when the
great force had just set off, taking fright at the fearful rumours they heard
of the news of how the *Chos-'khor dPon-po* and the very powerful chiefs
(10a) of Ku-ri-lung had previously been instantly defeated, many parties of chiefs
and all the communities along the way were terrified and lost their courage
and so they were placed in subjection. The King of sTong-phu had prepared
arrangements for offering resistance after making weapons for a stockade
but at the very instant the great force advanced he was destroyed so that not
even his name was left. When it arrived at gZhong-sgar the rulers and officers
of sNga-tshang [and] Phyi-tshang [32] together with their retinues were
fighting and contending, having [previously] separated into two factions,
and at this time of turmoil both were astonished by the strength of the
great force. Thinking that whoever should be first to seek protection and
assistance would be accorded special favour and preference, both factions
scrambled to make acts of submission. Among them King Dar-'jam [33]
together with his [cousin-] brothers and chief councillors came from sNga-

dpung gnyen sus zhu ba de / kha 'dzin* zhing ngo che ba yong bsam *btsan
nas / gnyis ka hab* thob kyi 'bab zhus byung ba la / snga tshang *has
nas rgyal po dar 'jam spun chas dang gtso las rnams / phyi tshang
nas rgyal po zla'u la spun chas dang gtso las / ba geng bre mi he
long nas (10b) rgyal po rdo re dang yong nas / de nas bzung chos
rje 'brug pa'i bka' ci gsung* 'grub rgyu yin zer nas khas blangs so / *gsungs
gnyis ka'i zhu tshig zhabs 'dzul la khyad par med kyang / sngar nas
bla ma rnam* sras dang drin** shin tu che ba'i gshis*** kyis**** / *rnams **'drin ***shis ****kyi sra
dmag dpon gnyis snga tshang pa la dag snang dkar tsam mdzad / de
nas dmag dpon gnyis gzhong sgar du rdzong gi bshams ra mdzad
nas bzhugs / bla ma rnam sras kyis* dmag dpung kha 'thor shig *kyi
'khrid nas / U dza rong weng li zam pa la sgar bcas nas sdod / rtseng
mi tsho lnga / bkra shis sgang pa / skang lung pa / kha ling pa
rnams la mi sna bang chen btang / khyed rang rnams 'bab zhus
byed rgyu yin nam / dmag bcug rgyu* yin gyi lan gsal gtong zer ba *gyu
dang / bla ma rnam sras dang kha ling pa sngar nas ma cham pa'i
zhe khon* yod pa'i gzhis** kyis / kha (IIa) ling pa'i dmag dpung *khyen **shis
U dza rong la yong nas / kha ling pa rnams kyis* U dza rong pa la *kyi
smras pa / khyed rang tsho sa rgyus* dang ri rgyus legs par ston** *rgyud **bton
pas* chog** / dmag dpung gi stobs dang 'khrugs rtsal gyi shed *pa'i **mchog
nged tshos the tshom med par bya'o* zer bas / ngar skad byas nas *byas so
'khrugs pa'i 'dzing* ra bshams nas yod pa'i skabs la / bla ma rnam *jings
sras kyi dmag dpung gi* dkyil nas / dmag mi khal gsum tsam gyis* *gyi
chu la rkyal rgyab nas grang ma'i chu tshur la 'thon byung ba dang /
der yod pa'i kha ling pa'i mi thams cad kyi bsam pa la / dmag mi
de rnams chus mi thub mes mi thub yin pa 'dra bsam nas / rgol ba
la the tshom byas pa dang / lhag par du ba geng rgyal po rdo re U
dza rong pa dang nye ba drung po yin pa'i gshis* kyis / phan sems *shis
kyis bslab* bya smras pa la / kha ling pa'i kha la (IIb) nyan nas *slab
'brug pa'i dmag la rgol ba'i rtsis* ma byed cig / bum thang chos *rtsi
'khor dpon po dang / ku ri lung gi dpon chen stobs che ba rnams
kyi rgol bas* ma thub par bcom pa yin / lhag par du kha ling pa *ba'i
rnams dgun gyi dus su rgya'i las sgo la 'dzul 'gro bas khyed rang
tsho cig pos zam pa srung mi tshug / de bas da lta nas 'bab zhus
byed pa drag* zer ba bzhin / U dza rong pas 'bab zhus byas nas *grags
weng li'i zam sna btad pa dang / kha ling pa dang / rkang lung* *omitted
pa rnams kyang bya thabs* med par phyi ltar du kha las 'bab zhus *theb
kyi tshul tsam byed pa ma gtogs / nang ltar du 'bab zhus byas pa
la / blos rangs* pa med cing 'og tu 'dzul ba'i bsam pa cig kyang *rang
med pas / de'i rgyu rkyen gang yin na sngar kha ling rgyal po bde
ba dang / bla ma rnam sras gnyis ma 'cham* (12a) par yul thon *cham
song ba dang / lhag par du shar phyogs lung pa 'dir / kha ling pa
rnams mi dpung rgya che ba dang stobs mnga' thang mgu nas ma

tshang, King Zla'u-la [34] together with his [cousin-] brothers and chief
(10b) followers came from Phyi-tshang and King rDo-re came from Ba-geng
Bre-mi He-long and they made a promise saying: "From this time on we
shall fulfil any command given us by the Hierarchs of the 'Brug-pa."
Although there was no difference in the acquiescence expressed in the
letters of each faction, the two commanders showed some favour to the
people of sNga-tshang since they had been extremely kind to *Bla-ma*
rNam-sras in the past. Then the two commanders made preparations for
[building] a fortress at gZhong-sgar and resided there.

Bla-ma rNam-sras, taking with him a detachment of the army,
established a camp at the bridge of Weng-li in U-dza-rong and stayed there.
Envoy couriers were sent to the Five Hosts of rTseng-mi, to the people of
bKra-shis-sgang, sKang-lung and Kha-ling to whom they declared: "Send
clear replies as to whether you are going to make acts of submission or
whether you are going to come forth to battle." Thereupon, because of the
feelings of resentment that existed between *Bla-ma* rNam-sras and the
(11a) people of Kha-ling due to their former discord, the army of the Kha-ling
people came to U-dza-rong and the Kha-ling people said to the U-dza-rong
people: "You can show us properly the lie of the valleys and mountains. We
shall [together] use the strength of our army and the power of our battle
skill." Saying this they let loose yells. At a time when they had prepared a
stockade for battle, about three score soldiers from the centre of *Bla-ma*
rNam-sras' army swam and reached the near side of the Grang-ma'i Chu
river so that all the Kha-ling people who were there thought to themselves:
"It seems that neither water nor fire can do any harm to those soldiers."
They hesitated in offering resistance and, moreover, King rDo-re of Ba-geng,
because he was a close mentor to the U-dza-rong people, spoke words of
(11b) counsel to them benevolently, saying: "Do not make schemes to offer
resistance to the army of the 'Brug-pa having paid heed to the words of the
Kha-ling people. The *Chos-'khor dPon-po* of Bum-thang and the powerful
great chiefs of Ku-ri-lung were defeated as their resistance could not cope.
What is more, since the Khaling people proceed to the Indian *duars* in winter
you will not be able to guard the bridge alone. Instead of that it would be
better to make acts of submission as from now." When, in accordance with
these words, the U-dza-rong people had handed over the bridge of Weng-li
after making acts of submission, the Kha-ling and rKang-lung people too
had no course except simply to pretend to make verbal expressions of
submission outwardly; apart from this, as for their internal acts of submission, they were discontented and had no thought whatsoever of capitulating.
If [it be wondered] what the cause of this was, [firstly] King bDe-ba of
(12a) Kha-ling and *Bla-ma* rNam-sras, [these] two, had not been in accord and so
[the latter] had left his home. [Secondly], moreover, the Kha-ling people
delighted in their large force of men and in their strength and dominion in
this region of the Eastern Province and so they would not give ear [to
commands]. And [thirdly], Pho-brang A-chi, [35] King of the rKang-lung
people, both father and son, and *Bla-ma* Nag-seng of Me-rag [36] had great

nyan pa dang / rkang lung pa'i rgyal po pho brang A chi pha spad gnyis / me rag bla ma nag seng stobs mnga' thang che zhing / dga' ldan pa'i kha lo bsgyur mi dang nye ba drung po yin pa'i gshis* kyis rgyab rten dpung nyen la yid ches nas 'og tu 'dzul mi nyaṇ pa'i rtsa ba de yin 'dug / de nas rtseng mi'i rgyal po stobs ldan dpon chen gtso rgan rnams yong nas / nged rnams ni pha* spun snga tshang rgyal blon rnams kyis* ji ltar byed pa bzhin phyag phyir zhu'o zer nas 'bab zhus byas so / de dus bkra shis sgang pa dang / bus mkhar pa gnyis sa cha'i nang nas ma cham par 'khrug pa'i skabs yod pa la gzhong sgar nas chos mdzad dkar po gdung* gis bkra shis sgang pa la (12b) smras pa / khyed rang rnams dang sbi mkhar pa ma cham pa las / khyed rang gi rgyab rten zhu sa chos rje 'brug pa la byas na* kha drag dang dbang che ba yong zer ba dang / bkra shis sgang rgyal blon spun cha rnams gros sdur nas / tshe dbang rgyal po dang / slang nga gnyis weng li zam pa la bla ma rnam sras kyi drung du yong nas / nged kyi skyabs mgon zhu sa khyed rang byed pa yin / nged kyi yul sa 'dus* che** zhing rdzong sa btsan po yod pas* der byon pa zhu zer ba dang / de dus rgyal po snga tshang phyi tshang dang / nyi ma che rigs chung rigs thams cad 'dzoms nas / tshig chad rdo byed pa la / sngar phan chad dga' ldan pho brang pa'i* mnga' 'og yin kyang / dus da** res nas bzung chos rje 'brug pa'i zhabs la 'dzul ba yin no zer nas / rgyal blon gtso las mi sna rnams rang rang so so'i yul du 'gyes so / de nas bla ma rnam (13a) sras yang dmag dpung dang bcas gzhong sgar du log nas / dmag dpon gnyis la 'bab zhus kyi nor gser dngul rnams phul nas / gnas tshul rnams zhib par zhus pas / dmag dpon gnyis kyi zhal nas / da lan re zhig la de ltar yin gsungs so / de nas yang nub phyogs stung la 'bi nas gdung nor bu dbang phyug zer ba'i dpon g.yog kha shas zhig gzhong sgar du yong nas / dmag dpon gnyis la zhus pas / nged kyi lung pa kheṅg rigs rnam* gsum gyi rgyal khams thams cad la / nya mkhar gdung gis* dbang sgyur nas gzhan gyi mi sde 'phrog / mnga' 'bangs mi sde thams cad la mi 'os* mi 'tshams pa'i sdug po mang po gtang gis yod pas / de gdul ba la byon par zhu / dmag gi sna 'dren dang lam rgyus* ri rgyus ni ngas bya'o zer nas khas blangs so* / (13b) dmag dpon gnyis kyis zhal gyis** bzhes nas / dmag dpung bcas der* phebs pas / gdung nor bu dbang gi spun chas rnams dang / blon 'bangs rnams kyis* lam du sha chang gis* bsu nas zas kyi bye brag mang po bsnen bskur zhab tog dpag tu med pa drangs nas / yul du sleb pa dang che 'byor gyi phyag mjal* 'bul ba re phul / da** nas bzung chos rje 'brug pa'i zhabs la 'dzul ba yin pas / pha tshe bu rabs rim pa ltar la thugs rje brtse ba mi 'dor ba zhu zer zhing dmag dpung gi sna khrid byas nas rim par song bas / go zhing phang mkhar / su brang / go phu /

*shis
*phu
*kyi
*drung
*nas
*dus **chen
*yod pas (rdzong tu pa) der byon
*pas **de
*rnams
*gi
*'od·
*rgyud
*so pas **gyi
*la
*kyi
*gi
*mnga' **de

strength and dominion and due to the fact that they were close mentors to the rulers of the dGa'-ldan-pa they trusted them as allies in their support. Those were the basic reasons for their refusing to capitulate.

Then King sTobs-ldan of rTseng-mi together with great chiefs and headmen came forth and declared: "We, father and [cousin-] brothers, shall render service in accordance with whatever the king and officials of sNgatshang do," and so they made acts of submission.

At that time the people of bKra-shis-sgang and the people of Bus-mkhar, [these] two, were not in accord over the question of land property and so they were contending. When these circumstances were prevailing *Chos-mdzad* dKar-po-gdung from gZhong-sgar said to the bKra-shis-sgang people: "Rather
(12b) than quarrelling with the sBi-mkhar people, if you go to the Hierarchs of the 'Brug-pa for support then great strength and power will come to you." Thereupon, after the king and officials of bKra-shis-sgang, [cousin-] brothers, had held a discussion, Tshe-dbang rGyal-po and Slang-nga, [these] two, came before *Bla-ma* rNam-sras at the bridge of Weng-li and said: "We look to you for our protection. The land of our home is rich and there is a strong place for a fortress, so please come there." At that time the kings of sNgatshang [and] Phyi-tshang and all the people of Nyi-ma Che-rigs [and Nyi-ma] Chung-rigs assembled and in the words of promise they made it was declared: "Although up till recently we have been subjects [37] of the dGa'-ldan Pho-brang-pa, from this time on we submit to the authority of the Hierarchs of the 'Brug-pa." The kings and officials, the chief councillors and the envoys then departed each to their own homes.

(13a) Then, after *Bla-ma* rNam-sras too had returned to gZhong-sgar together with the army, he offered to the two commanders the tribute wealth, the gold and silver, and on reporting the news in detail the two commanders declared: "Now that's how it is for the time being."

Then a chief called *gDung* Nor-bu dBang-phyug came with a few servants to gZhong-sgar from sTung-la-'bi in the west and said to the two commanders: "Having gained power throughout all the realms of our homeland in Kheng-rigs rNam-gsum, the *gDung* of Nya-mkhar is seizing the communities of others and causing much unlawful affliction to all the subjects and communities. [38] Please come to subdue him. I shall act as the army's guide, [using my] knowledge of the paths and mountains," he
(13b) promised. The two commanders agreed and went there with the army. On the way the [cousin-] brothers of *gDung* Nor-bu dBang[-phyug] and his officials and subjects welcomed them with meat and ale and served them many kinds of food with infinite respect. On arriving at their homes each made offerings of rich gifts. "Since from now on we submit to the authority of the Hierarchs of the 'Brug-pa, we beg you not to forsake showing loving mercy during the lifetime of [we] fathers and for successive generations of [our] sons," they said and, leading the army on its way, they proceeded by stages. Of all the *gDung* and chiefs of Kheng-rigs rNam-gsum, including those of Go-zhing, Phang-mkhar, Su-brang, Go-phu, Ta-li and 'Bu-li, who involuntarily [surrendered], some bowed down with

ta li 'bu li bcas pa'i / kheng rigs rnam* gsum gyi gdung** dpon *rnams **ddung
thams cad rang dbang med par la la ni dag snang mos gus kyi sgo
nas zhabs la btud / la la ni 'jigs shing dngangs* skrag nas btul / la *dangs
la ni gtam gyi ngar* (14a) sgras btud / nya mkhar gdung gi mkhar *sngar
sa btsan po la sleb pa dang / nya mkhar gdung de sngar nas stobs
mnga' thang che zhing kheng rigs rnam* gsum la dbang sgyur nas *rnams
gzhong sgar gyi mkhar sa btsan po la dmag rgyab nas bskor ba
dang / bu brag gi rdzong sa btsan* po la gsang dmag rgyab nas *brtsan
bcom pa'i nga rgyal gyis rgol ba'i 'jigs ra bshams shing 'thab pa'i
grab 'grigs nas yod pa la / dpung chen rnams kyis dus cig la dpa'i
ngar skad sgrog pas / gnam sa 'khol ba tsam byung ba dang / me
mda' thams cad dus cig la rgyab pa'i 'ur sgras stong gsum gang ba
byung bas / rgyal blon 'khor dang bcas pa thams cad dngangs* *ngangs
shing skrag nas ha las 'das par gyur te / 'dar zhing dpa' 'khum nas
rang dbang med par bros pa las (14b) slar yang zhabs la btud nas /
bu chen dang nor rdzas dpag tu med pa* phul nas / mi sde yul *omitted
'khor thams cad mnga' 'bangs la bcug cing / de nas slar* log nas *slar repeated
krong gsar du byon pa'i lam kar* / re phes** bla ma rgyal mtshan *mkhar **phas
gyis* bka' la mi brtsi bar gnya' reng byed** nas bros song ba yang *gyi **byad
phyi nas rma bya gdang sa la 'khrug tu yong bas / de yang srog la
thug nas ming med du btang ngo / de nas dpung chen rnams krong
gsar du sleb / dpon slob mi 'gyur brtan pas dga' ston* gyi gnang *rton
sbyin nor rdzas dpag tu med pa gnang nas / tshim zhing rgyas pa
bde zhing skyid* pa'i ngang las rang rang so so'i yul du log go / *bskyid
de nas yang zla ba kha shas nas bla ma rnam* sras** kyis*** shar *rnams **omitted ***kyi
phyogs lung pa la sngar gyi dam bca' ba'i tshig chad rdo bzhin yod
med dang mnga' (15a) zhabs yin pa nas / khral 'u lag gi rgyun re
btsug dgos bsam nas / tsha se A zhang tshos rtsar byon nas bzhugs
phyogs mtha' la mi sna btang nas / khral dang 'u lag dgos pa'i lung
gtong ba dang / de yang dga' ldan pho brang pa'i 'og la sdod dus /
khral dang 'u lag rgyug pa'i rgyun cher med pa dang / mi sde rnams
kyi sems 'tsher snang lta bu'i khral rnams phral du rang yong ma
nyan pa dang / bla ma'i phyag g.yog sgar pa rnams so sor btang nas
dbang shugs che ba'i* ngos nas khral 'dus yong bas / kha ling rgyal *bas
po chang lo dpal rgyal blon 'khor bcas / btsan mkhar rgyal po pho
brang A chi pha spad / gcen mkhar rgyal po sangs rgyal po rnams
blos ma rangs* par / khong gsum gros bsdur nas ngo log pa'i rtsis *rang
(15b) byed pa dang / bla ma rnam sras* kyis** skad cha thos nas *omitted **kyi
gzhong sgar phan tshun gyi [. . .] [1] rtsa mang dang / snga tshang
dang phyi tshang dang / rtseng mi tsho lnga / bkra shis sgang pa
bcas pa'i dmag bkug pa dang / kha ling rgyal po chang lo dpal gyis* *gyi
kha ling phyi 'khor* nang 'khor** las*** dmag mi*** bsam**** *bskor **skor ***omitted ****bisam

1. Approximately two words seem to have been omitted here.

devotion and reverence, some were subdued in terror and fright, while some
(14a) bowed down at the fearful sound of rumours. When [the army] arrived at
the strongpoint occupied by the *gDung* of Nya-mkhar's castle, that *gDung*
of Nya-mkhar, having previously acquired great strength and dominion and
gained power over Kheng-rigs rNam-gsum, was feeling proud at having then
waged war and surrounded the strongpoint occupied by the castle of
gZhong-sgar, and at having attacked with a secret force and conquered the
strongpoint occupied by the fortress of Bu-brag. So he had layed out a
stockade to offer resistance and had prepared arrangements for battle.
Thereupon the soldiers of the great force simultaneously let loose such
brave cries that the sky and earth boiled and the roar of all the muskets
being fired simultaneously filled the three voids. [39] Terrified, the ruler
and his officials together with their retinues, all of them, were astonished.
(14b) Trembling and losing courage, they fled involuntarily but then once again
having bowed to authority they offered an infinite number of hostages
and articles of wealth. Thereafter all the communities and village districts
of Kheng were made subject.

Then [the army] returned and along the path it took to Krong-gsar, *Bla-ma* rGyal-mtshan of Re-phes behaved obstinately, refusing to comply with orders, and although he took flight he later came to rMa-bya-gdang-sa in order to contend, so he too met with his end and was rendered nameless. [40]

Then the great forces arrived at Krong-gsar. *dPon-slob* Mi-'gyur brTan-pa gave them the boon of a celebration and an infinite number of articles of wealth. Satisfied and enriched, each then returned to his own home in a state of happiness and contentment.

Then after some months *Bla-ma* rNam-sras thought [enquiries should be
made to determine] whether or not the words of the oath which had
previously been taken in the region of the Eastern Province were [being
(15a) observed] in accordance with the promise. Also since it was a subject area,
a custom of taxation and corvée should be introduced. So he went to his
maternal uncles' place at Tsha-se [41] and resided there. Despatching envoys
in all directions, the proclamation that taxes and corvée would be required
was sent around. However, when the area was subject to the dGa'-ldan Pho-
brang-pa, the custom of implementing taxation and corvée did not exist in
large measure, so [now] the communities would not immediately deliver
up taxes which seemed to their minds oppressive. When, therefore, the
Bla-ma's servants and bodyguards had been sent out in various directions
and were proceeding around collecting taxes by means of great force, King
Chang-lo-dpal of Kha-ling, the ruler and his officials together with the
retinue, King Pho-brang A-chi of bTsan-mkhar, father and children, and
King Sangs-rgyal-po of gCen-mkhar were discontented; the three of them
(15b) held a discussion and devised a plan of rebellion. On hearing reports of this,
Bla-ma rNam-sras summoned an army from the districts around gZhong-
sgar, [namely] from rTsa-mang, sNga-tshang and Phyi-tshang, [and also]
from the Five Hosts of rTseng-mi and from the bKra-shis-sgang people.

gyis* mi khyab pa khrid nas / gcen mkhar du yongs nas rgol ba'i *gyi
'thab ra 'grigs / rgyal po pho brang gis pha phyi mang las rgol ba'i
'thab ra btsan chas bzos nas / grabs* thogs** med 'grigs nas yod *grab **thog
pa la / dbu mdzad dam chos rab rgyas kyis* dmag dpon byas nas / *kyi
gong gi dmag rnams khrid nas song bas / sngar pho brang A chi yis /
'dom mkhar rgyal po tshe ring las sngar nas blon po 'phrog zhe
khon gyis* / 'dom mkhar rgyal po tshe ring spun gnyis kyis** *gyi **kyi
dmag gi sna len dang gdong bsu (16a) byas nas khong gi yul du
bzhag / de'i sang* nyin gcen mkhar dang / pha chi mang gnyis la *gsang
'tshang kha rgyab pas / kha ling pa rnams kyis* dmag dpung gi *kyi
stobs la ma mgu bar / gcen mkhar grong gi 'thab ra'i nang las phyi
la 'thon* byung ba dang / grong stod rgyal po glang ngas lus la *mthon
khrab gon ral gri 'phyar zhing dbyugs* nas / dmag mi rnams rjes *kyi
bsnyag la the tshom med par rgyugs cing song ba dang / gdong
bsu'i dmag rnams dngangs* skrag nas grong gi 'thab ra'i nang la *ngangs
'dzul ba dang / rgyal po glang ngas kyang de tsho dang mnyam po
nang du 'dzul song bas nang nas gcen* mkhar rgyal po sangs *gcon
rgyas pos rgol du yong ba la / dbu mdzad dam chos rab rgyas kyis
me mda' rgyab nas der bsad pas / nang gi dmag mi rnams dngangs* *ngangs
skrag nas rgol* (16b) ma nus par yod pa la / rgyal po chang lo *rgol repeated
dpal gyis* mkhar mthon** mtho ral pa'i rtse la 'dzegs nas / mda' *gyi **'thon
rgyab pas phyi'i dmag mi rnams kyi reg tu ma nus par yod pa la /
tshe dbang rgyal po song nas / thabs kyis* bslus** nas slab bya *kyi **slus
smras nas khrid yong ba dang / mkhar* mthon** mtho ral pa'i *omitted **'thon
rtse la btsan dar 'phyar ba dang / pha phyi mang nas rgyal po pho
brang dang dmag mi rnams kyis* mthong bas / da ni rgyal po'i *kyi
dmag mi pham pa yin 'dug bsam nas / dmag mi rnams dngangs* *ngangs
skrag nas so sor bros song bas / rgyal po pho brang btson du
bzung / de'i sang* nyin bla ma rnam sras tsha se nas byon / rgyal *gsang
po chang lo dpal / pho brang pha spad gnyis btson du bzung nas /
gzhung spung thang bde ba can* la brdzangs / mkhar mthon** *chen **'thon
mtho ral pa rtsa ba nas bshig / (17a) blon 'bangs mi sde thams
cad mnga' 'og tu bcug / rdzong sa btsan po zhig btsal bas* / sngar *ba'i
dpon slob mi 'gyur brtan pas bka' bsgos* la yang / lung pa'i** 'dus *sgo **pas
che zhing sa btsan po beng mkhar la rdzong gtab* na phug su bstan *btab
pa la phan pa rgya chen* po yong** gsungs ba dang / beng mkhar *cher **yongs
pa rnams kyis* kyang rdzong nged kyi grong la rgyab pa drag zer *kyi
zhus kyang ma gsan par / beng mkhar du btsan sa bzung la dbu
mdzad dam chos rab rgyas bzhag / yul mkhar sa btsan po byi ri zor
la rdzong btab / shar phyogs lung pa'i rgyal po gtso las mi sna
drag* tshad thams cad der 'dus shing khrims ra bcas** nas / khral *grags **bca'
'u lag yang der sdus so / bla ma rnam sras kyi bsam pa la / ra ti jo
bo khams pa ma 'das gong du nga la bu mo ster zhing mag* (17b) *dmag
par bcug pa yin kyang / da ni 'das nas mi 'dug pas sgam ri lung pa'i

King Chang-lo-dpal of Kha-ling led forth an inconceivable number of
soldiers from Phyi-'khor [and] Nang-'khor in Kha-ling and, having come to
gCen-mkhar, prepared a stockade for offering resistance. King Pho-brang,
having made a stockade and defences for offering resistance from Pha-phyi-
mang, had prepared his arrangements without hindrance. Thereupon the
Precentor Dam-chos Rab-rgyas, acting as commander, led forth the troops
mentioned above and departed. Because of the hatred which King Tshe-ring
of 'Dom-mkhar felt for Pho-brang A-chi for his having previously seized one
of his officials, both King Tshe-ring [42] of 'Dom-mkhar and his [cousin-]
(16a) brother guided and welcomed the army and kept it in their home. On the
following day an invasion was made on both gCen-mkhar and Pha-chi-mang
and so the Kha-ling people, who were dispirited by the strength of the army,
issued forth from within the village stockade of gCen-mkhar in order to
capitulate. King Glang-nga [43] of Grong-stod, wearing armour and waving a
sword, unhesitatingly ran off in pursuit of the soldiers so that the soldiers
who had gone to welcome [the invaders] took fright and [re-] entered the
village stockade. After King Glang-nga had also entered together with them,
King Sangs-rgyas-po of gCen-mkhar came forth from within to offer
resistance but the Precentor Dam-chos Rab-rgyas fired his musket at him
and he was killed there. So the soldiers who were inside took fright and
(16b) were unable to resist. Thereupon King Chang-lo-dpal climbed to the top
of the mTho-ral-pa watch tower and fired arrows but he could not hit the
soldiers who were outside. Tshe-dbang rGyal-po then went and having
enticed him skilfully and spoken words of good counsel to him, he led him
away and when a banner was hoisted at the top of the mTho-ral-pa watch
tower King Pho-brang and his soldiers saw it from Pha-phyi-mang and
thought: "Now the king's soldiers have been defeated." The soldiers took
fright and fled in different directions and King Pho-brang was imprisoned.
On the following day *Bla-ma* rNam-sras came from Tsha-se. Having
imprisoned King Chang-lo-dpal and Pho-brang, both father and son, [44] he
sent them off to the capital at sPung-thang bDe-ba-can. [45] The mTho-ral-
(17a) pa watch tower was demolished from its foundations. The officials and
subjects and all the communities were brought into subjection. As for his
searching for a strongpoint for a fortress, *dPon-slob* Mi-'gyur brTan-pa had
previously declared: "If a fortress is established at Beng-mkhar, a place
which is rich and strong, it will eventually cause great benefit to the
Teachings." Even though the Beng-mkhar people had also made a request
saying: "It would be better to build a fortress in our village", he [*Bla-ma*
rNam-sras] would not listen but [merely] took control of the strongpoint
in Beng-mkhar and left the Precentor Dam-chos Rab-rgyas there. [Instead]
he established a fortress at the strongpoint [occupied by] the district
castle of Byi-ri-zor. All the nobility of the Eastern Province, [including]
the kings, their chief councillors and envoys assembled there and after a
court of justice had been established, taxes and corvée were also collected
there.

Bla-ma rNam-sras thought to himself: "Before he passed away Jo-bo
(17b) Khams-pa [46] of Ra-ti gave me his daughter and made me his son-in-law.

blon 'bangs rnams kyis* nga la dag snang ji ltar yod dam / me rag *kyi
bla ma nag seng dga' ldan bla ma dbu mched yin pas ji ltar byed
lta'o snyam nas / dmag dum* zhig dang bcas me rag phyogs la kha *'dum
gtad nas phyin pas bla ma nag seng grwa bu slob dang bcas yul
'thon nas la 'og yul gsum la song nas mi 'dug / me rag sag steng
dang sgam ri lung pa'i mi sde thams cad kyis* 'bab zhus byas mnga' *kyi
'og tu bcug pas / sbis mkhar chos mdzad yang bros song 'dug / bar
tsho gsum wang ser kung pa nas rgyal po zu gi*/ ser kong / rdo rje */omitted
rgyal po / ram geng ra nas sangs rgyas rgya mtsho / khong rgyal po
bzhi yis sna drangs nas slebs* byung ba dang / bzhan rnams kyis** *sleb **kyi
blos ma rangs* pa med kyang / rang bzhin (18a) gyis** zhor*** la *rang **gyi ***gzhor
bab* nas mnga' 'og tu bcug** go / de nas byi ri zor du log nas / *'bab **'jug
phyi mi ser gyi 'dzin skyong gyi sgrig rnam gzhag dang / nang du
rdzong rtsig pa dang / btsan chas byed pa la sogs pa'i gang la gang
'os kyi bkod pa bshams zhing byed nas zla ba brgyad tsam song ba
dang / me rag bla ma nag seng gis* sna bo** byas nas dmag dpon *gi **bon
phan yul drung 'tsho dang / sde pa 'dzam lha gnyis kyis khrid pa'i
bod kyi dmag dpung dang mon pa'i rigs kyi dmag thams cad yongs* *yong
nas / skyi ling shing la sgar bcas* nas / beng mkhar grong stod la *bca'
'tshang* kha rgyab byung ba dang / dbu mdzad dam chos rab *tshang
rgyas kyis* me mda'** yis*** mi gsum btud mar bsad**** pa *kyi **mda'i ***omitted ****gsad
dang / dmag rnams 'ur langs* nas 'tshang kha rgyab ma nus par *lang
skyi ling shing du log nas / dmag phal cher kha ling byi ri zor la
song nas rdzong (18b) bskor ba dang / kha ling pa rnams sngar las
blos rangs* po med pa'i khar** / bla ma nag seng dang bus mkhar *rang **kha la
chos mdzad kyis g.yo rgyu byas nas / khyed kyi rgyal po chang lo
dpal de / 'brug pa'i gzhung phyogs las nged kyi lag tu thob yod zer
nas / lung pa 'di phyogs kyi gos zas cha lugs* rnams bstan** pas / *lug **bsten
kha ling pa rnams yid ches nas ngo* log** pas bla ma rnam sras *ngog **omitted
kyis* tshugs** ma thub par tsha se la*** bros pas / lam du kha *kyi **tshug ***omitted
ling pas sgug* nas / bka' blon dbu mdzad nor bu der bsad** do *bsgrug **gsad
bla ma rang tsha se la 'dzul ba dang / dmag thams cad der
spungs* nas ra bas bskor nas mi thar ba dang / na rang thung pa'i *dpung
rgyal po nor bu A chi spun chas rnams dga' ldan pa'i blo gtad nang
ma yin pa nas / khong la ngo chen bcol nas srog la mi yong ba'i
srog nor ra ti khams pa'i g.yu chen 'bab g.yu skya dkar (19a) sbyin
nas nye skyon med par dmag mi bskor nas / skyi ling shing du dbu
mdzad nor bu'i mgo dang bcas dmag dpon gnyis kyi drung du slebs* *sleb
byung ba mig gis* mthong ba dang / sngar beng mkhar sa btsan pas *gi
brlags* ma 'khal** kyang*** / dbu mdzad dam chos rab rgyas dang *glags **khad ****The passage from* dbu mdzad nor bu *is repeated.*
beng mkhar rgyal blon rnams thams cad ci drag gi gros bsdur byas
pas / dbu mdzad kyi zhal nas da len bla ma dmag* mi'i lag tu tshud *omitted
pa las / nged rang rnams kyis tshugs*mi thub / da len re zhig la ngas *tshug

But now since he is dead and no longer, what sort of regard do the officials and subjects of the sGam-ri district feel for me ? *Bla-ma* Nag-seng of Me-rag is the clerical brother of the *dGa'ldan Bla-ma* [47] so I shall see what he is up to." Together with a detachment of soldiers he set off, proceeding directly towards Me-rag but *Bla-ma* Nag-seng was not there, having left his home [48] together with his monk disciples and gone to La-'og Yul-gsum. All the communities of Me-rag [and] Sag-steng and of the sGam-ri district made acts of submission and were brought into subjection, but the *Chos-mdzad* of sBis-mkhar took off in flight. The Kings Zu-gi, Ser-kong and rDo-rje rGyal-po from Bar-tsho-gsum and from Wang-ser-kung-pa, [49] and Sangs-rgyas rGya-mtsho from Ram-geng-ra – those four kings – guided [*Bla-ma* rNam-sras to their homes] and so he arrived there. The other [rulers],
(18a) although not discontented, submitted in the natural course of things and were brought into subjection.

Having returned to Byi-ri-zor,[50] about eight months passed during which he prepared and carried out as he saw fit plans for the 'external' regulation of [public] order and for the 'internal' building of the fortress, the construction of defences and so forth.

Then, with *Bla-ma* Nag-seng of Me-rag acting as guide, a Tibetan army and all the forces of the Mon-pa tribes led by the two commanders, the 'Phan-yul Doctor' and *sDe-pa* 'Dzam-lha,[51] came and established a camp at sKyi-ling-shing. When they made an invasion of Grong-stod in Beng-mkhar the Precentor Dam-chos Rab-rgyas killed three men in quick succession with his musket. Thereupon the forces became agitated and being unable to attack, they retreated to sKyi-ling-shing. Most of the
(18b) forces then went to Byi-ri-zor in Kha-ling and surrounded the fortress. In addition to the fact that the Kha-ling people had since previous times been disaffected, *Bla-ma* Nag-seng and the *Chos-mdzad* of Bus-mkhar deceived them, saying: "Your King Chang-lo-dpal has come into our hands out of the 'Brug-pa's capital," and on showing them local articles of dress, food and apparel, the Kha-ling people believed them and rebelled. Being unable to do them any harm, *Bla-ma* rNam-sras fled to [his home in] Tsha-se. The Kha-ling people ambushed [his party] and the Minister, Precentor Nor-bu, was killed there. The *Bla-ma* himself entered Tsha-se, whereupon all the forces gathered there and surrounded it with a fence so that he could not escape. Since Nor-bu A-chi, King of Na-rang-thung-pa, and his [cousin-] brothers were the trusted confidants of the dGa-ldan-pa, he
(19a) [*Bla-ma* rNam-sras] used them as negotiators and having given them Khams-pa of Ra-ti's large pale-coloured turquoise as a ransom lest he should lose his life, he was surrounded by the soldiers without injury. At sKyi-ling-shing he saw the head and other limbs of the Precentor Nor-bu which had been brought before the two [Tibetan] commanders.

Although Beng-mkhar had not previously been brought to destruction due to the strength of its position, the Precentor Dam-chos Rab-rgyas and all the rulers and officials of Beng-mkhar held a discussion as to what would be best done, during which the Precentor said: "Now that the

gzhung krong gsar du song nas dpung rgyab kyi dmag zhus nas
bsleb* yong** / de'i bar la khyed rang rnams 'bab zhus nas sdod *slebs **yongs
zer zhing / dbu mdzad rang gzhung la byon / beng mkhar (19b) pa
rnams kyis* rdzong ni sprod ma nyan par 'bab zhus byas pas / ma *kyi
'gyur dang bu chen blongs* nas da ni dga' ldan pho brang gi mnga' *len
zhabs yin no zer / bla ma rnam sras dang ma 'gyur dang bu chen
rnams khyer nas* dmag dpung rnams so sor phye** nas so so'i yul *nas repeated **'phyes
du log go / bla ma rnam sras lha sa la khrid nas / btson khang du
bzhag* pa las bros pas bdas mod** / rjes bsnyags kyis***zin nas *bzhags **mos ***kyi
bkrongs* 'dug / dbu mdzad kyis kyang / krong gsar dpon slob mi *krong
'gyur brtan pa la dmag mi gnas tshul zhib par zhus pas / dpon slob
kyi zhal nas sngar ngas slab pa bzhin / rdzong sa beng mkhar du
bzung na yong rgyu yin pa la da res cung zad nor 'dug gsungs nas /
gang ltar bla ma'i lung bstan yod pa la da rung* bstan pa 'tshugs** *ru **gtsug
rgyu yong gsungs nas / gzhung tsho chen gyi dmag dum (20a) zhig
dang / dbang 'dus pho brang gi mnga' zhabs gang yod kyi dmag
dang / mang sde lung pa'i dmag gang yod bcas la / dmag dpon sku
drung pad dkar chos 'phel dang / gnyer pa long ba gnyis kyis byas /
dbu mdzad kyis* sna khrid** nas dpung chen btegs nas yong bas / *kyi **khrin
gnam sa 'khol ba tsam gyi 'jigs sgra byung ba dang / rtseng mi rgyal
po stong ldan gyis* sna len dang gdong bsu** byas nas / zla ba *gyi **su
gnyis pa'i nang* la dmag dpung gi dkyil sgar chen mo gong thung* *omitted
du bslebs* dang / dag pa be mi'i** dmag mi rnams sa bsrung kha *sleb **ma'i
gnon byed pa la bar tsho gsum du bslebs* byung ba dang / gong *sleb
thung nas dbu mdzad dam chos rab rgyas kyis dmag dum zhig
khrid nas song bas / dag pa'i dmag rnams mkhar sing pa'i rtse la
btsan sa bzung nas / 'brug pa'i dmag dang sna phrad nas 'dzing* *'dzings
(20b) grabs byed pa la / dbu mdzad kyis me mda' cig rgyab pas* *pa'i
chos skyong gi nus mthu yin nam / tshe snga ma'i las gang yin ma
shes par 'phrul 'khor lta bus / dag pa mi khal lnga tsam dngangs* *ngangs
skrag cing 'ur langs nas mkhar sing pa'i brag gi rtse las / g.yang la
lhung nas shi* bas** dmag mi gzhan rnams 'jigs shing skrag*** nas *shis **ba'i ***sgrag
bros pas / shar phyogs kyi mi 'go mnga' 'og tu mi 'dzul ba'i* bsam *bas
pa* nga rgyal dang ldan pa rnams kyang dpa' 'khum par 'gyur to / *pa'i
beng mkhar du byon nas btsan sa bzung zhing / phyogs bzhi mtha'
dag la pho nya ba bang chen btang nas* / khyed rang rnams 'bab *na
zhus byed pa yong rgyu yin nam / so so'i yul du dmag sgar gdeg* *btegs
rgyu yin gyi lan gsal tong* zer bas / kha ling phyi 'khor** nang *gtong **skor
'khor* / U dza rong pa las pa** los pa / sgam ri lung pa me (21a) *skor **omitted
rag sag stengs / bar tsho gsum thams cad 'bab zhus byed pa la kha
'cham* nas / rgyal po gtso las mi 'go thams cad dbu mdzad kyi *cham
drung du* slebs byung ba dang / dbu mdzad kyis mi ser rnams la *omitted
'bab sha 'bab nor phyag mjal 'bul ba dang bcas / gong thung du
dmag dpon gnyis kyi drung du khrid khyer bas / dmag dpon gnyis

Bla-ma [rNam-sras] has fallen into the hands of the soldiers, there is nothing we can do about it. I shall now for the time being go to the [provincial] capital at Krong-gsar and after requesting the forces of a supporting army I shall arrive back. Until then you make acts of submission [to the Tibetans] and remain here." The Precentor himself went to Krong-gsar. The Beng-
(19b) mkhar people made acts of submission but, as for the fortress, they refused to hand it over. After their pledges and hostages had been received, they declared: "Now we are under the authority of the dGa'-ldan Pho-brang."

Taking with them *Bla-ma* rNam-sras, the pledges and hostages, the armies separated in different directions and returned to their various homes. *Bla-ma* rNam-sras was taken to lHa-sa and put in prison, from where he fled and was chased. His pursuers caught and killed him.

As for the Precentor, after he had reported in detail all the news about the soldiers to *Krong-gsar dPon-slob* Mi-'gyur brTan-pa, the *dPon-slob* said: "You have committed a small mistake as it would have gone well if you had taken control of a site for a fortress at Beng-mkhar as I had said previously. In any case," he said, "since we have the prophecy of the *Bla-ma* [Ngag-dbang rNam-rgyal], we shall establish the Teachings once more." *sKu-drung* Pad-dkar Chos-'phel and the 'Blind Steward', [52] these two, acted as
(20a) commanders of a detachment of the Great Hosts [53] of the capital, of all the available forces under the authority of dBang-'dus Pho-brang [54] and of all the available forces of the Mang-sde-lung people. With the Precentor guiding it, the great force set off and proceeded on its way, so that fearful sounds as if the sky and earth were boiling came forth. After King sTong-ldan of rTseng-mi had guided and welcomed it, the army arrived in the second month [of the lunar calendar] at its great central camp at Gong-thung. When the Dag-pa [55] soldiers of Be-mi came to Bar-tsho-gsum in order to harass the defenders, the Precentor Dam-chos Rab-rgyas led a detachment from Gong-thung and went there. The forces of the Dag-pa took control of a strong-point at the top of mKar-sing-pa and, on first coming into contact with the
(20b) forces of the 'Brug-pa, made preparations for battle. When the Precentor fired a shot of his musket, about five score men of the Dag-pa took fright at [what they saw as] a sorcerous device, not knowing whether it was caused by the magical power of the 'Protectors of Religion' or by the *karma* of their previous lives; raising a commotion, they all fell from the top of the mKhar-sing-pa rock into a ravine and died.

The other soldiers were terrified and fled, with the result that the leaders of the Eastern Province who had been arrogant in their unwillingness to subordinate themselves to authority lost their courage too. After [the army of the 'Brug-pa] had gone to Beng-mkhar and taken control of the strong-point, envoy-couriers were despatched in all four directions, declaring: "Send clear replies as to whether you are going to come to make acts of submission or whether you are going to maintain military camps in your various homes." All the people of the Phyi-'khor [and] Nang-'khor of Kha-
(21a) ling, of Las-pa [and] Los-pa in U-dza-rong(-pa) and of Me-rag [and] Sa-stengs in sGam-ri-lung(-pa) agreed and so all their kings, chief councillors

kyis zhal nas / khyed rang rnams dmag dmangs* gis 'khrug** *dmang **'khrul
rtsod* byed ma dgos** par / gros khyab che ba'i sgo nas 'dir yong *brtsod **gos
ba shin tu legs gsungs so / de nas dam tshig gi dam bca' byed pa la
lha dpang du bka' srung* dam can chos skyong thams cad gsol *bsrung
mchod kyis* mnyes par byas nas dpang du btsugs** / mi dpang du *kyi **btsug
tsho chen gyi rgan 'go / dbang 'dus* pho brang gi rgan 'go / mang *dus
sde lung pa'i rgan 'go / chu stod kyi chos mdzad rgyal mo / (21b)
gzhong sgar chos mdzad dkar po gdung / snga tshang* rgyal po dar *tsha
'jam / phyi tshang rgyal po zla'u la / ba geng rgyal po* rdor re / *omitted
rtseng mi rgyal po stong ldan rnams / zas nor gnang sbyin gyis* *gyi
tshim par byas nas mi dpang du btsugs*/ lha mi dpang** du *btsug **dpangs
btsugs* pa'i drung du / shar phyogs lung pa'i rgyal po gtso las / *btsug
mi 'go thams cad mna' tshig dor* ba la / dus de** ring nas bzung / *'dor **'di
dpon dga' ldan pho brang pa rgyab skyur zhing / chos rje 'brug pa
mdun du len nas / bka' gang gnang gsung ci grub byed rang mi
byed re* zer nas mna' bkal zhing mna' bor / gang la gang 'os gnas *ri
skabs dang bstun pa'i bu chen dang / btsun khral* rnams bsdus *khras
nas gnyer pa long ba dmag dpung dang bcas* nas gzhung la** log / *chas **lo
sku drung pad dkar chos 'phel 'khor dang bcas pa beng mkhar du
byon nas grong stod rgyal (22a) po* lha lnga'i khyim du bzhugs *omitted
nas rdzong gi btsan cha bzos / grong stod la ltag rdzong brtsigs* / *btsig
grong smad la rdzong gi dbu rtse lcags ri 'khor yug dang bcas pa
bzhengs nas der phebs cing bzhugs / rgyal khrims chos khrims gnyis
kyi khrims bca' / dbu mdzad kyis* thabs kyi 'khor lo sgyur nas / *kyi
bka' blon mdzad / mtho ba khrims kyis gnan* / dma' ba thabs** *gnon **thams
kyis skyong / bka' khrims drang po nor rdzas dang rang 'dod ngo
lta la ma 'khri bar / khrims dang nyi ma gzhung rgyugs kyis* / *kyi
bzang po la bya dga' bster* / ngan pa la khyad gsod** byas pas / *ster **sod
steng nas 'phrog sa med / 'og nas bslu ba med par byas / ma nyan
par byung na nag gcod drag po lus srog gi* steng du btang bas / *mi
'jigs shing skrag pas grags pa'i* steng du khyab pa'i stobs las / dus *pa
ding sang gi bar du bstan (22b) pa'i ring* lugs** shar phyogs su *ringpung **omitted
yod pa ni / sku drung dang dbu mdzad gnyis kyi phyag rjes yin
'dug / de'i dus su gung gdung rgyal po yang / sa ri rong dog cing sa
zur chod thag ring ba dang / 'og tu 'dzul ma* nyan par gnya' rengs** *ba **re
byas nas yod pa la / phyis nas lo kha shas song ba dang / sku drung
pad dkar chos 'phel dang gsol dpon bstan pa don ldan gnyis kyis* *kyi
dmag gung gdung la bcug / rgyal po btul nas mnga' 'bangs la bcug
pa yin / phyis nas sa skyong rdzong dpon rim par phebs cing / bstan
pa rin po che la 'dzin skyong spel gsum lugs* gnyis kyi sgo nas / *lug
gces spras* rje cher mdzad pa las / bstan pa'i ring lugs kyi mdzad *spros
khyon* mnga' thang nam mkha'i gong du 'phags pa las / mnga' *khyod
'bangs* mi sde yangs pa'i rgyal khams thams cad / zas nor longs *'bang
spyod kyi dpal (23a) 'byor dar zhing rgyas* pa dang / phan tshun *rgyal

and leaders came before the Precentor. Thereupon the Precentor brought [these] subjects, together with their 'tribute-meat', 'tribute-wealth', gifts and offerings, before the two commanders at Gong-thung. The two commanders said: "There being no need for you to contend with your popular forces, it is very good that, through broad counsels, you should have come here." Then in order to swear oaths they called as their divine witnesses upon all the 'Guardians of Commandments', the 'Oath-bound' deities and the 'Protectors of Religion' after pleasing them with supplications and offerings. For their human witnesses, after satisfying them with gifts of food and articles of wealth, they called upon the elders of the 'Great Hosts', the elders of dBang-'dus Pho-brang, the elders of Mang-sde-
(21b) lung(-pa), [56] *Chos-mdzad* rGyal-mo of Chu-stod, [57] *Chos-mdzad* dKar-po-gdung [58] of gZhong-sgar, King Dar-'jam [59] of sNga-tshang, King Zla'u-la [60] of Phyi-tshang, King rDo-re [61] of Ba-geng and King sTong-ldan [62] of rTseng-mi. In front of the gods and men they had called upon to witness, all the kings, chief councillors and leaders of the Eastern Province pronounced the words of the oath, each declaring: "As from today onwards we cast behind us the dGa'-ldan Pho-brang-pa as our lords and receive before us the Hierarchs of the 'Brug-pa. We shall fulfil whatever commands are given and whatever we are told to do." Thus they took the oath and pronounced it. Having collected hostages and 'monk levies' in accordance with circumstances as was seen fit, the 'Blind Steward' together with the army returned to the capital. [63]

sKu-drung Pad-dkar Chos-'phel with his retinue went to Beng-mkhar
(22a) and having taken up residence in the house of King lHa-lnga of Grong-stod, the defences of a fortress [64] were constructed. At Grong-stod an upper citadel was built. At Grong-smad the fortress' central tower together with its encircling rampart walls was built, after which he [Pad-dkar Chos-'phel] went there and took up residence. He instituted the laws of both secular law and spiritual law. The Precentor [Dam-chos Rab-rgyas] acted as minister, turning the wheel of method. He pressed down on the upper orders with laws and protected the lower orders with skilful measures. Without regard to wealth, personal desires or status [in issuing] fair edicts, the laws and the discharge of government affairs showed favour to the good and contempt for the evil, thus eliminating the possibility of acts of plunder committed from above or acts of cunning committed from below. If there were disobedient persons, severe punishments were meted upon their bodies and lives, so that people were terrified; reports of this were not only noised
(22b) abroad but spread everywhere and because of their force, the order of the Teachings [65] exists up to present times in the Eastern Province, a token to the achievements of both the *sKu-drung* and the Precentor.

During their time the King of Gung-gdung, whose land and hills were made up of narrow ravines, cragged and remote, acted obstinately, refusing to subordinate. Later, after some years had gone by, *sKu-drung* Pad-dkar Chos-'phel and *gSol-dpon* bsTan-pa Don-ldan both invaded Gung-gdung with a force. The King was subdued and brought into subjugation.

Later, as the ruling *rdzong-dpon*(s) [of bKra-shis-sgang] succeeded each other by turn, they acted with increasing love, upholding, guarding and diffusing the Precious Teachings by means of the dual system so that the sphere and dominion of the Teachings' order was raised up to the heavens.
(23a) Thereafter, in all the broad realms of the subjects and their communities

'thab cing brtsod pa med pa / phyogs bzhi mtha'* dag nas las sgo'i *mtha'i
kha 'phye nas / bka' khrims drang po'i gdugs dkar dgung* la** btegs *dgongs **omitted
cing skor bas mthu stobs chen po'i bsil grib las / rgya bod shar nub
phyogs bzhi mtha' dag* gi gzhi lam 'bras**gsum / sa yul gang du *omitted **byed
phyin kyang 'phrog bcom rkun jag med par / rang nyid stabs bde
ba'i ngang las gang la gang 'dod nor rdzas kyi longs spyod la / rang
rang so so'i ci la ci 'dod kyi dngos po dka' las med par 'bad med lhun
gyis* grub** pa'i bsam don yid bzhin gyi nor bu lta bur len nas / chu *gyi **'grub
me shing 'dzoms pa'i sa bde skyid* ngal bso zhing nyes skyon med *skyi
par / rang rang so so'i gnas su log pa dang / yul du 'ang sngar med
kyi so* nams kyi (23b) las la brtson 'grus che shing / gna'** dus *bsod **gnas
kyi snga phyi mig ltos kyang zhing 'debs la / mkhas pas lo thog
rnams kyang je cher 'phel zhing rgyas pa dang / rgyal* khrims gser *rgyas
gyi gnya' shing chos bzhin skyong ba / dbang chen mtho non nye* *nyer
ring med par bde skyid* phun sum** tshogs pa dang ldan par *bskyid **gsum
byung ba ni / dpal 'brug pa rin po che ngag dbang rnam* rgyal gyi *rnams
thugs rje dang sku drin yin no / gzhan yang sangs rgyas la* khro *omitted
ba yod kyang 'dzin pa med pa'i dpe bzhin / sngar gong stobs kyis* *kyi
'khor los* bsgyur** ba'i rgyal po chen po rnams kyis dbang ma *lo **sgyur
sgyur ba'i gshis* / rang rang so so'i lung pa la dbang sgyur ba'i *shis
stobs mnga' thang la mgu nas / shar phyogs kyi yul khams 'dir nga
che nga drag snyam pa'i nga rgyal gyis mnga' 'og tu 'dzul mi nyan
pa / ku ri lung nas / rgyal po dga' ba / dpon (24a) chen dar ma /
kha ling rgyal po / stong phu rgyal po / gung gdung rgyal po / nya
mkhar gdung / bla ma rgyal mtshan gyi mi brgyud dang gzhan
yang bka' la mi 'khri ba rnams kyang / sngar byas spangs shing da
byas dang du len pa'i 'gyod snang gi zhabs phyi ci 'gyur zhu ba la /
thugs rje brtse* bas gzigs nas / btson dang bu gter bzhag pa las *btso
dgongs* yangs** sku drin*** bskyangs**** nas / rang rang so *gong **yang ***mgri ****skyangs
so'i yul du gang yod kyi khang zhing nor rdzas blon 'bangs dang
bcas pa gang yod rnams gnang nas / mi brgyud rim* par bded cing *omitted
ding sang gi bar du skyid* par** yun du longs spyod cing bde bar *skyi **phar pha
sdod rgyu byung ba ni / dpal ldan 'brug pa'i thugs rje phyogs ris
mi* mnga' bas [ngan* pa*] tshar gcad [bzang* po*] rjes su 'dzin *omitted
pa las dge legs kyi dpal du gyur pa yin no //

the abundant enjoyment of food and wealth increased and among them there was an absence of strife and contention. Trade routes having been opened up in all four directions, each person [is now able to] obtain spontaneously as if [by means of] a wish-fulfilling gem, without difficulty or exertion, his heart's desire of whatever goods he wants [after having searched] easily for the rich abundance of whatever articles he should desire, without theft or banditry wherever he goes, to India or Tibet, to the east or west – at the starting point, on the way and at the destination, [these] three, throughout the four directions – under the powerful cool shade of the white parasol of fair edicts that is hoisted and revolved in the heavens. Then, having rested contentedly at places where water, fire and wood abound, each person returns without harm to his own place.[66] In their homes too, because they work with great diligence in agriculture as
(23b) never before and due to their skill in cultivating by being attentive to the timing [of ploughing, transplanting etc. observed] in former ages, harvests are also caused to increase and multiply. And the golden yoke of secular law administered according to religious principles is devoid of partiality in pressing down on the powerful higher orders. That [all of this] has come forth with abundant happiness is due to the mercy and kindness of the Precious One of the Glorious 'Brug-pa, Ngag-dbang rNam-rgyal.

Furthermore – in accordance with the example of the Buddha who, although having a wrathful aspect, has no 'clinging' – because the great *bāla-cakravarti-rājas* of former times did not gain power [over the whole area], each delighting in the strength and dominion [they acquired] from gaining power in their own lands, [the petty rulers] in this region of the Eastern Province used to refuse to subordinate themselves to authority on account of their pride in thinking: "I am great, I am better." But on seeing with loving compassion that King dGa'-ba[67] and the Great Chief Dar-ma[68]
(24a) of Ku-ri-lung, the King of Kha-ling,[69] the King of sTong-phu,[70] the King of Gung-gdung,[71] the *gDung* of Nya-mkhar,[72] the descendants of *Bla-ma* rGyal-mtshan[73] and, moreover, all those who had not abided to commands were [now] performing whatever works of service that came their way in a state of repentance that forsook their previous actions and purified their present deeds, those that had been imprisoned and those sons who had been kept as hostages were favoured with remissions and [re-] granted whatever houses, fields, articles of wealth, officers and subjects they each had in their various homes. So their descendants follow in succession and that they should up to the present be enjoying contentment for long periods and living happily is due to the impartial mercy of the Glorious 'Brug-pa(s), [a mercy] which, having eradicated the evil and assisted the good, has become a glory of virtue.

Thus it has been said.

zhes kyang smras so / dpal (24b) 'brug par lung lha'i gdung rgyud
kyis bstan pa'i ring lugs* / lho mon kha bzhi las nyi ma shar phyogs *lug
su byung zhing* rgyas pa'i lo rgyus** gsal ba'i me long 'di ni / dbu *omitted **rgyud
mdzad dam chos rab rgyas sku dngos kyi zhal nas ji ltar gsungs pa
dang / rgan pa mig mthong rgyus* yod rnams kyis smras pa bzhin / *rgyu
shākya'i btsun pa ban rgan wa gindra'i ming gis yi ger 'khrul med
bkod pa'o // //

(24b) This *Clear Mirror [containing] the Story of How the Order Prophesied to the [School of the] Glorious 'Brug-pa by its Divine Lineage Came and Spread in the Eastern Province of the Sun Within the 'Southern Mon Country of Four Approaches'* was set down in writing unerringly by the reverend one of the Śākyas, the old monk named Wa-gindra (Ngag-dbang)[74] in accordance with whatever the Precentor Dam-chos Rab-rgyas [75] recounted in person and with what was related by elderly persons who had themselves witnessed and experienced [the events recorded herein].

Notes to Text II

1. *nyi-ma* ('sun') here and in the text below has a purely rhetorical function. The area referred to as the Eastern Province is the region between Krong-sar and the eastern border of the country. *lHo Mon Kha bZhi* is the old name for Bhutan (Aris 1976: 43 note 63).
2. The first *Zhabs-drung* (1594-?1651), founder of the Bhutanese state.
3. This relates to the defeat in 1642 of the gTsang ruler, bsTan-skyong dBang-po, by Guśri Khan, chief of the Qośot Mongol tribe who is referred to here by a Mongolian title, Dalai Bātur. The *phyag-mdzod* of the dGa'-ldan-pa (= dGe-lugs-pa) school, who is here given the name of *sDe-pa Nang-so* A-bo, can be identified with bSod-nams Chos-'phel, 'regent' of the 5th Dalai Lama, who played a vital part in inviting Guśri to attack the gTsang forces and place his master on the throne. On the events leading up to and following this crucial event in Tibetan history, see Shakabpa 1976: 397-462.

   This opening passage of the *Lo-rgyus* is important for its assertion that the gTsang-pa rule had extended south into this region of Bhutan. No doubt, however, the connection was as tenuous as that which existed later under dGe-lugs-pa rule, as we see on f. 15a below.
4. See *rGyal-rigs*, f. 19b.
5. See f. 5a-b below and the notes thereto.
6. Mi-'gyur brTan-pa was the first governor (or *dpon-slob*) of Krong-sar. The date of his appointment is not certain but must have taken place some years before 1651 when the *Zhabs-drung* went into retreat. Mi-'gyur brTan-pa later succeeded as the third *'Brug sDe-srid* in 1667 and reigned for fourteen years down to 1680. Accounts of his rule are found in *LCB* I, ff. 94b-96a, and ff. 68b-70a of the *rnam-thar* of bsTan-'dzin Rab-rgyas. The annexation of eastern Bhutan is always regarded as his personal achievement, though it is clear from this text that he never took to the field himself, but instead directed the whole operation from his stronghold in Krong-sar. The exact date of the annexation cannot be determined from this account but it seems likely to have been in the 1650's during the *Zhabs-drung*'s 'retreat', there is no mention of the *Zhabs-drung*'s direct involvement in the campaign and he only appears here (ff. 4b-6b) at its prelude, some three years before it began in earnest. The whole campaign is briefly alluded to in *PBP* (ff. 144b) in a passage describing the areas taken over by the 'Brug-pa authorities during the 'retreat' of *Zhabs-drung*. More specifically, the *rnam-thar* of bsTan-'dzin Rab-rgyas (f. 59a) maintains that the Eastern Province was ceded to the new realm in the year 1655. That seems to be the interpretation warranted by: *shing-mo-lug lor shar-phyogs Kha-ling tshun 'brug-lung dkar-mor bsgyur-ba'i bar-du*. This appears in a passage on the first *sde-srid* and derives from the *bstan-rtsis* quoted in *PBP*, f. 145b.

   During Mi-'gyur brTan-pa's tenure of the office of *'Brug sDe-srid* (1667-1680), the western border of the country was extended westward towards the area around Kalimpong in West Bengal. (This used to be referred to as British Bhutan, following the annexation of 1865-6). The westward movement brought the government of Bhutan into conflict with the authorities of Both Sikkim and Tibet. Shakabpa (1976:447-8) has used some interesting Tibetan documents which deal with this period (1668-78), particularly with the role played by the Lepcha chieftain Mon-pa A-lcog, the main opponent of the Bhutanese.
7. sPung-thang is the literary name for sPu-na-kha, the winter capital of Bhutan. The *rdzong* there was built in 1637 (*LCB* I, f. 35b and *PBP*, f. 97b).
8. bsTan-'dzin 'Brug-rgyas, the Ist *'Brug sDe-srid* (ruled 1651-56). For accounts of his rule see *LCB* I, ff. 92a-93b and ff. 58a-59b of the *rnam-thar* of bsTan-'dzin Rab-rgyas.
9. It is worth introducing at this point a long passage (ff. 20b-22a) from the undated biography of Kun-dga' rGyal-mtshan (1689-1713) by the 9th Head Abbot of Bhutan, Shākya Rin-chen (regn. 1744-55). It provides a quite different, and very likely apocryphal, account of the parentage of *Bla-ma* rNam-sras. According to this version his father is said to have been the 'illegitimate' son of bsTan-pa'i Nyi-ma (1567-1619), father of the great *Zhabs-drung* Ngag-dbang rNam-rgyal. bsTan-pa'i Nyi-ma is said to have had a large number of tantric consorts; the 2nd *'Brug sDe-srid* bsTan-'dzin 'Brug-grags (regn. 1656-67) is claimed to have been the product of one such union. However, the similar claim here was doubtless made to aggrandize the pedigree of Kun-dga' rGyal-mtshan, the first in a line of incarnations who re-embodied the *Zhabs-drung*'s own son 'Jam-dpal rDo-rje (1631-?1681); according to this tradition, our *Bla-ma* rNam-sras was the step-brother of Kun-dga' rGyal-mtshan's grand-father. It provides a good example of the strong temptation to reinforce the slender threads of incarnational succession by backing it with family ties. The passage is also important for providing independent corroboration to the story of the

eastward expansion of the Bhutanese state as told here in the *Lo-rgyus*. It is interesting to note that when the passage was written a treaty between Tibet and Bhutan was in force, in contrast to the period when these events took place. The treaty in question was no doubt the one drawn up by the Bhutanese and Pho-lha-nas, the Tibetan ruler, in about 1730.

Perceiving that there was a special need to bring benefit to the Teachings in the future, he [bsTan-pa'i Nyi-ma, 1567-1619] attended on various wise ladies who possessed the signs of *ḍākinīs* of gnosis as his 'companions on the path' (*lam-gyi grogs*). Consequently a son was born in the region of Yam-'brog and by stages he came to the residence [of the 'Brug-pa at Ra-lung]. He was given the name Thugs-dam Pad-dkar and was bestowed with the precepts of maturation and release. Having resided in meditation at various hermitages, he then went to Grwa sDing-po-che (see Ferrari 1959: 55 and map), the seat of the great Omniscient One Padma dKar-po [1527-92]. He surrendered himself to the great scholar-sage Rin-chen dPal-bzang [cf. sNyan-grags dPal-bzang in the *Lo-rgyus*]. By command of that lord he was commissioned to tame the beings of the Eastern Realm of the southern region (*lho-rgyud shar-phyogs-kyi rgyal-khams*), and so he brought great benefit to beings by means of the six-syllable *mantra*, the essence of Ārya Mahākaruṇā. He became known as the King of Tsha-sa and so received honour. This lord also took to himself a girl possessing the signs [of a *dakini*] and *Bla-ma* rNam-sras was born to them. Then on his return [to Tibet] he built a monastery at the restful abode called Brag-dkar in La-'og Yul-gsum [in Kameng] and stayed there in meditation. There too a son was born to him and he gave him the name of Chos-skyong.

At that time the Precious One of the 'Brug-pa, the Mighty *Dharmarāja* Ngag-dbang rNam(-par)-rgyal(-ba) [1594- ? 1651], had himself come to these Southern Lands and was gradually establishing the teachings of religion and the state. It was then that *Bla-ma* rNam-sras came to be on bad terms with King bDe-ba of Kha-gling and consequently he hastened to the presence of *Chos-rgyal* Mi-'gyur bsTan-pa [3rd *'Brug sDe-srid*, 1667-80] who was then residing as the *spyi-bla* [see glossary] of Chos-'khor Rab-rtse [Krong-sar]. Out of broad and loving regard, the latter gave him great assistance and said to him: "It is at present a time when *Zhabs-drung Rin-po-che* [Ngag-dbang rNam-rgyal] is continuously giving the precepts of maturation and release at the residence of sPungs-thang [sPu-na-kha rDzong in western Bhutan]. It would be proper for you to go and receive them too." When accordingly he [*Bla-ma* rNam-sras] was on his way there, the *Zhabs-drung Rin-po-che* saw him clairvoyantly and declared: "A son of our *Yam-'brog-pa* Thugs-dam Pad-dkar is coming here. He will be a help to Mi-'gyur bsTan-pa in subjugating the eastern districts." He [the *Zhabs-drung*] is also said to have given further prophecies from his clear view of the distant future. Before long [*Bla-ma* rNam-sras] came before him and he treated him with love. Having given him properly the precepts of maturation and release, he then sent him back to Chos-'khor Rab-rtse.

For the duration of seven years he [*Bla-ma* rNam-sras] stayed as the servant of *Chos-rgyal* Mi-'gyur bsTan-pa, at which time he assisted in the work of taming the arrogant rulers and officers [of the districts] as far as bKra-shis-sgang in the east, who included among them the *Chos-'khor dPon-po* of Bum-thang [see the *Lo-rgyus*, ff. 6b-8a]. He thus took upon himself the great burden of the Teachings with such courage that he did not shy from far-ranging endeavours which included the work of bringing [the districts and their rulers] under the broad white parasol of the religion and state of the 'Brug-pa hierarchs. Then together with the person called *dBu-mdzad* Dam-chos Rab-rgyas, he went to protect the subjects of 'Brug bKra-shis-sgang. Before long he fell into the hands of a large Tibetan force which had invaded, and so he died [see the *Lo-rgyus*, ff. 14b-19b].

Then his incarnation was born at the monastery of Brag-dkar as the son of *Bla-ma* Chos-skyong [his step-brother]. He received the name of 'Brug Phun-tshogs. The younger brother of this incarnation was the great being *dBon-po* rDo-rje, the father of the *rGyal-sras bDag-nyid Chen-po* [Kun-dga' rGyal-mtshan 1689-1713, incarnation of the *Zhabs-drung*'s son 'Jam-dpal rDo-rje, 1631-?1681], a natural yogin who untied all the artificial fetters. Due to the fact that during those times there was no treaty (*chings-'jags*) between Tibet and the South [Bhutan], great hostility was being shown by the [dGe-lugs-pa] monastery of rTa-wang [in Kameng]. *dBu-mdzad* Dam-chos Rab-rgyas therefore warned him [*dBon-po* rDo-rje] to come in this direction. Accordingly he came towards bKra-shis-sgang with his retinue. [The 'Brug-pa authorities gave him the monastery of Tsham-'brog which is said to have been associated with the figure of 'Brug-pa Kun-legs (1455-1529). He settled there and married Karma lHa-mo who gave birth to their son Kun-dga' rGyal-mtshan, the Ist *rGyal-sras sPrul-sku* of Bhutan.]

10. I have not been able to identify sNyan-grags dPal-bzang (Rin-chen dPal-bzang in the above passage). He is perhaps the person referred to as *Bla-ma* sKu'i-skyes in the Addendum [III] of the *rGyal-rigs* (f.51a); Thugs-dam Pad-dkar (the same as Thub-bstan Pad-dkar here) and he jointly occupied the position of *bla-ma* in the tripartite system of clan rule (*bla-ma, wang-ma* and *gtso-rgyan*). It is not clear which branch of the 'Brug-pa school the monastery of Grwa sDing-po-che belonged to. It can be assumed from the above passage that it was from this monastery that the incumbents to the office were appointed before the annexation of eastern Bhutan.

11. The foundation of these 'Brug-pa monasteries in eastern Bhutan must have paved the way to full 'Brug-pa rule in that area in the same way that the 'Brug-pa monasteries did in the west of the country. However, none of the eastern ones are at present identifiable.

12. More correctly sNa-dkar-rtse, on which see Wylie 1962:74, 145 Note 277.

13. The dual system of 'religious law' (*chos-khrims*) and 'royal law' (*rgyal-khrims*). See the *Khrims-yig* below, passim.

14. See Aris 1979: 118-19.

15. This place lies at the top of the sTang valley in Bum-thang.

16. On the role played by bSod-nams dBang-po in recognising the second *sGang-steng sPrul-sku*, bsTan-'dzin Legs-pa'i Don-grub (1645-1726), see f. 28a of the latter's biography. On the hereditary office of the *Chu-smad gDung*, see Aris 1979: 117.

17. On the office of *mi-dpon*, see *ibid.* 119, 199. sDom-mkhar is a village at the western end of the Chu-smad valley, close to the palace of bKra-shis Chos-gling.

18. This is the same lCags-mkhar that appears in the story of the 'Sindhu Raja' (Aris 1979: 43-59, and f. 8a below). The title *gnas-po* (pronounced 'nep' in the vernacular) is rarely used now except with the meaning of 'host'. It also signifies the guardian spirit of a particular locality.

19. On the militia still drawn today for ceremonial purposes from the 'Eight Great Hosts of the Wang People' (*Wang Tsho-chen brgyad*) see Aris 1976: 615-617, 625 note 61.

20. 'Brug rNam-rgyal was the 'steward' (*gnyer-pa*) of Ra-lung, the chief 'Brug-pa monastery in Tibet. He seems to have been appointed to this position by *Zhabs-drung* when the latter entered retreat at lCags-ri in 1623. In about 1645 Ra-lung was formally taken over by the dGe-lugs-pa in reprisal for their military defeat in Bhutan. 'Brug rNam-rgyal fled south to his master in Bhutan and soon rose to the position of *gZhung mGron-gnyer*, the fourth incumbent to that office. As commander-in-chief of the forces of western Bhutan, he not only played a vital part in the annexation of Eastern Bhutan, but was also responsible for subjugating the area of Dar-dkar-nang (*LCB.* ff. 30a, 42a, 47b). He is not to be confused with the person of the same name who ruled as the 21st *'Brug sDe-srid* from 1799 to 1803.

21. Wa-can rDzong in the Shar district of western Bhutan was built by descendents of Gar-ston, son of *Pha-jo* 'Brug-sgom Zhig-po (1208-76), who had been appointed by his father to control the three districts of gDung, Had and sDong (f. 31a of *Pha-jo's* biography). Of these, only Had ('Ha' of the map) can now be located. The family of the *Wa-can Zhal-ngo* had control of the Wa-can rDzong and seems to have been the most powerful of all those in Shar claiming descent from Gar-ston, among whom stood the *Zhal-ngo* families of Khyen, Wa, Shar-ngos and sTod-lu (*Hūṃ-ral gdung-rabs*, f. 3b). The *Wa-can Zhal-ngo* became the ally of *Zhabs-drung* Ngag-dbang rNam-rgyal, and the traditional powers of the family must have been absorbed quite soon into the new 'Brug-pa regime established in the west (*LCB* I, ff. 26a-b, 32b). It is clear from this passage of the *Lo-rgyus* that at the start of the eastern campaign the Shar district was still being administered by the 'Brug-pa authorities from Wa-can, and not from the new *rdzong* at dBang-'dus Pho-brang (built in 1638) which later took over control of the entire district (see f. 20a below).

22. This is the *gDan-sa* Yu-ba-shing visited by Padma Gling-pa (f. 186b of his *rnam-thar*). The present inhabitants of Bum-thang were unable to give me its location.

23. There is some confusion about what really happened to the remains of Padma Gling-pa. According to a local tradition in Bum-thang, the *gTam-zhing Chos-rje* who had charge of the portable *stūpas* containing the remains of both Padma Gling-pa and his son Grags-pa rGyal-mtshan, employed a ruse to deceive the 'Brug-pa commanders into taking away to sPu-na-kha the wrong *stūpa*, i.e. that of Grags-pa rGyal-mtshan. This is denied by the 'Brug-pa government which maintains that the *stūpa* still kept today in the *rdzong* at sPu-na-kha is the right one. A further *sku-gdung mchod-rten* of Padma Gling-pa is housed in the palace of g.Yung-drung Chos-gling in Mang-sde-lung and is said to have been moved there this century from its original location in Kheng mTha'-ma.

24. The 'Blind *gNyer-pa*' is unlikely to have been *gNyer-pa* 'Brug rNam-rgyal, the commander-in-chief (see f. 7b above). The designation of *rdzong-bdag* for a fort-governor has recently been revived in Bhutan.

25. See *rGyal-po sindha ra-dza'i rnam-thar*, f. 19a.
26. On the legendary origins of these chiefs see *rGyal-rigs*, f. 43a.
27. 'Phakidung' of the maps. *gZhung* ('capital') suggests the place had some precedence over other communities in Ku-ri-lung, but the kings of Phag-gi-gdung are not mentioned in the *rGyal-rigs*.
28. This is usually contracted to lHun-rtse.
29. This is similarly contracted to Yang-rtse.
30. See *rGyal-rigs*, f. 20b.
31. See *rGyal-rigs*, f. 43b.
32. See *rGyal-rigs*, f. 16b.
33. See *rGyal-rigs*, f. 17a and f. 21b below.
34. See *rGyal-rigs*, f. 17b.
35. See *rGyal-rigs*, f. 20a.
36. See ff. 17b-18a below. *Bla-ma* Nag-seng of Me-rag may be identified with Blo-gros rGya-mtsho, the fourth incarnation of bsTan-pa'i sGron-me of the Jo-bo clan (*rGyal-rigs*, f.30b). Sarkar (1975: 35-39) has provided an interesting account of the life of 'Lote Gyatso' (sic), also known as 'Mera Lama', apparently based on an oral tradition that survives in the rTa-wang area. Born in the same household as bsTan-pa'i sGron-me, he is particularly remembered today for the part he played in constructing the great rTa-wang monastery (or *rdzong*) under the directions of the 5th Dalai Lama. This occurred sometime after "the Nyingmapa and the Dukpa and Karmapa sub-sects of the Kargyupa had combined against the Gelugpa and directed their attack against his religious establishments" (op. cit., 36).
37. Cf. f. 15a below. The dGe-lugs-pa rule in this area of eastern Bhutan must have been the natural successor to the gTsang-pa rule which collapsed in 1642.
38. See Aris 1979: 117-18.
39. Perhaps 'outer, inner and middling' (*phyi nang bar gsum*).
40. I.e., he was killed.
41. Cf. f. 5a above. *Bla-ma* rNam-sras' father had married a lady of Tsha-se.
42. See *rGyal-rigs*, f. 20a.
43. The name is spelt Slang-nga on f. 12b above and lHa-lnga on f. 22a below.
44. See note 55 to the *rGyal-rigs*.
45. sPung-thang bDe-ba-can (or -chen) is the name of the *rdzong* at sPu-na-kha. See note 7 above.
46. Presumably a descendant of Kra'u who established this branch of the Jo-bo clan (*rGyal-rigs*, f. 29b).
47. The 5th Dalai Lama, Ngag-dbang Blo-bzang rGya-mtsho (1617-1682). On the relationship between the *Me-rag Bla-ma* and the 5th Dalai Lama, see Sarkar 1975: 36-39.
48. His birthplace was actually Ber-mkhar in La-'og Yul-gsum. Me-rag was the site of one of the monasteries founded by the first of his line, bsTan-pa'i sGron-me (*rGyal-rigs*, f. 30b).
49. See *rGyal-rigs*, f. 18a, 36b.
50. See f. 17a above.
51. This invasion may perhaps have formed part of the large scale attack on Bhutan by the dGe-lugs-pa forces of Tibet in 1657, the third dGe-lugs-pa invasion (*LCB* I, ff. 51b-52a and f. 64b of bsTan-'dzin Rab-rgyas' *rnam-thar*; also Shakabpa 1976: 443-5). The Bhutanese sources affirm that one column of this invasion was directed towards bKra-shis-sgang in the east, led by a certain lHa-rgya Ras-pa (a name that appears elsewhere as lHa-rgya-ri-pa). It may eventually be possible to identify him with one of the two Tibetan commanders mentioned here. On the lHa-rgya-ri princes see Tucci 1949: 649 and Petech 1973: 50. Members of the family appear quite frequently in the 5th Dalai Lama's *rnam-thar*.
52. The *rdzong-dpon* of Bya-dkar in Bum-thang. See f. 8a above.
53. See note 19 above.
54. See note 21 above.
55. This is the tribe, closely allied to the Mon-pa of Kameng, which inhabits the easternmost confines of Bhutan. The 'Dakta' (sic) have been briefly described by Cooper (1933b). See also note 95 above.
56. All these 'elders' must have been the officers of the regional detachments of the 'Brug-pa army from Western Bhutan.
57. See f. 6b above.
58. See ff. 9b, 12a above.
59. See f. 9b above and *rGyal-rigs*, f. 17a.
60. See f. 10a above and *rGyal-rigs*, f. 17b.

61. See f. 10b above.
62. See ff. 12a (sTobs-ldan), 20a above and *rGyal-rigs*, f. 17a.
63. This is Krong-sar, capital of eastern Bhutan.
64. The *rdzong* of bKra-shis-sgang, which stands to this day.
65. I.e. the teachings of the 'Brug-pa school.
66. This passage emphasises the importance of trade in the traditional life of the eastern Bhutanese.
67. See ff. 8b-9a above.
68. See loc. cit.
69. See ff. 2a-5b above on King bDe-ba of Kha-ling, and ff. 15a-b. 16b, 18b on King Chang-lo-dpal of Kha-ling (who is probably the king referred to here).
70. See f. 9b above.
71. See f. 22b above.
72. See ff. 13a-14b above.
73. See f. 14b above. *Bla-ma* rGyal-mtshan seems to have been the only one of the rebel leaders listed here who lost his life in the campaign.
74. Cf. *rGyal-rigs*, f. 47b.
75. See ff. 16a-22b passim.

TEXT III

// (100b 1.4) gnyis pa 'brug mthu chen chos kyi rgyal po'i bka'i khrims yig bshad pa la / de yang sprul pa'i sku gong sa mi pham dbang po gser khrir 'dzeg pa nas / kha bzhi'i rgyal khams 'di gong ma'i bka' khrims ltar lugs gnyis kyis bde bar skyong ba'i dgongs pa gtad de / bka' gnang la khyed kyis rgyal rabs dang chos rgyal mes dbon nas zhabs drung rin po cher brgyud pa'i khrims yig sde pa dbu mdzad sogs kyis ma nyams par bskyangs pa'i khrims lugs kyi yig cha zhig cis kyang gyis shig ces gsung pa las / nged kyis kyang rgyal rabs chos 'byung / srong btsan sgam po / khri srong lde btsan / khri ral pa can / zhabs drung rin po che / sde pa dbu mdzad sogs kyi bka' khrims ji ltar rnyed pa rnams (101a) zin bris su bgyis te phul ba yin te / de ni sde srid phyag mdzod rim byon gyi lo rgyus rjes su bka'i khrims yig 'di nyid kyang bshad pa skabs su babs shing / lhag par dpal 'brug pa'i bstan 'dzin rim par 'byon pa tsho'i nges rgyu dmigs rkyen mchog la phan phyir 'dir yang bkod pa las de yang 'di ltar /

dPal 'brug pa rin po che mthu chen ngag gi dbang po'i bka' khrims phyogs thams cad las rnam par rgyal ba'i gtam /

PART I

chos srid phan bde'i lung bzang pos //
sman ljongs legs lam gyis 'tsho ba'i //
dkar rgyud zhing khams rgya mtsho'i dkyil //
mthu chen 'jigs med grags des skyongs //

dge legs rab 'byams chos kyi 'khor lo'i dbyangs //
sku gsum rgya cher bshad pa'i nges legs klung //
zhing khams rgya mtshor spyod mkhas zas gtsang sras //
mchog gsum snyan pa'i 'phreng bcas gtsug na rgyal //

rlabs chen tshogs gsum smon 'jug ye shes kun bzang spyod pa'i klu dbang gis //
sgyu 'phrul nor bu'i bang mdzod yongs 'gengs phyogs bcu'i nam mkha'i mthar thug par //
legs lam zab rgyas rin chen mchog de char du snyil la 'gran bral khyu //
dkyil 'khor kun gyi rnam rol gcig 'chang dkar brgyud pa zhes grags la 'dud //

[Preamble]

(100b 1.4) Secondly, as to explaining the decree of the legal code of the Mighty
Dharmarāja[1] of the 'Brug-pa, now when the incarnation Lord Mi-pham
dBang-po[2] had ascended the golden throne he voiced his thoughts about
the propitious rule of this Realm of Four Approaches by means of the dual
system [of royal and religious law] in accordance with the legal decrees of
the ancients. He issued a command, saying: "You must at all costs prepare
a record of the legal customs which were maintained intact by the *sDe-pa
dBu-mdzad*[3] and others [and which were based on] legal codes handed
down from the royal lineage and the ancestral *Dharmarājas* to *Zhabs-drung
Rin-po-che.*" I myself,[4] therefore, drew up and offered a draft of the laws
of Srong-btsan sGam-po, *Khri* Srong-lde-btsan, *Khri* Ral-pa-can, *Zhabs-
drung Rin-po-che,* the *sDe-pa dBu-mdzad* and others, just as they were
(101a) discovered in the royal and religious histories. Now, following the account
of the successive [incumbents to the office of] *sDe-srid Phyag-mdzod,*[5]
the time has come to explain this same decree of the legal code. Furthermore, it is also set down here in order to bring benefit as an excellent
example of what should be known to the successive upholders of the
teachings of the Glorious 'Brug-pa, and so it is as follows:

The Legal Decree of the Glorious 'Brug-pa Rin-po-che,
the Mighty Ngag-gi dBang-po[6] **[entitled]**
The Discourse, Victorious in All Directions

[PART I: Introduction to the principles of theocratic rule]

By good pronouncements, beneficial to religion
and the state,
Mighty 'Jigs-med Grags[-pa] [7] protect
In the centre of the ocean, the realm of the
dKar-rgyud[8]
Which is sustained by the way of deliverance in
the Land of Medicine![9]
Virtuous and all-encompassing sound of the
Dharmacakra,
Excellent river of extensive teaching in your
three bodies, [10]
Son of Śuddhodana, [11] skilled in action in the ocean
of realms,
With sweet-sounding series of the triple gem [12]
rule over my head.
I bow to those known as the dKar-brgyud-pa, holders
of the enjoyment of all the *maṇḍalas;*
The matchless company who rain down these very
precious things, profound and vast, of the way
of deliverance
As far as the ends of the sky in the ten directions of
space; who are completely filled with magical
stores of jewels

mkhyen rtogs brtse ba'i nus ldan rigs gsum gyis //
bsil ba'i ljongs der mi nub phan bde'i lung //
gzhal med bka' drin gter gyis sa skyong ba //
chos rgyal mes dbon rim byon rnams la 'dud //

khyad (101b) par nges gsang snying po'i bstan pa yis //
'dab chags rgod kyis nyin mor snyed brtol ba //
snyan pa'i ba dan cher bskyod sprin gyi dbyangs //
brgyud par bcas pa'i zhabs la phyag bgyi'o //

bstan la gnod byed ma rungs g.yul //
mthar byed ye shes mgon lcam dral //
mngon spyod ral gri'i 'khor lo'i mtshon //
dgra srog bcod la dam bzhes dgongs //

rgyal khams kun tu phan bde 'byung mi 'byung //
rgyal khrims chos bzhin bca' la rag las phyir //
rgyal srid chos kyi 'khor los bsgyur ba'i lung //
rgyal bstan tshad mar 'dzin las gzhan du ci //

de phyir thub gzhung gser gyi mngal //
tshangs pa'i 'khor lo sde bzhi'i 'phrin //
rnam dpyod mang bskur sgyur rgyal gyis //
bsod nams chen por longs su spyod //

ces pa ltar / spyir nam mkha' dang mnyam pa'i sems can mtha' dag gi bde skyid rgyal ba'i bstan pa gang du dar ba de nyid la rag las / bye brag tu bdag cag lnga brgya pa rnams la bcom ldan 'das shākya'i rgyal po'i bstan pa 'am / ston pa de nyid kyis bcas pa'i khrims yin cing / de yang / nyan thos kyi khrims / byang chub sems dpa'i khrims / bde bar gshegs pa'i khrims lugs zhes bsgrags pa'i bstan pa rin po che 'di nyid 'dzin skyong spel zhing bsrung ba las / phyi ltar lugs bzhin spyod pa'i rgyal khrims / nang du bshad sgrub gtan la phab pa'i dge 'dun / gsang bar dam can rgya mtsho'i tshogs kyis dngos dang rdzu 'phrul gyi mthus rim par skyong zhing bsrung ba las / deng sang gi bar du ma (102a) nyams pa mtho ris dal 'gro'i rgyun bzhin yod pa 'di'o // de la dgongs te bcom ldan 'das kyis kyang gser 'od dam pa'i mdor /

By the lord of the *Nāgas,* who exercises the perfect
wisdom, the fulfilled desire pertaining to the
extensive Three Assemblages.[13]
I bow to the succession of ancestral *Dharmarājas,*
Those who ruled with the treasure of immeasurable
kindness
And beneficial, undiminishing authority in that Cool
Land[14]
By means of the three kinds[15] of wisdom, which have the
the power of loving kindness.
(101b) In particular I do obeisance at the feet of the one
possessed of the lineage
Of the melody of clouds[16] [that resembles] the sweet
sound of a banner waved strongly,
Of the winged vulture[17] which reaches as far as [its
destination in a day]
By means of the doctrines pertaining to the essence
of secret truth.
Oh Ye-shes mGon[-po] lCam-dral,[18] who brings to an end
The wars of malignant spirits who injure the teachings,
Armed with a circle of magic swords,
Remember the oath you took to sever the lives of
enemies.
Since the appearance or non-appearance of benefit
and happiness throughout the realm
Depends on whether state laws are promulgated in
accordance with religion,
As to authority for governing the state by means of
the *Dharmacakra,*
What else is there for it but to hold to the teachings
of the *Buddha* as a model?
On that account the golden womb of *Muni's*
scriptures,
The divine action of the fourfold[19] wheel of Brahmā,
Was enjoyed meritoriously
By the discriminating Mahasaṃmata.

In accordance with these words, in general the happiness of all beings who are as limitless as the sky's extent depends on those very places where a *Buddha's* teachings have spread. In particular, for us of the age of decline[20] it is the teachings of the Śākya king or the laws established by that same teacher [which hold sway]. In that regard, the precious doctrines known as the *Śravaka* discipline, the *Bodhisattva* discipline and the *Sugata* discipline have been upheld, guarded and diffused; externally, the state laws of proper conduct, internally the *Sangha* which systematises the explanation and realisation [of the teachings] and, secretly, the ocean of
(102a) oath-bound divinities with real and magical powers have progressively protected and guarded them. So to this day they exist, having the quality of an unimpaired, slowly flowing heavenly stream.
Thinking of that, the *Bhagavat* said in the *Suvarṇaprabhasa sūtra:*[21]

bdag dang gzhan la phan gdags phyir //
yang dag chos kyis yul bskyang bya //
g.yo rgyu byed pa mthong gyur na //
chos bzhin chad pas bcad par bya //

zhes gsungs pa ltar / sangs rgyas kyi bstan pa'i dar rgud rgyal khrims lci yang gi khyad par gtso che zhing / rgyal khrims rgyal brgyud rim pa'i lugs srol ma nyams par byed dgos pas / de'i phyir rgyal brgyud rin po che'i rgyal rabs kyi khungs kyang / snod bcud ma chags pa'i sngon 'od gsal lha'i gzhal yas kyi khang par las snang rang byung gi tshangs pa chen po gser mngal can du bskrun / de las khams gsum pa'i 'od gsal gzugs khams kyi gnas rigs bcu bdun / 'dod lha rigs drug gi chos nyid rim par gdal ba'i mthar 'dzam bu'i gling du babs pa las / bdag rkyen gyis thog mar snga ba mang bkur rgyal po // de nyid kyi rigs su sngon gyi rgyal po lngar grags pa dang / 'khor los bsgyur rgyal sde lnga / de'i rgyal brgyud kyi rabs su rgyu mtshan gyi sgo nas bu ram shing pa'i brgyud dang shākya'i brgyud du'ang 'dogs shing / de la mang bkur rgyal po nas sras sgra gcan 'dzin gyi bar rgyal rabs sa ya gcig dang 'bum khri lnga brgya yod pa 'dul ba las gsungs / de las du mar gyes pa'i chos rgyal mya ngan med nas rim par bod yul gyi rgyal por snga ba gnya' khri btsan po // de'i rgyal rabs su gnam (102b) la khri bdun / stod kyi lteng gnyis / bar gyi legs drug / sa la lde brgyad / 'od gi btsan gsum / zhes grags pa'i rgyal rabs nyi shu rtsa bdun na / 'phags pa kun bzang gi rnam sprul lha tho tho ri snyan btsan byon pas dam pa chos kyi dbu brnyes / de'i rgyal rabs lnga par 'jig rten dbang phyug srong btsan sgam po byon nas / de bzhin gshegs pa'i 'khor lo bcu dang / chos kyi rgyal po'i 'khor lo bcu zung du 'brel bas skyong bzhin par / 'jam dpal dbyangs khri srong lde'u btsan yab sras na rim nas / gsang ba pa'i tshogs kyi gtso bo mnga' bdag khri ral pa can la sogs pas / bod yul lha ldan gyi rgyal khams thams cad dam pa chos kyis dbang bsgyur bar byas shing / der ma zad / rgya gar / rgya nag / kha che / li bal nor 'dzin gyi char yang / rgyal khrims 'khor lo'i rtsibs su rgyal bstan nor bu'i gdugs dkar bkod pas dge zhing yun ring gnas pa ni / lung las /

mi yi chos lugs bzang po de //
dam pa chos kyi gzhi ma yin //
gzhi ldan chos la spyod pa de //
bde nas bde ba thob par 'gyur //

For the benefit of myself and others
I shall protect the land with pure religion.
If the practice of deceit should become apparent
It shall be stopped by punishments that accord
with religion.

In accordance with these words, since a degree of strictness [in the administration] of the state laws is most important for the fortunes of the *Buddha's* teachings, the state laws and the customs of the successive rulers must be maintained unimpaired.

In that respect, as to the origins of the lineages of precious royal families: before the world and its inhabitants came into being, the great Brahmā of the golden womb was produced as the spontaneous appearance of activity in the heavenly palace of the gods of clear light. From him there spread out in succession the clear light of the third realm, the seventeen abodes in the realm of form and the essence of the six groups of gods of desire. Finally, after he had descended to Jambudvīpa, by his favour the first [ruler to appear was] King Mahasaṃmata, in whose family the so-called 'five ancient kings' and the five classes of *Cakravartin* kings [came forth]. In the succession of their royal lineage they came to be known, from [various] causes, as the lineage of the Ikṣvāku and also as the Śākya lineage. It is said in the *Vinaya* that among them, from King Mahasaṃmata to Prince Rahula, there were one million one hundred and ten thousand five hundred generations of kings.[22] After [the time of] the *Dharmarāja* Aśoka, when many of these had gone by, [there appeared] gNya'-khri bTsan-po, the first of the
(102b) kings of the Tibetan land, and in his royal lineage [there arose] the so-called 'Seven *Khri* in the Sky', 'Two *lTeng* of the World Above', 'Six *Legs* of the Intermediate Space', 'Eight *lDe* on the Earth' and 'Three *bTsan* of the Underworld'.[23] In the twenty-seventh generation of these kings lHa-tho-tho-ri sNyan-btsan, the incarnation of Ārya-Samantabhadra, came forth and the holy religion was begun. After Srong-btsan sGam-po, the lord of the world, had come forth in the fifth generation from him, in ruling by means of joining together the ten cycles of a *Tathagāta* with the ten cycles of a *Dharmaraja*,[24] from [the time of] *Khri* Srong-lde'u-btsan the Mañjuśrī, his son and the line of his successors, [down till the time of] the ruler *Khri* Ral-pa-can who was the chief of the secret host, and others, all the realms of Devavān[25] in the country of Tibet were governed by means of holy religion. Not only there but also in the countries of India, China, Kashmir, Khotan and Nepal the white parasol of the precious doctrine of the *Buddha* was placed on the spokes of the wheel of state laws. As for the fact that they thereby remained for a long time as fields of virtue, it is mentioned in scripture:

The good religious observances of humans
Form the basis of holy *dharma*.
The practice of the *dharma* together with its basis
Will gain one happiness on happiness.

zhes 'byung ba ltar / rgyal kun snying rje'i rang gzugs 'phags mchog spyan ras gzigs dbang de nyid chos kyi rgyal po srong btsan sgam por sprul zhing / khrims lugs ji snyed pa'i sgo nas spang blang gsal bar 'god cing bod khams dag pa'i zhing du bsgyur ba dang / de mtshungs de yi rnam sprul ye shes rdo rje grags shing / lha mi'i (103a) 'gro ba'i mchod gnas gdung dang na bza'i mtshan can chos kyi rje gtsang pa rgya ras pa de nyid kyi rigs su kha bzhi'i rgyal khams gdul bya'i zhing du yod ces / ma 'ongs pa na rang nyid 'byon pa'i brdar pha jo 'brug sgom zhig por lung gi gnang ba stsal te / nyid kyi gdung brgyud dri ma med par sprul pa'i sku nyid du bsam bzhin skye ba bzhes pa dpal 'brug pa rin po che mthu chen ngag gi dbang po phyogs las rnam rgyal 'jigs med grags pa'i sde'i mtshan du byon pa de la / khrag 'thung gi rgyal po ye shes mgon po lcam dral dregs pa'i dpung dang bcas pas / kha bzhi lho'i rgyal khams chen po 'di nyid chos gzhis kyi tshul du phul nas 'phrin las bsgrub pa'i bka' nod cing / rig 'dzin chen po padma 'byung gnas kyis kyang /

lho bha ga'i sbugs su yul btab nas //
sgo btags su chu bo phyogs bzhir 'gyed //

ces lung bstan pa la dgongs / dpal ldan 'brug pa rin po che rgyal sras bdud 'joms rdo rje'i gdul bya 'phrin las bzhi'i chibs kyi kha lo sman ljongs kyi grong khyer chen por bsgyur te / ma rungs bdud bzhi'i g.yul ngo rmeg med dang bcas pa bcom zhing / lugs gnyis chos kyi rgyal srid dri ma med pa'i 'dzin skyong spel gsum la mnga' dbang bsgyur nas / rten gsum gtsug lag khang gi bkod pa rgya mtshor 'jug cing / lho phyogs nor 'dzin gyi yul gru mtha' dag nyid kyi bka' 'bangs su bsdus te / lho khrims med la khrims dang / rdza lung med la lung btags nas / chos khrims (103b) dar mdud bzhin du bsdams / rgyal khrims gser gyi gnya' shing lta bu'i ljid kyis gnon te / lugs gnyis kyi bka' khrims chen mo bca' ba nas brtsam / mi bdag rim byon gyis kyang / chos bzhin rgyal khrims kyi srol ma nyams par skyong bas / kha bzhi'i rgyal 'bangs thams cad bde zhing skyid pa'i dpal yon du longs spyod chog pa 'di byung ba yin cing / yin pa de bzhin rgyal brgyud snga ma'i phyag len ma nyam pa zhig byed dgos rgyu yin / de yang sngon chos rgyal chen po'i khrims yig gi thog mar / srog mi gcod pa'i khrims gshin stong dang gson stong / ma byin par mi len pa'i khrims dkon mchog gi nor brkus na brgya 'jal / rgyal po'i nor la brgyad cu 'jal / 'bangs kyi nor la brgyad 'jal du bcas / bdag po can gyi chung mar log g.yem mi byed pa'i khrims rmad 'jal dang byi chad bcas / brdzun spong ba'i khrims lha srungs chos skyong dpang du bzhag nas mna' bsgag pa sogs kyi khrims dang / spyir mi dge bcu spong ba'i steng du pha la phar 'dzin pa / ma la mar 'dzin pa / dge sbyong dang bram ze la dge sbyong dang bram zer 'dzin pa / rigs kyi rgan rabs la

As it thus happened, Ârya-Avalokiteśvara himself, the embodiment of all the *Buddhas'* compassion, incarnated himself in the *Dharmarāja* Srong-btsan sGam-po who clearly laid down by means of many legal observances what was to be abstained from and what was to be adopted and so he turned the realm of Tibet into a pure land. Likewise the Realm of Four
(103a) Approaches existed as the field of conversion for the family of his own reincarnation who was known as Ye-shes rDo-rje, [also known as] the Hierarch gTsang-pa rGya-ras(-pa) who possessed the name of his lineage and of his apparel [26] and who was the object of worship by beings, gods and humans [alike]; thus did he [gTsang-pa rGya-ras] give a prophecy to *Pha-jo* 'Brug-sgom Zhig-po [27] as a sign that he would go there himself in the future. And so he [gTsang-pa rGya-ras] took birth according to his will in an incarnation body within his own stainless lineage and came forth as the one named the Glorious 'Brug-pa Rin-po-che, the Powerful *Ngag-gi-dbang*-po Phyogs-las-*rnam-rgyal* 'Jigs-med-grags-pa. [28] To him the blood-drinking king Ye-shes mGon-po lCam-dral together with his proud army offered this Great Southern Realm of Four Approaches in the manner of a religious estate and accepted orders to fulfil his actions. Bearing in mind the prophecy which the *Mahāvidyadhara* Padmasambhava had also made, saying:

Having founded a home in the womb cavity of the South
Rivers will disperse to the four quarters at the named doors, [29]

he turned the bridle of his horse of the four actions towards the great city of the Medicine Land, the sphere of conversion of the Glorious 'Brug-pa Rin-po-che, the *Bodhisattva* bDud-'joms rDo-rje. [30] Having defeated the four atrocious demons [31] together with their disorderly battle lines and having gained control of the upholding, guarding and diffusing of the stainless theocracy of the dual system [of religious and secular government], he began the laying out of vast numbers of 'triple supports' [32] and temples, and subjected to his authority all the districts of the South. Having introduced laws where there had been no southern laws and fixed handles
(103b) where there had been no handles on pots, [33] he constrained by means of religious laws like a silken knot and pressed down with state laws as with the weight of a golden yoke. Beginning [from the time of] the introduction of the great law of the dual system, the successive rulers also preserved intact the observance of state laws in accordance with religion and it is due to this that the possibility has arisen for all subjects of the Realm of Four Approaches to enjoy themselves in the glory of happiness and contentment. This being so, there is a need for maintaining unimpaired the practices of the early royal lineage.

Now, foremost in the legal code of the great *Dharmarāja* [34] [there occurs] the law of not taking life, manslaughter-fines for the dead and the living; the law of not taking without being given – the hundredfold restitution for stealing religious goods, the eightyfold restitution for the king's goods, with the eightfold restitution for the goods of subjects; the law of not committing adultery with married women, with fines for fornication and penalties for adultery or rape; the law of abstaining from falsehood, the law of calling the guardian deities to witness when swearing oaths etc., and in general, in addition to abstaining from the Ten Unvirtuous Actions, showing filial respect for one's father and mother and due respect to *śramaṇas* and *brahmins*, honouring the elders of the family, returning kindness done to phud du bkur ba / rang la gzhan gyis phan btags pa'i byas pa drin du gzo ba / bre dang srang la sogs pa'i ngan pa'i g.yo spong ba ste mi chos gtsang ma bcu drug khrims su bca' ba 'di mdzad 'dug cing / de bzhin lho phyogs kun bzod kyi khyon 'dir yang snga thog tu zhabs drung rin po che'i sgrigs rnam gzhag ces lugs gnyis (104a) bka' khrims shin tu dam pa'i dper byed 'dug kyang / bar skabs sgrigs rnam gzhag phal cher snyoms las rang gar spyod 'dug par / 'di rigs de lam du bzhag tshe / bya ba dang bya ba ma yin pa'i khrims mi 'ongs / khrims med na sems can la bde skyid mi 'byung / sems can la bde skyid med na chos rje 'brug pas lugs gnyis kyi bstan pa 'dzin pa'i don med cing / des na bstan pa rin po che snying la bcang zhing nye 'gyangs phyogs lhung med pa'i drang thig sor bzhag gi khrims lugs chos rgyal gong ma srong btsan sgam po lta bu byed dgos / de yang /

'gro ba'i bde skyid rgyal ba'i bstan pa dang //
bstan pa de yang bstan 'dzin skyes bur rag //

ces 'byung ba ltar / bstan 'dzin gyi skyes bu ni sems can yongs la bu gcig ltar bsam pa'i lugs gnyis kyi rnam gzhag gang yang gtan la dbab pas bstan 'gro'i bde skyid tshugs pa zhig dgos rgyu yin kyang / da skabs so so nas log pa'i dran 'khrul tshod 'dzin med pa'i ngan pa gnya' rengs kho nas bka' khrims gnyan po ras su bor / dge sdig rgyu 'bras kyi spang blang skad cig kyang mi bsam par / nor phyir snyad med snyad btags kyis brdung thag bkyigs thag 'og khang la bcug pa sogs chad pa 'phral bkog byas nas / sbyin bdag kun mi yul gyi yi dags dngos su bsgyur ba dang / gros mi spyi dpon sogs nor yod ngo can 'gas kyang / g.yon can snyan par smra te dpon la gus tshul gyis nor sug sogs mgo bskor (104b) 'ba' zhig dang / la las bden brdzun sna tshogs gzhung sar 'phen pa'i 'bangs gyen log sogs / bstan la mi 'tsham pa'i spyod ngan byed pa mang pos rgyal khrims phan bde'i rol mtsho rnyog par 'dug pas / gtso bo khrims kyi bdag pos / 'di yin 'di min gyi rtsad gcod zhib mor btang nas / chos dang chos min 'byed pa'i khrims kyi srol bzang po gtod dgos pa / ji skad du /

rgyal ba kun la mkhas pa yis //
bran g.yog legs par brtag par bya //
bden dang chos la gzhol ba yis //
rtag tu yul 'khor bskyang bya zhing //

zhes pa ltar / rgyal khrims chos bzhin bskyang dgos pas chos 'gal gyi las nag byed pa bkag cing / rang 'dod khong 'tshang bag med smyo spyod dam tshig gnyan po khyad gsod nyams pa bdun dang zhing bcu tshang ba'i rigs tshar bcad rjes su 'dzin pa mdo rgyud kyi dgongs pa yin cing / rgyal ba nyid kyi lung las /

oneself by others, abstaining from false cheating with regard to weights and measures – he performed this enactment by law of the Sixteen Pure Rules of Human Conduct.

In that manner the so-called "regulation of [public] order"[35] of
(104a) *Zhabs-drung Rin-po-che* acted in previous times throughout the whole of this land of the South as a most sacred example of a legal code pertaining to the dual system; however, in the meantime this regulation of [public] order has been largely treated with indifference and if such things are left to continue in that manner, laws relating to what should and should not be done are not practicable. If there is no law, happiness will not come to beings. If beings do not have happiness there is no point in the Hierarchs of the 'Brug-pa upholding the doctrine of the dual system. Therefore, holding the precious doctrine in one's heart, it is necessary to enact legal observances like those of the *Dharmarāja* Srong-btsan sGam-po which establish a justice devoid of bias or partiality.

Furthermore:

The happiness of beings depends on the doctrine
And the doctrine on beings who uphold it.

Thus it happened, and so for beings who uphold the doctrine there is cause for desiring an establishment of happiness in the doctrine and among beings by setting up whatever is fundamental to a dual system [of legal administration] under which all beings are looked upon as an only child.

Yet nowadays, due to sheer obstinate wickedness on the part of various persons [characterised by] bad, confused thoughts and lack of due measure, the bodeful laws have been repudiated. Without thinking for a moment about discrimination between good and evil, or between cause and effect, penalties and summary confiscations have been meted out for the sake of [acquiring] wealth by making false accusations against the innocent, beating and tying them with ropes and throwing them into dungeons, and all the 'patrons' have really become ghosts in the land of humans. The beneficial, enchanted lake of the state laws has been stirred into turbidity by many evil deeds not consonant with the doctrines, such as plain trickery, including bribery, on the part of a few wealthy and important people who include among them [village] counsellors and messengers[36] [who do this] while speaking sweet
(104b) sounding deceits in pretence of respecting officialdom; also uprisings of subjects pushed towards the capital by some of them [with] all sorts of truths and untruths. Therefore, having investigated in detail what is what, the chief master of the laws[37] should turn towards good legal usages that distinguish religion from irreligion. As it is said:

The *Jina* skillful in all things
Should consider well his servitors.
With application to truth and religion
He should always protect the provinces.

Since it is necessary therefore to preserve the state laws in accordance with religion, acts of evil that transgress religion are to be suppressed; the pursuit of terminating all such things as selfishness, anger, fecklessness, wild behaviour, fierce oaths, contempt, the 'Seven Defects' and the 'Ten Realms'[38] is the intention of the *sūtras* and *tantras*.

According to the word of the *Buddha* himself:

'di dag bsgral bar byas nas ni //
dmyal ba'i gnas su yun thung 'gyur //
rnal 'byor bsgrub la bar chad med //
theg pa chen po'i mthu dar zhing //
sangs rgyas bstan pa rgyas par 'gyur //

zhes gsungs shing / byang phyogs sā la'i sman ljongs su sngon nas byon pa'i chos kyi rgyal po rnams ni byang sems sha stag bka' drin gyi gnas yin mod / phyis kyi sde srid kha cig kun slong zhe gnag gi phyogs 'dzin dam pos / kar 'brug gnyis kyi mgo gnon gang thub dang 'di pa 'tsho'i ring lugs ngan pa yin phyir bsnub par byed sogs pa'i khrims yig 'dod sbyar byas pa'ang 'dug cing / de 'dra (105a) ni /

ci sbyang dregs pa'i skad 'byin yang //
ri dags rgyal po snying rje skyes //

ces sam /

skyes mchog rang gi skyon la blta //
skye ba ngan pa gzhan skyon 'tshol //

zhes gsungs pa ltar ro // de bzhin lho phyogs kyi rgyal khab 'dir yang 'ga' zhig rang 'dod du lhung bas / chos srid bstan pa'i 'dab brgya dkar po zum dus su nye zhing / de'i phyir bstan pa rang mdun ras su bor bar mi bzod pa'i bsam khur snying khong rus pa'i dkyil nas gzhen btab ste / chos srid 'phrin las kyi gdugs dkar 'di nyid 'dzin skyong spel zhing bsrung ba la / rgyal sras zur phud lnga pa khri srong lde btsan gyi mkhyen rab dang snying stobs kyi rjes su 'jug dgos / zhes dpal 'brug pa rin po che mthu chen ngag gi dbang po'i chos kyi rgyal srid spyi'i rnam par gzhag pa'i gleng gzhi thog mar dge ba'i bkra shis dang po 'jig rten kun la khyab gyur cig /

By cutting to pieces these things,
The sojourn in hell will become short,
There will be no obstacles to achieving *yoga,*
The power of the Mahāyana will expand
And the Buddhist doctrines will extend.

Thus it was said, and in the Northern Medicine Land of Sāla the *Dharmarājas* who came forth in early times were certainly nothing other than *Bodhisattvas* and abodes of grace. But later one section of [Tibetan] rulers,[39] as a result of their severe favouritism [characterised by] frenzy and evil temperaments, oppressed both the Kar[-ma-pa] School and the 'Brug[-pa] School as much as possible and even achieved their will [by promulgating] ordinances to the effect that since the order of these schools was evil they were to be annihilated. For example:

(105a) Even though the jackal howls with arrogance,
The lion bears [him] compassion.[40]

Or again:

The great being examines his own faults;
The bad man looks for faults in others.[41]

It was as said in these words. Similarly, even in this state of the Southern Land a few have fallen into selfishness and so the time draws near when the hundred white petals of the doctrine of religious and secular government will close. Exhorting, therefore, from one's innermost heart the sense of duty that cannot bear [to see] the doctrine repudiated before one, it is necessary to take after the wisdom and courage of the *Bodhisattva Pañcaśikha, Khri* Srong-lde-btsan, for the sake of protecting and of upholding, guarding and diffusing this white parasol of the action of religious and secular law.

[Here ends] the preliminary introduction to the general fundamentals of the theocratic rule of the Glorious *'Brug-pa*
(105a *Rin-po-che,* the Mighty Ngag-gi dBang-po. May the first
1.4) virtuous blessing contained herein fill the whole world.

PART II

// bde dang phun tshogs 'jig rten la //
rgyal thabs spyod pa'i lung 'chang ba //
skyes chen ma la ya rlung gi //
mdzad pa'i dri bzang 'di nas spel //

da ni lugs zung bstan pa'i sgron me khrims lugs 'phrin las kyi bdag po sde srid phyag mdzod pa'i bgyi 'os kyi gtso bo / bcom ldan 'das kyis mdor /

rgyal po chos la dga' bar gyur na ni //
tshe rabs gnyis kar bde ba'i lam 'di yin //
rgyal pos spyod bzhin du ni 'bangs kyang spyod //
de bas chos bzhin sa la gnas par slob //

ces dang / (105b) rgyal ba gnyis pa chen pos /

pha ma'i brgyud dag 'bangs kyis 'khur mkhan mang //
spyod pa ya rabs mna' tho chad la 'dzem //
mnga' thang skyong shes dgra 'joms dpung pa can //
mi chen rgyal po mchog la dgos pa yin //

[PART II: The duties of rulers and ministers]

(105a 1.4) Those who hold the authority of royal measures taken
In this happy and prosperous world,
May these great beings diffuse from here
The fragrance of their deeds on the Mālaya winds.

Now, as to the chief actions befitting a *sDe-srid Phyag-mdzod,* who is the illuminator of the doctrine of the joint system [of religious and state law] and master of the practice of legal observances, the *Bhagavat* has said in the *sūtras:*

If the king becomes enamoured of religion,
It is the path to happiness both in this and future lives
Subjects will also act as the king acts;
Therefore he must learn how to live in accord with religion.

(105b) Also the Second Buddha [Padmasambhava] has said:

A pure parental lineage, many supporting subjects,
Noble behaviour, heed to promises made in an oath-list,
Ability to guard one's dominion and possession of an army to overcome one's enemies,
These are the requisites of an excellent king, a great man.

ces pa ltar / lho phyogs kyi rgyud 'di nyid mnyam med dpal 'brug pa rin po che'i 'dul zhing yin pas / rgyal ba'i khyab bdag mthu chen ngag gi dbang po'i zhabs kyi padmo gtsug tu mchod pa'i sgo nas bstan pa dang skye 'gro'i bde skyid la thugs bskyed mi dman pa dgos nges / sangs rgyas kyi bstan rtsa dge 'dun yin phyir gar bzhugs bkur sti'i bzos sgo ci 'gyur byed pa'i / chos spyod bcu dang gar thig dbyangs sogs bskyed rdzogs kyi nyams len la zhabs bskul yang dag byed / sgra snyan pa dang mtshan nyid grwa sde'i slob sbyang gi dpe rgyugs 'phral 'phral du len nas deb dang bstun pa'i gnang sbyin stsal / gdan sa mtha' dag gi dngos po'i phyag rdzas ci yod rgyal ba'i sku gsung thugs rten sogs dkon mchog gi mchod rdzas dang dge 'dun gso ba las gzhan du chud zos mi gtong ba'i bka' khyab lo ltar bzhin phebs / bzo rigs grwa sde dang / sgar nang gzan gyi rigs la'ang / yi ge 'bri mchod sbyin pa dang sogs spyod bcu gtso bor 'don pa'i so so'i las ka dang bstun pa'i rgyugs len cing bstan pa'i zhabs 'degs gang 'gyur du 'jog / nyin re bzhin mnga' 'bangs spyi'i skyid sdug dri rtsad byas pa'i 'thus ma 'thus kyi skabs 'phral du bde ba'i thabs kho nar bkod / yul gru (106a) so sor srog gcod rku 'phrog spangs pa'i ri rgya lhungs rgya bsdams pa sogs / chab 'bangs dge bcu'i khrims su sbyor ba'i blo gros kyi shes rgya 'das ma 'ongs dpyad tshugs pa dgos / 'jig rten skyid sdug rgyal 'pham kha mchu'i gcod sdom dang khral 'ul dos skyal de rang gtso bas / drag zhen su thad nas kyang zas nor ngor bltas pa'i nye ring phyogs lhung yod med rgyun du rtsad gcod drag por btang / rdzong mgron spyi bla sogs nor yod ngo can 'ba' zhig dang nye 'khor zhabs 'bring ba'i rang 'dod zhus dbang du mi btang bar rgyal khrims dpang thub gtso bor bton ngos / mtha' bzhi'i sa mtshams kyi las 'dzin rnams kyang / dbus kyi bde skyid mtha' la rag las pa bzhin / rang sdes gzhan phyogs su Ár jag dgra rkun shor nas rang khrims mi btsan par byas shing / chings dan gyi khra 'gal du 'gyur na / de'i lan rtsa rang la thug par ma zad bstan 'gro spyi'i 'gal tshabs* tu 'gyur bas / de bzhin mi 'gyur bar bde 'jam byed dgos pa'i bka' khyab yang yang gnang / lhag par rdzong kha gar yang

*tshab

In accordance with these words, since this southern range is itself the unequalled and glorious 'Brug-pa Rin-po-che's field of conversion, there is a definite need for not inferior designs to further the happiness of beings and of the doctrine by honouring on high the lotus feet of the Mighty Ngag-gi dBang-po, the *Jina*'s ruler.

Since the *sangha* is the basis of the Buddhist doctrine, measures should be taken to do it honour as the occasion arises, giving pure exhortations towards [the cultivation of] the meditational procedures of the *utpatti [-krama]* and *sampanna[-krama]* [42] including the Ten Religious Practices [43] and the study of sacred dance, *maṇḍalas* and chanting. Textual examinations on studies completed by the students of grammar and poetry and by the College of Logic should be held at frequent intervals and rewards should be given in accordance with the works [on which they are examined]. An annual proclamation should be issued to the effect that instead of otherwise squandering whatever material objects there are in all the residences, they are to be used as offerings to the [Triple] Gem, including the body, speech and mind-supports of the *Jina*, and for the upkeep of the *sangha*.

In the College of Crafts and also among the bodyguards and household servitors, examinations are to be held in accordance with their respective work in which emphasis should be placed on the Ten Religious Practices consisting of writing, making offerings, giving alms and so forth; and they should be employed in whatever works of service are undertaken for the doctrine.

When, in carrying out a daily investigation into the general welfare of the subjects, [it becomes evident that it is] favourable or unfavourable,
(106a) they should be brought exclusively to states of happiness. Enquiries should be entered into concerning how in time gone by the wisdom of good counsel caused subjects to adhere to the laws of the Ten Rules of Virtuous Conduct [and how this could also be done] in the future [such as was done in the past by] the enactment of prohibitions against hunting and fishing and so on, whereby killing and thieving were abstained from in the various districts.

Since the victory or defeat of worldly welfare depends chiefly on judgements passed on litigation and on [matters concerning] taxation, corvée and the [compulsory] transportation of [government] loads, strict measures should be taken continuously in order to enquire into and root out any prejudiced relations that have been formed with an eye to [the acquisition of] food and wealth, whoever it may be [who indulges in this], great or small. The ability to call the state laws to witness must be given prime importance, [44] without being influenced solely by what is said by [the incumbents to the offices of] *rdzong[-dpon]*, *mgron[-gnyer]*, [45] *spyi-bla* [46] and others who are wealthy and important, and [without being influenced] by the selfishness of personal servants in [one's own] retinue.

In this regard, as to the officials on the frontiers of the four borders, just as the happiness of the centre depends on the outer limits, if the terms of a treaty should be violated, one's own laws being treated laxly and acts of brigandage by one's own people occurring on the other side, not only will we meet with reprisals for these things but also it will turn into a serious transgression against the doctrine and beings in general. Lest this should happen, orders are to be issued repeatedly concerning the need for peaceful conduct.

rtswa khral shing khral des sbyin bdag sdug po rang zhig 'dug pa / 'di rigs la rta'i rtsis bdag dang rtswa khral 'di thob kyi rim pa sngar khyun bzhin byed du bcug dgos / mdor na phyi mnga' 'bangs kyi bde thabs / nang las tshan spyi'i dpang 'jog / don skyabs gsum 'dus tshogs spel ba'i mdzad bzang 'phrin las bzhi'i rnam par rol ba dus gcig tu dbang bsgyur ba'i bio gros kyi nyin mor byed pa'i 'phrul 'khor shes dgos pa / mthu chen seng ge'i (106b) nga ro las /

dbus zlum zhi ba phyi gru bzhi //
dung bzhi 'phrin las rgyas pa dang //
khams gsum dbang sdud nga ro'i sgra //
mngon spyod ral gri'i 'khor lo bskor //

zhes dang / bstan dgra 'joms pa'i spu gri las //

gang zhig skye bo mi bsrun pa //
mthu mi bu lon ltar snyeg pa //
de la mngon spyod las kyi mthu //
gnam lcags 'dra ba 'di phob cig //

ces bka' stsal pa ltar / bzang po bzang thog tu srol gtod / nyes pa nyes thog tu tshar ma bcad na / rgyal khrims chos bzhin du spel mi nus pas / rgyal khrims drang por bcad pa rgyal po'i dgos don gyi gtso bo yin cing / de yang rgyal po la gces pa khrims zer ba bzhin / rgyal po gcig gis rgyal khrims drang por skyong bar byed na de'i 'bangs rnams nyin gcig la bde bar bkod nus shing / de ni sngon dus chos rgyal mes dbon rim pas bsil ldan gyi 'gro ba rnams cig car chos srid lung gis 'tsho bas dang / zhabs drung rin po ches rmug rgod lho phyogs kyi rgyud 'di 'dul sbyong nus pa'ang rgyal khrims chos bzhin bskyang ba'i mthu las yin no // spyir rgyal khrims bca' ba'i rgyu mtshan / yul gru so so'i rgyal 'bangs bde ba'i ched nyid dang / sgos su rgyal dbang thub pa'i 'dul khrims bstan rtsa dge 'dun gyi 'dzin skyong spel phyir bcas pa yin 'dug kyang / bar skabs su rnam par dbye bas 'phongs te / dge slong sdom nyams srog gcod ma byin len sogs bstan pa'i phung gzhi byed kyang rtsad gcod mi gtong / des ni mig ltos ngan par ma zad bstan 'gro'i legs lam nub par (107a) lung bstan las /

'dul khrims nyams pas dam nyams lung pa gang //
de yi rgyu las skye 'gro'i bde skyid nub //

Furthermore, if there should be any 'patrons' in any of the districts under the administration of a fort who are particularly oppressed by [the need to render] grass-tax and wood-tax,[47] such persons must be allowed to take charge of [government] horses and supply grass-tax at rates of liability fixed according to the custom which prevailed in previous times.

In brief, one must know the mechanism which illuminates the mastery of controlling at one time the play of the Four Actions [of pacifying, multiplying, ruling and subduing in order to fulfil], externally, the means by which the subjects are brought to happiness; internally, the commission of all officials; and in truth, the good deeds which diffuse the Three Refuges
(106b) [and] the monastic community. In *The Mighty Lion's Roar* it is said:

In the centre a peaceful circle, on the outside,
a square,
Prospering with the works of the four conch-shells,
The lion's roar which subjugates the three
realms.
Turning the wheel of the magic-working sword.[48]

And in *The Razor which Defeats the Enemies of the Doctrine* it is said:

Any malignant being
Will be overtaken by magic power like a debt.
Bring down like a meteorite
Powerful works of destructive magic upon him.

As it is thus commanded, the custom of heaping good on good is instituted. If the heaping of evil on evil is not brought to an end, the state laws will not be able to spread in accordance with religion and so the principal requirement of a king is the fair discharge of state law. Moreover, just as one speaks of 'the law beloved of the king', so if a single king administers the law fairly he can bring his subjects to happiness in a single day. Now, the fact that the succession of ancestral *Dharmarājas* in previous times sustained the beings of the Cool Land by means of the simultaneous discharge of religious and secular authority and the fact that *Zhabs-drung Rin-po-che* was able to tame this wild area of the South is due to the power [they obtained through] administering state laws in accordance with religion.

In general the reason for instituting state laws is for the very sake of the happiness of subjects in the various districts. In particular it is for the purpose of upholding, guarding and diffusing the *sangha* which [abides to] the *Vinaya* rules of the Buddha and [forms] the basis of the doctrine. However, in the meantime it has declined in some of its aspects and monks have broken their vows, taken life, taken that which is not given, and so forth. Although acting as the cause of the doctrine's decay [such persons] are not rooted out. Not only is this a bad example but it will also cause the good
(107a) path of the doctrine and of beings to decline as prophesied:

When the *Vinaya* rules decline the land is
filled with oath-breakers.
This causes the happiness of beings to diminish.

ces dang /

chos khrims zher pas ma mgon dbyings su gshegs //
dam sri spun gyi kha rlangs dum bur 'phro //
mi yi chos lugs zher bas lha rnams nyams //
nag po bdud kyi rigs rnams ha har rgod //

ces sogs dang / lhag par de bzhin gshegs pa nyid kyis nyi ma'i snying po'i mdor / lnga brgya tha ma'i dus rab tu byung ba'i khrims kyang / rgyal khrims dang bstun par gsungs ba bzhin / rang phyogs blos ma bzod par 'dug pa'i da cha nas gzung / dge slong bslab par skyon tshad 'dul lugs dang mthun pa'i chad pa gcod cing / rtags dang cha lugs bskyur dgos thag chod yin zhing / gzhan yang bdud kyis yo lang bshams pa'i zas ngan tha ma kha zer ba 'di da ltar sgar lto gzan sogs mi nag skye bo kun gyi nyin mtshan du spyod par 'dug mod / 'dis ni sku gsung thugs rten grib kyis non par ma zad / steng lha nyams / bar btsan 'khrugs / 'og klu la gnod cing / rgyu des 'jig rten khams su nad mtshon mu ge'i bskal pa rgyun du 'byung bar / slob dpon chen po padmas lung bstan mang po gsungs 'dug pa ltar / rdzong mgron sku tshab las tshan gros mi spyi dpon tshos / yul phyogs gar yang phung zas tha ma kha'i nyo 'tshong dang 'thung mi byung tshe / rtsad gcod drag por ma btang na rang rang so so'i steng khar yong rgyu thag chod dang / rgya drung tshos kyang las sgo rang nas bkag pa sogs de lugs (107b) kyi rtsis bdag byed pa gal che / de bzhin snyigs ma'i yid can gyi las dbang lta bus / da lta'i skabs 'dir chab 'bangs skyid sdug mi snyoms pa'i mtho dman sna tshogs kyi lo rgyus thos tshe / bde thabs yod bzhin snyoms las su bskyur na / bdud kyi rgyal po dang khyad par ci yod / rang gzhan su thad nas kyang / drang gsum 'khar ba mdun btsugs dkon mchog dpang gsol ma gtogs / kha mchu'i bslab don khral 'ul sogs la nye ring rgyab mdun byas 'dug na drag po'i khrims la sbyar rgyu thag chod yin zhing / de bzhin byed dgos pa lung las kyang /

ji ltar rgyal srid bskyang ba dang //
sdang ba'i dgra rnams 'dul ba dag //
'bangs la re ba ma 'jog par //
zhal bzhugs tshe na myur du mdzod //

ces dang /

rtsub pas rtsub pa thul 'gyur gyis //
zhi bas 'dul ba ga la nus //

And:

When religious law is discarded the main protector
departs to heaven.
It is broken to pieces by the exhalations of the
demon brothers.
When the religious customs of humans are discarded
the gods decline.
The classes of black devils laugh 'Ha ha!'

Moreover the *Tathāgata* himself has said in the *Sūryagarbha Sūtra*[49] that the laws of monks during the final age of decline will accord with the laws of the state. Accordingly, from this time on when things have become intolerable for us, punishments are to be meted out in conformity with the customs of the *Vinaya* in right measure [for each] fault against the monastic precepts and it is certain that [such monks] must be deprived of their tokens of office and their robes.

Furthermore, this evil sustenance called *tha-ma-kha* (tobacco) which is a cunning trick prepared by demons, is now being used continuously by all the people and the peasants, including the bodyguards and menials; not only does this pollute the body, speech and mind-supports but also it causes the gods above to decline, it disturbs the spirits of intermediate space and injures the *nāgas* of the underworld. From this cause there continuously arises in the world the fate of diseases, wars and famines and so it conforms with many prophecies given by the great teacher Padma[sambhava]. If people in any of the districts should be found to be indulging in the trading and smoking of tobacco, this ruinous sustenance, and if this practice is not forcibly eliminated by the *rdzong[-dpon]*, *mgron[-gnyer]*, government representatives[50] and officials, the village counsellors and messengers, then things will definitely fall on their own heads. The officials on the Indian frontier[51] must prohibit [the import of tobacco] at the *duars*[52] them-
(107b) selves. Control through these measures is important.

Similarly, when accounts are heard about the unequal and varying degrees of welfare among subjects during these present times, rather as a result of the karmic propensities of beings in the Age of Degeneration, and if [a ruler] should then discard with indifference those means towards the obtainment of happiness that do exist, then what difference is there between him and a king of devils ? Apart from planting the staff of the Three Truths[53] before one and calling upon the [Triple] Gem to act as one's witness, if anyone at all, whoever he might be, has shown partiality and discrimination in his judgements on litigation or in matters of taxation, corvée and so on, then it is certain that he himself will meet with severe laws. That one should act in such a manner, it has been said in the scriptures:

Protecting the realm by whatever means,
Taming the hated enemy,
And not forsaking the hopes of the subjects:
Do these quickly during your lifetime.

And:

The rough tamed the rough
But how will the gentle be able to tame.[54]

zhes gsungs pa bzhin / rtag tu dkar po dge ba'i las la brtson zhing las 'bras kyi rtsa ba chod pa dgos na'ang / ma yin ma 'thus pa'i nag can la snying rje ma bzhag par srog lus la tsa ra phyis lam khegs pa dgos / de yang ngo tsha dang snying rje'i dbang du bzhag tshe blo bsam mi bsrun gyi rigs rnams je 'phel du song na rgyal por gces pa khrims dang / de 'og nas 'tshang rgya zer ba bzhin yin pas / rdzong sdod sku tshab rim pas rang 'bangs rnams la / rgyal khrims chos bzhin skyong mi skyong snyan lam du gsan spyan gyis gzigs pa'i / byung ma byung gi skabs 'phral 'phral du tshar bcad rjes su 'dzin pa (108a) ni sde srid phyag mdzod rim byon gyi mdzad par shes dgos so // de yang /

dam pa dpon du bkod gyur na //
don grub pa dang bde skyid thob //

ces gsungs pa ltar rgyal po khri thog tu 'tshang rgya ba de byung ng ba yin no // bstan 'dzin chos kyi rgyal po de nyid kyi zhal lung 'chang ba mgron gnyer / gdan sa'i rdzong dpon / spyi bla rnam gsum / de'i bya bzhag gi rim pa / rgyal dbang kun mkhyen 'brug pas /

yas kyi rjer gus mas kyi 'bangs la byams //
spyod pa mdzangs thon kha 'jam zhe mi gnag //
'khrugs na dpa' la gzhan zhig chog shes ldan //
rgyal po'i gnang chen byed na dgos pa yin //

zhes pa ltar / lnga brgya pa rnams kyi gtsug rgyan dpal 'brug pa rin po che rgyal sras ngag gi dbang po'i chos srid kyi zhabs 'degs spyi dang / khyad par sa dbang chen po'i bka' lung spyi bor nod pa'i gus btud mdzes khyad sngon du song ba'i / rgyal srid phyi nang bar gsum du dge skyon spo bzhag gi babs yul byung dus rgyu mtshan zhu / sngar rgyun bstan 'gro'i sku rim dang lung pa'i bde thabs kyi rtsis sdoms / mtha' mtshams kyi zhu sna 'gangs chen rigs snyan 'bul zhib par zhu dgos / kha mchu'i skor phag tu nor sug dang kha drag shed yod kyi dbang du mi btang bar / bden brdzun gsal por phye ba'i drang gtam lugs mthun snyan du 'bul / rgya bal bod sogs grub mtha' mi gcig pa'i rigs kyis zhu yig dang ngo ma mjal dgos byung tshe / de rang du zhib rtsad dris pa'i de bstun gyi bdag rkyen sprod / bstan la byas pa can gyi rigs blo pham du ma bcug par gong sar snyan gsan phab nas (108b) las tshan gang 'os su bton / gnyer las

In accordance with these words, one must cut off at its roots the karmic effect of deeds while forever striving in virtuous actions. Evil criminals [55] should not be regarded with compassion but retributions [56] [should be visited upon their] bodies and souls [in order that] the future practice [of such deeds] be eliminated. If, however, on account of shame and pity they are allowed to continue, malevolent persons will multiply. That being so and since it is just as it has been said that Buddhahood [subsists] under the law beloved of the king, when it comes to be established [by a ruler], on the basis of either what he has himself seen or of what he has heard of in reports, that the different grades of officials who reside in the *rdzong* and the government representatives either have or else have not been administering the state laws to the subjects in accordance with religion,
(108a) they are forthwith to be either eliminated or supported; and it must be known that this is a duty of the successive *sDe-srid Phyag-mdzod.* Furthermore:

> If a holy man is appointed chief
> Aims are realised and happiness is gained.[57]

In accordance with these words, Buddhahood comes from a reigning king.

As to the order of employment of those holding the authority of the *Dharmarāja* who upholds the doctrine, (i.e.) the *mgron-gnyer,* the *rdzong-dpon* of the seats of residence and the three *spyi-bla* [of sPa-gro, Krong-sar and Dar-dkar-nang], *rGyal-dbang Kun-mkhyen 'Brug-pa* [=Padma dKar-po] has said:

> Devotion to the lord on high and affection
> for the subjects below,
> Noble behaviour, gentle speech and a pious
> disposition,
> In combat brave and able to take others on;
> These are the requisites when fulfilling the
> great commissions of a king.

Accordingly, on arrival in a place to which he has been transferred, [an official] should give reports on the merits and defects of government in its external, internal and middling undertakings [in that place]; [this should be done] in general as a service rendered to the theocratic rule of the Glorious *'Brug-pa Rin-po-che,* the *Bodhisattva* Ngag-gi dBang-po who is the crown ornament of those [living in] the age of decline, and in particular as a primary act of reverence of special value for the orders received on high from the great ruler. Detailed reports should be submitted on the accounts for previous expenditure on ritual ceremonies performed for the benefit of the doctrine and of beings and on the welfare of the district; also any very troublesome suits concerning the frontiers.

Regarding law-suits, honest statements which do not contradict each other and which clearly distinguish truth from falsity are to be submitted without being swayed by bribes and great haughtiness.

When it becomes necessary to receive petitions from or have personal meetings with people who [pursue] philosophical systems different [from our own], including those from India, Nepal and Tibet, careful enquiries should be addressed to such persons, in accordance with [the outcome of which] help should be rendered to them.[58]

Persons who have worked for the doctrine should not be made despond-
(108b) ent but brought to the notice of the ruler and raised to official posts in accordance with their merits.

'dzin / bzo rig chibs bzhon / sgar lto gzan gyi nang khrims rgyun du rtsad gcod gtong zhing sngar lugs kyi thun khar btsud / che phra gang la yang bzang kha rang nyid kyis byas pa'i ngan kha gzhung srid skyong dang bcas par mi bcol / gzhung don bya ba'i rigs su gyur par rang don dang khyad med kyi ru nga grub rtsol gang cher byed dgos shing / gal chen don yod kyi rigs rnams bslab ston ma zhus par rang nyid kyis blos bcad mi byed / nag po sdig las dang gal chung don med kyi rigs zhu zhu mang ba thugs dam gyi sad rgyur 'dug pas blo thag gcod pa las 'os med / mnga' 'bangs spyi'i skyid sdug blta zhing dge bcu'i khrims la sbyor ba'i snyan bskul sogs / rlabs chen spyod pa'i bgyi ba dus gcig la 'phrin las bzhi bsgrub nus pa'i bka' nod cing / lhag par mtha' zad sbugs ral du mi 'gyur ba'i phyi rdzong gi gad bdar / nang mdzod kyi gsog 'jog / bar khrab mtshon gyi bsgrub lugs / dgra nam 'ong med / grab thung med kyi dpe bzhin / gang la yang ring thung med pa'i sa mtshams su mig gis bltas / rna bas nyan pa'i dgra zon la g.yel ba med pa gcig dgos rgyu yin / yang / drag po g.yul gyi las la zhugs dgos tshe / skyabs gnas kyi ngo bo bla ma rin po che dang bstan don kho nar bsam pa'i snying stobs / dpa' mdzangs des gsum cang rig khyug gsum brtan brling bkyel che'i thabs tshul gyi sgo nas / gcan gzan gyi khongs na seng ge ltar (109a) brjid pa'i dpa' gdengs chen pos / 'khor gsum mdo drug tshang ba'i dmag mi dmag gral du 'khod par / longs spyod gya noms pa bstab pa'i mthar / skabs dang bstun pa'i bkod bshams rang sde dpa' nus bskyed cing dgra dpung klad* 'gems nus pa'i kha lo *kled
bsgyur te / dgra sde thal bar rlog kyang rgyal ba'i sku gsung thugs rten la me brgyag pa / bshig cing brdungs pa la sogs mtshams med kyi las yin pas dang thog nas bkag / dmag gral thob rigs thob mkhan gyis khyer chog / mtshon kha sprod dus stobs ldan brgya thub la g.yu dang khang gzhis stsal ba'i bka' khyab / mi gsad re gnyis mar

Continually holding enquiries into the internal discipline of the storekeepers, the officials, the craftsmen, those entitled to ride horses, the bodyguards and cooks, they should be placed in shifts as of previous custom.

No person great or small should be entrusted with government powers if he [takes credit for] the good while blaming others for the evil he has himself committed.[59] When one comes to perform governmental duties one should endeavour as much as possible to fulfil them meticulously[60] just as if they were identical with one's own private affairs.

As to matters of great importance and significance, one should not decide on them oneself without having requested instructions. Since [however] to submit many reports concerning evil crimes and unimportant matters of no significance would disturb the concentration [of the ruler], it is unfitting to do more than decide on these matters oneself. Giving admonishments which inculcate the observance of the Ten Rules of Virtuous Conduct among the subjects while looking to their general welfare and so on, one should accept the command to fulfil on a broad scale acts [such as these] which can accomplish simultaneously the Four Actions.

Furthermore, lest decay on the border should lead to internal destruction[61] and in accordance with the saying: "Cleaning of the fortress without; hoarding and depositing [of provisions] in the stores within; furnishing armour and weapons in between – [since] there is no certainty when the enemy will come, do not minimize preparations." – so vigilant heed should be taken against enemies by watching and listening on the frontiers wherever they may be and without regard to their distance [from the fortress.] Also when it is necessary to take part in fierce warfare [one should display] the brilliance of great and confident bravery like a lion amidst wild beasts, by means of steadfast and prudent methods [using] humility, intelligence and alertness, [these] three, with resoluteness, courage and wisdom – these three [qualities][62] – which look only to the precious lama as the essential refuge and to the
(109a) doctrine's gain. By these means the soldiers, each with a full set of armour, weapons and helmet[63] and with a horse[64] [apiece] are to be arrayed in the battle line where abundant revels should be held, at the conclusion of which dispositions [are to be made] as the occasion demands. Once one's own side has summoned forth its courage and dexterity and once [one has oneself] become a leader capable of surprising the hostile army, then the enemy side is to be destroyed to ashes. Since, however, it would be a frightful crime if the body, speech and mind-supports of the *Jina* [belonging to the enemy] should be burnt, wrecked and smashed, such actions are to be stopped at their inception. Booty obtained in the battle line may be carried off by those who obtain it. When handing out weapons, orders are to be circulated to the effect that turquoises, houses and land properties[65] will be granted to those champions who can take on a hundred [of the enemy]. Those who have killed one or two persons should be treated

dpa' dar rgyab bkab sogs gang 'os byed pa'i / dmag dpon / mda' dpon / lding dpon / sgar gnyer / go mtshon / dmag mi sogs drag po g.yul gyi las la 'jug pa'i bkod pa bshams lugs mang yang skabs thog dang sbyar ba gnad che'o // gtso chen rgyal srid kyi bya ba la rje dang 'bangs kyi bar du legs lam gyi mtshams sbyor sgrigs shes dgos pa / ji skad du /

blon po blo ldan drang po yis //
rje dang 'bangs kyi don kun 'grub //

ces dang /

blo chung gros nyes 'khrugs pa'i tshe //
blo ldan thabs kyis bde bar gso //

zhes pa ltar / rdzong mgron bka' bgros pa'i rigs dang zhabs 'khril sku gshogs pa sus kyang / phyi'i bya bzhag nang du ma dgongs pa'i rigs sba gsang med par snyan du zhu zhing / nang gi skad cha phyir skyel med pa'i blo ngag shin tu dam por byed /

blo (109b) gsal ngag nyung nye gnas te //
phra ma 'jug na stor shing yin //

zhes dang /

gsang gros thub pa grogs yin te //
gzhan la 'chad na zangs thal yin //

gsungs pa bzhin gsol gzims sogs thugs nang dag dgos de bzhin ma byas na /

chen po rnams la dgra bas kyang //
rang gis 'khor gyis gnod pa mang //

de bzhin gzims 'gag pas nyin mo bag med dang snga phyi gu yang sogs mi byed cing lus ngag yid kyi kun spyod chos dang rjes su mthun pa dgos / des na rgyal srid phyi nang bar gsum gyi sgrigs rnam gzhag mthu chen ngag gi dbang po'i bka' khrims spang blang 'dzol med byed dgos tshe / chu 'go nas rnyog na mi dangs pa bzhin /

rgyal po nyid kyis ma rtsis na //
thams cad mkhyen pa'ang bkur mi 'gyur //

zhes pa ltar / gtso bo khrims kyi bdag po sde srid phyag mdzod gong du mtshungs pa las / gzhung phan tshun gyi rdzong dpon spyi bla / gangs ri'i rdor 'dzin sogs la bdag rkyen mthong srol khyad according to their merits and given 'hero sashes', mantles and so on. With regard to the commanders, 'arrow captains', officers, quartermasters, armourers and soldiers, since there are many tactical dispositions to be prepared when they enter upon fierce warfare, it is vital that these should be arranged promptly.

Above all, the ability to establish the cohesion of good relations between the ruler and his subjects is required when undertaking government work. As it is said:

> An intelligent and honest minister
> Fulfils all the interests of the ruler and his subjects. [66]

And:

> When petty-minded, ill-advised people quarrel
> An intelligent person restores them to happiness
> by skillful means.

In accordance with these words, those *rdzong[-dpon]* and *mgron[-gnyer]* who take part in deliberations and those followers who attend on the lord, whoever they may be, should give reports without concealment about those external businesses that are not being considered within [the court] and observe a strict watch on their thought and speech to avoid conveying outside the internal discussions [of the court].

(109b)
> As for the companion of clear intellect and
> few words,
> If slanders are committed they are like pieces
> of wood that have been misplaced.

And:

> Someone who can be trusted with secret counsels
> is a friend;
> If told to others they are unimpedable. [67]

In accordance with these words the butlers-in-chief, stewards-in-chief and others must have pure hearts. If they do not act in that manner, then:

> Even more than by enemies are great men
> Harmed by their retinues. [68]

Similarly, the household guards should not be careless during daytime and must not take breaks too soon or too late; they must make their general behaviour conform in body, speech and mind to religious principles. Accordingly, at times when it is required to show unerring discernment in one's choice of action [according to] the laws of the Mighty Ngag-gi dBang-po [which contain] the fundamentals of government administration in its external, internal and intermediate aspects, then just as water is not clear when disturbed at its source:

> If the king himself does not render honour
> Even the Omniscient One will not be held in esteem.

In accordance with these words, apart from the *sDe-srid Phyag-mdzod* at the head who is master of the law and who should conform to the above [principles], [69] the *rdor-'dzin* of Gangs-ri [70] and other [officials are to be med / rdzong dpon mgron gnyer gsol ba thab tshang du lhan cig bzhes dgos rgyu / gnyer las 'dzin gang gi thad la'ang sngar rgyun las bdag rkyen gsar bcos mi byed / gsol ba dkar mo'i rigs dang 'brel tshad snga phyi rim par phye ba'i gsol bskor byas mi chog / phyogs mtshams kyi rdzong dpon mtha' dang / rgya drung shar nub / gzhan yang phyi mgron gyi rigs sku tshab che chung gang yin rung / gzhi len gyi rnam pa'i mthong srol ma gtogs gzhan gsol ba dkar mo'i gral du yin / gzhung don kha mchu bcad pa dang 'gro dgos kyi rigs la bod (110a) gsum bzhi las lhag pa mi 'khrid / rdzong kha che phra so sor lto gzan gsar rnying 'jug bton gyi skor dang chos gzhis nas 'bru 'di thon dang / sbyin bdag nas khral dang dbang yon 'di yong lto gzan grangs dang bstun pa'i mgron 'thud kyi steng nas / lo star gyi 'bru dang zong nor bka' rgya re bcug pa'i gsal cha gong sar dgos rgyu / phyogs mtshams gar yang lde mig gnyer pa ngo bo rang ma gtogs / rang gi zla bor mi bcol / bzo rig gi sdeb ma gtogs drags zhen su la'ang phogs byin mi chog / rdzong kha so so'i 'bru mdzod dang gnyer tshang gi skor yun ring bzhag kyang chud zos su 'gro bas / gong sar snyan sgron zhus pa'i lo star bzhin mnga' 'bangs su sbyin gtong sogs bde ba'i thabs kho na 'ba' zhig byed pa la / gangs can skye bo'i skyid sdug lan gsum snyoms pa'i chos rgyal mu ne btsan po dang khri ral pa can gyi rjes su 'jug dgos / zhes dpal 'brug pa rin po che mthu chen ngag gi dbang po'i chos kyi rgyal srid skyong ba'i bka' blon spyi'i rnam par gzhag pa'i gzhung don bar du dge ba'i bkra shis gnyis pa 'jig rten kun la khyab gyur cig /

accorded] identical entitlements and customary privileges. The *rdzong-dpon* and the *mgron-gnyer* are required to eat their meals together in the kitchen. Alterations are not to be made from previous practice with regard to the privileges of the store-keepers and officers, whoever they may be. All those entitled to the various sorts of 'white rations' [71] are not permitted to eat turn by turn, earlier or later [instead of together]. All the *rdzong-dpon* of the provinces, the *rgya-drung* of the east and west and moreover those of the rank of *phyi-mgron* [72] whether they are major or minor [government] representatives, belong to the class of [those entitled to] 'white rations', except in the case of the various customary privileges [that are admissable in terms of a special feast] when taking up residence.[73] Not more than
(110a) three or four attendants are to be taken with one when it is necessary to go on government duty to try law-suits.

Detailed accounts must [be rendered] to the ruler [in compliance with] proclamations that are issued annually regarding [the revenue to be derived in terms of] grain, goods and wealth; [these accounts are to be drawn up] in respect of each district under the administration of a *rdzong,* whether great or small, on the basis of the appointment and dismissal of old and new servants, the specific measure of grain realised from the ecclesiastical estates, the specific amount of taxes and 'initiation fees' [74] obtained from the 'patrons' and the entertainment allowances [reckoned] in accordance with the number of servants.

Throughout the districts keys should be held only by the store-keeper in person and not entrusted to one's own kinsmen.

With the exception of the team of craftsmen, it is not permitted to give [ration-]salaries to any person, strong or weak.

If the contents of the granaries and store rooms in each of the districts under the administration of a *rdzong* are left for a long time they go to waste; annual distributions should therefore be made to the subjects, the matter being reported to the ruler. In performing measures such as this simply and solely to bestow happiness, one should take after the *Dharmarājas* Mu-ne bTsan-po and *Khri* Ral-pa-can who on three occasions reduced the disparities of joy and misery among the beings of the Land of Snow. [75]

[Here ends] the middle main section concerning the general fundamentals of [the system whereby] the ministers administer the theocratic rule of the Glorious 'Brug-pa Rin-po-che, the Mighty Ngag-gi dBang-po. May the second virtuous blessing contained herein fill the whole world.

PART III

// rgyal phran bye bas mngon btud ral pa'i khrir //
longs su spyod pa gang gi bka'i tham ka //
bsrel 'os las 'dzin du ma'i blang dor gyi //
rnam dbye sngon gyi rabs bzhin 'dir brjod bya //

gang yang bkod pa'i mi dang 'dzugs pa'i shing du gleng ba ltar / lung pa re la khrims bdag re bkod pa'i rgyu mtshan des / (110b) ding sang sems can gyi skyid sdug sku tshab las tshan gyi rigs gtso che ba 'dug par / de dag gi spang blang sgrigs rnam gzhag rim par phye ba'i nges rgyu 'di ltar / sku tshab tsho gnyis ma dang / bla gnyer sbrel ma rnams la bod gnyis dang A drung re / sku tshab yongs la bod re dang A drung re / de las lhag pa'i zur gsos gzhis kar 'dug tshe / bkyigs thag dang / sku tshab phogs bcad / las tshan gyi rigs 'gro 'grul mang po des sbyin bdag kun la gzan sgo cher 'dug pas / da nas spo 'jog byung na ma gtogs gom kyang snyad btags byas 'gro mi chog / chur mo brdung chag sprod dgos rigs sdeb bsags kyis sprod pa las / rgyun par mi sprod / de yang rgyus gang ldang las lhag pa'i mi len / sngon dus kyi mchod gzhis 'gang can ming du thogs pa yod na ma gtogs / gzhan ma sbyin bdag yul babs dang bstun pa'i bsdu thun la gtong / mi ser la gser g.yu khro zangs rta nor rten mchod chas sogs dngos po'i rigs tshong la snyad pa'i spus btsug mi 'phrog / phyag mdud rgyab bkab byin nas nor mi slong / lung pa'i sde thang gis bcad pa'i nyo tshong ma gtogs / dbang tshong byas mi chog / tshwa mar mi sprod / bal 'thag mi sprod / lug rgyab mi slong / rdzong kha sku tshab dgon sde'i bla mas sbyin bdag las bsod snyoms rgyugs rigs

[PART III : The duties of government officials]

(110a 1.5)
I shall speak here about the principal aspects,
such as [prevailed in] ancient times,
Of the discerning behaviour [to be observed by]
the multitude of officials who are worthy of
being trained
[By] the seal of the command of he who experiences
enjoyment
On a throne [formed by] the tresses of millions
of petty rulers who openly bow down [before
him].

Just as one speaks of someone as 'an appointed man, a planted tree',
(110b) the reason for appointing a master of the law to each district is because the various kinds of government representatives and officers are vital for the welfare of sentient beings in present times. That which they must know to be the fundamental rules governing their behaviour, analysed each in turn, is as follows.

Second-class [government] representatives and those holding the joint office of *bla[-ma]* and *gnyer[-pa]* [are entitled to] two attendants and one groom. All [ordinary] government representatives [are entitled to] one attendant and one groom. If it is [found] that on the estates there are [attendants and grooms] in excess of these [entitlements] who have been maintained on the side, [they shall be] bound with ropes and the government representative's salary in kind is to be stopped.

Since much travelling around by the various classes of officers is the occasion of great oppression to all the 'patrons', as from now, except when transfers occur, it is forbidden to take even a single step on false pretexts.

Paddy that has to be given for husking must be given only after a large measure has been saved up and not in dribbling quantities. Moreover, no more should be taken than that which is yielded by the sheaves [after threshing].

Apart from ancient religious estates which bear official responsibilities and which are properly designated, others should be subjected to the common tax collections [76] [reckoned] according to the [number of] 'patrons' settled there.

Material objects, including gold, turquoise, bronze, copper, horses, cattle, images and religious objects are not to be seized from the public as false shares in kind for trading ventures. Apart from trading [at rates] determined by the local prices in [each] district, it is not permitted to force people to trade [at extortionate rates]. Salt and butter is not to be handed over [as barter]. Wool yarn is not to be handed over [for weaving]. Fleece [77] should not be demanded.

As from now [the habit of] those government representatives belonging to the districts under the administration of a *rdzong* and those lamas grong bshal sogs da nas rbad gcod / chug khol nyo tshong byas mi chog / ma nges pa'i nyo 'tshong byed mi byung kyang lung dpon la brda sprad pa'i / des kyang gong ma (IIIa) gtso bor snyan sgron dgos rgyu / tshwa chu sman chu'i skor / yas phyin mchog phebs zhor dang / 'phags pa'i dge 'dun gong bkur / grub mtha' mi gcig rigs gang 'os / gzhung phan tshun dang spyi bla sogs kyis mtshon las 'dzin che phra lto gzan sogs na tsha dos drags mig zin rigs rnam pa lta rgyu tsam las / gzhan tshwa sman skor la rang rdzas dang mthun 'tshol ma gtogs gnyer tshang dang dos 'ul zhag babs kyi lto chang sogs rbad gcod yin / tshwa sman 'gro 'dug la brten gzan rtsa nas bkal mi chog / rang don du song phyin phar phyir shar rgyag 'gro ba las rdzong du 'thon mi chog / gzhan yang dos 'ded kyi rigs rdzong kha sku tshab gang yin nas / dos 'di song gi zhu yig gong sar dgos rgyu dang / sa rims tshigs so so nas kyang / zla tshes 'di la mi 'di'i dos 'di song gi 'dzin tho gong sar dgos rgyu / de ltar med pa'i dos 'ded byung tshe / tsa ra nag chad so sor yongs rgyu / sku tshab pas rtsis rta gcig dang rdzong nas gso rta re sprod 'dug na dang / de steng 'bul ba ṭaṃ ka brgya skor thud las / rta re 'go dpon gtso bor zhus nas gso ba ma gtogs / zur rdzas kyis rta nor gsos mi chog / gso mkhan byung na rdzong khar 'phrog / de bzhin rta gsum tshun gso ba las / sku tshab pas sbyin (IIIb) bdag nas rtswa khral shing khral dos skyal 'u lag gi rigs bkod mi chog / 'bul thus kyi rta'ang nyo tshong byed par las sgor mi ser btang mi chog / sku tshab pas khral pa'i kha mchu gcod pa'i chang skyel la / ming don mthun pa'i chang zo re ma gtogs / che ba ma ṭaṃ dang chung ba sman kha tsam yang len mi chog / de bzhin thug gsher gyi rigs rdzong khar rang la of the monastic communities who tour around begging alms from the 'patrons', roving the villages and so on, is to be suppressed.

It is not permitted to indulge in slave trading. If anyone trading suspiciously should come, the matter is to be explained to the district
(111a) chief and it is required that he too informs his chief overlord.

With regard to saline and mineral springs, apart from just those who fall under [the following] categories, [it is forbidden to use the hot springs]: *yas phyin mchog phebs zhor* (?); [78] the holy *sangha* [for which it is] a mark of honour; those according to their merits [who pursue] philosophical systems different [from our own]; and those officers, great or small, for example [the *rdzong-dpon* of] the various provincial capitals and the *spyi-bla,* [their] servants and so on, whose severe illness has been duly recognised. Besides otherwise [taking] one's own provisions and looking for assistance, [the practice of demanding] board and lodging, compulsory transportation of loads, food and ale during overnight stays and so forth is to be eliminated. It is absolutely forbidden to take servants on account of one's own going to the saline and mineral springs. In going there of one's own accord, apart from going straight there and back, it is forbidden to enter the *rdzong.* If [persons] should come [into the *rdzong*], the rules forbid them to be given provisions, audience or succour. In travelling there, unless the road guards possess orders [to the contrary], those persons who are fit to go to the saline and mineral springs may be permitted to proceed after they have been stopped and individually passed.

Furthermore, as to the various kinds of load transport, the government representatives in the districts under the administration of a *rdzong,* whoever they may be, are required [to send] written reports to the ruler concerning the specific number of loads transported. It is also required [to send] to the ruler a list of receipts [which specify] the various distances over which such and such a number of loads belonging to so and so were transported on such and such dates. If loads are not transported in this manner, reprisals and severe punishments are to be imposed individually.

As government representatives are given one horse for them to look after and one horse which is maintained [for them] by the *rdzong,* in addition to these they may, after requesting the chief civil officer, maintain each a horse on payment of a due of one hundred *ṭaṃka.* Besides this, it is not permitted to maintain horses and cattle on one's private means. If persons are found to be doing so, [the horses and cattle] will be seized and taken to the *rdzong(-kha* ?). Apart from thus maintaining up to three horses, it is forbidden for a government representative to impose on 'patrons' any
(111b) grass-tax, wood-tax, transportation of loads, and the various kinds of corvée. It is not permitted to send members of the public to the border trade marts in order to trade in the horses that have been collected as dues. [79]

With regard to the presents of ale sent to a government representative while he is judging cases, apart from a single vessel of ale reckoned from each litigant, it is not permitted to take as much as a *ma-ṭaṃ* or as little as a square of *sman[-rtse]*. [80] Similarly, apart from holding trials in the

skyel ba ma gtogs / che chung gang yang sku tshab pas thag bcad
mi chog / sku tshab pas lo thog bsdu btab zhing rtsig* bskor ba sogs *tshigs
la snyad btegs kyis grong bshal gyi rigs byed mi chog / sku tshab
pas zhing rtsig* rtswa phran thog phran bza' shing sogs las / nges *tshig
med mi ser gyi rta phyugs phran bu'i kha thal cung zad la'ang / za
'dod snyad gtser gyi chad las 'os med mi byed / sku tshab las tshan
'gan yod rigs kyis smyo zas kyi chang 'thung ba / bud med brten pa /
khyad par bdag can gyi bud med la log par g.yem pa sogs / bstan
pa'i ru drar 'dug pas sku tshab laṣ tshan nas 'phral 'don byed / sha
khral mar khral bsdu khral la* sogs pa khral rgyug gi 'dzom 'dzom *omitted
byed dgos rigs / sku tshab rang gi gzhis kar rgad po spyi dpon
rnams 'dzom te / dpya 'di phog gi zhib rtsis bsdur nas 'go dpon
gtso bor snyan sgron phul nas rgyug pa ma gtogs / sbyin bdag nas
spyi sger gyi khral rigs rgyugs mi chog / sa mtshams zhag babs
rnamṣ su mgron 'thud bzhag kyang / mgron babs sbyin bdag la
bkod 'dug pa thus rgyu min / gzhan yang sbyin bdag la ma nges
pa'i lto (112a) 'babs rigs / bdag yod mgron la sbyar ba las ja chang
sha la sogs pa'i spros pa mi byed / lto 'thud gzhi kha* len mi chog / *khad
sku tshab pas zhu rten phyag mjal sogs len nas / dpa' gzas chad
'thud 'u lag khral rkang sogs yang mi chog / sku tshab pas shi gson
gyi ston mo'i phud mi len / gnyen dga' bral dga' sdom byed pa la
phyag mjal len mi chog / mar khral lta bu las tshan phyin dgos rigs
la / bod dang spyi dpon gsum 'dzom gyis go bcad / der brten gyi
khral rigs med / nor dang rdzi bo'i phyag mjal mi len / ru pa pho
mo gcig las med na she ma gcig dang rdzi bo gcig gzhan bza' tshang
las pher bcas yod na she ma rdzi bo rbad gcod / 'u lag chad 'thud

rdzong(-kha?) itself, it is not permitted for a government representative to decide on them [elsewhere], whatever the degree of their importance.

It is not permitted for government representatives to rove around the villages on false pretexts such as inspecting the boundary walls of fields during times of harvesting and planting. If horses and cattle belonging to the public should happen to stray and eat a little of the grass, grain-crop or fruit trees [within] the boundary walls of the government representative's fields, he is not to [mete out] false and tormenting punishments in order to obtain whatever he should desire or commit [other such] unworthy deeds. Since the behaviour of those government representatives bearing the responsibilities of office who consume intoxicating liquor, cohabit with girls and commit adultery with married women constitutes the arch-enemy of the doctrine, such government representatives are to be summarily dismissed from office.

With regard to the administration of taxes [for the levy of which] meetings are required to be held, such as for meat-tax, butter-tax, harvest-tax and so forth, the village headmen and messengers must assemble on the property of the government representative himself and they are to be levied [only] after submitting to the chief civil officer [a demand roll in which are entered] the detailed accounts of specific tax liabilities that have been adjudged; [81] apart from this it is not permitted to levy from the 'patrons' various kinds of taxation, public or private.

Although an entertainment allowance is provided during overnight stays on the borders [between districts], 'patrons' have [sometimes] been [summarily] appointed [to supply] board and lodging for guests; [the entertainment allowance] is not to be realised [in this manner]. Further,
(112a) with regard to chance visits paid on 'patrons' for meals, apart from preparing for the guest whatever one might have at hand one should not occupy oneself [with providing] tea, liquor or meat. It is not permitted to take fields in lieu of the food allowance.

It is also not permitted for a government representative, after accepting gratifications, presents and so forth [to grant remissions from] military service, penal labour, [the provision of government] allowances, corvée, [or to show favour in matters relating to] tax estates and so forth. Government representatives should not take the prime portions in feasts held either for the dead or for the living. It is not permitted [for them] to accept presents during the festivities held to celebrate marriages and divorces.

In matters that require officials to go on tour, as in the case of butter-tax, decisions are to be taken by an assembled group [consisting of the official himself], an attendant and a village messenger – [these] three. It is not [permitted to impose other] kinds of tax on their own account.

Presents should not be accepted from cow [-owners] and herdsmen. In the case of there being no more than a single couple [working as] pastoralists, [they may be allowed to employ] one dairyman [82] and one herdsman; if they [the couple] can manage the work within their own family, it is prohibited for them to employ a dairyman and a herdsman.

'u lag rang bkod pa ma gtogs rgyu dngos mi len / gros* mi spyi dpon bla ma zhal ngos las sner slebs pa rnams kyis gzhung sogs byes 'gro'i rigs la / mi ser nas zla bo mi 'khrid / phyag mjal la snyad pa'i khral bsdud byed mi chog / gzhi nas las tshan 'gan yod che phra rnams na rgas dbang pos ma lcog pa dang nad cong gis zin pa mig mthong rigs gang 'os / gzhan dgongs pa grol rigs rdzong du zhag gsum las lhag pa sdod mi chog / lung par mi rigs mi gcig pa byung tshe / lung dpon gang yin la brda* ma sprod par mi btang / de dag gi sna len gdong bsu mi byed / Ar jag gi gnas tshang byung na rkun mo dang khyad med pa'i nag chad / khol bros nyams mi dga' ba'i rigs / babs yul nges can rnams kyis 'dzin (112b) 'chang ma byas par gtong tshe khol tshab sgrigs / 'dzin 'chang byas pa'i khol jor 'byor 'phrod byung tshe / sa thag ring thung zhag yun sogs dang dpags pa'i lto rngan lung pa'i sde thang byin / gzhan yang sbyin bdag bu yod pa bu dang / bu mo yod pa bu mos za / de yang khral rkang gnyis sbam byed mi chog / sbyin bdag bud med dang g.yog rigs med pa'i rgan rgon sogs yod tshe / ngo bo ma yol bar du skam khral gang 'byor re byed bcug / ngo bo yol tshe sha rus gang nye'i mi phros yod pa nas khral rkang rtsa lhongs byed / pha ma mi dga' ba'i gnyen mi bya / gzhan ma khral zhing khral khyim dngos po yod bzhin du / khral pa gnyis gsum sbam zhing / de yang skam khral la thab thus kyis bsgyur nas / yongs la gnod pa'i dpe ngan gcig 'dug pa / de rigs kyang de rang la bu dang bu mo'i phros yod na khral rkang so sor btsugs / mi phros med na rang gis blos 'phos pa'i mi phros yod pa la / khral 'ul dmag tsho res 'phel nges bcug / gzhis khang gzung nas grong khar khral med yod tshe / gzhis dang dpag pa'i khral 'ul gang pher re bcug / mi shi'i skor srog gcod mang du byed pa / shi gson gnyis kar ma bzang 'dug pa / da nas me btang bla ma'i gdong len dkar dro byed na 'gab 'dug pa'i dkar dro byed tshe / gzhung gi sku bkal mgo zug

*grol

*omitted

Apart from actually conscripting persons in corvée, punishments and the provision of government allowances, goods should not be taken [from them in lieu of these obligations.]

Those persons who have come to the end of their work, such as village counsellors and messengers, lamas and noblemen, and who travel to the capital and elsewhere, should not take with them companions from among the public. Nor are they permitted to levy taxes on the false pretext of [their having to procure] presents [to offer their superiors in the capital] Basically those officials, great or small, bearing government responsibilities who are unable [to continue in service] on account of infirmity and old age and those, according to their merits, whose chronic illness has been duly recognised and, furthermore, those who have been retired, [all such persons] must not stay in the *rdzong* for more than three days [after receiving their dismissal].

If foreigners come to a district they are not to be permitted to proceed without informing the district chief, whoever he may be. Such persons are not to be harboured or welcomed. Those who have sheltered brigands [are to receive] severe punishments identical to those for thieves.

If unhappy slaves [83] who run away are not seized and held by the
(112b) inhabitants of those places where they stop but rather are allowed to proceed, then they [the inhabitants] shall themselves have to arrange substitute slaves [in replacement]. If a slave who has been seized and held is delivered up to the slave owner then food and rewards and the hospitality of the district should be given to the person responsible, fixed according to the distance and number of days [spent in returning the slave].

Furthermore, if a 'patron' has a son, that son shall inherit and if he has a daughter, that daughter shall inherit. They are not permitted to combine two tax estates. If there is a 'patron' who has no daughters or servants of any kind, he should be made to supply 'dry tax' [84] to whatever extent possible for as long as he is living. On his decease the tax estate should be transferred to the kin most closely related to him by flesh or bone. [85] Marriages should not be contracted against the wishes of the parents. Also the practice whereby two or three taxpayers combine their taxable houses, taxable fields and all their material possessions causes a confusion with regard to 'dry tax'; this sets a bad example, injurious to all. If such persons themselves have male or female issue, then separate tax estates must be established. If they have no issue, then they must designate someone as their 'issue' who must without fail be made to deliver taxes, take part in corvée and in the militia. Any persons possessing land property and houses who reside in a village district untaxed should be made to deliver taxes and take part in corvée on suitable terms fixed according to the size of his land property.

With regard to deaths, if much killing [of animals for funerary feasts] takes place, this is not good either for the dead or for the living. Therefore in entertaining the lama who performs the cremation, it is sufficient to offer him a 'white meal'. [86] If this is done, then the government share is to be tshab la phyed ṭaṃ gi 'gong / bla ma'i sku bkal ras yug gi 'gong / yang / gshin po'i zas (113a) bsngos tsam las dkar dro ma 'byor tshe / gzhung dang bla ma'i sku bkal gong bzhin / gsung chog pa'i sha bkal tshab la chur mo phul bzhi re zong byin kyang de rtsis byed / yang / srog gcod ma byed ka med rang byung tshe / srog gcig bcad nas gzhung dang cho ga pa sogs nye ba 'dzom rigs kyi gdong len des khyab par byed / de las lhag pa'i srog gcod byed mi chog / nye ba'i lto byin dang ras bkab kyi sha de bcad / dge ba yul tshan de rang las gzhan du mi spros / stong rtsi zhabs tog gi rgyu'ang skam rlon gang 'byor sbyin bdag rang gi 'dod sbyar byed / dgon sde'i bla mas sger dbang gi mi shi'i phung po dbyar ka zhag gcig dang dgun ka zhag gnyis ma 'gyangs par / me btang dgos pa'i cho ga pa'i grangs dang yo byad sogs gzhung dang cha 'dra yang / bla ma ngo bo byon ma tshugs pa dang dus 'gyangs pa sogs byung tshe / bla ma gzhung nas dge rtsa'i cho ga btsugs skor sbyin bdag rang gi yo byad gang 'byor mtshan ma re dgon par skyel ba las yul du btsugs mi chog / chos pa'i lto bkal sa zhing bcad nas btsong mi chog / 'jig rten pas chos pa'i rgyags mi bcad / chos pa rang rkang can grong bshul sbyin bdag nye gnas sha tshas dge bar gang 'gro byed / lto gzan zur bzhugs chos pa'i rigs grong rjes su rten mchod chas rnams gong sar dgongs rdzogs su phul / de lhag dge bar gang 'gro byed / chos pa'i mtshams khang brdung dgos rigs / chos sde'i khongs su ma gtogs grong ltag ri bsul gang byung (113b) brdung mi chog / dgon sder pho mo sdom pa'i bu tsha bcas byung tshe / 'jig rten byed pa grong khar yin pas / yul sde'i khral tshab dgos par bcug / grwa rigs bsod snyoms don spyod bla ma'i brel ba gong du phud pa'i / bag med gu yang la zla phyed brgal tshe / khyim pa so nam gyi brel bas / yul

reckoned to the value of half a *[ma-] ṭaṃ* in lieu of the head and quarter of
an animal and the lama's share to the value of one roll of cotton. If, however,
(113a) besides simply the 'blessed food' offered to the deceased himself, 'white
meals' cannot be provided, the shares for the government and for the lama
are to be reckoned as above and the monks assisting in the ritual are to be
given four *phul* measures of rice or a piece of cloth in lieu of their shares of
meat. If, however, it happens that there is nothing for it but to kill an
animal, then a single animal may be butchered and used in a manner
sufficient for providing the government [share] and for the entertainment
of the monks assisting in the ritual and all the kinsmen assembled there. It
is not permitted to butcher more than that. [The distribution of] meat to
the relatives as a feast and [a similar distribution made] when the pall is
placed [on the corpse] is prohibited. Acts of merit [for the deceased]
should be performed in his own village and not elsewhere. As for the
materials used in acts of service 'reckoned to the thousandfold', [87] these
may accord with the desire of the 'patron' himself and consist of whatever
'dry' [cash] or 'wet' [food] he has at hand. Lamas of monastic communities
[acting] in their private capacity must cremate the corpses of the deceased
before one day has elapsed in summer and two in winter; the number of
monks assisting in the ritual and the material necessities are equal to [those
prescribed for funerals performed by] the government. In cases when the
lama cannot come in person or is delayed, the 'patrons' must take to the
monastery whatever provisions they have at hand, and of good quality, as
the food required for the lama and the government when introducing the
ritual of 'The Root of Virtue'; apart from doing this, it is not permitted to
introduce [such rituals under these circumstances] in the home [of the
deceased]. It is not permitted to set aside part of one's land and fields [in
order to raise] the food shares of the religious persons [conducting a
funeral]. Lay persons are not to reduce the provisions offered to religious
persons. The personal property left by a deceased religious person who was
himself the possessor of a tax estate should be disposed of by his loving
patrons and attendant disciples in whatever meritorious works they can
accomplish. After the death of a retired orderly who has devoted himself
to the religious life, his religious objects and ritual implements are to be
offered to the ruler for his funerary memorials. If there are more things
besides these, they should be disposed of in whatever meritorious works
can be accomplished.

As to the requirements governing the building [88] of hermitages for
religious persons, these should be built only within range of a monastic
(113b) community and not above villages or in any random side valley. If men and
women who cohabit in monastic communities should bear children, [they]
should be forced to settle in district communities where substitute taxpayers [89] are required [in order to replace previous tax-payers who had
died there without issue] since the village is where worldly actions should
be performed. If monks spend more than half a month in heedless
loitering, except in the case of their going on begging tours, pursuing their

babs sku tshab pas dos skyal 'u lag bkol / de bzhin dgon sde'i bla ma tsho'ang / lo dus kyi dbang chos tshes bcu ma ṇi'i brel ba gong du phud pa'i bcad rgya kho nar bzhugs dgos rgyu / yul sde rnams su bslab shes kyi rig gnas khung thub yin na ma gtogs / gang dran glur blangs kyis gzhan mgo bskor ba'i mo rtsis sngags ban sman pa sogs bkag / gzhung pa rdzong kha'i ma ṇi bas mtshon / ma ṇi ba'i rigs la / dad 'bul ma gtogs / khral rigs bkod mi chog / mi ngan 'khrul lag can gzhung nas bskrad par che phra sus kyang brten brdzi rgyab skyor byed pa med / khyad par rkun ma nges can rku thog tu bsad pa la / nag chad dge stong med / gri 'bal la gri chad / 'thab na 'thab chad / gsod res byung na shi gson mnyam sbrags / ma thub tshe nam zin la dmar gsod gtong ba'i / bu gzhis rnams tshe rabs su rang yul las gting 'don mtha' la bskrad / yang / lam brdung jag chom rkun ma g.yo khram nges can gsod pa dang / yul grur gnod pa'i gcan gzan gsod pa dang / dgra phyogs las thob pa phul byung na phyag mdud rgyab bkab sogs gang 'os byed / las sgo so (114a) so'i zong rigs sngar lugs ltar spus dag dgos rgyu dang / las sgo'i 'go pa do dam gang bkod des kyang tshad ldan dang / tshong pa sogs su thad nas kyang de ka'i ngag 'khril dgos rgyu dang / don gyi snying por che phra su thad nas kyang / 'di don la mi rtsi ba'i ngan pa mtshang rdol byung ba dang / bka' shog gi rigs la 'dra brdzus 'bru log dang / sa rim gyis gtong bar 'then thogs / gtan tshigs bkram pa'i don las 'gal ba sogs mi 'tsham pa'i bya ba byed mkhan byung na / rke mig srog gsum rang la gtong nges yin zhing / de bzhin gtso bo mi rje chos kyi rgyal po nas gzung / bla dpon sde rigs las tshan che rim rnams la de lugs kyi khur bzhag med cing / mnga' 'bangs skyid sdug mi blta / rang 'og mi non / rgyu 'bras khyad gsod nag po sdig las kyi bya ba byas pa phyogs mtshams mtha' bzhi gang nas byung zhing thos kyang /

own [legitimate] affairs or their lama's business, then just as householders engage themselves in agricultural work, [so also should] the government representative in the district where such monks make their halt put them to work in the transportation of loads and in corvée. Similarly, the lamas of monastic communities are to reside solely in states of seclusion, except when they are engaged in the annual and seasonal initiations, teachings, *tshes-bcu* [90] rituals and *ma-ṇi* recitations. Besides [propounding] in the district communities those spiritual precepts which are well-founded in learning, the diviners, astrologers, spell-binders, false monks and doctors who deceive others by singing whatever comes to mind are to be prohibited. Apart from devotional offerings, it is not permitted to render any kind of tax to the various sorts of *ma-ṇi-ba,* [91] for instance to the licensed *ma-ṇi-ba* attached to the districts under the administration of a *rdzong.*

Evil and deceitful persons who have been banished from the capital are not to be given harbour or support by anyone, great or small. In particular, there are no penalties or manslaughter-fines for killing a real thief while in the act of theft. For drawing a knife, 'knife penalty', and for fighting, 'fight penalty' [will be incurred]. If murders take place, the dead and the living are to be bound together. [92] If this cannot be done, [the murderer] is to be executed upon his arrest and his children and family are to be expelled from their home and exiled to the border for all their lifetime. Furthermore, any person who kills an actual highwayman, robber, thief or deceitful liar, and any person who kills a wild beast that has been committing injuries in the districts, and any person who comes to offer goods won from the enemy side, [all such persons] should be rewarded appropriately with consecrated ribbons, mantles and so forth.

(114a) As of previous custom, the various goods in the different border trade marts [93] must be of good quality and whoever is appointed as the superintendant official of the border trade mart must himself be judicious in character. The traders and others, whoever they may be, must abide closely to what he says.

Essentially, if any person at all, great or small, should commit capital crimes such as perpetrating evil deeds and sins that contravene the substance of these rules, counterfeiting written orders or altering their sense by reshaping their letters, impeding the dispatch by stages of such orders, or transgressing the substance of decrees [94] that have been duly circulated and other such things, then it is certain that such people will be bound by the neck, blinded and executed – [these] three. Similarly, if anyone from the chief *Dharmarāja* ruler at the top, down to the lamas and officers who hold important posts should, without acquiescing to such provisions as these, fail to look to the welfare of the subjects or keep a hold on those beneath them or if they should commit evil sinful deeds in contempt of the doctrine of karmic retribution – and if accounts of such things occurring anywhere within the four cardinal points should be heard, then:

'di la mngon spyod mi mdzad na /
dam can srung mas ci zhig bya //

zhes sogs dang /

dge ba su spyod sun 'byin pa //
'di 'dra bsgral ba'i 'os lags so //

zhes pa'i lung bzhin du ye shes mgon po'i dmar rgyan du 'bul rgyu thag chod yin pas / der ma song ba'i rang rang so so'i thad du go shes yang dag yod pa'i mu nas / lha dpang dkon mchog gsum dang / mi dpang phyag mdzod rang du bcol ba'i bstan pa phyi nang gsang gsum gyi zhabs 'degs ci 'gyur dang phan sleb gang che byas shing / mtha' na lus (114b) srog gi steng khar babs kyang ci gsung bsgrub pa'i snying stobs kyi go cha gyon te / chos dang srid kyi bslab ston 'gan bzhes chos blon mgar lta bu'i phyag phyi zhu dgos / zhes dpal 'brug pa rin po che mthu chen ngag gi dbang po'i chos kyi rgyal srid phyogs mthar spel ba'i las tshan spyi'i rnam par gzhag pa'i yan lag tha mar dge ba'i bkra shis gsum pa 'jig rten kun la khyab gyur cig //

gang 'dir chos srid lugs brgya'i bum bzang gtso //
phan bde'i lung gi rin chen ma nyams par //
rgyal brgyud lha dbang dgyes pa'i mchod sprin du //
'gro gsum mtho ris rten du bkod pa yin //

zhing khams rgya mtshor dge legs rab 'byams khungs //
bde 'byung nor bu'i khrir 'dzegs chos rgyal du //
longs su spyod chog dam pa'i legs bshad 'di //
sa spyod du ma'i rgyan du cis mi gzung //

srid par rlabs chen 'jug pa'i rnam thar 'phreng //
nyin gcig bzhin du spyod cing nges 'dod na //
blo ldan gang zhig 'di la che bzhir dang //
rgyal po khri thog sangs rgyas nyid du 'gyur //

de lta'i mthu las 'jig rten khams kun tu //
dpal ldan dbyar rnga'i chos srid rab rgyas te //
gnas skabs mthar thug mi bslu phan bde'i 'bras //
rdzogs ldan ngo mar spyod pas 'da' gyur cig //

If destructive magic is not performed on him
What can the oath-bound Protectors do?

And so forth. Also:

Those who offer insults to persons engaged in
virtue
Are worthy of being dispatched in this manner.

In accordance with this command, it is certain that such persons should be offered to Mahākāla as his meat sacrifice.[95] And so, lest it should come to such a pass, each on his own part should with pure conscience endeavour to fulfil whatever works of service to the doctrine – in its external, internal and secret forms – befall him and so bring benefit to the doctrine as much as possible, calling on the Triple Gem as his divine witness and on the *Phyag-*
(114b) *mdzod* himself as his human witness. Even though he should lose his life in the end, he should wear the armour of fortitude in accomplishing whatever he is commanded and render service like the religious minister mGar,[96] bearing the responsibility of giving admonitions on matters pertaining to the religion and the state.

[Here ends] the final section concerning the general fundamentals of [the system whereby] government officials diffuse to all directions and limits the theocratic rule of the Glorious 'Brug-pa Rin-po-che, the Mighty Ngag-gi dBang-po. May the third virtuous blessing contained herein fill the whole world.

Lest the jewel of the authority of beneficial happiness
should decline,
He who is here chief of good vessels [encompassing] the
hundredfold forms of the religious state
Established the Three [Classes of] Beings[97] as supports of
paradise [and]
As a cloud of offerings which delights the royal lineage and
the divine rulers.
Why should not these holy aphorisms be upheld as the
ornament of worldlings,
[Aphorisms] such as may be used for the sake of a *dharmarāja,*
He who has ascended the throne of jewels from which
happiness arises,
And who is the source of extensive virtue in the ocean of
heavens?
If [a man in his] string of lives which billow into existence
Should genuinely aspire to act as if he had but a day,
Then any such wise person would here and now become a witness
[to the Buddha]
And an enthroned king would become an actual Buddha.
From such power as this may the religious state of the
Glorious Drum of Summer[98]
Flourish widely throughout all realms of the world
And may it achieve and surpass the real *satyayuga*[99]
Which is the goal of temporal circumstances, the sure result
of beneficial happiness.

ces dpal 'brug pa rin po che mthu chen ngag gi dbang po'i bka' khrims phyogs thams cad las rnam par rgyal ba'i gtam 'di yang / chos rgyal gong ma'i khrir sngon gyi smon lam rten 'byung gis grub pa / bdag ngag (115a) dbang bstan 'dzin mi pham dbang po'i sdes / rgyal ba'i gong bu ngag dbang bdud 'joms rdo rje 'phrin las bzhi'i 'khor lo sgyur ba'i gzhal med khang / 'brug spungs thang bde ba chen po lugs gnyis dge bar skyong ba'i rgyal khab nas / rab byung zhes pa sa mo bya'i lo rgyal bas gsang sngags chos 'khor ston pa'i dus kyi zla ba'i yar tshes bzang por bris pa dge legs su gyur cig / ces pa lta bu ni blo ldan bstan la brtse zhing 'gro la phan bzhed lugs nyis skyong ba rnams la sman 'gyur cher srid snyam nas 'dir dka' yang dang du blangs pa'o //

[Colophon]

Thus this *Legal Decree of the Glorious 'Brug-pa Rin-po-che, the Mighty Ngag-gi dBang-po* [entitled] *The Discourse, Victorious in All Directions,* completed on the strength of aspirations made in previous lives on the throne of the Lord *Dharmarāja,* was written by myself, Ngag-dbang
(115a) bsTan-'dzin Mi-pham dBang-po, in the capital of 'Brug sPungs-thang bDe-ba Chen-po where the dual system is virtuously administered, the palace where the *Jina's* essence, Ngag-dbang bDud-'joms rDo-rje, turned the wheel of the Four Actions, on the later auspicious dates of the month in which the *Jina* revealed the *Dharmacakra* of the *Mantrayana,* in the year called *Rab-byung* of the Earth Female Bird (1729).[100] May it become a work of virtuous merit.

Thus, even though difficult, these words are submitted here since I [bsTan-'dzin Chos-rgyal] think they can be of great expediency to those wise persons who administer the dual system, who are enamoured of the doctrine and desirous of benefitting beings.

Notes to Text III

1. This could be taken to refer either to the Ist *Zhabs-drung,* Ngag-dbang rNam-rgyal (1594-?1651) or to one of his two incarnations alive when this code was composed: 'Jigs-med Grags-pa, the first *thugs-sprul* (1724-1761) or Phyogs-las rNam-rgyal, the first *gsung-sprul* (1708-1736). In a more general sense, it might refer to all three. However, in the formal title below we see the decree promulgated in the name of the founder whose memory over-shadowed his living incarnations.
2. Mi-pham dBang-po (1709-38) was the first of six incarnations of the great bsTan-'dzin Rab-rgyas (1638-96) who had ruled as the 4th *'Brug sDe-srid* from 1680-95 and who had been one of the most serious claimants to the guardianship of the throne of the Ist *Zhabs-drung.* Mi-pham dBang-po's biography by Shākya Rin-chen unfortunately has nothing to say on the matter of his 'legal decree', merely pointing out that at the start of his reign as the 10th *'Brug sDe-srid* he used "all sorts of measures to bring sentient beings to happiness" (f.36a). No doubt the decree was intended to be one such measure.
3. bsTan-'dzin 'Brug-rgyas, the Ist *'Brug sDe-srid (regn.* 1651-56).
4. bsTan-'dzin Chos-rgyal, 10th Head Abbot (*regn.* 1755-62), the author of *LCB* I.
5. See *LCB* I, ff. 92a-100b.
6. *Zhabs-drung* Ngag-dbang rNam-rgyal.
7. 'Jigs-med Grags-pa is both one of the names of Ngag-dbang rNam-rgyal (see f. 103a below) and of the Ist *thugs-sprul* (the 2nd *Zhabs-drung*). Perhaps it is intended to refer to both here.
8. The 'mother school' of which the 'Brug-pa is a part.
9. *sMan-ljongs* ('The Land of Medicinal Herbs') is a common expression for Bhutan.
10. On the *dharmakaya, saṃbhogakaya* and *nirmanakaya* see note 36 to the *Relação* below.
11. The historical Buddha, Śākyamuni, son of Śuddhodana.
12. Buddha, Dharma and Sangha.
13. This presumably refers to the three 'Paths of Assembling Merit' (*tshogs-lam,* Skt. *sambhāramārga*): small, middle and great.
14. Tibet.
15. The categories referred to here are probably: 1) 'memory of one's abodes in previous lives' (*sngon-gyi gnas rjes-su dran-pa*), 2) 'divine sight' (*lha'i mig*), and 3) 'knowledge that one's afflictions are ended' (*zag-pa zad-pa shes-pa*).
16. An allegorical expression referring to the 'Brug-pa ('thunder-dragon') school.
17. An allusion to the prophecy that the school of the 'Brug-pa would extend to an area covered by eighteen days flight of a vulture.
18. Mahākāla and his consort.
19. 'Pacifying, enriching, overpowering and destroying' (*zhi, rgyas, dbang, drag*).
20. *lnga-brgya-pa* is a confusing term which could easily be taken to refer to the last five hundred years in the duration of the *dharma,* a period when certain enlightened beings achieve full karmic realisation in the face of the doctrine's apparent collapse (see for instance the *Vajracchedikā*). However, Jamyang Namgyal (1971:96) notes: "The usual Lamaist scholastic explanation for this expression is *snyigs-ma lnga, tshe-lo brgya* ['the five decays, and the lifespan of a hundred years']. The five snyigs-ma (kaṣāya) are: 1) *tshe'i* (āyuh); 2) *lta-ba'i* (dṛṣṭi); *nyon-mongs-pa'i* (kleśa); 4) *sems-can-gyi* (sattva); 5) *dus kyi* (kalpa). During this degenerate age, the life of man is no more than a hundred years." The dual signification of the term cannot be put into convenient English, hence my vague rendering as 'us of the age of decline'.
21. Tōhoku Nos. 556 and 557.
22. Cf. the extended account of the lineage of King Mahasaṃmata in the *Blue Annals,* Ch. I.
23. On this 'prehistoric' line of Tibetan kings, see Haarh 1969.
24. This theme is fully amplified by the *gTsang mKhan-chen* who adapts it particularly to his life of the Ist *Zhabs-drung* (PBP).
25. lHa-ldan (Devavān, 'The Abode of Gods') is thought to refer to lHa-sa, the capital of Tibet.
26. Ye-shes rDo-rje (1161-1211), the effective founder of the 'Brug-pa school, derives his epithet of *gTsang-pa rGya-ras* from the name of his family or clan (rGya) and the white cotton of his yogin's dress (*ras*).
27. On this important figure who is said to have been the first 'Brug-pa teacher in Bhutan, see Aris 1979: index.
28. By Bhutanese reckoning *Zhabs-drung* Ngag-dbang rNam-rgyal was the fourth incarnation of *gTsang-pa rGya-ras* Ye-shes rDo-rje. The three preceding him were *rGyal-dbang-rje* Kun-dga' dPal-'byor (1428-76), *'Jam-dbyangs* Chos-kyi Grags-pa (1478-1523) and *Kun-mkhyen* Padma dKar-po (1527-92).

29. LP tries to resolve the problem of *sgo-btags-su* in this prophecy by taking *sgo* ('door') to refer to the 'approaches' (*kha*) which are 'named' (*ming-btags*) in the term (*lHo Mon*) *Kha bZhi* ('The Southern Mon Country of Four Approaches', i.e., Bhutan). The many images which this prophecy conjure up are explained in his long gloss: *lho-rong-gi yul 'di-ni sbas-pa'i yul-gyi nang-tshan zhig yin yul-'di'i bkod-pa rdo-rje rnal-'byor-ma ḍākki-ni wa-ra-hi'i gsang-ba'i padmo'i sbubs lta-bur yod-pas gsang-sngags-kyi chos thams-cad 'byung-ba'i gnas rdo-rje btsun-mo'i bha-ga rang-bzhin lhun-gyis grub-pa'i gnas-kyi lte-ba thed-thim-gyi yul-du (yul-lam pho-brang ste) rdzong btab-nas / dpal-ldan 'brug-pa'i phrin-las rnam-pa bzhi chos-srid-kyi bstan-pa kha-bab-kyi chu-bo chen-po bzhi'i yon-tan dang-mtshungs-par phyogs dang phyogs-su spel-ba'i kha bzhi-las 'dzam-gling kun-tu khyab-pa'i rten-'brel phyogs-bzhir kha bzhi'i ming-btags-pa'i sgo chen-po bzhi dang-ldan-pa de yin //*
30. Another of Ngag-dbang rNam-rgyal's names, in fact the one he himself most often used.
31. The demons of: 1) 'the *skandhas' (phung-po),* 2) 'obscurations' (*nyon-mongs-pa*), 3) 'the Lord of Death' (*'chi-bdag*), and 4) 'the son of the God of Desire' (*['dod-] lha'i bu*).
32. Images, books and *stūpas,* which are classed as physical, verbal and mental supports of the faith, in that order.
33. The 'fixing of handles on pots' seems to be an allusion to Ngag-dbang rNam-rgyal's success in bringing the material benefits of civilization to Bhutan. The expression, which is not to be taken in a literal sense, is much favoured by later writers (Aris 1976:628 note 66). It would be interesting to discover its origin.
34. It is beyond question that Srong-btsan sGam-po promulgated laws, but not those listed here. Uray (1972:65) maintains that the *Mi-chos gtsang-ma bcu-drug* were first compiled "... to justify the codifications of *Tshal* and/or that of *tai si-tu Byang-chub-rgyal-mtshan* from the historical and ideological point of view." The 'restitutions' listed here (and which vary greatly from period to period) perhaps have their prototype in what appears to be the provision for a nine-fold restitution for the theft of royal property in the 'Four Fundamental Laws' (*rTsa-ba bzhi'i khrims*), which are similarly attributed to Srong-btsan. These have been mixed up here with the 16 *mi-chos* and the 10 *lha-chos.* For the original lists of all these sets see *Ma-ṇi bka'-'bum,* Vol. *E,* f. 103a-b.
35. The word *sgrigs* ('order') is heard most commonly now in the compound *sgrigs-khrims,* a term which covers all the unwritten rules governing the formal behaviour required of government officers and the public at the royal court or in a *rdzong.* These rules were originally of monastic origin, though that is nearly forgotten now. The term is today never applied to the state laws or administration in general. The *sgrigs rnam-bzhag* must have evolved in the *rdzong* monasteries of western Bhutan during the time of the 1st *Zhabs-drung* and his immediate successors. bsTan-'dzin Chos-rgyal, the author of this decree, seems to have extended the true meaning of the term to include both 'laws' and 'administration' in general simply because there were no real state laws at the start of the Bhutanese theocracy. Much of the vagueness in the first two sections of his decree seems to derive from the absence of true legislation dating from the period of the state's founding.
36. I have assumed that the *spyi-dpon* in the 18th century had the same function as he does now in the 20th century, namely the carrying of messages from the *rdzong* to his village, the office rotating around the village. He stands at the very bottom of the administrative scale today but he may'have been truly included at that time among the "wealthy and important" with whom he is linked in this text. *ngo-can* (lit. 'one having face'; 'important person') is a word often used specially of an influential person to whom contending parties will take their dispute for settlement. The *gros-mi* ('counsellor') has disappeared, if indeed his office was ever of a formal nature. DS (179) notes "Kyomi in Sikkim".
37. Presumably the *'Brug sDe-srid.*
38. Neither of these are identified and the translation is tentative.
39. The dGe-lugs-pa authorities of Tibet.
40. *Sa-skya legs-bshad* No. 52.
41. *Sa-skya legs-bshad* No. 109.
42. The 'Stages of Generation' and the 'Stages of Perfection' in the practice of tantric yoga.
43. For a list of the 'Ten Religious Practices' see Aris 1977: 226 note 66.
44. LN: *rgyal-khrims dpang-thub gtso-bor bton-ngos zer-ba-ni / bya-ba gang-yin-kyang rgyal-khab-kyi khrims-yig dpang-por bzhag-ste khrims-yig-la cha-'jog gtso-bor bton-pa'i ngos-nas (thog-nas) bya-gal che-ba zer-ba-yin /*
45. Apart from the *gZhung mGron-gnyer* ('Government Chamberlain'), all the provincial governor (the *rdzong-dpon* and *spyi-bla*) had their own *mgron-gnyer.* Broadly speaking, their duties seem to have covered all matters external to the governor's courts, while the *gzim-dpon* ('Steward-in-chief') looked after the internal affairs.

46. *sPyi-bla* is the literary form for *dpon-slob* ('Governor'), of which there were three, i.e. those of sPa-gro, Dar-dkar-nang and Krong-sar. The office of *Dar-dkar dpon-slob* has lapsed and the remaining two are usually held by members of the present royal family. Both forms of the title reflect their monastic origin.
47. I.e. the requirement to provide the *rdzong* with fodder and firewood.
48. The form of the *Zhabs-drung*'s seal known as 'The Sixteen I's' (*Nga bcu-drug-ma*) is derived directly from the symbolism contained in this verse. See Aris 1979: 213-14.
49. Tohoku No. 257.
50. The *sku-tshab* were almost certainly the government representatives appointed to the control of groups of villages, known as the *drung-pa*. See Aris 1976:616, 627.
51. The *rGya-drung* are called 'subha', 'soubah' etc. in the British records.
52. See the Glossary under *las-sgo*.
53. The 'Three Truths' are perhaps the same as the 'Three Kinds of Validity' (*tshad-ma gsum*): 1) the validity of quotations from scripture, 2) the validity of visible proof, and 3) the validity of reasoning.
54. *Sa-skya legs-bshad* No. 162. Cf. No. 328: "By mildness one conquers the mild and by mildness one also conquers the rough."
55. LN: *ma-yin ma-'thus-pa'i nag-can zer-ba-ni / chos-srid-kyi khrims dang-mthun-pa ma-yin-par bka'-khrims-kyis ma 'thus-par khrims-'gal-gyi mi-de nag-can yin-pas /*
56. See Glossary under *tsa-ra*.
57. *Sa-skya legs-bshad* No. 32.
58. Cf. f. 112a below: "If foreigners come to a district they are not to be permitted to proceed without informing the district chief, whoever he may be. Such persons are not to be harboured or welcomed."
59. LN: *bzang-kha rang-nyid-kyis byas-pa'i ngan-kha zer-ba-ni / gzhung-don gang byed-kyang bzang-kha (legs-shom) nged-kyis byas-pa-yin bya-ba ngan-pa'i rigs byung-na nga min kho yin zer gshan-la mi-'gel-ba dang /*
60. See Glossary under *ru-nga(-bo)*.
61. DS (171): "literally, so that things may not look frayed and worn both at the edges and rent in the centre."
62. LN: *des-gsum cang rig khyug gsum brtan rling bkyel che'i zer ba ni / des-pa-ni sems-rgyud zhi-dul bya-ba gang-la-yang cang-grung shes-rig khyug-pa dran-pa brtan-po dang-ldan-pa brling-ba-ni sems-kyi gting zab-cing bkyil-che'i* (sic) *sems-la dran-pa-rnams lam-sang kha-nas ma-thon-par sems-la bkyil-te gtam bzang-ngan lab-dgos-pa-yin /*
63. This is TR's definition of *'Khor-gsum: rmog, khrab, mtshon-cha*. Cf. the entries in Das and Jaschke.
64. See Glossary under *mdo-drug*.
65. DS (172): 'Jagir' (?).
66. *Sa-skya legs-bshad* No. 201.
67. *zangs-thal* (lit. 'to pass unhindered') is according to TR a term usually employed in describing the miraculous power of being able to pass through solid objects, hence my translation by 'unimpedable'.
68. *Sa-skya legs-bshad* No. 261.
69. LN: *gong-du mtshungs-pa-las zer-ba-ni / 'brug sde-srid rang-nyid khrims dang mthun-dgos-pa ma-zad /*
70. The *Gangs-ri'i rdor-'dzin* was the official appointed to control the area surrounding Kailash in western Tibet which had been granted to the Bhutanese authorities by the king of Ladakh when this region still formed part of Ladakh. Relations between Ladakh and Bhutan were consolidated by *Byams-mgon* Ngag-dbang rGyal-mtshan (1647-1732) and the grant probably dated from his lifetime. The government derived considerable income from the donations of pilgrims to Kailash and from the monastic estates which it administered there (Kawaguchi 1909:168). The post of *Gangs-ri'i rdor-'dzin* (or *Gangs-ri bla-ma*) was last held by *Drag-shos* bSod-nams Rab-rgyas who continued in office until 1959 when the Tibetan revolt took place.
71. *gsol-ba* ('siu' in the vernacular) is the honorific for *lto*, 'rice' and, more generally, 'food'. The term *gsol-ba dkar-mo* may refer to the high grade of white rice known as *sbo-'bras*, the issue of which seems to have been a privilege of senior government officers. The lower ranks would have received the coarser grade of reddish coloured rice.
72. We may conjecture that the office of *phyi-mgron* (lit. 'External Chamberlain') would have been held by certain officers on special deputation to a district.
73. LN: *gzhi-len-gyi rnam-pa'i mthong-srol zer-ba-ni / dpon-khag gsar-pa bskos-pa dang phyogs-gzhan-nas gzhung-gi mgron-po gsar-pa phebs-mi-rnams-la gzhi-len zer-ba lto-chas gang-zab drang-rgyu dang gzhi-tshugs zer gnyer-tshang sogs sprod-srol yod-pa zer-ba-yin /*

TEXT IV

Title fol. 1 ***The Report which Father Estevão Cacella of the Society of Jesus sent to Father Alberto Laercio, Provincial of the Province of Malabar of East India, about his journey to Catayo* [Cathay] *until he came to the Kingdom of Potente* [Bhoṭanta=Tibet].**

Fol. 6 Para. 2 This city [of Pargão[1] = sPa-gro] begins in a beautiful plain wide and pleasant, set between mountains on either side of it, which are cheerful to look at and there are well laid out fields of wheat and rice with which it was then covered; the plain is divided by two great rivers[2] which make it good to see, principally with the freshness imparted by great willows and by irrigation channels which come out of the rivers; with the plain begin the buildings, very big and high houses which are often of three, four or five storeys having very thick walls with windows and verandas which adorn them; these buildings are not in such a way that they form streets but are divided one from another over the plain and amidst the foothills of the mountains in such a way that they make a city but so long that even the part we covered and saw would be at least three leagues and there was quite a lot more which we did not see; because the valley goes on in the way I have described until it ends up in a mountain which divides it into two, down which come the two rivers one on each side, which irrigate the valley and around this mountain the city forms two long arms which go uphill along the rivers quite a long way. The people are innumerable and if one were to add them up the very least number that live there would be more than five hundred thousand souls;[3] it is possible for so many people to live there because of the way which they have of living in those houses, because in each house there are many dwellers divided up by the storeys and the divisions which they make for this purpose; on the 25th of March we entered this city, the day on which the Eternal Word clothed in our humanity entered this world and from its infinite goodness we hope that our entry on that day into that land may constitute for that whole people their recognition by their Saviour. We could not come immediately to the house of the companion[4] who was guiding us and when on the next day we entered it we found ourselves robbed that morning of everything that we had for our sustenance; he put us in a house of his that was so dark that even at midday we could not see each other and it looked more like a prison than anything else. Immediately we asked him to find us what we needed because he was

acting as our guard in order to convey us in safety; but he, feeling very secure and independent, replied to us that he was going to rest and that afterwards he would do his duty. In all this he showed how little he cared about being unfaithful to us even after we had trusted him, and so he became obviously cross when we spoke to him about this business, saying
fol. 7 that that business was not the work of one day but that it would last months, and that when the man who had done business with us in Runate [Rangamati = Jaigaon] [5] had come he would do what seemed best to him. When we saw the damnable resolution of this man and other signs which he gave of having a heart infected with evil plans from which the lord [later] freed us and which we afterwards got to know, we decided to leave his house in which there were great difficulties but after two days, seeing that he was often out of doors, we left his house -- on which his relatives came up and stopped us and took news to him of what was happening; it was notable the anger with which this man came to impede us and to try once again by force to put us in his house; he made use of weapons and everything that he could against us; but God our Lord was pleased that with patience we should overcome him, resisting him only with this patience, that is resisting the passion and rage with which he came over-filled. And since at this time many people came up who saw the unreasonable way in which that man was acting towards us, they took pity on us, trying to quieten him down, and having taken him back to his house, we were thus rid of him; and that night we went into the house of a good old man who for the love of God our Lord made us welcome and on the next day a lama (*Lamba*) with authority with whom the Father João Cabral had previously talked sent us horses and people who took us to his house which was very far from this staging-post; but when we reached him we found him altered because he was afraid to quarrel with the man who had stolen from us, if he were to shelter us in his house: however, our Lord was pleased to encourage him not to notice this problem, although after we had been in his house because of the same man he prevented us from going onwards to such an extent that when another lama wished to take us, this man's people prevented him from doing this by force with weapons. Seeing us in such a state and in many other circumstances of difficulties and problems which I refrain from recording, in a country where no one takes any action, every one of these men being an absolute lord in his own house, without there being anyone outside it who can ask him for an explanation of what he is doing, we met the principal lama[6] that the King [*Zhabs-drung* Ngag-dbang rNam-rgyal] has here and who, when he knew of the impediments which we had preventing us from reaching the King, said that by his influence we would go there since it was he who was there in charge of the King's business, and he said that immediately we should go to his house; which we did with the agreement of the lama with whom we had been sheltered, and indeed he himself [later] took us and accompanied us to the King; but even here the enemy did not refrain from making his normal efforts to impede us in such a way that, while we were talking with the principal lama about

how we wanted to go on, the lama tried to persuade us that we should not go on but we should wait for the King there and he said that he [the King] would come within a month (which was quite false since now six months have gone by without the King going there). When we saw that this change of heart also had its origin in the man who had robbed us we bade farewell to the lama and we began to walk alone, determined to carry on our journey, confident that our Lord would guide us and guard us, for having done everything we could we saw no other way of going ahead. The lama, seeing our resolution, was obliged to ask us to wait a few more hours to get us ready and to prepare his safe-conducts and we were to go by his means to the King because if the King were to see us there without our journeying as we should or if on the way some accident should happen to us the King would punish him severely. So we waited for the day and he gave us people and horses for the rest of the journey and in the company of the first lama we left Pargão [sPa-gro] on the second octave of Easter, the fifth of April [1527].

After three days journey we found in a village a lama, a relative[7] of the King, who came from the King to look for us with people and horses and he accompanied us; this person wrote immediately to the King that we were coming and so he sent other lamas who were to wait for us at the next staging-post with two horses, very well equipped, and journeying thus with all that company a good way before we arrived he sent more of his people inviting us to tea, which he and his people use a lot, and continuing our road afterwards which led through high mountains, coming near now to the place where he was, he sent other youthful lamas on their horses who entertained us with many races which they held in a staging-place where the mountains allowed it and then we saw through the trees a great multitude of people who were waiting for us and their shawms and trumpets were playing, because the instruments which they use in their festivals have
fol. 8 some similarity with these. Here were a hundred lamas[8] all young from twelve to twenty years old who came to meet us lined up in two lines. In the middle were three small lamas with incense which they were carrying in thuribles, which is an honour only the King has. Thus they took us to the place which they had made ready for us which was a very well made tent lined with Chinese silk with an altar-hanging and a place where we could lie down; and a little later the King sent us a note that we could proceed [to his presence] and we found him in another tent, very well decorated with silk, and he was sitting in a high place clothed with red silk embroidered in gold; on his right and very close to him in another appropriate place there stood an image of his father[9] with a lamp alight [before it] which was always burning there; there were also two high places for us, no other lama however important having a place there except on the mats which were spread on the ground. He received us with a demonstration of great benevolence, signifying this in the joy which he showed on seeing us and on knowing where we were coming from, where we were from, i.e. from what country and nation, and he asked the other questions normal at a first

meeting: we were able to tell him that we were "Portuguese" because since no foreigners ever come to these mountains, nor do they remember ever having seen or heard of similar people passing there, [10] the name of *Franguis* [Franks] has not reached them, which is the name which the Portuguese have in all the Orient.

It was no mean lack of consolation to find us here almost without a language because although we brought with us someone who knew Hindustani very well, Parsee and the language of the Koch people (*cocho*), however we found here only one lama from Chaparangue [rTsa-brang] [11] very beloved of the King who could understand something, but very little, of Hindustani; through him we spoke as best we could with much trouble and difficulty, and also on the King's part who desired very much that we should be able to make ourselves clear in the lengthy conversations which he had every day with us; but knowing from us how we came there with orders to preach to him the faith of Christ our Lord because we had heard that of old they had been Christians and afterwards as the years went by and with lack of teachers the Christian religion was forgotten but that they still had some elements of Christianity, [12] he showed himself to approve of our coming and said that we should learn his language so that we could speak to him and that he could not possibly not accept what we would teach him for those must be very good things for which we had come from so far away to search for him and so he ordered that lama from Chaparangue [rTsa-brang] to continue teaching us every day and the King for this purpose relieved the lama of his other duties.

The King who is called Droma Raja *[Dharmarāja]* [13] is thirty-three years old, the King and at the same time the chief lama of this Kingdom of Cambirasi,[14] the first of those of Potente [Bhoṭanta] in this area, which is very great and populated; he is proud of his gentleness for which he is highly reputed, but less feared, and at the moment he has in his house a lama, [15] a relative of his, who did him a notable disservice but he treats him well and told us that he would let him go immediately and that he had no heart to give him any other punishment although he knew that when he was freed from prison he would certainly rise up against him as he was accustomed to do. The King is also very celebrated for his abstinency in never eating rice or meat or fish, maintaining himself only with fruit and milk,[16] and also for the solitary way in which he lived during the three years before we came here, withdrawing into a hut which he made very small in the middle of the mountains on top of a great rock, now not seeing or allowing himself to be seen by anyone and they put his food on two ropes which from his hut went down to others which were below and he pulled the food in without speaking all this time to anyone;[17] he occupied himself, as he told us, in praying and in his spare time he made various objects which he has and he showed us one of them which was the best, being an image of the face of God in white sandalwood, small but very well made and this is an art of which he is very proud, as also that of painter at which he is good and he showed us some of his paintings which were very good and seeing a St Raphael

on a panel which we brought he wanted to make a copy of it and began straight away and went on with it very well, although because of his many
fol. 9 occupations he has not yet finished it.[18] This King has also a great reputation as a man of letters and as such all the other great lamas reverence him and the Kings send him presents and he is sought out from all these places, having with him lamas from very distant Kingdoms.[19] The reason why we found him lodged in tents in these mountains is because the people of the villages are each one accustomed to call him to their village and so he sets himself up in some staging-place[20] from which he can go to many villages and they then offer to him great presents of horses, cattle, rice, cloth and other things which are his principal revenue, and those who do not invite him to visit them because they live too far away come themselves to find him with their offerings. For this reason he was in the mountains with the school of his lamas which he always takes with him and he has more than a hundred who are well practised at learning and performing their ceremonies; these are called *Guelõis [dge-slong]*[21] and they are the principal lamas for they do not marry and do not eat more than once before midday after which they cannot eat rice, nor fish, nor meat, nor do they ever drink wine and in this they are different from the other lamas[22] who are not so strict; they spend the whole day in the school in which they eat and sleep, all of them coming out twice a day, once in the morning the other time in the afternoon, and then going back immediately in order one after the other in a composed and modest way, so well taught and accustomed to this are they and yet it was a great grief to see them so occupied in the errors which they are taught for they spend a great part of the day in their prayers and at night they all get up when a signal is given and they pray for a space of half an hour and again in the early morning, singing like clergy in the choir.

In these mountains and others we accompanied him *[Zhabs-drung* Ngag-dbang rNam-rgyal] for two months until we came to his house[23] which is in those mountains where he spent his period of retreat without having with him anyone else apart from his lamas, nor is the place capable of being populated because to make a house it is necessary to break many stones and to flatten with great trouble some part of the mountain which is very steep; and it is a place he chose to defend himself against a King who is eight days journey from there and he is the greatest King of Potente [Bhoṭanta] who is called Demba Cemba *[sDe-pa gTsang-pa]*[24] and he fought with him in the past because he *[Zhabs-drung]* did not want to give him, as he said, a bone of his dead father[25] which the King asked him for and for this reason he does not live in a city of his, great and good, which is called Ralum [Ra-lung][26] and this is five days journey away; he looked after us very well in his house in a part of it where we were able to make and decorate very nicely a chapel to which we invited him on the day of our Holy Father Ignatius[27] and the Lord consented that despite two robberies we still had all the apparatus which we brought for the altar and all the images for although in the first of the robberies they took away a picture of our Virgin

Lady on a board, all the same a lama who found it in possession of one of those who robbed us brought it to us along with another Bible which they also had there; the King came to see the chapel with his master [lHa-dbang Blo-gros] [28] who is a very old lama for whom he has great respect and with the rest of the lamas and they were all very pleased with what they saw, spending some hours in seeing and asking about everything.

In these months we took every diligence to learn the language[29] and although we were staying in tents and going on roads and in strange houses which took up our time, all the same God our Lord did for us in this matter as in all others the greatest mercies; the worst trouble of all was the lack of a master because we could only make ourselves understood with great difficulty with the one that we had because he was not from this Kingdom but from Chaparangue [rTsa-brang] and did not know the language of this area, of which at the present time we had more necessity because while all these Kingdoms have the same language there is a great variation in the pronunciation and in the endings and the corruption [30] of it in some parts makes it almost another language, especially in this Kingdom which because it is in this corner having little contact or commerce with other Kingdoms the language is very different; however all the lamas and generally the people also understand the language of the rest and so with what we know we can communicate in all these areas and also we take a great deal of trouble to instruct ourselves well in the language of this very Kingdom in which the Lord is pleased that we should make our first stay and thus at the moment
fol. 10 thanks to God our Lord we understand quite a lot fairly well and we talk about the things of our Holy Faith and we compose prayers and necessary instructions in this language and we have them written in their characters so that they [the lamas] may learn more easily; and it helps us very much that we already know how to read their books even though we do not yet understand them well since they are written in the best and most polished form of the language; they were in all these times very frequent, the conversations we had with the King about the things of our Lord and which he enjoyed listening to; but realising as well that between us and him there was a great distance about what we believed of our Holy Faith we saw clearly in him dislike and coldness towards our things;[31] and thus we said to him, after thanking him very much for the love which he had shown to us, that he should be graciously pleased to give us permission and company in order to go forward to the Chaparangue [rTsa-brang] area because in this Kingdom there was nothing for us to do: the King was very embarrassed with this request and putting off the reply for some days he used the time by getting other lamas to try and persuade us from going on; but when we insisted on what we had asked he himself gave us a reply saying that it was a discredit to him that we should leave him and go on because all these Kingdoms knew that we were with him and having us here was a great honour and for this reason we were not to go on, particularly since we had said to him that we would be here always, nor would we leave him. To this we replied that our being here would be conditional on his taking pleasure in there being

preached in the Kingdom the true Law of Christ our Lord and more particularly if he accepted it and made himself a Christian, and because we saw in him little pleasure in this business which is the only thing for which we were looking here there was no reason why we should stay here. To this he said it was true but that he was afraid that if he was now to embrace our Law he would die immediately because his forefathers had had the law which he had and they were never Christians, but he said we should go on reading his books and that we should talk more deeply about the matter of the law and that for the moment we should begin to make Christians and preach our Holy Faith which was a very good one and this was his view and he said that soon we should have many Christians which was what we wanted and so that we could begin he said he would give us, and indeed he did, in his presence a young lama of twenty years, very close to him and the first co-brother of another lama [32] who is the whole government of the King and he said that he would soon give us two more and that many would follow these and he would build us a house and church in Pargão [sPa-gro]. When we saw the resolution of the King we said that we would like to please him because he had pleasure in our staying in his Kingdom with the hopes that he was giving us of extending in it the Faith of the Lord and we thanked him very much for the lamas which he had given us and who wanted to become Christians and we thanked him also for the church which he wanted to make in Pargão [sPa-gro]; as for the matter of dying immediately if he took up the Faith of the Lord he would see the contrary in those whom we made Christians because being Christ our Lord, the true life of souls, He did not kill bodies but rather with Him he would have all the goods of the body and the soul.

I will tell Your Reverence about the religion of this Kingdom which we learnt from conversations with the King and with his old master. They say in the first place that they were never Christians, nor do they find in their books that their forefathers in all this Potente [Bhoṭanta] knew Christ our Lord or held his Law but they say they are not pagans, rather they laugh and mock pagan things like adoring animals and they abominate sacrificing cattle in pagodas and other ceremonies of the pagans; they speak very badly of the Moors [the Muslims] and it is a name they use when they want to describe a very bad man. [33] They say that they adore only One God and they have of him very well made images and one of them the King showed to us, very well made, modest and authentic of golden metal who had between his hands a small pot of water and he said that that water meant how God washed the souls of sin. [34] He also showed us another image of God on cloth all of dark blue and when we were surprised by the colour he said that they painted God in that way not because God had any colour but because his dwelling place was in the sky and for that reason they painted him
fol. 11 with that colour of the sky: they also showed us another panel in which the sky was painted, in the middle of it a square house [35] in which they said God lived: although in their ordinary speech they know of God as immense and being such he is everywhere; they say that in God there are three who are one God and two of them have no body and one has a body and the

one that has a body they call *Togu [sPrul-sku]* [36] which means Son and in the way they talk about his birth they give us to understand that they mean that his mother was a virgin and they will show us the image of a woman who they say is the mother of God. [37] They are aware of the blessed state where the good go and of hell where the evil are punished in which they say there are great torments of fire and cold. One can clearly see in these things that somehow the light of the Holy Gospel has arrived here, and other ceremonies and blessings which they use show a great similarity with things of Christianity; but they have other things very much spoilt; they say that six hundred years ago there was no one in this Potente [Bhoṭanta], that it was all water, but when it dried the earth had trees but only two monkeys [38] from which they say all the people of Potente [Bhoṭanta] are descended and that these monkeys afterwards went to heaven, and that in the beginning of these Kingdoms there was a King who had twelve heads. [39] And when we laughed at this and said that that was all falsehood and mockery he replied, sticking to what he had said, that this was what his books told him. Also they pretend that there are three paradises [40] where the good go from one to the other until they become completely spiritualised and those who go to heaven say that they enter into God himself and become Gods; and so they adore their masters and Kings whom they have as Holy like God after they are dead; for this reason it is that this King uses all his art and care in making images of his father and decorating them very nicely and making festivals for him and this image he has in a house which he made here for his prayers in which there is only this large image in a good and beautiful sepulchre of silver. [41] When they heard us say that only in the Law of the Lord Christ is there salvation they affirmed it to us that many fore-fathers of this King had gone to heaven in body and soul in the view of many people and this did not happen in the distant past but only a few years ago here, [42] and that the father [Mi-pham bsTan-pa'i Nyi-ma] of Droma Raja [Dharmarāja = *Zhabs-drung* Ngag-dbang rNam-rgyal] was so holy that where he put his foot on stone sometimes foot-prints [43] were made and he told us other things about his forefathers with which the devil has kept them blind and deceived. About the Son of God whom they say has been born they affirm it to be their Chescamoni [Sakyamuni] which is a pagoda [44] very famous in these places and it is twelve days journey away and they say that he was born two thousand years ago and that he spent twelve months in his mother's womb: this the principal lama [45] told us, who is the one who governs the house of the King, the King having first told us that Chescamoni [Sakyamuni] was not God and that the educated lamas did not adore him but only the common people and those who were ignorant; and when the King heard the lama say this he did not contradict him, rather both of them were embarrassed and confused, not knowing who it was who was this God the Son whom it seems they knew and they did not know anything about him concerning whom we gave him very different news; nor up till now have we discovered that they have any knowledge of any of the other mysteries of the life of our Lord, nor do we find any other signs of the Holy Cross

apart from a similarity in the name; because what we call cross they call *cruca* [46] but they do not regard this holy sign as a sacred object. Everyone esteems the King and the great lama [47] greatly and they give of what they have when they die so that he may send them to heaven; the ceremony is that when they are near to death and in their final agony the King is called and he is present at the death and prays, and when they die the King pulls them by the hair of their head and then he does for them that which they consider a great act of mercy in sending their soul to heaven. [48] And when I asked one of these lamas on the occasion of the death of another one who died here if he pulled him by his hair before he died or afterwards the lama was very surprised at my question saying that to pull the hair before death would be a very serious sin. After the man has died they share out what they find amongst the rest of the people so that the soul can get on well in the other life and those who are absent when a relative dies take to the King the principal possessions of the dead man and they bring him to perform his supplications over him. [49] Such, more or less, is the cult of God whom all these Kingdoms of Potente [Bhoṭanta] adore as we learn it from the King
fol. 12 and the lamas who are here from all these Kingdoms. We took every trouble to ask questions about the Kingdom of Catayo [Cathay] and we have no knowledge of it by that name which is completely unknown here; there is however a very well known Kingdom which they say is very big and is called Xembala [Sham-bha-la] [50] and he has asked us about it many times. We believe that Catayo [Cathay] [51] may be of this Kingdom because the Kingdom of Sopo [Sog-po] [52] is that of the Tartars, as they understand through the war which this King says that Kingdom continually has with China, adding that the King of China has more people; however the people of Sopo [Sog-po] are stronger and thus normally defeat the Chinese, all of which tallies with what is so well known about the war of the Tartars with the Chinese, [53] and since the Kingdom of Catayo [Cathay] is very big and the only one which is on this side next to the Tartars as the maps show, it seems that we can with some probability think that it is what they call here Xembala [Sham-bha-la], nor is it a reason against this the fact that no other name is known here because neither China nor Tartaria nor Tibet are known by these names of which they have no knowledge; and China they call *Guena* [rGya-nag], Tartaria *Sopo* [Sog-po], and Tibet *Potente* [Bhoṭanta]; they say there are many difficulties on the journey to the Kingdom of Xembala [Sham-bha-la]; however I trust in the Lord who has so far brought us with our eyes fixed on that Kingdom, that he may bring us to where we may see it more closely so that next year I may send to Your Reverence news about it. It will not be possible for Father João Cabral and me to go together because of the resolution of this man that we should not go any further and thus if it pleases God our Father Father João Cabral will stay in this house and church which the king is making for us, preaching the Holy Gospel to this people with the help and company of the three men whom the King has given us and seeing together the fruit which may be obtained in the souls of this Kingdom so that in conformity with

this we may deal with the setting up of this mission; and I with the help of the Lord will try to go to the Kingdom of Xembala [Sham-bha-la] which may be either in that one [which we have heard about] or in one of the others which are around here and may God our Lord provide occasions for us to perform greater services for him, and next year I will let Your Reverence know about everything concerning which we are able to have knowledge. [54]

The King gave us two more lamas which he promised us, one of whom is an agreeable boy of twelve years who is clever and another is nineteen who is particularly good in learning what is taught him: we are catechising and instructing all three in the matters of our Holy Faith. Also there is another lama twenty-seven years old, a very important one and with many relatives who all these months was here with the King, helping him in his works of painting, sculpture and masonry in which he is always occupied for the decoration of the image of his father and he has promised me to become a Christian many times as soon as he should finish the King's works which will be in about a month and a half from now. I use this man to help me write and put into good language the prayers and Christian doctrine; and one of these days when he was writing the chapter of the catechism concerning the Holy Cross being the sign of Christ, and other things about the birth of Christ our Lord, and about the purity of our immaculate Virgin, Our Lady, he was very pleased and told me afterwards that he kept it in his heart and it contented him greatly. Also another man who came here from another village, seeing the chapel which we have and hearing some things about our Lord, told us that he would like to stay with us and that by going to our house he would stay with us so that our Lord might forgive him a sin which kept him very unhappy and that was that by an accident with an arrow he had killed a man; this person has been back again and persists in the same intention. Also others who have an affection for our things have promised us to bring us their children so that we can teach them and one of these is particularly grateful to us for the mercy which he says our Lord did him by giving one of his children health, a child whom he brought to us sick when we were with the King in the tents and when he asked us for a holy object for a cure Father João Cabral gave him a relic to which the man attributes the health of his child and others often ask for holy water with which they say they are cured of their afflictions. And the lamas and other people who come here to see us also with their offerings of fruit and milk, when they see the images and decoration of the chapel they are
fol. 13 amazed and prostrate themselves many times before the image of our Virgin Lady and of Christ our Lord, kissing the base of the altar with much devotion. All this happens inside the King's house next door to this house where the pagoda is which is adjacent, where there goes on continuously the war which the devil wages against souls with the singing and praying of the lamas of the King's school and the sound of the various instruments with which they are always occupied in their cult and with the presence of the King himself who knows of everything that is happening here and his

people compare our things with his and they prefer ours, of which it is clear that the King is very disapproving; and so from having this beginning here we can conjecture that there will be improvements in the good of souls, trusting in God our Lord who, coming out of this fortress which the devil has here, may give us many victories over him, stripping him of the souls which he has subjected here: because besides this there are no other pagodas or very few and when we went through these mountains for the first sixteen days journey we did not find a single one except that on the top of a mountain there was a lean-to, badly made of stones piled on top of each other with some pictures of the devil and idols; [55] and in Pargão [sPa-gro], although it is a city as I said, we did not see more than one small house belonging to one lama which was his pagoda and so if churches are made to which the people can come en masse one may hope with the help of the Lord for fruit in the good of souls, in which one may see the thirst which is caused by the propensity which they have for the knowledge of their creator, [and this can be seen] in the good will and pleasure which they show in hearing the things of the Lord which we tell them and in the piety and reverence which they show to any image which we tell them is of God and to the things of his divine service and this good thing will be greatly helped by the liberty which there is in this Kingdom which is large, broad and well populated, and the people have a very voluntary subjection to their King without any obligation on their part to refer to him or without any obligation to follow his doctrine, nor does he have power over the people to make anyone do anything; rather since his principal revenue is in what they give him voluntarily he does not wish to have any of his subjects discontented and every one of them is very free to do what he wants, as the King himself said to us on many occasions when he was talking to us even about his own lamas who are the people who are most subject to him. [56]

[Paragraph omitted. Cacella explains how pleased he is to be putting his religious training into practice and how much the Lord has favoured him in this.]

fol. 14 So far I have failed to tell Your Reverence in this letter of any informa-
1st para. tion concerning the country in itself and about its climate; the climate is very healthy and after we came into these mountains we were always in good health and I never had such health in India; and this is common to everyone because one very rarely finds any sick man here and indeed there are many who although very old are healthy and vigorous; some servants whom we brought with us became indisposed and had previously been ill but here they recovered perfect health: we have been some seven months in these mountains and all the time the weather was very temperate without cold or excessive heat; in the four months from November to February it is colder but for these months there are very good woollen cloths which everyone wears. The country is very abundant with wheat, rice, meat, all of which are very cheap, of fruits which are many and good, pears of various sorts, some of them very big, all of them good, excellent peaches, apples, nuts, quinces in great abundance and there are also not lacking the

rose-apples of India. There are also peas and very good turnips besides other things and fruits which are only found here. There is no fish here but good dry fish comes from the Salt Lake where they also get salt and that is nearby, or also it comes from the Kingdom of Cocho [Cooch Bihar] from where they also bring salt; and some things which are not in this land can be found in other places which are not very far away, such as grapes of which there are none here but they are found in a city called Compo [Kong-po] which is some twenty days journey from here and there they also make wine. [57] And this land is supplied with things from China such as silk, gold and porcelain which all comes to that city of Compo [Kong-po] and from there it comes down here, and also from Caximir [Kashmir] via Chaparangue [rTsa-brang] there is commerce with the lands which abut on to this Kingdom, and many foreigners come to Guiance [rGyal-rtse] which is the Court of Demba Cemba *[sDe-pa gTsang-pa]*, the most powerful King of this Potente [Bhoṭanta] and that is eight days away and Laca [lHa-sa] which is the city where the pagoda Chescamoni [Sakyamuni] is frequented by yogis and merchants of other places; however, to the mountains where we are no foreigner comes and they only have memory of the very occasional yogi [58] who has passed this way nor does anyone come here from Cocho [Cooch Bihar] apart from the captives who are brought here by those who come down from this Kingdom to that one; and one uncle of the King of Cocho [59] [Cooch Bihar] who some years ago out of curiosity and a desire to see the world came into these mountains and for some time they kept him prisoner and made him work at the plough and when the King of Cocho [Cooch Bihar] heard about this he ordered all the people of this Kingdom to be taken prisoner who were in his Kingdom and proposing to do justice on them if they did not hand over his uncle, however this obliged them to hand him over and they did so. This land is not more than a month's
fol. 15 journey from the Kingdom of Chaparangue [rTsa-brang] and so after we arrived here we have occasionally had news of the fathers who are there, not directly from them because it seems they do not yet know of our arrival in these mountains but through the lamas who have come from there and through others who have gone there we have already written three times to the fathers [60] and also I sent to them letters for them to send to Your Reverence via Goa. The peoples of this Kingdom are white even though since the people are not clean they do not appear to be white; they all grow their hair in such a way that it covers their ears and part of their foreheads. Normally they do not allow any hair to grow on their faces and they have very well made tweezers around their necks whose function is solely to pull out any hair which appears; their arms are naked and from their necks to their knees they are covered with one of these woollen cloths, having another big one as a cape; [61] they have leather belts with plates very well made as also are very well made and worked the bracelets which they normally have on their arms and the reliquaries which they wear over their shoulders; normally they are barefoot but they also have leather boots or socks made of their cloth specially for journeys; their weapons are bow and

arrow, short swords and daggers of excellent iron which they decorate with great care and well. The lamas have no weapons and they cut all the hair of their heads; some, but a few, let their beards grow; the King has a long beard [62] and some of its hairs reach his waist and which he normally has wrapped up in silk, and on festival days he takes them out of their wrappings and they are visible, and this he did when he received us; the hair on his head is so long, almost two ells; it seems he is very proud of these and he has them as a mark of grandeur; however he told me he intends to cut them off as soon as he has a son who will succeed him in his Kingdom [63] and that then he would retire and leave the world because he did not wish death to come upon him with his hair long as one ancestor of his, another King, died and this was a matter for scandal, that he had not cut his hair until that time. [64] All the lamas are dressed in oriental tunics which cover their chests well, leaving their arms uncovered and the rest of their body down to their feet they have well covered with another large cloth, yet another being a cape; which they never take off, nor do they walk about naked. May God our Lord set upon all of them the eyes of his divine mercy and bring them all to his divine knowledge, compelling them to make use of the mercy which he does them in knocking on their doors with the news of the Holy Gospel, for which I beg Your Reverence once more a continuation of the prayers and sacrifices of all that Province; and I recommend myself to the blessing of Your Reverence.

From this Kingdom of Cambirasi and the house of the King, 4th of October 1627.

Son in Christ of Your Reverence, Estevão Cacella.

Notes to Text IV

1. Pargão is an Indianised form of the Bhutanese place-name sPa-gro, the largest valley in western Bhutan. The ending *gao* derives from Bengali *gram* ('village'), a word pronounced *gaon* in the northern area of Bengal which adjoins western Bhutan (e.g. Jaigaon, Shipgaon, Palarigaon etc.). Other Indian adaptations or usages found in the *Relação* are: 1) *Lamba (bla-ma)*, misapplied to all monks; 2) Droma Raja *(= Dharmarāja)* for the *Zhabs-drung*; 3) Potente (= Bhoṭanta) for Tibet, which here includes Bhutan; and 4) Cocho (= Cooch Bihar). All these terms must surely have been used by Cacella's Cooch Bihari attendants and they provide a clue to the origin of the term 'Cambirasi' (see note 14 below) which appears only in this text to designate the area of Bhutan.
2. These are the sPa-ro Chu (or sPa-chu) and its tributary, the river which descends the side valley of Dol-po Shar-ri ('Dopshari').
3. This is a wild guess on Cacella's part. It is quite inconceivable that the sPa-gro valley could ever have supported such a population. The 1969 census gives the figure of 63,032 (Rose 1977:41).
4. This companion had joined the party at the village of 'Rintam' near the Indian border and was a relative of a Bhutanese they had met at Jaigaon with whom they had arranged for the journey. That arrangement had embroiled the Jesuits in an earlier adventure described in Wessels 1924:132.
5. See Wessels 1924:135.
6. This cannot have been *Chos-rje* La-sngon-pa bsTan-'dzin 'Brug-grags who was appointed the first *dpon-slob* (or *spyi-bla*) of sPa-gro, presumably not before the establishment of the new *rdzong* there in 1645. More likely, it was one of two brothers from Zangs-dkar in La-dwags who came south with the *Zhabs-drung* and whom the latter appointed to sPa-gro as his representative. This person (either *Chos-rje* dNgos-grub or *Chos-rje* Klu-klu, it is not clear) finds brief mention in the biography of his descendant, Ngag-dbang Tshe-ring of rDzong-khul, an important lama of the 'Brug-pa school in that area. See *dPal-ldan bla-ma dam-pa 'khrul-zhig rin-po-che ngag-dbang tshe-ring-gi rnam-thar kun-tu bzang-po'i zlos-gar yid-kyi bcud-len*, f. 6a, repeated on f. 4b of the continuation of the *rnam-thar* by bSod-nams 'Brug-rgyas.
7. This relative of *Zhabs-drung* is likely to have been the *Chos-rje* La-sngon-pa referred to in note 6 above. He was the half-brother of *Zhabs-drung*, the first *sPa-gro dPon-slob* and later the second *'Brug sDe-srid*, ruling as such from 1656 to 1657 (*LCB* I, ff. 93b-94b, and ff. 59b-68b passim of the *rnam-thar* of bsTan-'dzin Rab-rgyas).
8. The number of monks in *Zhabs-drung*'s personal retinue had greatly increased from the figure of thirty when he first established the community based at lCags-ri (*LCB* I, f.29b). These later became the core of the state monastery founded in the *rdzong* at sPu-na-kha, which was built to hold a total of more than 600 monks in 1637, ten years after the events described in this narrative (*LCB* I, f. 36a).
9. Mi-pham bsTan-pa'i Nyi-ma, who had died some seven or eight years previously (*LCB* I, f. 29a).
10. This seems to be quite correct as there is no account of any Europeans coming to Bhutan prior to Cacella and Cabral. Even if the Portuguese described in *LCB* I (ff. 34b-35a) and *PBP* (ff. 96b-97a) were a quite different party to their own, the Bhutanese accounts place this visit sometime after the years 1634 when a Tibetan force had temporarily occupied the *rdzong* at Srin-mo-dho-kha ('Simtokha'). See 'Background to texts'.
11. On the Jesuit mission to rTsa-brang ('Tsaparang') see Wessels 1924:69-93.
12. It was not very long before the Jesuits were disabused of the notion, current in north India during this period, that a corrupted form of Christianity was still practised in a vague area beyond the Himalayas. In a letter dated June 17th, 1628, written from Hugli after his return, Cabral said: "I begin to believe that these countries are pagan, both because they say they are, and because I have found that they have the same pagodas as the kingdom of Nepal and some kingdoms of Bengal. They only differ from the latter in not having their superstitions of caste and food" (Wessels 1924:156). Cabral was at Arakan in Burma four years later and noticed some of the features common to the forms of Buddhism practised there and in Tibet and Bhutan. It has been argued that Cabral was therefore the first "... to realise that besides Hinduism and Mohammedanism there was a third great religion in Asia" (Collis 1943:191). The passage in Cabral's letter from Ceylon dated November 12th, 1633, in which he announces this discovery, also that of the ethnic affiliations of the Tibetans and Burmese, is worth quoting in full: "There in Arracan, I discovered that the religion of the Magha [= Mogos = Arracanese] and that of Tibet are

identical, and that there is very little difference in their language. The gods are represented in the same manner, and with the same features; they have the same names, the same worship, and the same manner of prayers, and use the same ceremonies as the *lamas*. Talking with them on that subject, I was told in confidence that they are the same, and that those of Tibet are true Maghs, from whom they themselves are descended." (Luard 1926-7:421) Cabral eventually became rector of the Professed House of the Jesuits at Goa. It was left to the great Desideri (1684-1733) to produce the first coherent account of Tibetan Buddhism in his well-known *Notizie Istoriche del Thibet*, but four bulky manuscripts containing his defence of Christianity written in Tibetan still remain unexamined in the archives of the Society of Jesus in Rome.

13. This is doubtless the first recorded use of the title *Dharmarāja* as applied later to the *Zhabs-drung* and his incarnations by the Indian and British authorities. Cabral noted in his letter from Hugli that the Tibetans referred to him as 'Lamba Rupa' (*Bla-ma 'Brug-pa*) and that he ranked fifth in the Tibetan hierarchy (Wessels 1924:335). The statement that Ngag-dbang rNam-rgyal was thirty-three years old in 1627 is quite correct by western reckoning; he was born in 1594. By Bhutanese or Tibetan reckoning he would have been thirty-four.

14. 'Cambirasi' was presumably a local name for Bhutan used by the people of Cooch Bihar which Cacella learnt from his attendants. It cannot be found in any source except this one where it appears just twice. As Cabral wrote in his letter cited in note 12 above, they later heard in Tibet that the proper name for the country was the unspecific term *Mon*. Wessels (1924:143) speculates that 'Cambirasi' may be related to 'Chumbi', the name used by the British for the Gro-mo valley between Bhutan and Sikkim. This seems most implausible. The ending 'rasi' may well be the same as 'Razi' ('mountain'), as found in the names of many of the peaks which lie on the border of Tibet and Burma (e.g. Pasaung Razi, Gwelang Razi, Dindaw Razi, etc.). The highest of these is Kakabo Razi (19,315 ft), perhaps derived from the Tibetan *Gangs dkar-po* ('White Snow-Mountain') + 'Razi'. The latter element, obviously a word in one of the many tribal languages of Northern Burma (Lissu, Rawang?), could perhaps have been transmitted westwards to northern Bengal through the medium of the Ahom people of Assam.

15. Unidentified.

16. "He is an ascetic, eats only plantains, drinks only milk and indulges in no pleasures whatever." Thus did a Bhutanese captured by the Moslim invaders of Cooch Bihar describe the Zhabs-drung in 1661, as recorded in *Fathiyab i Ibriyah* (Blochmann's translation in Wessels 1924:141).

17. This tallies perfectly with information found in *LCB* I (ff. 30a-31a) and *PBP* (ff. 52b-53a). In 1623 *Zhabs-drung* entered a three-year retreat in complete seclusion at lCags-ri at the top end of the Thimphu valley. The cave (known as bDud-'dul Phug-pa) where this occurred is incorporated into a retreat house standing on the hillside just above the main temple.

18. *Zhabs-drung*'s artistic skills are well attested in all the literature, for instance in *LCB* I (f. 19a) where we find him at an early age "contesting with the styles of India and China" in making an image of Hevajra for the head of the Sa-skya school, bSod-nams dBang-po. None of the *Zhabs-drung*'s paintings or images have yet come to light.

19. This is also evident throughout the biographical literature. The greatest influx of Tibetan lamas seems to have occurred after the dGe-lugs-pa school won complete authority in Tibet in 1642. This event caused several great figures to take refuge at *Zhabs-drung*'s court, most prominent of them being the *gTsang mKhan-chen* who was chaplain to the family of his old rival, the *gTsang sDe-srid*.

20. This practice is called *sgar-'khor 'phebs-pa* ('going around in camps'). For long periods *Zhabs-drung* enjoyed a peripatetic existence accompanied by all his monks, as we see below. This particular tour took him to the Shar district where he met the traditional patrons of the 'Brug-pa school in that area. Unfortunately the account (in *LCB* I, ff. 32a-b) has no mention of our Jesuits.

21. Sanskrit *bhikṣu*, a fully ordained monk.

22. Cacella here refers to the many existing communities in Bhutan, some of whose leaders were opposed to the *Zhabs-drung*.

23. lCags-ri rDo-rje-gdan, whose construction had been completed four years before the arrival of the Jesuits in 1623, just before the *Zhabs-drung* entered his three-year retreat (*LCB* I, f. 29a and *PBP*, f. 47b).

24. This is Phun-tshogs rNam-rgyal, the *gTsang sDe-srid* (or, as here, *sDe-pa gTsang-pa*), the old enemy of the *Zhabs-drung*. See Aris 1979: 208.

25. The bone, a vertebra, was actually a relic of *gTsang-pa rGya-ras* (1161-1211), founder of the 'Brug-pa school and a remote, though direct, ancestor of *Zhabs-drung*. The relic is the famed *Rang-byon Karsapani*, still kept in the *rdzong* at sPu-na-kha today. The highly decorated reliquary in which it is kept was made by Newari artisans employed by the *Zhabs-drung* (*PBP*, f. 75a). See Aris 1979: plate 22.
26. For a description of Ra-lung see Tucci 1956b: 53, 60-63.
27. July 31st.
28. On *Zhabs-drung*'s long association with lHa-dbang Blo-gros, the great astrological scholar, see particularly *LCB* I, ff. 16a, 29b, 33a, 34a. In 1627 he would have been about seventy-nine years old (in 1632 he was eighty-four; *LCB* I, f. 34a).
29. As we see below, Caçella's grasp of the relationship between the language of the 'Ngalong' of western Bhutan and classical Tibetan (both of which he and Cabral tried to learn) is perceptive.
30. This must refer to the odd set of verbal complements used in Bhutan and the way in which two syllables in standard Tibetan are fused into one in Bhutanese.
31. This feeling of antipathy towards the Jesuits increased. Cabral wrote that later the *Zhabs-drung* sent two emissaries to the court of the *gTsang sDe-srid* to warn him of the Jesuits' true aims "... by giving out that the main object of our visit was to pull down their pagodas and destroy their religion" (Wessels 1924:153). This is somewhat surprising in view of the strained relations between the two rulers at this time, though it is possible that efforts were being made to patch the old quarrel.
32. This is undoubtedly the first *'Brug sDe-srid*, bsTan-'dzin 'Brug-rgyas who ruled the country from 1651 to 1656 at the start of the *Zhabs-drung*'s final retreat. (See *LCB* I, ff. 92a-93b, and ff. 58a-59b of the bsTan-'dzin Rab-rgyas *rnam-thar*.)
33. The word is probably *mu-stegs-pa* ('heretic') which includes both Hindus and Moslims.
34. This must have been the Buddha of Boundless Life Amitāyus (Tshe-dpag-med) who holds the vase containing nectar.
35. Perhaps a *maṇḍala*.
36. The Christian trinity does bear these rather superficial resemblances with the theory of the three 'Bodies' of the Buddha, which consists in the 'Body of the Doctrine' existing on a transcendent, absolute level (*dharmakāya*, *chos-sku*), the 'Body of Bliss' on the heavenly plane (*sambhogakāya*, *longs-sku*), and the one mentioned here, the 'Manifested Body' on the mundane level (*nirmaṇakāya*, *sprul-sku*).
37. Queen Māyā, from whose right side the Buddha Śākyamuni was born in the Lumbinī Grove. The Jesuits were of course hoping that her image would resemble the Virgin Mary.
38. See *rGyal-rigs*, ff. 5a-6a.
39. This should be eleven, a reference to the eleven-headed form of Avalokiteśvara.
40. Probably the three 'realms' (not paradises) of 'Desire, Form and Non-Form' (*kāmadhātu*, *rūpadhātu*, *arupadhātu*; *'dod-khams*, *gzugs-khams*, *gzugs-med-khams*).
41. This is the *dNgul-'bum mChod-rten* containing the remains of *Zhabs-drung*'s father, Mi-pham bsTan-pa'i Nyi-ma. The silver for it was offered to Zhabs-drung by his patrons at sKya-khra ('Chapcha') and the *stūpa* itself made by Newari artisans who had been brought for this purpose from the Kathmandu valley by way of central Tibet. The principal temple at lCags-ri was built to contain it (*LCB* I, ff. 28b-29a). *Zhabs-drung*'s own minute description of the *dNgul-'bum mChod-rten* is quoted verbatim in *PBP*, ff. 45a-47b.
42. This is a reference to *'ja'-lus 'pho-ba chen-po* ('the Great Transference by the Rainbow Body').
43. Stories about bsTan-pa'i Nyi-ma's footprints (*zhabs-rjes*) are still told in Bhutan today and no doubt find mention in his *rnam-thar* which I have been unable to trace.
44. Cf. f. 14 below. The temple is of course the Jo-khang of lHa-sa, containing the famed image of the Crowned Buddha, Śākyamuni.
45. bsTan-'dzin 'Brug-rgyas (see note 32 above).
46. *sku-ru-kha*, a punctuation mark shaped like a cross, signifying 'as before' in ritual and devotional texts (see Jaschke 1881:22).
47, lHa-dbang Blo-gros (see note 28 above).
48. A reference to the rite of *'pho-ba* ('the transfer of consciousness').
49. Cf. *bKa'-khrims*, f. 113a where the same practice has become institutionalised under the law.
50. All the itineraries to Sham-bha-la place this mythical kingdom in the far north (Tucci 1949:598, 617 note 289).
51. Despite the travels and discoveries of Bento de Goes in 1602-7 which had determined the identity of Cathay and China, the Jesuits were still seeking this fabled land of Christianity. The notion was derived from a distant memory of Nestorians at the Mongol court at the time of the Franciscan missions in the 13th and 14th centuries, and from garbled accounts of Chinese Buddhism. See Wessels 1924: Ch. I.

52. Mongolia.
53. The Tartars here are the Manchus who in fact belonged to a different stock from the Mongols. Their repeated attacks on the Chinese Ming dynasty culminated in 1644 with their establishment of the Ch'ing dynasty.
54. If this letter was ever written, it has not survived.
55. This statement, like the one above on the population of sPa-gro, passes belief. There must have been several hundred temples and monasteries in Bhutan by this date. Could it be that both of these extraordinary statements derive solely from Cacella's wish to portray the country as ripe for Christian conversion?
56. It should be noted that this tolerant, even permissive, trait in the complex personality of the great *Zhabs-drung* was recorded during the period before he started to impose his will directly on the country by constructing or appropriating fortresses that commanded the western valleys. Much of his success seems to have been derived from the uncompromising way he treated all opponents, external and internal, while apparently leaving his subjects to fulfil their obligations out of faith rather than by coercion. It is still not clear at which point his subjects were extended beyond the 'patrons' of the 'Brug-pa school to include the entire population.
57. Wine is called *rgun-'brum-gyi chang* ('the ale of grapes') in Bhutan, though it is not drunk there. That it was known to be found in Kong-po was the main factor behind the establishment of the Capuchin mission there.
58. Hindu *yogins* or *sadhus* do seem to have penetrated occasionally to the mountains of Bhutan. Speaking of the 'bad old days' before the imposition of 'Brug-pa rule, *LCB* I (f. 7b) says: "Indian yogins on pilgrimage were sold as slaves."
59. This king may perhaps be identified with *Rāja* Padma Narayan of Cooch Bihar who sent gifts to the *Zhabs-drung* on three occasions (*LCB*, ff. 28a-b, 47a).
60. There were a total of seven Jesuits in Tsaparang in 1627, headed by the famous Antonio de Andrade. Their church had been built there in the previous year. See Wessels 1924: 71-72.
61. This description of Bhutanese costume shows how much it has changed since the 17th century. The sleeveless, knee-length garment known as 'pakhi', which was worn with a belt and knotted or buckled at the shoulders, is today only worn by a few groups in the south of the country. The cloak mentioned here is now only seen among some pastoral groups of the northern highlands. The standard article of dress for men is now the 'ko', basically the same as the Tibetan 'chuba' but hitched to the knees to form a pouch at the waist. By contrast, the women's dress has probably remained unchanged.
62. We can be positive, therefore, that the iconography of *Zhabs-drung*'s figure, as seen in countless paintings and images throughout the country, is based on a physical likeness.
63. This is perhaps the single most important statement in the *Relação* from the point of view of Bhutanese history because it confirms the fact that it was *Zhabs-drung*'s aim to leave a son who would succeed him as ruler of Bhutan. The idea of incarnational succession must have had little appeal for him in view of the protracted quarrel over his own recognition as the embodiment of Padma dKar-po. His son, the sickly 'Jam-dpal rDo-rje, was born in 1631 four years after this account was written. True to his intention recorded here, *Zhabs-drung* then received the tonsure of a fully ordained monk in the following year from his old master lHa-dbang Blo-gros (*LCB* I, f. 34a, *PBP*, f. 89a).
64. The only member of the rGya lineage who is depicted with long hair in the thankas is Nam-mkha' dPal-bzang (1398-1425). He was one of two 'holy madmen' in this branch of the 'Brug-pa school, the other being the much more famous 'Brug-pa Kun-legs (1455-1529).

GLOSSARY

This glossary includes only the following: (1) unusual administrative terms, (2) certain kinship terms, (3) rare words and rare meanings, (4) some standard terms whose every occurrence I wished to note, and (5) Bhutanese usages. For many of these I have relied closely on my informants in Bhutan, among whom LN, LP and TR (see below) are specifically mentioned. The order of entry follows that of the Tibetan alphabet.

Abbreviations

I	*rGyal-rigs 'byung-khungs gsal-ba'i sgron-me*
II	*Lo-rgyus gsal-ba'i me-long*
III	*Khrims-yig*
BU	Bhutanese Usage
J	Jäschke's *Tibetan-English Dictionary*
LN	*Slob-dpon* Nag-mdog
LP	*Slob-dpon* Padma-lags
S	Stein (1974)
TR	sTobs-dga' Rin-po-che

---

kar-rdzi, perhaps an official who had charge of herds belonging to a clan ruler in eastern Bhutan, I: 51a, 53b.

klad-'gems (emended from *kled-'gems* = J: *klad-pa 'gems-pa*) = 'to surprise', lit. 'to destroy the brain', III: 109a.

dkar-dro = lit. 'white meal', i.e. a bloodless, vegetarian meal, III: 112b, 113a.

bka'-blon = 'minister', II: 18b, 22a.

bka'-blon nang-ma (= *nang-blon*) = 'household official', II: 7a.

bka'-khrims / *bka'i khrims-yig* = 'legal decree', 'the decree of a legal code', III: 100b (x 2), 101a (x 2).

rkang / *khral-rkang* = 'tax estate', III: 112a, 112b (x 3).

rkang-can = 'the possessor of a tax estate', III: 113a.

skam-khral = lit. 'dry tax' levied in cash, as opposed to *rlon-khral* ('wet tax') levied in kind. (LN: *skam-po dngul dang rlon-pa rgyu-dngos*), III: 112b (x 2).

skam-rlon = 'dry (cash) or wet (food)', III: 113a.
sku-drung (= J: *dge-brkos*) = 'monastic prefect', II: 20a, 21b, 22b (x2).
sku-tshab = 'government representative'', particularly the *drung-pa* ('drūm' in the vernacular) an official appointed to the control of groups of villages, III: 107a, 107b, 109b, 110b (x 5), 111a (x 3), 111b (x 5), 112a (x 3), 113b.
sku-tshab tsho gnyis-ma = 'second-class government representatives', III: 110b.
Kha-khra = lit. 'Striped-Mouths', unidentified people of Arunachal Pradesh, I: 49b.
Kha-dkar = lit. 'White-Mouths', unidentified people of Arunachal Pradesh, I: 28a.
kha-mchu = 'law-suit, litigation'; the broader sense of 'quarrel, strife, dispute' (J: *kha-mchu* 3 and J: *zhal-mchu* 3, sub *mchu*) is not known in Bhutan; (cf. *kha-mchu'i gcod-sdom* / – *bslab-don* = 'judgements passed on litigation'), III: 106a, 107b, 108a, 109b, 111b.
Kha-nag = lit. 'Black-Mouths', the Aka people of Arunachal Pradesh, I: 28a.
kha-lo sgyur(-ba) = 'to rule, govern, lead' (see J2), I: 27a, 41b, 43b; III: 109a.
kha-lo bsgyur-mi = 'ruler', II: 12a.
khungs ma-chod-pa = 'unfounded, groundless, unproven', I: 11a, 45a (x 2).
khungs-bcad = 'have been substantiated', I: 46b.
khungs - - dpyad = 'have examined . . . the grounds' (of oral traditions), I: 47b.
khol-jo = 'slave-master' (cf. *chug-khol* q.v.), III: 112b.
khol-tshab = 'substitute slave' delivered to a slave owner by a community which failed to capture and return to him his runaway slave when the latter stopped in their territory (cf. *khral-tshab* q.v.), III: 112b.
khyug-bde-ba = 'agile', I: 34a.
khra = 'terms' (of a treaty, *chings-dan-gyi* –); from *khra-ma* = 'judicial decree' (J2), III: 106a.
khral-rgyug = 'taxation', 'administration of taxes', III: 111b.
khral-pa = 'taxpayer', III: 112b.
khral-tshab = 'substitute taxpayer' settled in a district by the authorities in order to provide a replacement for a previous taxpayer who had died without issue but whose obligation to render taxes is still borne by the community (cf. *khol-tshab* q.v.), III: 113b.
khral-zhing khral-khyim = 'taxable fields, taxable houses' forming part of a single tax estate, III: 112b.
khrims-ra = 'court of justice' (J), II: 17a.
dkhyil-sgar = 'central camp', II: 8b, 20a.
'khus-lan btab-pa = 'to return an insult', II: 4a (x 2).
'khor-gsum = 'armour, weapons and helmet' (lit. 'three wheels'), TR,III: 109a.
Gangs-ri'i rDor-'dzin, the official deputed to control the Bhutanese enclave in the Kailash area of Western Tibet; also known as the *Gangs-ri Bla-ma,* III: 109b.

Gu-se Lang-ling, name of deity from whom the *gDung* (q.v.) families claim descent, I, 32a, 36a.
go-mtshon(-pa) = 'armourer', III: 109a.
gri-chad = 'knife penalty', a fine for unsheathing a knife or sword (*gri* is pronounced 'gi' in the vernacular; cf. *'thab-chad, byi-chad* q.v.), III: 113b.
grong-bshul (= J: *shul* 3) = 'the personal property left by a dead person', III: 113a.
gros-mi = '(village) counsellors', III: 104a, 107a, 112a.
dgon-lag = 'branch monasteries', II: 5a (x 2).
mgron-gnyer (abbreviated to *mgron*) = 'chamberlain', III: 106a, 107a, 108a, 109a, 109b.
mgron-'thud (LN: *gzhung-gi mgron-po khag-la sprod-rgyu'i lto-mthud*) = 'entertainment allowance' due to government guests and officials on tour and realised in kind from selected households (cf. *lto-'thud* q.v.), III: 110a, 111b.
mgron-babs (LN: *mgron-por sprod-rgyu'i babs-sgo*) = 'board and lodging' for government officials on tour (cf. *lto-'bab* and *zhag-babs* q.v.), III: 111b.
'go-pa do-dam = 'superintendent official' of the border marts, III: 114a.
rgad-po = 'village or district headman' (pronounced 'gap' in the vernacular), III: 111b.
rgan-'go = 'an elder', II: 21a (x 3).
rgya-drung, government officials appointed to control the frontier districts bordering on India; the 'subha', 'soubah' etc. of British records, III: 107a, 109b.
rgyab-bkab = 'mantle', III: 109a, 110b, 113b.
rgyal-mkhar = 'royal castle', I: 10b, 13a, 14a, 13b, 15b, 15b-16a (x 2), 17a, 17b, (x 2), 18b (x 2), 19a, 21a, 23a (x 3), 23b, 24b, 25b (x 2), 26b, 27a, 27b, 28b, 31b.

yul-mkhar = 'district castle', I: 31b, 42a (x 2), 42b; II: 17a.

mkhar = 'castle', I: 39a; II: 14a (x 2).

rgyal-mkhar bzung-mkhan / 'dzin-mkhan = (royal) 'castellan', I: 23a, 31b, 43a.

mkhar-mthon (emended from *mkhar-'thon*) = 'watchtower, turret' (T), II: 16b (x 3).

rgyal-rabs [1] (= *rgyal-brgyud-kyi rabs,* III: 102a) = 'dynasty', 'royal lineage', 'generations of kings', I: 6a, 3a; III: 100b, 102a (x 3), 102b.
rgyal-rabs [2] = 'royal genealogy, history', I: 10a-b, 47b; III: 100b.
rgyal-rigs = 'royal family' (cf. *rje-rigs* = 'noble family', I: 48a), I: 3a, 10a, 10b, 17a (x 2), 17b (x 2), 18a, 18b (x 3), 19a, 20a (x 2), 20b, 20b-21a, 25b, 26b (x 2), 28b, 31b, 32a, 40a, 43b, 46a, 47a (x 2), 47a-b.
rgyal-sa = 'royal site, seat, throne', I: 3b, 15a, 16b (x 2), 18a, 20b, 25b, 27a, 28b, 29b.
rgyal-srid = 'government' in its secular aspects (cf. *chos-gyi rgyal-srid* q.v.), III: 108a, 109a, 109b.

rgyas-btab (-'debs-pa) = 'to seal (a matter with prayers)', I: 16a.
rgyugs len-pa = 'to hold an examination', III: 105b (x 2).
rgyud-tshig = 'traditional words', I: 48b.
brgyud-khung = 'ancestral origins', I: 2b, 28b, 40b.
brgyud(-pa) = 'line of descendants, lineage', 'lineal descendants', I: 3a (x 3), 13b, 17b, 19a, 19b (x 3), 20a (x 2), 24b, 26a, 28a, 28b, 31a, 31b, 35b, 36a, 43a (x 2), 43b, 44b.
nye-bar brgyud-pa = 'close lineal descendants', I: 28b.
mi-brgyud = 'descendants', I: 41b; II: 24a (x 2).
sgar / sgar-pa = 'bodyguard', II: 15a; III: 105b, 107a, 108b.
sgar-gnyer = 'quartermaster', III: 109a.
sgor-ba = ? 'plot, patch' (of grass), I: 34b.
sgrig(s) rnam-gzhag = 'regulation of (public) order', 'fundamentals of administration'; the term *sgrig* seems to have been used first in regard to monastic administration and the customary discipline of monks in the state monasteries. It was later used in reference to public administration in general, II: 18a, III: 103b, 104a, 109b, 110b.
ngag-rgyun = 'oral traditions', I: 2b, 36a.
nges-rtags = 'sure evidence, certain proof', I: 10b, 11a.
ngo-can = 'important (person)', lit. 'having face', III: 104a.
ngo-ma (= ngo-bo) = 'actual, real', 'face to face, in person' (BU), III: 108a.
mngon-spyod = 'destructive magic', lit. 'manifest action', III: 106b (x 2).
bcad-rgya = 'retreat', 'state of seclusion', III: 113b.
chad-khungs = 'genesis, origin' (of families, lineages etc.), I: 2b, 28a, 32a, 36a, 40a, 43b, 46b.
(dam-bca'-ba'i tshig) chad-rdo (byed-pa) = 'promise'.
(*chad-rdo* is related to *brjed-rdo*, an inventory, an aid to memory *(mi-brjed-pa'i dran-rten)*. In both cases *rdo* ('stone') acts as a *tshig-grogs*, an auxiliary or qualifying element suggesting the indissoluble nature of the promise or inventory (LP). *chad-rdo* seems unconnected with the meanings given by J (1): 'the stone which is broken in the ceremony of *rdo gcog-pa' or* J (2): 'monument, memorial of a covenant'), II: 12b, 14b.
mna'-tho(-'i) chad = 'promises made in an oath-list', III: 105b.
chings-dan = 'treaty' (LP), III: 106a.
chibs-bzhon, government officials entitled to ride horses, III: 108b.
che-dgu = ? 'all one's most precious possessions', I: 24a.
chug-khol / khol = 'slave' ('zap' in the vernacular), III: 110b, 112a.
chur-mo = 'husked paddy', 'rice' BU, ('chum' in the vernacular), III: 110b, 112a.

chos-kyi rgyal-srid / *chos-srid* = 'theocratic rule', III: 105a, 108a, 110a, 114a.
chos-mdzad (honorific for *chos-pa* ?), title of a semi-ordained religious practitioner from a noble family, I: 47b, 48a; II: 6b (x 2), 12a, 17b, 18b, 21a, 21b.
mchod-gzhis (= *chos-gzhis*) = 'religious or monastic estate', III: 110b.
rje-rgyal(-po) = 'lord-king' (especially used of gNya'-khri bTsan-po), I: 2a, 3a, 10a, 14b.
rje-dpon = 'lord-chief' (i.e. petty ruler), I: 5b, 6a (x 2), 14a, 14b, 15b (x 2), 17a, 18b, 21a, 23a (x 2), 23b, 24b, 26a (x 2), 28a, 29a (x 2), 29b (x 4), 31a (x 2), 31b (x 2), 32a (x 4), 32b (x 2), 33a, 33b, 34b, 36a-b, 40a.
rjes-'jug = 'successor', I: 46b.
'jigs-ra (= 'thab-ra q.v. = *'dzing-ra* q.v.) = 'battle-fence, stockade', II: 14a.
nya-khral = 'fish-tax', I: 23a.
nye-ba drung-po = 'close mentor', II: 11a, 12a.
gnyen-du sdebs-pa = 'to intermarry', I: 14b.
gnyen-zla = J: 'fit for matrimonial alliance' (as to birth etc.), I: 14b.
gnyer-pa = 'steward', II: 7b, 8a, 20a, 21b.
snyad-btags / – *-btegs* = 'false pretext' (cf. S: *snyad brko-ba* = 'pretexter'), III: 110b.
ṭaṃ-ka / *ma-ṭaṃ* / *phyed-ṭaṃ*, various Bhutanese coins, III: 111a, 111b, 112b.
gtam-rgyun (= gtam-rgyud = ngag-rgyun q.v.) = 'oral traditions' (cf. *gtam-rgyus* = 'news', II: 7b), I: 10b, 22a, 25b, 29a, 40a, 45b (x 2), 46a, 46b, 47b.
ltag-rdzong = 'upper citadel', built in positions overlooking some of the principal *rdzongs* situated on hill sides (as in sPa-gro, Krong-sar and bKra-shis-sgang), they serve as a final point of defence from which a last-ditch stand could be made, II: 22a.
lto-'thud = 'food allowance' = (cf. *mgron-'thud* q.v.), III: 112a.
lto-'bab = 'meal visits', paid on households by government officials (cf. *mgron-babs* and *zhag-babs* q.v.), III: 111b-112a.
lto-gzan / *gzan* = 'menial' 'orderly', lit. 'eater of (the master's) food' BU (cf. *nang-gzan* q.v.), III: 107a, 118b, 110a (x 2), 111a (x 2), 113a.
stung (= *gzeb(-mal)),* a box or pannier made of split cane, LP (Tsangla dialect) I: 21b, 22b. sTung-sde, name of clan, I: 22b et seq.
stong [1] = unidentified Bhutanese fruit (*mon-gyi shing-'bras*), I: 33a (x 2), 33b, 34a (x 2).
stong [2] / *dge-stong* = 'manslaughter fine', III: 103b, 113b.
tha-ma-kha = 'tobacco', III: 107a (x 2).
thug-gsher = 'trial' (LN: *lab-gzhi dang rtsod-gzhi rigs kha-mchu rtsis-gzhi'i rigs-la zer-ba-yin*), III: 111b.
thun-kha (= J: *thun*) = '(work) shift', III: 108b.
tho-chems = 'testamentary record', I: 48b.

mtha'-khob = 'barbarian border region' (cf. J: *yang-khob* = '. . . a still more distant and barbarous country.' Also cf. *mtha'-'dul, yang-'dul* etc.,), II: 6a.
mthong-bkur = 'privilege and honour', I: 32b.
mthong-srol = 'customary privileges', III: 109b.
'thab-chad = 'fight penalty' (cf. *gri-chad, byi-chad* q.v.), III: 113b.
'thab-ra (= *'dzing-ra* q.v. = *'jigs-ra* q.v.) = 'battle-fence', 'stockade', II: 10a, 15b, 16a (x 2).
'thud = 'allowances' supplied in kind by the public to officials on tour (cf. *mgron-'thud* q.v.), III: 112a (x 2).
dong-pa (= J: *dong-po, ldon-po*) = 'tube' (of bamboo), I: 37b.
smyug-dong, I: 37b (x 2).
gdung [1] = 'clan', lit. 'bone' (honorific for *rus* q.v.), I: 14a, 15b, 23a, 35b; III: 103a.
gdung-rus = 'clan' (pleonastic compound), I: 28a.
gdung [2], hereditary title and family name of the ancient ruling nobility in Bum-thang and Kheng (*bum-thang sde-bzhi'i gdung; gdung rin-po-che; rje-dpon gdung; gdung grags-pa dbang-phyug* etc.,). I: 32a, 32b, 33a (x 3), 33b, 35b (x 5), 36a, 40a (x 2); II: 6b, 13a (x 2), 13b, 14a (x 2), 24a.
gdung-brgyud = 'line of descendants, lineage' (honorific for *brgyud-pa* q.v.), I: 6a. 6b. 3a. 10b, 32a, 46a; III: 103a.
gdung-rabs = 'generations' of a royal or noble family (honorific for *mi-rabs* q.v.; cf. *rgyal-rabs* q.v.), I: 1a, 2b, 3b (x 2), 10a, 10b, 11a, 32b, 48a.
mda'-dpon = 'arrow-captain', III: 109a.
mdo-drug (= *mdo-'phrug* ?) = 'horse' (epic term, frequent in Ge-sar and Tun-huang literature), III: 109a.
rdo-phong (= J: *pha bong*) = 'boulder', I: 24a.
lding-dpon = captain', II: 4a (x 3), 4b; III: 109a.
'dus-che(-ba) = 'rich, prosperous' (in reference to a locality), I: 13b; II: 9b, 12b, 17a.
'dra-brdzus 'bru-log = 'counterfeiting (written orders or altering their meaning by) reshaping their letters', III: 114a.
sde-thang = 'local price', III: 110b.
sde-pa [1] (= *sde-srid* 1 q.v.), title by which the secular rulers of Bhutan were known; pronounced 'deb' in the vernacular; hence the 'Deb Rājas' of the British, II: 4b; III: 100b (x 2).
sde-pa [2] = the provincial rulers or district governors of Tibet, I: 36a.
sde-srid [1] / *sde-srid phyag-mdzod* / *phyag-mdzod*, the 'Deb Rājas' of Bhutan, III: 101a, 105a, 107b.
sde-srid [2], the 'Kings' of gTsang and, later, the 'regents' of the dGe-lugs-pa, II: 2a (x 2), 2b; III: 104b, 114a.
sdeb [1] = 'team', i.e. of craftsmen etc., III: 110a.

sdeb [2] = 'measure' i.e. of grain that has been saved up, III: 110b.
bsdu-khral = ? 'harvest tax', levied on grain after the harvest *(lo-thog bsdu-ba)*, III: 111b).
bsdu-thun = 'common or general tax collection', III: 110b.
na-rim = 'successive (generations)', I: 28b.
nag-gcod / *nag-chad* = 'severe punishment', perhaps 'execution'; lit. 'black severance', 'black punishment', II: 4b, 22a; III: 111a, 112a, 113b.
nang-gzan = 'household servitors' in government employ (cf. *gto-gzan* q.v.), III: 105b.
gnam-lha / *gnam-gyi lha* = 'The God of Heaven' (the deity 'O-de Gung-rgyal), I: 12a, 32a, 33b, 36a.
gnas-po = 'landlord' (used as a title as in *lCags-mkhar gNas-po;* 'nep' in the vernacular), II: 7a.
gnas-mo chen-chung = 'senior and junior wives', I: 16b.
dpa'-dar = 'hero sash', awarded to soldiers as a mark of bravery in battle, III: 109a.
dpa'-gzas = 'military service' (cf. *dmag-tsho* q.v.), III: 112a.
dpung-rgyab-kyi dmag = 'the forces of a supporting (or auxiliary) army', II: 19a.
dpon-mo = '(hereditary) chieftainess', I: 35b.
dpon-slob [1] (= *spyi-bla* q.v.), lit. 'chief-teacher'; probably *slob-dpon* reversed; title of the three regional governors of sPa-gro, Krong-sar and Dar-dkar, II: 4b (x 2), 6b (x 2), 7a (x 2), 7b (x 3), 8a, 14b (x 2).
dpon-slob [2] = 'the lord and his disciple(s)', II: 5b.
dpya (= *khral*) = 'tax', III: 111b.
spus-dag = 'pure quality', in reference to merchandise, III: 114a.
spus-btsug = 'share-in-kind' in a trading venture, III: 110b.
spo-bzhag / *spo-'jog* = 'transfer', on government duty, III: 108a, 110b.
spyi-dpon = lit. 'general officer', the lowest grade functionary on the village level whose main duty is to carry government messages between the *rdzong* and the village; hence, 'village messenger' ('pshipon' in the vernacular), III: 104a, 107a, 111b, 112a.
spyi-bla (rnam-gsum) (= *dpon-slob* [1] q.v.) = the three 'regional governors', lit.'head *bla-ma'*. (Use of this term is confined to literary works whereas *dpon-slob* is used in common parlance), III: 106a, 108a, 109b, 111a.
sprin-gyi dbyangs = 'the melody of clouds', i.e. the thunder which is said to be the sound of dragons (*'brug*); an allegorical expression used in reference to the 'Brug-pa school. (cf. *dbyar-rnga* q.v.), III: 101b.
pha-mes (= *yab-mes* q.v.) = 'ancestors', lit. 'fathers and grandfathers', I: 45b.
pha-spad = 'father and son(s)', I: 28a; II: 12a, 16b.
pha-spun = 'paternal siblings', I: 13b, 31b.

pha-tshan = 'family' (lit. 'paternal relatives'), I: 45a; II: 7a.

phul, the smallest measure of grain (= 1/6 *bre* ?), III: 113a.

pho-ngar (= J: *ngar-po*) = 'strong', I: 43b.

pho-mnyam = ? 'men of standing equal' (as in *ya-rabs pho-mnyam* = 'nobles of equal standing' and *pho-mnyam gzhon-pa* = 'young men of equal standing), I: 4b, 47a.

pho-rengs (= J: *pho-yan, pho-rang, pho-hrang*) = 'bachelor' (cf. *yug-sa-ma rengs-mo / mo-rengs-mo* q.v.), I: 38a, 38b (x 3), 42b.

pho-res (= LP: *re-res*) = 'individually', I: 42b.

(*gser-dngul-gyi*) *phya-thag* = '(gold and silver) *phya*-cord' (cf. *rmu-thag* q.v.), I: 45b.

phyag-mjal = 'gifts' offered to a superior, II: 21a; III: 112a (x 2).

phyag-rjes = lit. 'hand-print', used figuratively with the sense of 'a token to someone's achievements', II: 22b.

phyi-mgron = 'commissioner', lit. 'external chamberlain', a government representative on temporary (?) deputation, III: 109b.

'phrul-'khor = 'sorcerous device', 'mechanism', II: 20b; III: 106a.

'phrul-thabs = 'magical (or mechanical) devices (or means)' (probably in reference to skill in warfare), I: 26a, 47b (x 2);

'phros-gtam = 'legend', I: 11b.

ba-spu = 'Babu', a title used in reference to those Eastern Bhutanese who settled in or near the Assam Duars and gained a measure of control over the local Indian populations, I: 24b, 28a (x 3).

bu-chen = lit. 'big son', the eldest son delivered as hostage to guarantee the good behaviour of his relatives, II: 14b, 19b (x 2), 21b.

bu-gte = 'sons (kept as) hostages', II: 24a.

bu-brgyud = 'issue, progeny, descendants, scions' (cf. *sras-brgyud* q.v.), I: 11b, 17a, 17b (x 2), 18a (x 2), 18b (x 3), 19a (x 2), 20a (x 3), 20b (x 4), 24b (x 2), 25a (x 4), 25b (x 2), 26a (x 2), 26b (x 2), 27a, 31b (x 3), 42a (x 3), 42b, 43a (x 3), 43b (x 2), 45b.

bu-rabs rim-pa = 'successive generations of sons', II: 13b.

bod = 'attendant' BU (? from J2: *'bod-pa* = 'to call [summon] a person'), III: 109b, 110b.

Bon Thang-la 'Od-dkar = name of an unidentified *bon-po* deity or saint, I: 36a.

bya-bzhag = 'employment', 'business', III: 108a, 109a.

byi-chad = 'penalty for adultery or rape' (J); (cf. *gri-chad, 'thab-chad* q.v.), III: 103b.

bran(-pa) (= *shes-pa* or *go-ba*) = 'to know, understand' a dialect word from E. Bhutan; pronounced as written, not 'dren'), I: 22a.

bla-gnyer sbrel-ma (LN: *blaṁ dang gnyer-pa gnyis-sbrags-kyi go-sa-can-gyi dpon-khag*) = 'those holding the joint office of *bla-ma* and *gnyer-pa'*, i.e. those monastic officials who bear secular responsibilities of government, III: 110b.

dbang-yon = lit. 'initiation fee', here signifying an additional tax imposed on the public, ostensibly for blessings bestowed on it by the state monks (BU), III: 110a.
dbang-tshong (byed-pa) = 'to force someone to sell at extortionate rates'; in the vernacular 'bangchen tshongwa' means simply 'to extort', 'to force someone to do something against his will', III: 110b.
dbu-mched (= mched-grogs=chos-spun) = 'clerical brother', II: 17b.
dbu-rtse, the central square tower of every *rdzong* comprising a tier of temples several stories in height, II: 22a.
dbon-sras (= sras-dbon ?) = 'descendants' (lit. 'grandsons (and their ?) sons'), I: 45b.
dbyar-rnga = 'the drums of summer', an allegorical expression used in reference to the 'Brug-pa school, the dragon (*'brug*) being associated with the thunder of summer (cf. *sprin-gyi dbyangs* q.v.), III: 114b.
'bab-g.yu skya-dkar, a particular kind of pale-coloured turquoise (the function of *'bab* is unclear), II: 18b.
'bab-zhus = 'acts of submission' (cf. *zhabs-'dzul* = 'acquiescence' II: 10b), II: 9a, 10a, 10b, 11b (x 4), 12a, 13a, 17b, 19a, 19b, 20b, 21a.
'bab-sha 'bab-nor = 'tribute meat, tribute wealth', offered on making submission to the 'Brug-pa authorities, II: 21a.
  'bab-zhus-kyi nor, II: 12b.
'bul-ba [1] = lit. 'offering', used in a special sense when referring to tributes delivered to the authorities on behalf of districts or groups of villages; (pronounced 'biu' in the vernacular), II: 21a.
'bul-ba [2] = 'due', 'fee', III: 111a.
  'bul-thus = 'dues collected', III: 111b.
ma-'gyur = a 'pledge' which is retained by the authorities if a promise remains 'unfulfilled' (*ma-'gyur*) TR, II: 19b (x 2).
ma-ṇi-ba = 'bard' ('manip' in the vernacular), III: 113b (x 2).
ma-yin ma-'thus-pa'i nag-can = 'evil criminal', III: 107b.
mar-khral = 'butter-tax', III: 111b.
mi-khyim = 'habitation, household', I: 4a, 13b, 14a.
mi-'go = 'leader', II: 20b, 21a, 21b.
mi-sde = (secular) 'community' (under the control of a local ruler or civil official; as opposed to *lha-sde,* a community under the authority of a monastery), I: 10b, 19a, 21a, 24a, 24b, 25b, 32b (x 2), 39a, 41b, 42b, 43a (x 2), 43b; II: 7b, 10a, 13a, 14b, 15a, 17a, 17b, 22b.
mi-nag = 'peasant' (BU), lit. 'black man' (pronounced 'minap' in the vernacular; cf. J = 'layman'), III: 107a.
mi-sna = 'envoy', II: 2b (x 3), 3a (x 2), 4a, 15a, 17a.
  mi-sna bang-chen = 'envoy courier', II: 10b, = *pho-nya-ba bang-chen,* II: 20b.

mi-dpang = 'human witness' to an oath (cf. *lha-dpang* q.v.), II: 21a, 21b; III: 114a.

mi-dpon = 'overlord' or 'headman' of a village or district, I: 32b; II: 7a.

mi-rabs = 'generations' of a family (cf. *gdung-rabs* q.v.), I: 1a, 2b, 13b, 31b, 43b, 46b.

mi-rigs = 'human race', I: 2a, 10a.

mi-brgyud = 'human race', I: 43b, 44b.

mi'i skad-gtam = 'human speech', I: 38a.

mes-po (emended from *mes-pho*) = 'ancestor', lit. 'grandfather', I: 36a, 42b.

mes-dbon = 'grandfathers and grandsons', 'ancestors' (cf. *dbon-sras* q.v.), I: 48a; III: 100b, 101a, 105b.

yab-mes (emended from *yab-med*) = 'ancestors', lit. 'fathers and grandfathers' (honorific for *pha-mes* q.v.), I:40a.

mo-ma = 'diviner', possibly 'female diviner', I: 4b.

dmag-gral = 'battle-line', III: 109a (x 2).

dmag-dpon / dmag-dpon chen-mo = 'commander', 'commander-in-chief', II: 7b; III: 109a.

dmag-dum = 'a detachment of the army', II: 17b, 19b-20a, 20a.

dmag-dpung kha-'thor shig = *idem,* II: 10b.

dmag-dmangs (= *dmangs-kyi dmag* ?) - 'popular forces' (TR), II: 21a.

dmag-tsho = 'militia' composed of ordinary taxpayers (*khral-pa*), one of whose common obligations is to take up arms during times of war (cf. *dpa'-gzas* q.v.), III: 112b.

dmar-rgyan = 'meat sacrifice', lit. 'red ornament' offered to Mahākāla; here used euphemistically for 'execution' (cf. next item), III: 114a.

dmar-gsod = 'execution', lit. 'red killing', III: 113b.

rmad-'jal (= *smad-'jal* ?), a fine for fornication, III: 103b.

(lha'i) rmu-skas (emended from *rmu-skad*) = '(divine) *rmu*-ladder', I: 45b.

(lha'i) rmu-thag = 'the (divine) *rmu*-cord' (cf. *phya-thag* q.v.), I: 32a.

rMu-btsan lHa-gnyan Chen-po, the name by which the deity Gu-se Lang-ling (q.v.) was known in the land of rMu, I: 36b.

sman(-rtse) = a yellow silk cloth with a printed floral pattern ('damask'?), III: 111b.

tsa-ra = retribution, reprisal (TR says this is a Khams-pa term; LN suggests, unaccountably, = *rtsad-dpyod / zhib-dpyod,* 'detailed enquiry, investigation'), III: 107b, 111a.

gtso-rgan = '(village or district) headman', used only in Eastern Bhutan (cf. *rgad-po* q.v.), I: 21b, 27b, 28a; II: 12a.

gtso-las = 'chief councillors', II: 10a, 12b, 17a, 21a, 21b.

btsan-chas / btsan-cha = 'defences, embattlements', II: 15b, 18a, 22a.

btsan-sa = *(sa btsan-po,* II: 14a) = 'stronghold, fastness', I: 17b; II: 20a, 20b.

btsun-khral (emended from *btsun-khras*) = 'monk levy', the obligation incurred by families having three or more sons to send one of them to join the state monastery located in the *rdzong,* II: 21b.
rtsa-lhongs (byed-pa) = 'to transfer' a tax estate, 'to settle it upon someone else', III: 112b.
rtswa-khral = 'grass tax', the obligation to provide fodder for government horses, III: 106a (x 2), 111b.
rtsis-rta = 'a horse handed over to the charge (*rtsis-sprod*) of a government official for his use' (cf. *gso-rta* q.v.), III: 111a.
rtsis-bdag = 'charge, responsibility, control', III: 106a, 107b.
tshwa-chu sman-chu (abbreviated to *tshwa-sman*) = 'saline and mineral springs', III: 111a (x 3).
'tshang-kha rgyab-pa = 'to make an assault, to storm', II: 7b, 16a, 18a (x 2).
'dzin-tho = 'list of receipts', 'account', III: 111a.
rdzong-kha = 'district under the administration of a *rdzong*' (the modern spelling is *rdzong-khag;* the term *rdzong-kha* has today the meaning of 'fort-language', i.e. the official language of Bhutan), III: 106a, 110a (x 2), 110b, 111a (x 2), 113b.
mdzad-mkhyon rlabs-che-ba (-chen) = 'extensive sphere of action', 'far-ranging endeavours' (S: *rlabs-chen* = 'de grande force, tres vaste'), I: 23b, 38b.
  bya-spyod-kyi rlabs = ? 'extensive activity', I: 42b.
  mdzad-mkhyon = 'sphere (of action)', II: 22b.
  rlabs-chen spyod-pa'i bgyi-ba = 'acts undertaken on a broad scale', III: 108b.
rdzong-dpon / – -bdag / – - sdod (abbreviated to *rdzong*) 'district governor', lit. 'fort-chief', 'fort-owner', 'fort-resident' (the term *rdzong-bdag* is the one in current use in Bhutanese government and administration), II: 8a, 9a, 22b; III: 106a, 107a, 107b, 108a, 109a, 109b (x 3).
'dzing-ra (= *'jigs-ra* q.v. = *'thab-ra* q.v.) = 'battle-fence, stockade', II: 11a.
'dzum-mu-le-ba = 'smiling', I: 34b.
wang (= sa-dong) = 'earth pit' (Tsangla dialect), I: 22a, 22b. Wang-ma, name of clan, I: 22b et seq. and Addendum.
za-ba = 'to inherit', lit. 'to eat', III: 112b.
zas-bsngos = 'blessed food' offered to a dead person as part of the funerary ritual, III: 112b-113a.
zur-chod = 'split up, sub-divided' (of land etc.); also 'cragged' (TR), I: 27b; II: 22b.
zlo(-ba) (LP = *'gran-pa*) = 'to contend, vie' (BU ?), I: 21a.
gzims-'gag = 'household guard', III: 109b.
gzims-dpon (abbreviated to *gzims;* = J: *gzim-dpon*) = 'steward-in-chief', III: 109b.
zhag-babs = 'overnight stay' on a journey (cf. *mgron-babs* and *lto-'bab* q.v.), III: 111a, 111b.

gzhi-len, a special feast admissable to a government guest or to a government official on taking up office. Cf. *gzhi-tshugs,* an issue of standard rations (LN / TR), III: 109b.
gzhis = 'family', III: 113b.
'ul (= *'u-lag;* S = *'u-la*) = 'corvee', 'conscripted labour', III: 106a, 107b, 111a, 112b (x 2).
'og-khang = 'dungeon', lit. 'lower house', III: 104a.
yan-po = 'bastard' (cf. I: 11b: *yan-pa* = 'unclaimed, unowned'), I: 11b.
yig-cha = 'personal documentary records', I: 28b.
yig-gter (= *gter-yig*) = 'treasure-writing' (hidden and rediscovered), I: 36a, 45b.
yig-tshang = '(? collected) records' (in modern usage = 'office'), I: 15a.
yug-sa-ma rengs-ma / mo-rengs-mo (= J: *yug(s)-sa-mo*) = 'widow' (cf. *pho-rengs* q.v.), II: 8b.
(g.)yas (= *zo-ba*) = 'trough, pail' (Tsangla dialect), I: 21b, 22b. Yas-sde, name of clan, I: 22b et seq.
ras-su 'bor-ba (LN = *yal-bar 'dor-ba* = 'to annihilate, annul' J2) = 'to repudiate' (*ras* is probably cognate to *dral-ba / hral-ba,* 'to tear to pieces', and to *ral,* 'torn'), III: 104a, 105a.
ri-rgya lhungs-rgya sdom-pa = 'to prohibit hunting and fishing'; lit. 'to seal up the hills and streams' (cf. J2: *ri-rgya lung-rgya 'dzug-pa*), III: 106a.
rigs [1] = 'family', I: 24b, 25a, 28b, 31b, 43a, 43b (x 2), 46b.
  'brogs-rigs = 'pastoral family', I: 42b.
rigs [2] = 'tribe', II: 18a.
rigs-brgyud = 'family lineage, genealogy', I: 14a, 40a.
rigs-rus (? abbreviation for *rigs dang rus*) = 'family and lineage (or clan)'; used loosely it seems to signify either 'clan' or 'family', I: 2b, 3a, 6a, 13b (x 2), 14b, 32a, 33b, 35a, 41b (x 2), 44a, 44b (x 3), 45a, 45b, 46a, 46b.
ru-nga(-bo) (LN: = gang-drag sha-tsha *che-tog-to* [BU: = *shin-tu che-ba*] = 'meticulous', 'assiduous', 'lovingly careful', TR (cf. S: *ru-nga-mo* = 'femme habile'), III: 108b.
rus (= *gdung* [1]) = 'clan, lineage', lit. 'bone', I: 11b, 14a, 14b (x 2), 15a, 22b (x 4), 43b, 44a, 44b (x 2), 45a (x 3).
  rus-chen = 'great clan', I: 32a, 44a, 44b (x 2).
  rus-rigs = 'clan-stock' (viz. Se, rMu, lDong sTong and some of their sub-divisions), I: 44a (x 2).
lan-rtsa = 'reprisal' (TR) (perhaps cognate to *tsa-ra* q.v.), III: 106a.
lab-rtsa (= J: *lab-tse*), the top of a pass where cairns are usually found, I: 12a, 52a.
lam-khral = 'road-tax, toll', I: 23a, 25b.
las-sgo / rgya-gar-gyi las-sgo = '(the Indian) trade-marts' (i.e. the Assam Duars), I: 18b, 19a, 24b (x 2), 28a, 28b, 37a, 42a (Tibetan *las-sgo*), 48a; II: 2b, 11b, 23a (in general): III: 107a, 111b, 113b, 114a.

(gnyen) sha-khrag[-gis] 'brel-ba = 'related by flesh and blood', (i.e., on the mother's side as opposed to the father's which is by 'bone', *rus* q.v.), II: 7a.

sha rus gang nye'i mi-phros = 'kin nearest related by flesh and bone', III: 112b.

sha-khral = 'meat-tax', ? levied in kind on animals slaughtered by the public, I: 23a, 111b.

shar-re-ba = 'in a flash', I: 38a.

shing-khral = 'wood-tax', the obligation to supply the *rdzong* with firewood, III: 106a, 111b.

she-ma = 'dairyman' (TR), III: 112a.

bshams-ra, sham-ra (= J(1): *shom-ra*) = 'plan, preparation', I: 23b; II: 8a, 10a, 10b.

bshal(-ba) = ? 'to rove, roam', I: 33b, 41b.

sa-rgyus dang ri-rgyus = 'the lie of the valleys and mountains', II: 11a.

lam-rgyus ri-rgyus = 'knowledge of the paths and mountains', II: 13a.

sa-brtsi ri-brtsi (= *sa-mtshams ri-mtshams,* LP) = lit. 'land-reckoning, hill-reckoning', i.e. the delineation of agricultural land and pastoral land belonging to people with adjoining estates, I: 25b.

sras-brgyud = 'issue, progeny, descendants' (honorific for *bu-brgyud* q.v.), I: 10b (x 2), 11a, 14a, 16a, 27b, 28b, 31a (x 2), 35a, 35b (x 2).

yab-sras-brgyud = 'father-son lineage', I: 48a.

srog-nor = 'ransom', lit. 'life-wealth, life-price', I: 53a; II: 18b.

gso-rta = 'a horse maintained by the government for the use of an official'. (cf. *rtsis-rta* q.v.), III: 111a.

gsol-ba dkar-mo = 'white rations', the finer quality white rice known as *sbo-'bras,* the issue of which to senior government officials was regarded as their customary privilege (the term may also include certain dairy products), III: 109b (x 2).

gsol-dpon (abbreviated to *gsol*) = 'Butler-in-Chief', II: 22b; III: 109b.

hab-thob (emended from *has-thob*) = 'to scramble for something'. (S: *hab-thob (byed)-pa* = 'se précipiter sur quelque chose, se disputer pour quelque chose'), I: 5b; II: 10a.

har-yangs = 'open, broad' (pleonastic compound), I: 12b.

hur-rgol = ? 'sudden raid', I: 35a.

hol-spyod = 'unexamined' (LP), I: 10b.

hrig-ge-ba = 'sharp-sighted' (cf. S: *rang-sems kyi ngo-bor hrig-ge-ba* etc.), I: 34a.

lha-dpang = 'divine witness' to an oath (cf. *mi-dpang* q.v.), II: 21a; III: 114a.

lha-btsun, title of royal descendants who pursue a religious life, I: 9b, 27b (x 4), 47a.

A-lce = 'Lady' (title of a female member of the nobility), I: 35b.

A-ya = 'a beauty', I: 36b.

Ar-po = 'a menial', I: 27b.

BIBLIOGRAPHY

A) Bhutanese Sources

Kun[-dga'] dBang-[-phyug], alias O-rgyan Tshe-dbang: *Grub-mchog hūṃ-ral drung-drung yab-sras-kyi rnam-thar mdo-tsam gleng-ba rin-chen do-shal;* (the *Hūṃ-ral gdung-rabs*) *dbu-can* ms. 71 ff., dated 1766.

dGe-'dun Rin-chen : *dPal-ldan 'brug-pa'i gdul-zhing lho-phyogs nags-mo'i ljongs-kyi chos-'byung blo-gsar rna-ba'i rgyan;* (a recently composed religious history of Bhutan) blockprint in 192 ff., completed in 1972.

Ngag-dbang bsTan-'dzin ? : *Pha 'brug-sgom zhig-pa'i* [= -po'i] *rnam-par thar-pa thugs-rje chu-rgyun; (gter-ma* biography of *Pha-jo* 'Brug-sgom Zhig-po) blockprint in 44 ff., ? 1580.

Ngag-dbang lHun-grub (1670-1730) : *mTshungs-med chos-kyi rgyal-po rje rin-po-che'i rnam-par thar-pa bskal-bzang legs-bris 'dod-pa'i re-skong dpag-bsam-gyi snye-ma;* (biography of bsTan-'dzin Rab-rgyas, 1638-1696) blockprint in 383 ff., dated 1720.

bsTan-'dzin Chos-rgyal (1701-67) : *rGyal-kun khyab-bdag 'gro-ba'i bla-ma bstan-'dzin rin-po-che legs-pa'i don-grub zhabs-kyi rnam-par thar-pa ngo-mtshar nor-bu'i chos-sdong;* (biography of the 2nd *sGang-steng sPrul-sku* bsTan-'dzin Legs-pa'i Don-grub, 1645-1726) *dbu-can* ms. in 123 ff.

bsTan-'dzin Chos-rgyal : *lHo-'i chos-'byung bstan-pa rin-po-che'i 'phro-mthud 'jam-mgon smon-mtha'i 'phreng-ba zhes-bya-ba / gtso-bor skyabs-mgon rin-po-che rgyal-sras ngag-dbang rnam-rgyal-gyi rnam-thar kun-gyi go-bde gsal-bar bkod-pa;* (the famous *lHo'i chos-'byung,* a religious history of Bhutan) blockprint in 151 ff., written in the period 1731-59.

Padma Gling-pa : *Bum-thang gter-ston padma gling-pa'i rnam-thar 'od-zer kun-mdzes nor-bu'i phreng-ba zhes-bya-ba skal-ldan spro-ba skye-ba'i tshul-du bris-pa;* (autobiography of Padma Gling-pa, completed by his son *rGyal-ba* Don-grub) 254 ff. in Vol. *Pha* of his collected works.

Padma Gling-pa ? : *rGyal-po sindha ra-dza'i rnam-thar;* 30ff. in a modern reprint, no date.

gTsang mKhan-chen : dPal 'brug-pa rin-po-che ngag-dbang bstan-'dzin rnam-rgyal-gyi rnam-par thar-pa rgyas-pa chos-kyi sprin chen-po'i dbyangs; (extended biography of *Zhabs-drung* Ngag-dbang rNam-rgyal, 1594-?1651) blockprint in 6 vols., no date. The last vol. (*Cha*) is a biography of Tshe-dbang bsTan-'dzin, alias rTa-mgrin rGyal-mtshan 1574-1643.

Shākya Rin-chen (1710-59) : *Byang-chub sems-dpa' chen-po kun-tu dga'-ba'i rgyal-mtshan dpal-bzang-po'i rtogs-pa brjod-pa dpag-bsam yongs-'du'i snye-ma;* (biography of the Ist *rGyal-sras sPrul-sku* Kun-dga' rGyal-mtshan, 1689-1713) *dbu-can* ms. in 126 ff., no date.

Shākya Rin-chen : *Byang-chub sems-dpa' sems-dpa' chen-po ngag-gi dbang-phyug bstan-'dzin mi-pham 'jigs-med thub-bstan dbang-po'i sde'i rtogs-pa brjod-pa dbyangs-can rgyud-mang;* (biography of the Ist *Khri-sprul,* Mi-pham dBang-po 1709-38) *dbu-can* ms. in 83 ff., no date.

B) Tibetan Sources

Kong-sprul Blo-gros mTha'-yas : *Zab-mo'i gter dang gter-ston grub-thob ji-ltar byon-pa lo-rgyus mdor-bsdus bkod-pa rin-chen bai-ḍū-rya'i phreng* (Lives of the 'text discoverers' in Vol. *Ka* of the *Rin-chen gter-mdzod*).

dKon-mchog dPal-bzang: *Bla-ma thang-stong rgyal-po'i rnam-thar gsal-ba'i sgron-me; dbu-can* ms. in 294 folios (no date). (The 'original' biography of Thang-stong rGyal-po from the monastery of rTa-mchog-sgang.)

'Gos Lo-tsa-ba gZhon-nu-dpal (1392-1481): *Deb-ther sngon-po* (1478); Yang-pa-can/Kun-bde-gling edition.

'Jigs-med Gling-pa (1729-98): *gTam-gyi tshogs theg-pa'i rgya-mtsho;* (the author's miscellaneous writings) blockprint, in Vol. *Nga* of his Collected Works.

Don-dam sMra-ba'i Seng-ge: *bShad-mdzod yid-bzhin nor-bu* (15th cent.); ed. Lokesh Chandra, *Śata-Piṭaka Series* 78. New Delhi, 1969.

dPa'-bo gTsug-lag 'Phreng-ba: *Chos-'byung mkhas-pa'i dga'-ston [lHo-brag chos-'byung,* 1565] ; ed. Lokesh Chandra, *Śaṭa-Pitaka Series* 9(4). New Delhi, 1962.

Bu-ston Rin-chen-grub (1290-1364) : *Chos-'byung* (1322). ed. Lokesh Chandra, *Śaṭa-Pitaka Series* 64 (Vol. *Ya* of his Collected Works). New Delhi, 1971.

Tshul-khrims 'Byung-gnas: *dPal-ldan bla-ma dam-pa 'khrul-zhig rin-po-che ngag-dbang tshe-ring-gi rnam-thar kun-tu bzang-po'i zlos-gar yid-kyi bcud-len;* 128 folios, dated *me-mo-phag* (1867 ?). Modern reprint, no date. (The biography of the 'Brug-pa teacher Ngag-dbang Tshe-ring (1717?-1794?) from rDzong-khul in Zangs-dkar. In the same collection there is a continuation of the *rnam-thar* by one bSod-nams 'Brug-rgyas, and a short *rnam-thar* in 9 folios of *Zhabs-drung* Ngag-dbang rNam-rgyal.)

Sangs-rgyas rGya-mtsho (1679-1703) : *Vaiḍūrya-ser-po* (1698); ed. Lokesh Chandra, *Śaṭa-Pitaka Series* 12 (1 & 2). New Delhi, 1960.

C) Modern Works and Western Editions

ALLEN, N. J. 1976. 'Studies in the myths and oral traditions of the Thulung Rai of East Nepal.' Unpublished D.Phil. thesis, University of Oxford.

ARIS, M. V. 1976. 'The admonition of the thunderbolt cannon-ball' and its place in the Bhutanese New Year festival.' *Bulletin of the School of Oriental and African Studies* 39: 601-635.

ARIS, M. V. 1977. 'Jamyang Khyentse's *Brief Discourse on the Essence of All the Ways :* a work of the *ris-med* movement.' *Kailash* 5(3) : 205-228.

ARIS, M. V. 1979. *Bhutan: The Early History of a Himalayan Kingdom.* Warminster and New Delhi.

BHUYAN, S. K. (ed. and tr.) 1933. *Tungkhungia Buranji or A History of Assam 1681-1826 A.D. An Old Assamese Chronicle of the Tungkhungia Dynasty of Ahom Sovereigns.* Calcutta

BLOCHMANN, H. 1872. 'Koch Bihár, Koch Hájo, and Asám, in the 16th and 17th centuries, according to the Akbarnámah, the Pádisháhnámah, and the Fathiya i 'Ibriya,' *Journal of the Asiatic Society of Bengal* 41 (I) : 49-101.

BOSSON, J. E. 1969. *A Treasury of Aphoristic Jewels, the Subhāṣitaratnanidhi of Sa Skya Paṇḍita in Tibetan and Mongolian.* Indiana University, *Uraic and Altaic Series* 92.

COLLIS, M. 1943. *The Land of the Great Image; Being Experiences of Friar Manrique in Arakan.* London.

COOPER, R. E. 1933. 'Daktas - people with a tail in the East Bhutanese Himalaya.' *Man* 33:125-128.

DAS, S. C. 1902. *A Tibetan-English Dictionary.* Calcutta.

DEVI, Lakshmi. 1968. *Ahom - Tribal Relations, a Political Study.* Gauhati.

DOUSAMDUP KAZI [Zla-ba bSam-grub]. No date. *A Complete Translation of the Lhohi-Chös hbyung [lHo'i chos-'byung]: Religious History of Bhutan.* 204 pp. of typescript. British Library A2 19999.h.17.

ELWIN, Verrier. 1958. *Myths of the North-East Frontier of India.* Shillong.

FERRARI, A. (tr.) 1958. *mK'yen brtse's Guide to the Holy Places of Central Tibet. (Serie Orientale Roma* 16).

GAIT, Sir Edward, 1926. *A History of Assam.* Calcutta.

HAARH, Erik, 1969. *The Yarlung Dynasty.* Copenhagen.

JAMYANG NAMGYAL. 1971. *'Vie et Chants de 'Brug-pa Kun-legs le Yogin,* a review.' Kailash I(I) : 91-99.

JÄSCHKE, H. A. 1881. *A Tibetan-English Dictionary.* London.

KAWAGUCHI, Ekai. 1909. *Three Years in Tibet,* Madras.

KENNEDY, R. S. 1914. *Ethnological Report on the Akas, Khoas and Mijis and the Monbas of Tawang.* Shillong.

KITAMURA, Hajime. 1965. *A Catalogue of the Tibetan Extra-canonical Works preserved in the University of Tokyo.* Tokyo.

KUZNETSOV, B.I. (ed.) 1966. *rGyal rabs gsal ba'i me long, The Clear Mirror of Royal Genealogies. (Scripta Tibetana* 1.) Leiden.

LUARD, C. Eckford (ed. and tr. with H. Hostens). 1926-7. *Travels of Fray Sebastien Manrique; A Translation of the Itinerario de las Missiones Orientales.* (Hakluyt Society, Second Series, 59 and 61.) Oxford.

MEISEZAHL, R. O. 1973. 'Die handschriften in den City of Liverpool Museums (1).' *Zentralasiatische Studien* 7: 221-265.

PAUL, G. 1958. 'Sherdukpens.' *Vanjayati* 6: 22-25.

PETECH, L. 1972. 'The rulers of Bhutan c.1650-1750.' *Oriens Extremus* 19 (1/2) : 203-213.

PETECH, L. 1973. *Aristocracy and Government in Tibet,* 1728-1959. (*Serie Orientale Roma* 25).

Political Missions to Bootan, comprising the reports of The Hon'ble Ashley Eden, 1864; Capt. R. B. Pemberton, 1837, 1838, with Dr. W. Griffiths's journal [1837-8]; and the account by Baboo Kishen Kant Bose [1815]. Calcutta. Bengal Secretariat Office. 1865.

ROSE, Leo, E. 1977. *The Politics of Bhutan.* Cornell.

SARKAR, N. 1975. 'Historical account of the introduction of Buddhism among the Monpas and Sherdukpens.' *Resarun* 1(1):23-44.

SHAKABPA, W. D. 1976: *Bod-kyi srid-don rgyal-rabs* (English title: *An Advanced Political History of Tibet*). 2 vols. Kalimpong.

STEIN, R. A. 1959a. *Recherches sur l'Epopée et le Barde au Tibet. (Bibliothèque de l'Institut des Hautes Etudes Chinoises* 8.) Paris.

STEIN, R. A. 1959b. *Les Tribus Anciennes des Marches Sino-tibétaines : legendes, classifications et histoire.* Paris.

STEIN, R. A. 1962. 'Une source ancienne pour l'histoire de l'épopée tibétain, le *Rlaṅs Po-ti bse-ru.' Journal Asiatique* 250:77-106.

STEIN, R. A. 1974. 'Vocabulaire tibétaine de la biographie de 'Brug-pa Kun-legs.' *Zentralasiatische Studien* 8: 129-178.

SURKHANG, Wangchen. 1966. 'Tax measurement and *lag 'don* tax.' *Bulletin of Tibetology* 3(1) : 15-28.

TOHOKU UNIVERSITY, 1934: *A Complete Catalogue of the Tibetan Buddhist Canons.* 2 vols. Sendai.

TUCCI, G. 1949. *Tibetan Painted Scrolls.* 3 vols. Rome.

TUCCI, G. 1956 *To Lhasa and Beyond; Diary of the Expedition to Tibet in the Year MCMXLVIII.* Rome.

URAY, G. 1972. 'The narrative of legislation and organisation of the *mKhas-pa'i dga'-ston.* The origins of the traditions concerning sron-brcan sgam-po as first legislator and organiser of Tibet.' *Acta Orientalia Academiae Scientarum Hungaricae* 26(1) : 11-68.

WESSELS, C. 1924. *Early Jesuit Travellers in Central Asia.* The Hague.

WHITE, John Claude. 1909. *Sikkim and Bhutan - Twenty-one Years on the North-East Frontier 1887-1908.* London.

WYLIE, T. V. 1962. *The Geography of Tibet according to the 'Dzam-gling-rgyas-bshad. (Serie Orientale Roma* 25).

YAMAGUCHI, Zuihō. 1970. *Catalogue of the Tōyō Bunko Collection of Tibetan Works on History,* Vol. I. Tokyo.